Insights, Experiences, and Hard Truths from
Expert Hazmat Responders:

BUILDING A HAZMAT TEAM

Training, Leading, and Sustaining the Nation's Best

The HazMat Guys

*Thank you to the hard work of our editors:
Toni Keyeck, Chris Pfaff, and Kim Salvesen*

© Copyright 2025 by The HazMat Guys

All rights reserved.

No part of this publication may be reproduced, distributed, or transmitted in any form or by any means, including photocopying, recording, or other electronic or mechanical methods, without the prior written permission of the publisher, except in the case of brief quotations embodied in critical reviews and certain other noncommercial uses permitted by copyright law.

ISBN: 978-1-7323609-4-5

Formatted and designed by Kamila & Co.

Printed in the United States of America

For permission request, contact the publisher as listed below.
The HazMat Guys
info@thehazmatguys.com
https://www.thehazmatguys.com

Inspirational Quotes

If your actions inspire others to dream more, learn more, do more and become more, you are a leader. - John Quincy Adams

Fall seven times and stand up eight. - Japanese Proverb

You may have to fight a battle more than once to win it. - Margaret Thatcher

Opportunity is missed by most people because it is dressed in overalls, and looks like work. - Thomas A. Edison

Until you start believing in yourself, even the easy will seem impossible. - Unknown

Fall seven times and stand up eight. - Japanese Proverb

Our days are numbered... - Billy Graham

Until you value yourself, you won't value your time. Until you value your time, you will not do anything with it. - M. Scott Peck

Never doubt that a small group of thoughtful, committed citizens can change the world... - Margaret Mead

Don't let weeds grow around your dreams. - H. Jackson Brown Jr.

The function of leadership is to produce more leaders, not more followers. - Ralph Nader

Honesty is the first chapter in the book of wisdom. - Thomas Jefferson

In order to have a winner, the team must have a feeling of unity... - Paul "Bear" Bryant

Success is to be measured not so much by the position... - Booker T. Washington

You are never too old to set another goal or to dream a new dream.
- C.S. Lewis

Only through focus can you do world-class things, no matter how capable you are. - Bill Gates

Use what talents you possess; the woods would be very silent if no birds sang there. - Henry Van Dyke

Rank does not confer privilege or give power. It imposes responsibility.
- Peter Drucker

Example is not the main thing in influencing others. It is the only thing.
- Albert Schweitzer

Only if we understand will we care. Only if we care will we help. Only if we help will we all be saved. - Jane Goodall

Never tell people how to do things. Tell them what to do and they will surprise you with their ingenuity. - Gen. George S. Patton

Education is the most powerful weapon which you can use to change the world. - Nelson Mandela

Opportunity is missed by most people because it is dressed in overalls, and looks like work. - Thomas A. Edison

Finding a job/resume is irrelevant; instead: Finding a leader means accepting responsibility before it's assigned. - Variant inspired by Ken Blanchard's leadership principles

Unless you try to do something beyond what you have already mastered, you will never grow. - Ralph Waldo Emerson

Success is not final, failure is not fatal: it is the courage to continue that counts. - Winston Churchill

Table of Contents

Foreword	i
Contributors	ii
Chapter 1: Selection of Personnel	1
Chapter 2: Training	41
Chapter 3: Tools	79
Chapter 4: Incident Frequency or Diversity	113
Chapter 5: Specialization	143
Chapter 6: Certification	175
Chapter 7: Continuing Education	207
Chapter 8: Culture	237
Chapter 9: Networking	269
Chapter 10: Conferences	295
Chapter 11: Outside Department Training	319
Chapter 12: Technology	345

Foreword

It's wild to think we've been doing this for nearly a decade - and honestly, we're still trying to wrap our heads around it.

When we started, the mission was pretty straightforward: build a better hazmat technician. That was the spark. But over time, we realized something bigger - something more scalable. We said, *what if we built a better instructor instead?* Because one solid instructor can train 25, maybe 30 people at a time. And if we could build better instructors, they'd turn around and build better technicians. That's when things really started to click.

What began as a conference-style show focused on teaching hazmat evolved into something much bigger. Today, it's a multi-day course that's been delivered hundreds of times - across the country, and even around the world. Just three years ago, we said, "Let's hit the road. Let's bring this right to people's doorsteps." And we did. From firehouses to bases to training centers, we showed up.

Everywhere we went, we got the same questions: *How do I teach this better? How do I get my team onboard? What am I missing?* These weren't just rookies asking - they were chiefs, officers, techs, cops, military folks. They were hungry for ways to improve, and we didn't have every answer - but we knew who to call.

So we did. We tapped our network - the best of the best. Hazmat leaders from big cities and small towns. Military instructors. Volunteer firefighters. Folks from the East Coast, the West Coast, and beyond. Makers, shakers, chiefs, supervisors—people who *do the work* every day. Our goal was to bring a wide range of voices together. I think we pulled it off.

And that's what this book is. It's a collection of those voices - the people in the trenches who've figured some of this out. Hopefully, there's something in here that helps you move the ball forward, even if it's just one quote that sticks.

Thanks for being part of this with us. We're The HazMat Guys - and we're always here if you need us. Let's get into it.

Special Thank You to Our Contributors

All contributors are listed here in alphabetical order by last name.

Dan Baker

Daniel J. Baker is Chief of Hazardous Materials for the New York State Office of Fire Prevention and Control. He holds a bachelor's degree from Siena College and was a small business owner prior to entering State service with OFPC in 2005.

Chief Baker has 31 years of fire service experience and currently oversees State Fire Instructors and Fire Protection Specialists who provide hazardous materials training and response support to public safety agencies across New York State.

Mike Callan

Michael Callan, a 50-year veteran of the Fire Service, served as a Captain with the Wallingford, Connecticut Fire Department for 20 years.

In 2013 at the International HazMat Conference in Baltimore, he received the prestigious John M Eversole Lifetime Achievement Award given annually by the International Association of Fire Chiefs (IAFC) to recognize a living individual who has had an exceptionally distinguished career in the field of hazardous-materials emergency response.

In 2010 he was the recipient of the prestigious Norman Y. Mineta Excellence in Transportation Award. The Mineta Award is given annually by the National Association of State Fire

Marshals (NASFM). In 2001, he was selected as the California Hazardous Materials Instructor of the Year.

Michael Callan is the author of the book *Responding to Natural Gas Emergencies*, *Responding to Electrical Emergencies and Responding to Utility Emergencies* (RTUE) used extensively by the Utilities Industries for training emergency responders and used as a traditional textbook and interactive training program called RTUE Online. He is also author of the popular *Street Smart Haz Mat Response* by Red Hat Publications.

In 1989 at the Fire Department Instructors Conference (FDIC) in Cincinnati, he was selected from 7,000 municipal and private sector instructors as the International Society of Fire Instructors' - George D. Post Instructor of the Year.

He is developer of traditional, interactive training and now Virtual Reality delivering training. He is the lead instructor on the video training series by Emergency Resources Inc., *Surviving the Hazardous Materials Incident*. He is co-author of *Hazardous Materials Exposures - Emergency Response and Patient Care* published by Brady and Prentice Hall.

John Cassidy

John Cassidy is a lieutenant and 29-year member of the Fire Department City of New York (FDNY). He is assigned to Hazardous Materials Company 1 with 22 years' experience responding to Hazardous Materials incidents.

Cassidy is an instructor at the FDNY's HazMat Technician School. He holds an associate degree in biomedical engineering from SUNY Farmingdale and a bachelor's degree in nursing from SUNY Stony Brook with 16 years of clinical practice in emergency nursing.

Dave DiGregorio

David currently serves as principal for D2 Emergency Management Consulting, LLC and serves as faculty as the Director of Hazardous Materials Response for the for the Beth Israel Deaconess/Harvard Medical School Disaster Medicine Fellowship. He contributes to the advisory board for First Line Technology.

David DiGregorio served as the director for the Massachusetts Department of Fire Services Hazardous Materials Emergency Response/Special Operations Division from September of 2016 through April of 2023 after holding the position of deputy director for two years. He retired from the US Army and Massachusetts Army National Guard after 32 years of service in 2014. Amongst his duty assignments, David served as a non-commissioned and commissioned officer with the 1st Weapons of Mass Destruction-Civil Support Team in the positions of Medical NCO, Physician Assistant and Deputy Commander. Prior to retiring, he held the position of Deputy State Surgeon for the Massachusetts National Guard, earning the Legion of Merit Award, Meritorious Service Medal and several Army Commendation and Army Achievement Medals. He has earned a MS degree in Emergency Management from the Massachusetts Maritime Academy as well as a BS degree and MS degree in Physician Assistant Studies from the University of Nebraska Medical Center. He served on the faculty of the Massachusetts Maritime Academy as a capstone advisor for the graduate level Emergency Management course from January 2015-August 2021.

Dave Donohue

Dave Donohue has over 40 years of emergency services experience, serving in Florida, Maryland, Washington DC, West Virginia, and Pennsylvania. He has served in roles from fire fighter, EMT and paramedic to department head.

He served, both active duty and reserve, in the US Coast Guard, retiring as a Chief Petty Officer.

He has been involved in training and education of emergency responders for over 35 years, most recently as a training specialist at the National Fire Academy. In his role as training specialist, he has designed and developed 17 courses delivered as in-person, self-study, and mediated on-line and provided oversight of the following curricula Planning and Information Management, Training, Leadership (acting), Executive Development (acting), Community Risk Reduction (acting), and Hazardous Materials. He has written for a variety of industry publications and has presented at regional and national conferences.

He holds a Master of Arts in Public Administration, Graduate Certificates in Educational Technology and Design and Disaster Science, Bachelor of Arts in Organizational Studies, Associates Degrees in Fire Science and Emergency Medical Services Technology, and Certificates in Weapons of Mass Destruction and Curricula Design.

Rick Edinger

Rick Edinger, EFO, has served in public safety for more than 50 years as both a volunteer and career firefighter, medic, and hazmat responder. Following his retirement in 2018 as Deputy Chief of a large, all-hazards fire and EMS department in central Virginia, Chief Edinger (ret.) remains active in hazmat response and serves as the Chairman of the NFPA Technical Committee for Hazardous Materials Response Personnel. He continues to develop course work, write, and provide instruction in the fire service and hazardous materials response fields.

During his career, Chief Edinger has worked as a hazardous materials technician, serving for 25 years as a member of the Chesterfield Fire & EMS Hazardous Incident Response Team. In addition to his hands-on experience, he holds a Bachelor of Science degree in fire science technology from Columbia Southern University and is a graduate of the

National Fire Academy's Executive Fire Officer Program. He also holds certifications in incident management disciplines and has deployed to state and national level incidents. His areas of expertise include incident and organizational management, organizational safety, and risk avoidance.

John Esposito

John M. Esposito is the Chief of Department of the New York City Fire Department (FDNY), overseeing the day-to-day work of more than 14,000 firefighters, fire officers, EMTSs, Paramedics, Fire Protection Inspectors and chiefs throughout New York City's 5 Boroughs. He is a 34-year veteran of the FDNY, who has served in various capacities, including leading Rescue, Marine and Hazardous Material Operations as the Chief of the Special Operations Command and previously as the Chief of Fire Operations.

The majority of his time as a Chief Officer was spent in mid-town Manhattan's 9th Battalion and Manhattan's 3rd Division where he was the incident commander for many large scale fires, high rise and other emergencies.

After joining the FDNY in 1991 and was assigned to Engine Company 324 in Queens and later worked as a firefighter in Engine Company 47 and Squad Company 18 in Manhattan, where he was involved in several technical rescue operations.

He was promoted to Lieutenant in March, 2001 and was assigned back to Squad 18 shortly after the 9/11 attacks after completing time as the Officer in Charge of Haz Mat Training.

He has also served as the Intelligence and Analysis Section Chief at the FDNY's Center for Terrorism and Disaster Preparedness and as a member of the National Fire Protection Association's (NFPA) High-Rise Building Safety Advisory Committee.

Chief Esposito holds a bachelor's degree from Stony Brook University and a master's degree in Security Studies from the Naval Postgraduate

School. He is a graduate of the FDNY's Fire Officers Management Institute and is an Eagle Scout.

Brandon Fletcher

Brandon Fletcher is the Chief of the Gilt Edge Fire Department in Tennessee and a 25-year student of the fire service. He is a second-generation firefighter with a background as both a volunteer and career firefighter in the rural, suburban, and airport/industrial settings.

Brandon holds a Bachelor of Science in Agriculture from the University of Tennessee Martin and is a graduate of the Texas A&M Fire Service Chief Executive Officer (FSCEO) program. He is a designated Chief Fire Officer (CFO) and Chief Training Officer (CTO) through the Center for Public Safety Excellence.

He is a contract instructor for the National Fire Academy and the Center for Domestic Preparedness, working in the HazMat programs for both organizations. Brandon has also served as a member of the Fire Service Occupational Safety (NFPA 1550) and Fire Officer Professional Qualifications (NFPA 1020) technical committees.

Chris Hawley

Chris owns FBN Training, which provides Hazardous Materials/WMD training worldwide. He is also the Chief Operating Officer for Emergency Management Solutions, a training and consulting group focused on emergency response. He was a founding partner of Blackrock 3, providing Incident Management Training for technology organizations. Previously, he was a Deputy Program Manager responsible for WMD and Counterproliferation courses within the DOD International

Counterproliferation Program (ICP). This cooperative program with the FBI and DHS provides threat assessment, Anti-Terrorism and HazMat training, and full-scale exercises worldwide. Before this position, Chris was the Special Operations Coordinator for the Baltimore County, MD Fire Department. Chris was a firefighter for 24 years and a HazMat responder for 37 years. He is the author of several HazMat and Terrorism response textbooks, and most recently published his 3rd Edition of Monitoring & Detection textbook with Jones & Bartlett Learning.

Mike Hildebrand

Mike Hildebrand has fifty-one years experience in hazardous materials emergency planning and response. He is a former U.S. Air Force firefighter and was an active volunteer firefighter for twenty years. He served as a Team Leader and founding member of the Prince Georges County Maryland Fire Department Hazardous Materials Response Team.

During his career he held professional positions with the National Transportation Safety Board, the International Association of Fire Chiefs, and the American Petroleum Institute. In 1989 Mr. Hildebrand co-founded Hildebrand and Noll Associates, Inc. with his business partner, Gregory G. Noll. Over 27-years their consulting firm completed more than 750 emergency planning and response projects throughout the United States and internationally.

Mike is the co-author of six textbooks and national level training programs on hazardous materials emergency response including, *Hazardous Materials: Managing the Incident*, 5th edition (2024) now in its 37th year of continuous print.

Mike holds a Bachelor of Science degree in Fire Safety Analysis and Investigation, from the University of Maryland at College Park. He is a Certified Safety Professional and the recipient of the International Association of Fire Chiefs Chief John M. Eversole Lifetime Achievement Award.

Bob Ingram

Bob Ingram began his fire service career with the Commack Volunteer Fire Department in November of 1974. He served in the ranks of Firefighter, lieutenant, and Captain and as a Fire Commissioner for 21 years.

In January 1982, Bob began his career with the FDNY and after graduating from the Academy, he was assigned to L-163 in Woodside, Queens. Bob was a Charter member of HMC1 in September 1984 until 1991.

He worked as a fire lieutenant in the 35 Battalian, a Captain in the 13th division and in E-273 in Flushing, Queens.

Bob established the FDNY HazMat School in 1997 under Chief Jack Fanning, and served as his Executive officer in HazMat Operations from 1998-99. Promoted to Battalion Chief in September of 2000 he was assigend as Executive Manager for Special Operations at HQ.

On September 11, 2001, he responded to the WTC attacks on Chief of Department Pete Ganci's staff and was assigned on September 12th to take command of HazMat Operations. With a great staff, they rebuilt, and re-organized HazMat capabilities for six years and in 2007 Bob moved to the Center for Terrorism and Disaster Preparedness where he worked his last 10 years serving as the WMD Chief for the FDNY.

Bob has a BPS in Fire and Emergency Management, SUNY Empire, and a MA in Homeland Defense and Security from the Naval Post Graduate School, Center for Homeland Defense and Security.

Bob Chaired the IAB for 5 years, served on the IAFC HazMat Committee for 9 years, and has presented numerous times in the U.S. and several international countries.

Phil McArdle

Phil started his career in the fire service when he was 18 years old. It was with the Edgewater Park Volunteer Hose Co. #1 Bronx, NY; this was one of 10 volunteer departments that existed inside the City of New York. He worked as a firefighter, company officer, safety chief and chief of the department (the youngest ever elected).

Phil entered the FDNY in June of 1982 and graduated as the valedictorian of his class earning him the option of selecting his first assignment which was Ladder 58 in the Bronx. After a short while, he was selected to be part of a newly formed Hazardous Materials Company AKA FDNY Haz-Mat 1.

His selection was based in part on the fact that his prior employment was as an Operating Engineer of heavy equipment and power plants. During his initial training Phil quickly realized that this was not enough. The more he learned, the more he realized he didn't know. He began going to school on his own. Phil eventually became an instructor, course developer and content matter expert in hazardous materials, WMD and the OSHA regulations. With his acquired knowledge and skills, he joined the adjunct faculty of a number of government & private institutions teaching and developing courses at the National Fire Academy, USDOJ, EPA, LSU, NFPA and the National Sherriff's Association as well as many others.

Phil was also an original member of FEMA's Urban Search and Rescue Task Force 1 where he deployed many times. He responded to the Oklahoma City Bombing, both WTC bombings as a rescuer and survivor. Phil is currently retired and enjoying his grandchildren.

Adam McFadden

Adam is a Hazmat Technician, Shift Training Instructor and Former Recruit Training Officer for Canada's Largest Fire Service; as well as a member of the Joint Response Hazmat & CBRNE Team.

He is also the owner of Firehouse Training, a private-industry fire service training company, developing various programs in the areas of electric vehicle and lithium-ion battery fire mitigation tactics and safety, hazardous materials spill remediation, flammable liquids and industrial fire response training.

Adam has over 20 years of experience in the Workplace Safety & Hazmat industry, he has completed Cargo Tank Hazmat Specialist Training, Incident Command & Hazmat Safety Officer training programs with the Michigan State Police Academy.

He has also completed his NFPA Pro-Board Certified Company Officer, in Massachusetts.

Adam has spoken previously at various Hazardous Materials & Fire Service Conferences across North America; including the Florida State Hazmat Symposium in Daytona Beach, New England Hazmat Conference, Continuing Challenge Hazmat Conference in Sacramento, California, Oklahoma State Hazmat Conference and the Ontario Hazmat Responders Association Hazmat Conference, in Kitchener, Ontario.

Mike Monaco

Since 1998, Michael Monaco has progressed from firefighting and specialized rescue to a key role in FDNY's Hazmat Company One in 2005, showcasing his knack for simplifying hazmat concepts. By 2008, he began teaching, shaping Hazmat education across various platforms. With a degree in Neurological Physiology from SUNY Stonybrook, Monaco's knowledge spans beyond firefighting. Married and a dad to three, his two decades focus on safety and education in hazardous materials.

Chris Pfaff

Chris Pfaff, a Fire Captain and prevention officer at West Pierce Fire & Rescue since 2006, has built a 20-year career as a firefighter, engineer, rescue technician, and hazmat technician.

With a Master's in Fire & Emergency Management Planning from Oklahoma State University, he holds multiple degrees in firefighting and emergency response.

As a prevention officer, Chris collaborates with agencies like the Washington State Patrol, ATF, and TEEX to advance hazmat safety protocols. His contributions include serving on International Code Council committees for fire safety and instructing and consulting for various agencies across North America.

As a certified hazmat and technical rescue instructor since 2009, he trains fire service, law enforcement, and EMS professionals through platforms like www.HazmatAndRescue.com.

Beyond his career, in his free time, Chris enjoys restoring classic cars, attending Tacoma AAA baseball games, and traveling to Blues Festivals, and once he bowled a near-perfect game of 298 at Pacific Lanes, Tacoma, the home of the late great Earl Anthony.

Rob Rezende

Chief Rezende has been with the San Diego Fire-Rescue Department for 18 years. He is currently the Battalion Chief assigned as the regional Alternative Energy Emergency Response coordinator.

Rob has been an active member of the hazmat team in all ranks since 2008. Rob has two (2) master's degrees from San Diego State University.

He has deployed as a Hazmat Specialist on many natural disaster responses on behalf of FEMA US&R and most recently as a lithium-ion battery expert to support the EPA at the Maui Fires.

Chief Rezende has been tasked by San Diego Fire-Rescue to spearhead the fire department's preparedness in managing lithium-ion battery emergencies. He is also a member of the EPA's Lithium-Ion Battery Task Force and FIRESCOPE's Lithium-Ion Battery Subcommittee. He sits on several industry panels for battery safety.

Bob Royall

Assistant Chief, Bob Royall with the Harris County Fire Marshal's Office retired in August of 2022 after a 48-year distinguished career in Emergency Services. He previously served as Sr. Captain and Assistant Coordinator for the Houston Fire Department HazMat Team, Emergency Management Coordinator for Harris County Public Health, and Task Force Leader for the Houston Marine Firefighting Task Force.

Chief Royall has more than 40-years of experience as a senior fire officer holding professional certifications as an Advanced Firefighter, Fire Officer, Hazardous Materials Technician, and Incident Safety Officer certifications through the Texas Commission on Fire Protection. He is also credentialed as a Type-1 Incident Commander and Type-3 Operations Section Chief and Planning Section Chief with the Texas Forest Service. Bob is a recognized subject matter expert on matters of Homeland Security preparedness, emergency management, hazardous materials response, marine shipboard firefighting, and disaster response.

Chief Royall proudly served as Deputy Area Commander for the Hurricane Katrina Astrodome Shelter Operation following the evacuation of New Orleans and as the Local On-scene Coordinator for the ESF-10 Hazardous Materials and Oil Spill response following Hurricanes Ike and Harvey. He has also responded to and directed an exceptional number of hazardous materials responses, major fires, shipboard firefighting incidents, and has developed and implemented plans and strategies to enhance emergency response operations within the busiest port and largest petrochemical community in the United States.

Bob is a long-time hazardous materials/WMD instructor, a published author and guest speaker, and serves on or chairs many national, state, and local committees including the NFPA 470/475 Technical Committee, the IAFC HazMat Committee, and the Texas Emergency Management Advisory Committee.

Bobby Salvesen

Bobby Salvesen, serving as a firefighter since 1994, quickly climbed the ranks to become Chief in 2014 at the East Meadow Volunteer Fire Department.

With a relentless pursuit of knowledge, he studied Chemistry at the New York Institute of Technology and is furthering his education at SUNY Old Westbury.

His career path took him from EMS to FDNY's Fire Department in 2000, and following 9/11, to a specialist role in Squad 288 within FDNY's Special Operations Command, focusing on Special Rescue and HazMat.

In 2013, he joined Hazardous Materials Company 1, continuously expanding his expertise. Bobby also passionately teaches at both the New York State and Nassau County Fire Service Academies, covering HazMat and Confined Space rescue.

Alongside his professional achievements, he is a dedicated husband and father of two.

Doug Schick

Doug Schick joined the Chicago Fire Department in 1996 and has seen a wide variety of assignments throughout the course of his career.

After graduating from the fire academy, he was assigned to Truck 29 on Chicago's west side where he worked for 8 years before he was transferred to Squad 1 in downtown Chicago, and eventually transferred back to the west side as a firefighter on Squad 2.

After being promoted he had assignments as on officer on Squad 7, Truck 3, Squad 1, and Hazmat 5-1-1. He is currently a Deputy District Chief and the Coordinator of Hazardous Materials for the department.

Over the years he has been an instructor at Chicago's Robert J. Quinn Fire Academy, the Illinois Fire Service Institute, the McHenry County College Fire Service program, and the Northeastern Illinois Public Safety Training Academy.

Jason Zeller

Jason Zeller served his nation with distinction for over 32 years on active duty across the United States Marine Corps, Army, and Army National Guard. Rising to Command Sergeant Major, he led at every level, from tactical ground operations to global missions. His career spanned some of the military's most challenging environments, including combat deployments, homeland defense, and 9/11 response.

Following the attacks on the World Trade Center, Jason served at Ground Zero as a member of the 2nd Weapons of Mass Destruction - Civil Support Team (WMD-CST), supporting emergency operations at one of the most pivotal moments in U.S. history. He also served on the New York State Governor's Executive Protection Detail during 9/11, ensuring security during a time of national crisis. Additionally, he held key positions within the elite Marine Corps CBIRF (Chemical Biological Incident Response Force) and later as the Senior Enlisted Leader for the 2nd and 24th WMD-CSTs, overseeing CBRN response missions nationwide.

Today, Jason continues consultation and training in CBRN downrange operations and emergency response for government and Department of Defense customers. A passionate mentor and advocate, he remains dedicated to veterans, mental health awareness, and helping others find renewed purpose and resilience beyond military service.

Jason lives in Maryland, staying active in the veteran and emergency response communities while continuing to lead, teach, coach, mentor, and serve in new ways.

Mark Zilch

Mark grew up in the Chicago suburbs and has always had a passion for scientific study and research. As an undergraduate student at Lewis University, he majored in Biology and minored in Chemistry. Mark continued his studies in the field of science and obtained a Master of Education from Western Illinois University.

In 2009, he joined the Chicago Fire Department. As a firefighter, Mark continued to further his knowledge by taking courses locally and traveling to FEMA and DHS CBRNE classes. He was assigned to 511-HAZMAT for six years, responding to Chicago's hazardous emergencies. He also joined the Illinois Urban Search and Rescue Team (USAR-ILTF 1). Later, he became an Engineer who relieved throughout the city, and was then detailed to the Quinn Fire Academy as a Hazardous Materials Class instructor. During this time, he was also a member of the Joint Hazard Assessment Team (JHAT) for CFD.

Currently, he is the Commander of Homeland Security for the Chicago Fire Department, under the Office of the Fire Commissioner and the Bureau of Special Operations. He is a CFD representative of the multi-jurisdictional Joint Hazard Assessment Team (JHAT). Primarily, Mark serves as the STC-Chicago Program Liaison/Operations Manager. His role includes being the radiological/nuclear subject matter expert and the operational coordinator of the STC Chicago Region. These duties include sweeps at pre-planned Special Events and responding to HazMat incidents after hours.

He oversees regional STC-related radiological training across disciplines and jurisdictions, including ongoing training of department and principal partner members.

Mark develops instructional materials to maintain the operational capability of primary and secondary screeners. He also assists with "onboarding" new partner members and participates in selecting and acquiring R/N detection equipment.

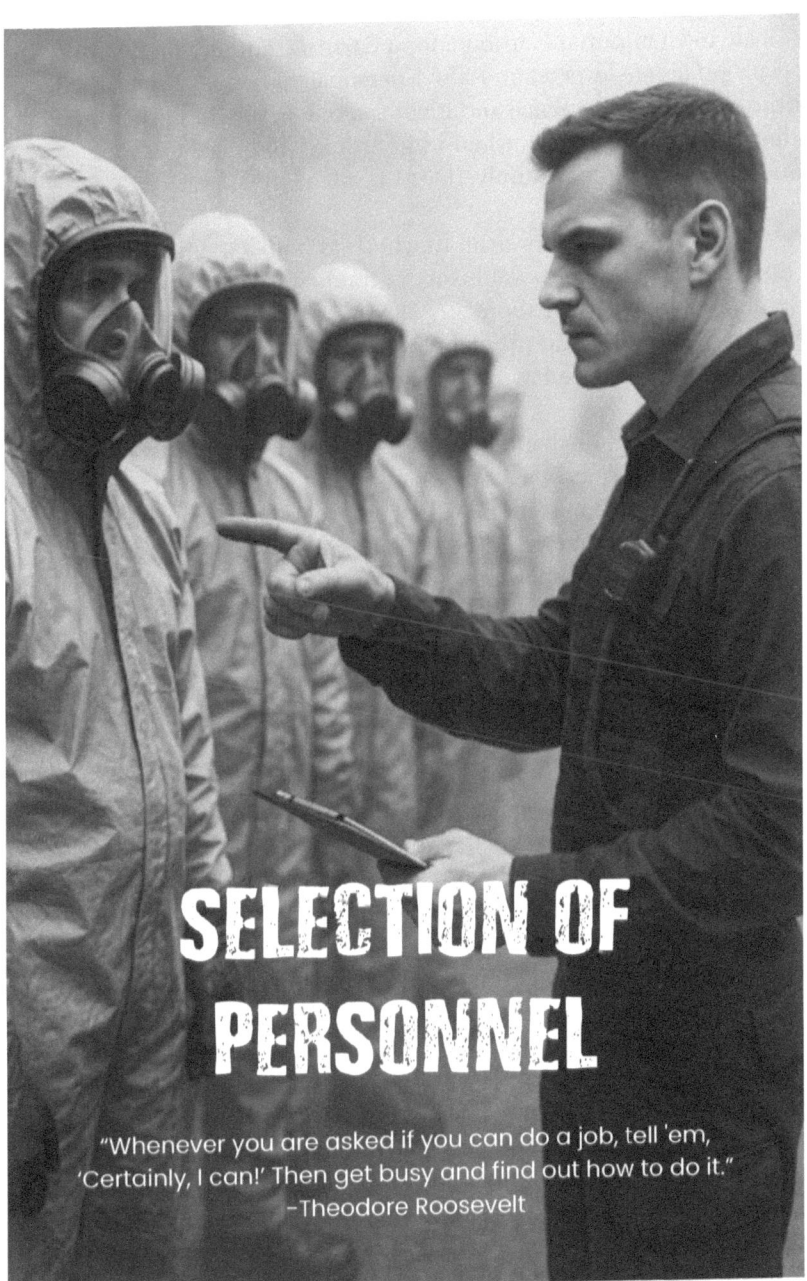

SELECTION OF PERSONNEL

"Whenever you are asked if you can do a job, tell 'em, 'Certainly, I can!' Then get busy and find out how to do it."
–Theodore Roosevelt

Dan Baker

The single most important attribute for a hazmat team member, especially on a state-level team, is their personality. Period. I've learned over the years that experience and training alone never cut it when building a solid crew. In fact, when I hire from civil service lists, our number one hiring rule is simply, "Don't be an a**hole."

Here's why that's crucial: our team functions as both a training and response unit. That gives us the luxury of training new members from the ground up. I can teach just about anyone to become a top-notch technician or specialist - no problem there. But you know what I can't teach? Basic human decency. I can't teach someone how not to be a jerk.

Believe me, I've seen firsthand how even the world's greatest technician can become a massive liability if no one wants to work with them. Toxic personalities don't just hurt morale; they unravel otherwise high-performing teams. Worse yet, they become genuine safety hazards when their disruptive behavior spills into critical incidents (trust me, I learned this the hard way).

Given the choice, I'll always go for someone who's decent, easygoing, and a team player - even if they're initially just a mediocre responder. You can train skills. You can't train attitude.

Now, evaluating someone's ability to handle stress can be tricky - our hiring system doesn't always nail that one down. But that's exactly where mentorship becomes indispensable. Pairing up a new recruit with an experienced mentor is hands-down the best approach to getting consistent, reliable results. Add in rigorous training - repetitions, repetitions, repetitions - and even the most stressful scenarios become manageable. If you've drilled something so thoroughly that it can't be done wrong, you minimize mistakes when the pressure hits.

Diversity also matters a lot to us, but it needs to grow naturally - not be forced. Each new team member starts by mastering the basics and taking a boatload of classes before they're fully operational as responders and instructors. That dual role - responder and instructor - is another huge part of our success. It creates a feedback loop: teaching makes you better at responding, and responding makes you a stronger instructor.

But once we've got someone trained up in the essentials, we give them the space to diversify. We let them explore their interests, figure out what they genuinely enjoy, and see what they're good at. It's not perfect - sometimes we wind up short-handed in certain specialties - but overall, it works pretty darn well. We end up with "meter guys," "propane guys," transportation experts, and folks fascinated by rail incidents. Even the complex equipment like the 908 or Gasmet systems naturally attract those who love diving into the intricacies. Give your people some autonomy, and you'll find they step up to the task.

Bottom line: hire smart, friendly, eager-to-work folks, then teach them the rest. It might sound simple, but trust me, it's how great hazmat teams get built.

Mike Callan

When OSHA first rolled out its regulations in 1910.120 in 1987, there were only two types of people they recognized: those on hazmat teams and those who were responders at the awareness level.

There wasn't any middle ground. You were either part of a hazmat team because you had already been involved in incidents, or you weren't. And back then, being part of a hazmat team was often a matter of pride. People wanted to be on the team because they were aggressive, eager to take on those roles.

But over time, that changed. As specialization grew, hazmat personnel found themselves competing with those in other high-demand roles like USAR, dive rescue, and high-angle rescue. This shift eroded the old dynamic. I mean, back in the day, especially in New York, a squad team was made up of all sorts of people - different personalities, different skills. It didn't matter if some members were more focused on modern approaches, others on cubist styles, as long as everyone could work together. No one had to go somewhere else for hazmat support; you knew you could rely on your squad.

But as specialization took hold, I didn't have to handpick the team anymore. I became more of an artist in the process, assembling a group based on what I believed would work. I remember meeting other "artists" at the National Fire Academy - people like Greg Noel, Jerry Gray, and Bill Hand. The Fire Academy played a crucial role in pulling us all together early on. One of the first hazmat classes I took there was all about chemistry, but it also marked the Fire Academy's first-ever hazmat class. Being part of something new, right at the beginning, helped shape the direction hazmat response took.

The diversity within hazmat response grew over time. We became more specialized, but one thing people weren't excited about? The paperwork. No one wanted to sit through community planning meetings. Back then, there were no Local Emergency Planning Committees (LEPCs); we had hazardous materials advisory councils, which were run by the Chemical Manufacturers Association. That's where we picked people for hazmat roles, and over time, it evolved.

Interestingly, I never really had a "named" hazmat team. We didn't operate with the structure that many of today's teams have. For many, the measure of being a hazmat team was having two things: a suit and a vehicle to get it to the scene. It became almost like a religion - those hazmat suits were treated like gods, and you had to have a chariot for them. Once you had that chariot, you could paint it, slap a name on it, and give yourself an identity. It's funny because teams would come up with all sorts of names - like "HIT" (Hazmat Incident Team) or "SRT" (Specialized Response Team). I remember joking around once that we were thinking of calling ourselves the "Special Hazardous Incident Team." But when we painted that on the truck, we realized the initials didn't work so well on a T-shirt. Sometimes, the branding didn't quite match the reality.

I know I've gone on a bit here, but the question about how to run a team? I didn't really have a traditional hazmat team back then. It wasn't what I had to do. Sure, I got involved in some ways. For example, when Frank Docimo was working with the Fairfield team, I tried to replicate that in Connecticut. The only truly organized hazmat team we had in the state, apart from the chemical companies, was in Fairfield.

Where I lived, there was an American Cyanamid facility, and we had a couple of pumps with foam - though we rarely used it. In those situations, we'd just call Cyanamid and say, "Hey, we've got a tanker fire. Can you come down?" And they'd show up and take care of it. But I tried to get regional teams together. I started with a proposal at the University of New

Haven for a Southern Connecticut Foam Vehicle and hazmat unit. It was a struggle - chiefs liked the concept, but we could only get four teams together in the New Haven area. And then there was the issue of arguing over who would manage the truck, where it would go, who would maintain it. That was a frustrating challenge.

But the thing was, the guys who wanted to be hazmat responders came to us. They were eager. The first group I trained - along with Frank - didn't have a standard to follow. But in 1986, we ran the first-ever Hazmat Tech class at the New Haven Fire Academy. We had 20 people in that class, and those 20 went on to become hazmat officers throughout the state. So, we didn't have a formal hazmat team, but we did have hazmat officers.

Looking back, if I were starting from scratch today, I wouldn't bother with a big truck or massive amounts of equipment. I'd get a Ford Blazer or something equally mobile, load it with meters, protective clothing, and foam, and use it to create a hazard assessment. The truth is, most of the time, you don't need a Level A suit. You can get by with Level B, especially since a lot of hazmat work is done from outside the hot zone.

That's how we evolved - towards bigger trucks, more equipment - but in the end, we often had everything we needed, but no real team to deploy it. It's an interesting situation, and when I think about where we go from here, it's clear that each chapter in the evolution of hazmat response has its place. Every piece plays a part, even if not all of them are necessary for success.

John Cassidy

At Hazmat 1, we've noticed something pretty consistent: most of our successful candidates already know someone on the team. That kind of personal connection makes a big difference. When an existing member recommends someone, there's a level of accountability baked in. If I'm vouching for Bob, I'm not going to bring him in unless I'm confident he can carry the weight - because if he flops, it reflects back on me. So those internal referrals? They tend to work out well because there's already been some real talk about what the team is, what we do, and what's expected.

That brings us to a key point - we're a dedicated hazmat company. We're not doing double-duty with fires or general emergencies like some teams. So, when someone comes in for an interview, it's really important they understand that. Our mission is different. We still go to fires, sure, but as a specialized resource and not a first due unit. We are expected to be the Haz Mat specialists or subject matter experts for the fire department.

Captain Hansen actually has a great way of surfacing this during interviews. He'll say something like, "Tell me about your best fire." And right away, the candidate lights up - they get animated, talk about how much they love the fire service. This thought exercise is important to ensure that the perspective candidate understands that this new role is different.

Now, personality-wise, we're looking for people who are comfortable being different. Hazmat 1 isn't your typical assignment - it requires folks who operate outside the norm. Every single member is expected to be a leader. That means strong communication skills are non-negotiable. In the interview, we pay close attention to things like eye contact, how clearly someone speaks, how well they express themselves. Those are not small details - they're critical.

We used to have this kind of "extra guy" setup to ease new members in. We don't do that anymore. Instead, there's a very clear progression pathway. First off, you've got to be a certified hazmat technician before you even ride with the company. That's the first filter - if you haven't passed tech school, you don't get in the rig.

Once you're in, the real work begins. We use sign-off sheets that cover every piece of equipment and the basic tactics we use. And you're not just memorizing stuff - you're expected to give presentations. That's where your communication and organizational skills come in. It usually takes a little over a year to complete the sign-offs, and the process pushes members to do research, think critically, and deliver information clearly and confidently.

Some of the early tasks might seem simple - like locating items on the rig - but we use those as a springboard. The pressure ramps up through follow-up questions and challenges designed to test your depth of knowledge. We're not looking for surface-level answers - we want mastery.

Before anyone presents to the full team, they'll usually run through their material a few times informally with peers. We also assign a mentor to help them fine-tune things. By the time they stand in front of the group for their official presentation, they've already practiced it plenty. That peer support and repetition builds confidence - and ultimately, competence.

Dave DiGregorio

When it comes down to it, I think this is probably the most important aspect. You can have all the policies and protocols in the world, but if you've got the wrong people on your team, that's where things start to fall apart. And to be honest, this might not even belong in the book, but let me share an experience from my past.

I had six teams, each with 45 guys. When a call came in, my guys would volunteer, and I'd look at who was on that call. I'd know right away if I had the A team or the B-minus team. When I had the A team, I didn't have to worry. I could trust that it was taken care of, sometimes without even needing to rush to the scene. But if I got the B team, there was a real sense of concern. So, yeah, having the right people on the team is crucial.

I firmly believe that any department that forces people to be on the hazmat team is making a mistake. If someone doesn't want to be part of the team, then they shouldn't be there. In Massachusetts, we had a waiting list to join, and that's the culture we built - this was a team you wanted to be on, not something you were "voluntold" for.

Then, of course, we had the JHIRT team, which was really a step above. That team had a reputation. People looked at it like it was Special Forces. But let's be real: I can teach skills, but I can't teach attitude. If I had someone with no hazmat experience but they were a go-getter - someone who would show up to every drill, volunteer, and be that person you almost had to turn away - those are the people I wanted. You can't teach that level of motivation.

I'd start by bringing in the highly motivated folks, even if they didn't have experience. Within three or four months, some of them were ready to fly solo. Others needed more time, sometimes even a year, to get up to speed, but it was all about how motivated they were to learn and grow in the hazmat field.

When I think about it, you also have to ask: Are they in it for the money, or are they truly dedicated to hazmat work? In Massachusetts, we tried to build something a bit different. For instance, when there's an incident, anyone who wants to volunteer for the hazmat incident can, but there's no rank involved. Even if a chief shows up and doesn't take charge as the incident commander, they could be assigned to DECON. Rank didn't matter on the hazmat teams.

To answer your question, having a good leader is paramount - someone who can take charge and command the team. But that's not all. You also need a team member who's got solid technical knowledge, especially in the science of hazmat. You want someone who's familiar with the equipment and can troubleshoot problems on the spot. There's always something that goes wrong with equipment and having someone who can handle that is crucial.

I've always believed in the value of personal interviews, too. I didn't do phone interviews. Each team had its leaders - team leaders, assistant team leaders, training coordinators - and those guys were responsible for deciding who would be on their team. After that, it came to my desk for a final review. I'd take a look and see if there was any reason not to accept someone. Occasionally, I'd call a team leader and say, "Have you thought about this guy's issues?" or I'd call the person directly and ask, "Why do you want to be on this team?"

That's how I ran things. It was about building a team that was motivated, skilled, and ready to handle anything that came their way.

Dave Donohue

When it comes to the qualities I look for in a team member, I'm definitely a "hire the heart, train the hands" kind of person. There are some intangibles that matter most to me, and these are the things that can't be taught in a textbook. First and foremost, the person needs to *want* to be there. They need to be passionate about the job. Being part of a specialty team can't just be a box to check off for rank or promotion - it needs to be something they truly care about.

Another big one is the ability to put service above self. This ties right back into that passion - it's about caring for others, not just for yourself or your advancement. They have to genuinely care about the team they're a part of and be willing to go above and beyond for those around them. Along with that, a lifelong learner mindset is critical. The day someone stops learning is the day they stop growing, and I'm not interested in working with anyone who's content to stop evolving. That learning also needs to be broad-based. It's not just about one discipline - it's about being able to draw connections across different areas of expertise and understanding how everything fits together.

Another important factor is understanding the community and why they need us. Often, it's not what we *think* they need, so it's crucial to have a strong grasp of the bigger picture and our role within it. They also need a life outside of the job. This might sound odd, but having something else in their life gives them balance, and it brings a different skill set to the table. Plus, it's important that they have something that provides meaning beyond the team itself.

As for the more definable traits, they need to be trainable. It's all about being willing to learn and make mistakes along the way. The real key is being able to learn from anyone, no matter their position. I've never met anyone who hasn't taught me something. Adaptability is also a must - they need to be able to think on their feet, adjust when plans go awry, and come up with creative solutions to problems. Self-motivation is huge too - there's a balance of persistence and focus, but they need to constantly be tinkering, trying to improve, and refining their skills.

When it comes to training, my approach is to start with building confidence in a low-stress environment. We do progressively more complex training scenarios, allowing for assessment without the pressure of high stakes. From there, they work their way into higher-stress situations, taking on more responsibility, but with mentorship and guidance every step of the way. As they progress, the mentorship is crucial - on-scene counseling and after-incident assessments, always with a focus on improvement.

Building a team like this is no easy task. We need both subject matter experts (SMEs) and generalists who can fill in wherever needed. It's hard to find and keep the right people, but you have to start with generalists.

They may not be the SMEs right away, but they have the skills to plug in to almost any position. Once you've got a solid general team in place, you can start developing SMEs. The value of an SME is that they bring detailed knowledge and expertise to handle complex situations, which is invaluable when things get more complicated.

Rick Edinger

I want people who *want* to be there. Not folks chasing a bump in pay or checking a box - people who are smart, solid thinkers, and have some real passion for this work.

We had incentive pay for our special operations team - hazmat, water rescue, tech rescue, all that - and while it attracted some great people, it also pulled in a few who were clearly just there for the bump in their check. No real interest in the work itself, and it showed. They did what was required, sure. But they weren't high performers. They weren't invested. So give me someone who's genuinely interested - someone who's ready to develop a passion for what we do. I can train that person. I can make them into a strong hazmat responder. But I can't train for or develop desire.

Assuming we're bringing someone in from within the organization - which is pretty standard in municipal or industrial setups - the first step is doing a bit of homework. I want to know how they perform under normal emergency conditions. How do they perform on a fire scene? Do their crews respect them? Do they make sound decisions under pressure?

Next step: we interview. Maybe even an informal assessment. We may bring them into a drill - nothing high-stakes or dangerous - and see how they handle it. Just let them blend into the scenario, not tell them it's a test, and watch. How do they move? How do they communicate? Can they think on their feet? One of our first filters was always: put them in a suit. If they can't tolerate being in the suit, that tells you something real quick.

Now, there's always that debate - do you want utility players or specialists? For me, it's not an either/or. You need both.

I want folks I can move around - drop into decon, entry, research, whatever the mission needs. But I also want a handful of people who are *outstanding* at one particular thing. My niche was research and planning. We had some real rockstars in detection and monitoring - people who knew the gear inside and out, stayed up on updates from the manufacturers, kept everything calibrated, and understood exactly what the instruments were telling us. I trusted them. I knew our equipment was squared away because those folks had it locked down.

Then we had others who were reliable, capable, and could plug in anywhere. They might not be a subject matter expert, but they'd get the job done. So yeah, I need pitchers and catchers, but I also need somebody who can play three positions in the outfield and not miss a beat. That's the mix you're looking for.

As for training? You've got to start with a strong foundation. That's non-negotiable. For us, it usually began at the state level - we'd send them to hazmat tech school in Virginia. They'd come out of recruit school with ops-level certs, and once they were on the team, they went to tech school. Everyone on the team had to be a technician.
From there, we build based on what we're actually going to respond to. What are the real-world risks in our community? Are we dealing with fuel tanker rollovers? High tech chemical facilities? A mix of both? That determines what knowledge and skillsets our folks need to master.

And for me, a big guiding document is the professional qualifications standard - NFPA 470. That's the baseline. Whether it's your state agency, municipality, employer, or whomever, if you're training to 470, you've got a solid footing. That standard lays out responder capabilities at different levels and gives you pathways into hazmat specialties.

But here's the deal - you can have all the training curriculum in the world, but if your trainers don't know what they're doing, it falls apart. Your cadre needs to be experienced. Not just warm bodies - people who've actually been there, done the work, and can communicate it. The right trainer doesn't just teach; they *transfer* knowledge and skills. That's the difference-maker.

John Esposito

When we were building Squad 8, we knew right off the bat you couldn't just go cherry-pick people who were already at the top of their game. If that's your only filter, you're going to miss the folks who, with the right training and experience, could become exceptional. So we didn't just look at skill - we focused a lot on attitude.

You need a baseline of competence, sure, but beyond that, it's about willingness to learn. That's the magic ingredient. I always go back to when I went to Squad 18 during the rollout of the new squads. They called it a "tryout day," but to me, it was more of an interview. You remember, you went to 288 - same thing.

So there was one evolution where you had to pick up a saw and cut something. Now, I was in a single-engine house back then. We didn't even have a saw in quarters. I pick it up, I'm staring at it thinking, "Is the switch supposed to be up or down?" I didn't have a clue. I looked over, saw Jerry Tracy, and I said, "Cap, we don't have a saw at my house." But once I figured it out, I got it running and completed the task.

If you were grading me just on starting the saw, I failed. But if you were looking at my willingness to figure it out and push through, that's a different story. That's what we looked for with Squad 8. During the interviews, we had three evolutions: the life-saving rope, forcing a door solo, and removing an unconscious firefighter. These aren't fancy tricks - these are things every firefighter is supposed to know. Some people nailed them, some struggled.

But we saw some young firefighters who did way better than expected. Meanwhile, we had seasoned truck chauffeurs who couldn't get through the rope evolution. So it came down to attitude. If someone had the right mindset and gave it their all, that mattered more than perfect execution.

And here's the other side of that coin - you can be the most technically solid person on the floor, but if you can't get along with the team, you're not going to help us. This is a team sport. You're not out there solo. Especially in our world - we ride with five, six, sometimes seven people. You've got to be able to function as part of that unit.

You also need to understand the significance of the work we do. That's something that sets special operations apart - whether it's hazmat or tech rescue. We don't just show up and follow an SOP like a checklist. We're problem solvers. Unique problem solvers.

I always tell the story of that sanitation truck that went through the side of a building - probably 10 or 15 years ago. We get on scene, and it's hanging 40 feet in the air. There's no SOP for that. But we had the officer, the senior firefighter, the newer guy - all huddled together, working through it using that API mindset: Analyze, Plan, Implement, Evaluate. And we cycle through that process together. No one's sidelined because they're the probie or a detail.

In hazmat and special ops, three different teams could face the same scenario and come up with three completely different solutions - each one safe, effective, and fast. That's what makes it special. The ability to think, adapt, and contribute, no matter your role.

And something else we're starting to put more value on - what people bring to the table from outside the job. There's more to someone than what company they've been assigned to. Take someone like George Howell - Columbia engineering background. And that's not unique. A lot of our guys own businesses, work trades like welding or steamfitting, or have military experience that's just unbelievably valuable.

That's why we've started asking for resumes. Not just your work history - I can look that up. I want to know what else you've done. What do you bring to the team that isn't on your fire record? Because it all matters. Every bit of it.

Brandon Fletcher

I'm all about finding motivated self-starters for the hazmat team. Intelligence, problem-solving, and the ability to work well with others are non-negotiable - Team Players are a must. I focus on people who not only ask "why" but are also eager to seek out the answer, not just settle for it being handed to them. In hazmat, so much of what we do revolves around understanding why something is happening, so that drive is essential.

Having come from small departments where everyone is expected to be at the Ops level and jump in when needed, I've learned that direct observation is key in deciding who gets "selected," "asked," or even "voluntold" to move up to technician and beyond. I tell my crew all the time: every day is an interview for your current and future position. Selection never ends! In a smaller department where everyone is expected to do a little of everything, we may not always have the luxury of being picky, but we absolutely can't accept slugs when it comes to something as critical as hazmat missions. That mentality drives our culture, and because of it, high performers across the board are usually the ones stepping up for more responsibility in hazmat.

A diverse skill set is essential for any solid team, not just hazmat. You need the "nerds" who can quickly pick up the science behind hazmat, the knuckle draggers with strength and endurance, and the mechanically inclined folks who know how things come apart and go back together. You need someone who can be the "adult" to keep things in check, and most importantly, you need a team willing to share knowledge and skills, helping each other strengthen any weaknesses.

Chris Hawley

In our department, the transfer system was essentially a "first come, first served" deal - whoever submitted their paperwork first got assigned to the hazmat unit. But I always thought it'd be more effective to have the ability to hand-pick your team. There's a lot of benefit in that, especially when you consider the importance of having the right mix of personalities. It's like running a circus - a three-ring circus, to be exact. You're trying to wrangle different people, each with their strengths and weaknesses, and get everything working smoothly. If you can choose the right mix of personalities for a given scenario, it can make a huge difference.

Take the tech side of things, for example. There's always the debate over what's really needed. Are we looking for someone with deep technical knowledge? Someone who knows how to disassemble and rebuild a valve? Me, personally, I'm great at taking a valve apart, but once it's apart? Not so much putting it back together. So, I need someone on the team who's got those mechanical skills. Ideally, you'd be able to pick the people who fit the job at hand - whether it's someone with a technical edge, or someone who's more hands-on. It's all about the disciplines, right? You need specialists for some things, generalists for others, but having the ability to choose those roles would be gold.

That leads me to another question that comes up a lot in the hazmat world - what happens when your key players are out? For example, every team relies on that one gas chromatograph operator, but what do you do when they're unavailable? The same goes for the hazmat team - when your go-to experts aren't around, things can get tricky. But it's about having a team that can keep things running even without the key person. You've got to make sure everyone can pitch in, at least at a basic level. Not everyone's going to be an expert, but everyone needs to be decent enough to keep things moving.

Do you think the job naturally sorts itself out, though? I've had the experience where you get a guy who's really gung-ho about wanting to be a driver, but when it comes to the hazmat suit, he's out. I had a guy once who told me, flat out, he wasn't interested in wearing the suit, but he just wanted to drive. But that's where your leadership needs to come in. I told him, "You may not want to wear the suit, but you need to know the equipment, how to set it up, and get everyone moving. If you can do that, I'm happy." It's about understanding the value in those roles. Some people are suited for setting up, not necessarily for going in the suit, but that doesn't make them any less valuable. He turned out to be an excellent driver who set up and maintained the equipment in an efficient manner.

One thing that's always stuck with me is how we handle the uncomfortable parts of the job. For instance, during recruit training, we had a fantastic instructor who was amazing at getting people comfortable with their gear. She'd take them off to the side, work with them on wearing the mask little by little until they could wear it for an extended period. It wasn't a one-time thing; it was about patience and gradual progress. Same thing with the hazmat suit. If you approach it with the right mindset, it's not impossible to get someone comfortable over time.

It's not about rushing someone into the suit; it's about the patience to build up their confidence and help them get there on their own. It's the same with the rest of the team - if you've got someone who is fantastic at setting up the decon station but isn't yet ready for a full hazmat operation, that's okay. They're valuable in their own right.

That's the real key: leadership. The leader's job isn't just to handle the technical stuff - it's about managing the people, making them feel comfortable, and knowing where each person's strengths lie. Once that's in place, the technical stuff is easier to manage.

Mike Hildebrand

Let me come at this from two types of experiences: First - how we built our team from scratch and second, our experience in assessing existing teams to help improve their operations. Greg Noll and I have done somewhere between 40 and 50 HazMat Team assessments. We've evaluated everyone from corporate hazmat teams, like BASF and DuPont, to at least 25 different refineries and chemical plants. Every one of them had some version of a hazmat team - some were solid, some just checked the box. We've also even assessed military teams. So, we've seen a pretty wide range of what works and what doesn't.

When you're selecting members for a team that you are building from the ground up, it comes down to two types of teams: people-dependent teams or system-dependent teams. Both can work. You just need to know which one you are now- or which one you *have* to be in the future.

People-dependent teams are all about individuals. You've got someone like you or Bobby on the call - experienced, sharp in judgment, not likely to get someone hurt. That's gold in a crisis. These are the folks you want when you've got to spin up a team fast, like post-9/11 scenario, or a quickly developing threat to the community like some foreign actor starts poisoning folks with nerve agents. You don't have time to train up or build a system - you need reliable people you can trust on day one and quickly make them operational.

But over time, you really want to move toward system-dependence. That's how you get consistency. Repeatability. Think about firearms on the American frontier. Before Winchester standardized firearms parts - there was no guarantee one gun's part would fit another even if it was made by the same gunsmith. Then Winchester changed the game by standardizing parts that were interchangeable. Same with Henry Ford. Interchangeable auto parts and standard operating procedures. That's what you want in a hazmat team - repeatability. No matter who's on shift, the outcome should be predictable because they have been trained to and are using a systematic approach to solving problems.

When we stood up our original HazMat Team with the Prince George's County, Maryland Fire Department, we weren't seeing consistent results across all shifts. If strong players like Greg Noll, Jim Yvorra, Chuck Thomas, or Craig Black were on the call, great – it would go well because these guys knew the job and had a track record of good decisions. But from duty crew to duty crew? Sometimes there are many variables. So, we had to define the system and develop Standard Operating Procedures. We wanted each member trained to the same level, knowing full well that some would excel in certain specialties. That's fine. But the baseline had to be solid. So, how do you pick the right people?

For either model - people-dependent or system-dependent - I'm looking for folks with a track record of hard work and continuous, incremental self-improvement. I'll take that over raw talent any day. Honestly, I think talent is overrated. There's a book I love called *Talent is Overrated* by Geoff Colvin. He was a Wall Street Journal business reporter, and he wrote about people that had accomplished great things from different backgrounds like violinists, chemists, business leaders. These were people that reached the top of performance, not because of some special gift, but because they practiced and refined their skills obsessively. They simply worked harder.

Incremental self-improvement – that is our world, too. Plan. Train. Exercise. Repeat.

I'm not looking for the smartest person in the room. Sometimes that's actually a problem. I'm looking for a risk evaluator, not a risk taker. I want someone who can think through a problem and operate outside the rigid command-and-control model when the situation calls for it. In traditional firefighting, the chief says do it, and you do it. No meetings, no discussions. It's just go time. But special ops - confined space, high angle, hazmat - those are different animals. The clock isn't always your enemy. There's room to think. So, your team needs to be comfortable working in that more flexible, collaborative environment.

When we started our team, I leaned on my military background. I did four years in the Air Force in crash rescue, but I didn't have special ops experience back then. So, I started studying military specialty teams like the Army Green Berets, Air Force Pararescue, and how those types of Tier 1 teams trained. Back in 1977 the U.S. Army Delta Force was brand new. The guy who started Delta Force was Colonel Charles Beckwith.

The U.S. military had no counterterrorism capability back then. Colonel Beckwith just got dropped into the deep end of the pool with no life vest. One of the first things he did was go straight to the British Special Air Service or SAS to learn how they operated.

Colonel Beckwith wrote an excellent book called *Delta Force* which explains the challenges he had politically selling his Delta Force concept, how he broke outside the rigid U.S. Army command structure, and adopted a standardized approach to training and qualifying team members. What stood out to me reading that book was that traditional rank structures took a backseat inside the SAS. You'd have officers and enlisted calling each other by first names. The command authority and rank were still in place for discipline but the rank and background barriers were less structured so team members were free to share ideas, contribute to decisions, and push back during discussions. That stuck with me.

In fire departments, especially combination departments, there's always that underlying friction: career vs. volunteer, union vs. non-union. We didn't want that baggage. Starting from scratch gave us a chance to build a different kind of culture.

So, we looked for folks who:
1. Had a track record of self-driven improvement
2. Could evaluate risk (not just take it)
3. Were comfortable operating in a flatter command structure

That third point? It's like the difference between a hazmat team in FDNY and a regular line company. It just *feels* different. It operates differently. We ended up with 30 original team members. Our Fire Chief told us, "You've got free reign - just make the problem go away." So we did. We divided the team into five squads - six people per team, each with a team leader. It wasn't a permanently staffed team. It was call-up based.

We organized our General Order to create three levels of incidents with 1 being the lowest skill level and capability to 3 as the highest. Level 1 calls were handled by line companies, Level 2 calls went to hazmat support units - folks trained to technician level. If the whole team was needed, the on-duty Level 3 squad would get activated. That team stayed on call for two weeks, whether they were on shift or not.

We interviewed for those 30 spots. Maybe 50 people applied. Some just weren't interested, and that worked in our favor - we got the folks who already had some background, who were *interested*. Many of our applicants were folks with bomb squad or fire investigator experience. They were self-motivated and already doing the homework.

During the interviews, we didn't just ask technical stuff like, "You've got a gas leak - walk me through the drill." Instead, we hit them with real-life chaos problems. "Your kid just pooped his pants. You're late for church. You dropped your keys in the snow. What do you do?"

We wanted to see how people worked through the problem and sorted through stress. There's no *right* answer - we just wanted to know how you think. I read a book about the creation of the World War-II Office of Strategic Service or OSS, the forerunner of the CIA. A lot of recruits were taken aback when they were asked weird questions during selection. The OSS was looking for the guy with a PhD from Stanford who could hold his own in a bar fight. They knew they could teach you how to blow up a bridge - but they couldn't teach the right *attitude*.

After 10 years of service as a company officer, one of our squad leaders quit the job and became an airline pilot. He went into his very competitive interview very nervous because he had limited flying experience. His United Airlines interviewer asked, "Why do you want to work here?" He said, and without hesitation, "Because you guys have the best damn television commercials." At that time, United had famed movie star Gene Hackman doing the voiceover with the tag "Fly the Friendly Skies". They *loved* the answer! Quick on his feet. That's what we were after. He didn't go into the interview with that answer in his head, it just came out because he had the *attitude*.

In the end, culture drives everything. People get promoted, retire, move on. But if you've built the right culture and evolve into a systematic organization, the new folks coming in don't know any different. It's like leaving an infantry battalion and going to a Green Beret unit - you walk into a totally different world. That's what we tried to build from day one.

And I think we got it right.

Bob Ingram

Determining what qualifies as an "Elite" hazmat team can be a tough call, especially given the variety of specialized units out there. You've got rail teams that excel at handling rail incidents and tank cars, RAD specialists who shine in RaAD facilities, and of course, the CA criteria with their Level 1, 2, and 3 teams based on personnel, equipment, training, and documentation. Then you've got FEMA's resource typing for hazmat teams when it comes to interstate requests. But at the end of the day, it really boils down to internal discipline and the funding available for maintaining skills.

The decision to determine which team qualifies as a "certified" team is in many cases decided by the Agency Having Jurisdiction (AHJ) and this language is used frequently in NFPA 470, "Hazardous Materials/Weapons of Mass Destruction (WMD) Standard for Responders."

Most Haz Mat programs follow the knowledge and skill competencies written in 470 which is a minimum level of guidance. Many teams are more advanced while others minimize specific areas of preparedness. For example, a jurisdiction without navigable waterways may not require any competencies on marine vessels. Another jurisdiction that has no rail within or near their response area may eliminate or minimize competencies in railcar planning, training, and response. And yet, these jurisdictions will certify their teams. I believe that this decision is acceptable, if they operate within their competency base (knowledge, training, and equipment).

In other programs, there are more rigid structures in place. The Federal Emergency Management Agency (FEMA) worked with hazmat leaders to develop resource typing language to standardize teams for deployment response into declared disaster areas.

The state of California's Governor's Office of Emergency Services (CalOES) oversees a "team typing" system broken into Type I, II, and III. Individual state, county, and local teams can request inspections from the Hazardous Materials Section of the Fire & Rescue Branch. These inspections will verify the agency's equipment inventory against the requirements for the team type they are requesting certification to. They also verify compliance with federal and industry standards, including NFPA, ASTM, OSHA, EPA, and others. The teams are subject to re-inspections to maintain their type certification.

Not many teams have a structured program like California's. It makes sense since California has resource typed and certified wildfire taskforces for many years for cross jurisdiction emergencies. New York City established work like this after September 11, 2001. We had fire and hazmat teams assisting us in the days and weeks after and the differences in how jurisdictions defined staffed, trained, apparatus, and equipment for engines, ladders, heavy rescues, and hazmat teams were not standardized. Mutual aid agreements were reviewed and revised to include standardized definitions.

So the question remains: how many teams can truly say they comply with every single element of NFPA 470?

For me, an "Elite" hazmat team needs to have a few key components:

1. A Dedicated Team
   This isn't a squad that's spreading itself thin across multiple missions. A true elite team is solely focused on hazmat response, and that focus is crucial.
2. Solid Firefighting Background
   It all starts with a solid firefighting foundation – 5+ years of experience at a minimum. You can't jump into hazmat work without knowing how to handle basic firefighting skills under pressure.
3. Diverse Team Members
   You cannot rely on a single type of education or skill set for a team to be effective. A mix of knowledge and skills is essential: plumbers, electricians, exterminators, bio and chem academics, code enforcement officers, welders, medics - these varied skill sets bring multiple perspectives, which is crucial when you're dealing with the unexpected.
4. Basic HM Foundation Training
   Hazmat training at the operational level during those initial firefighting years is a must. A solid 2-to-3-week Technician-level class should be part of the foundation, covering core areas of NFPA 470's Technician chapters, the mission the team is expected to perform, and the team's assigned equipment. More

time is necessary to become a good technician, but I would not train personnel beyond those 2 to 3 weeks in one period. They need time to develop skills and competence here, then add additional training during

5. Real-World Practice
   The first two years in the organization's hazmat company should be spent honing those basics, with a structured program of lessons that build on the core training. It's all about getting hands-on experience with basic level detection and monitoring, product control, local resources, and environmental rules and regulations. During those first two years an introduction to specialized equipment can also be part of the plan. National Fire Academy courses for hazardous materials such as Chemistry and Site Operations are a good fit during this initial level of training.

6. Second-Level Training
   Teams should be getting into more advanced, specialized areas of training and competence after mastering the basics in a documented program established by the agency. This next level should include advanced monitoring and detection, specialized product control equipment, equipment testing, maintenance, and repairs. Federal Consortium schools for live-agent training, radiological and biological response operations, advanced highway and rail containers, and energetic materials. These training programs and private training opportunities such as flammable liquid and gas and foam schools, and others, are in my opinion the gateway into the elite team level.

7. Instructor-Level Training
   It's critical that hazmat team members get trained as Level 1 or 2 instructors. This allows them to pass on their specialized knowledge to others and make sure the team stays sharp. Most teams cannot send the entire team to a distant school to attend a class. Funding and staffing are often not available to accomplish this. Members who attend initially and who are certified instructors can enhance the learning curve for those that follow. In-station training does not have to be done by the company officer. But it should be done effectively.

8. Networking and Community
   Second-level courses are also a great opportunity to network within the hazmat community, learning from others and expanding your resources. Personnel should also be approved to

attend any of the nationally recognized HazMat conferences to learn from their peers in various regions of the U.S. and other countries.

9. In-Service Training
Planned, systemic in-service training sessions covering equipment, SOPs, and practical team-building exercises are key. Annual refresher training should involve more than just drills - it should involve team-building scenarios that strengthen cohesion under pressure.

10. Incidents to Practice Skills
A solid, elite team needs to be involved in 100-300 incidents a year - real ones, not just the occasional stove gas leak or minor fuel tank spill. If you're not actively responding to incidents, you're not actively maintaining your skills.

11. Diverse Response Area
The geographic and scenario diversity of the team's response area plays a role, too. A team that operates in a variety of environments will develop stronger, more adaptable skills.

When it comes to team leadership, I believe the experience of being a firefighter really helps. Understanding how a candidate performs under stress, combined with evaluations from previous officers and unit commanders is vital to identifying potential leaders within the team.

And finally, diversity - again - can't be overstated. Not every team member has to be a chemist, and not everyone has to be a plumber. It's the mix of different skills and knowledge that makes a hazmat team truly elite. Each member brings a unique strength, which helps create a team with multiple instructors and experts in various areas, ultimately making the team stronger as a whole.

Phil McArdle

When selecting individuals for a Haz-Mat team, there are several key factors to consider. Motivation is one of the most important: Why does an individual want to join the team? Is it for financial gain, a change of pace, or to fulfill personal goals? Understanding their reasons for wanting to be part of the team will help ensure that their motivations align with the team's mission and culture. Equally important is what the department or team will gain by adding this person. What unique skills or knowledge do they bring that can enhance the team's effectiveness?

It's also critical to determine what special abilities will be needed for the role. What specific responsibilities will these individuals be expected to take on? Before making a decision, carefully consider the operational parameters of the team. What types of incidents will they be expected to respond to? Does the agency's Emergency Response Plan clearly outline the team's roles, responsibilities, and limitations? Assess whether the individual has the physical and mental strength to operate the tools and equipment safely and effectively. Additionally, are there any disqualifying factors, such as claustrophobia, colorblindness, or physical limitations that could affect performance?

A good example of this is seen with the FDNY Haz-Mat 1 team. One individual was selected due to his background as an operating engineer with experience in power plants and heavy equipment. His mechanical knowledge, understanding of HVAC systems, pumps, and machinery operations, as well as his expertise in rigging and handling large objects, made him a tremendous asset. His ability to assess which equipment needed to stay operational during an emergency and which could be safely turned off added another layer of strength to the team. His expertise demonstrated how specialized knowledge can contribute to a Haz-Mat team's success.

Next, consider whether the Haz-Mat team has a clear mission statement. Will the individual fit into that mission, or will they fall short? Can they grow under development and take on additional responsibilities? These are critical questions that need to be answered before moving forward with any selection.

Physical and knowledge assessments are essential for determining whether a candidate can perform under pressure. For example, after the Tokyo Sarin attack, the FDNY recognized the need to improve their Haz-Mat response capabilities. This led to mission-specific training where they expanded the number of personnel trained to wear Chemical Protective Clothing (CPC). They brought in units from various departments, including rescue companies, truck and engine companies, and battalion chiefs from special operations and safety divisions. Importantly, they ensured that all levels of supervisory personnel underwent the same pressure-filled training as the firefighters.

The training process followed a decision matrix, ensuring that individuals were equipped with the necessary knowledge and skills to perform the tasks, provided with the proper tools and equipment, and given the appropriate Personal Protective Equipment (PPE). The hazards and risks involved were thoroughly assessed to ensure that only after these criteria were met could individuals be expected to "work safely."

The FDNY's one-day training cycle included classroom sessions where personnel were taught about CPC, how to properly don and doff the gear, and self-extrication techniques. Additionally, they learned decontamination procedures and victim removal methods. After the classroom training, candidates applied what they had learned through a timed, task-oriented obstacle course simulating an emergency at Grand Central Station. The participants had to perform all tasks, go through decontamination, and self-extricate before running out of air. Anyone who couldn't complete the course failed. This hands-on training under pressure exposed weaknesses, such as claustrophobia or physical limitations, and those who passed proved they could handle high-stress situations.

A well-rounded Haz-Mat team benefits from the diversity of skills each member brings. Much like military special forces, each Haz-Mat team member possesses a foundation of knowledge, but specialized expertise is just as critical. Whether it's in communications, medical support, rigging, evidence collection, or operating heavy machinery, team members need to master aspects of various disciplines while understanding they cannot be experts in all of them.

Consider the different specialized roles within the Haz-Mat team: Should each mode of transportation have its own expert? What about specialized knowledge for various fixed facilities that might require unique expertise? Who is responsible for the maintenance, calibration, and inventory of equipment? Who ensures that the PPE is properly cleaned, sanitized, and ready for use? How will the team stay current on relevant laws, regulations, and the department's Standard Operating Procedures (SOPs)?

Understanding the potential hazards is also crucial. For example, who on the team has the expertise to identify and respond to drug labs? Who understands the equipment used in these labs, the chemical reactions involved, and the packaging and labeling of hazardous materials? As new threats emerge, the more you learn, the more you realize how much there is still to learn. The key is to maintain a team that is adaptable, diverse, and ready to take on new challenges.

In the end, a well-rounded and skilled Haz-Mat team that can adapt to evolving threats and challenges is essential for success. The team should be capable of handling a wide variety of situations while continuing to grow and learn, ensuring that they are always prepared for whatever comes next.

Adam McFadden

When I'm selecting people for a top-tier hazmat team, I'm not just looking for certifications or resumes - I'm looking for mindset. The people who thrive in this field are the ones who are genuinely committed to continuous learning. Hazmat is always evolving. You've got new threats, new technologies, and new mitigation tactics popping up all the time. So, I want folks who are hungry to stay ahead - who want to know more about chemical, biological, radiological, nuclear, and explosive hazards, and how to handle them smarter, safer, and faster.

Curiosity is a big one for me. The best techs are the ones always asking, *What if?* or *Why did that happen?* They're constantly thinking through scenarios from different angles, digging for better solutions, and pushing to refine the way we do things. You've got to be a problem-solver - someone who keeps their cool under pressure, adapts to the unknown, and understands that no two hazmat calls are ever the same. Flexibility isn't optional; it's mandatory.

And above all, they need solid situational awareness and the ability to work well in a team. Communication is critical. You have to be able to process complex information fast and pass it on clearly. This isn't a solo operation. We operate in dynamic, high-risk environments where teamwork and trust can make or break the outcome. The ones who succeed? They're sharp, confident in their skills, and humble enough to learn from every run, training session, and real-world experience. That's how you stay on the cutting edge in this game.

When it comes to evaluating someone's ability to perform under pressure, I look at how they function in chaos. Hazmat response means juggling multiple streams of data - what's leaking, how it reacts, what's happening environmentally, who's at risk, and what resources are available. And you've got to do that quickly and accurately, because hesitation can cost lives.

So during training and simulations, I throw candidates into high-stress scenarios. I'm watching how they process what's happening, how they prioritize, and whether they can make smart decisions under pressure without freezing up or rushing in recklessly. It's a balancing act - decisive but not impulsive. Fast but calculated. The people who excel are the ones who trust their training, stay calm, and adjust in real time. That kind of mental resilience and technical precision is what separates good techs from great ones.

Another thing that often gets overlooked is how important it is to build a team with a wide range of skills. A strong hazmat unit isn't just a bunch of people who know how to plug a leak. You need a foundation in firefighting principles - life safety, incident stabilization, and property conservation - that's your anchor. But beyond that, I'm looking for specialists.

Some of the best team members are the ones who bring something extra to the table. Maybe they've got a background in confined space rescue, industrial firefighting, emergency medical response, or they've done risk assessments or air monitoring. That cross-disciplinary experience is gold. It gives us depth and flexibility.

A hazmat call might involve a complex rescue from a contaminated zone one minute, then shift to decontaminating exposed victims, and end with managing an unstable chemical spill. That's three different skill sets in one call. So when you've got people who can step into those roles seamlessly, who understand both the tactical and the technical sides, your team is just better equipped - period. The more diversity you have in training and experience, the more adaptable and effective your response will be when things go sideways.

Mike Monaco

Whenever I sat in on interviews for new hazmat team members, there were a couple of things I was always looking for.

First off, I didn't care if they were chemical geniuses or had years of hazmat experience. That stuff can be taught. What mattered to me was whether they brought at least one or two solid skills to the table - something, anything, that could benefit the team. They didn't need to be an electrician or a plumber or know the periodic table by heart. But they had to have *something* they were good at that could be valuable in the field. Period.

As for personality traits, I leaned toward people who could figure things out on their own. Once someone gets trained up to the technician level, the expectation is that they can step back, see the big picture, and know how to move forward. You want folks who don't need their hand held - people who can operate independently and stay plugged in to what's happening around them.

Now, here's the thing about stress. You can't sit across a table from someone and really get a read on how they'll perform under pressure. Interviews are just too clean, too controlled. The only real way to know how someone reacts in the thick of it is to talk to someone who's *seen* them in it. That's where references become crucial. We'd reach out to people who've worked with them - captains, supervisors, whoever - and ask: "Have you seen them in a tough spot? How'd they handle it? Did they see it through?" That's how you find out if someone's got the grit.

And when it comes to building a well-rounded team? Diversity of skills is everything. You *need* the plumbers. You *need* the chemists. You need the people who live in between. The truth is, there's no such thing as the perfect hazmat technician. The person who's incredibly strong in chemistry usually isn't very mechanical. And the mechanical wizards?

They're often not too sharp on the chemistry side. So, you're either looking for someone who's well-rounded across the board, or someone whose strength in one area is deep enough to make up for the gaps elsewhere. That balance is what makes a team truly effective.

Chris Pfaff

So, when I was sitting there looking at it and thinking about it - and I've talked about this throughout my instruction - selection of personnel, one of the key qualities and attributes when selecting members is passion. But it's passion, passion for the craft, passion for anything. And this isn't just hazardous materials - this is technical rescue, paramedicine. You know, we've heard so many times in the fire emergency response field, "You don't become a paramedic for the pay." And you see paramedics or hazmat technicians or rescue technicians or anyone on a specialty team who joined just because they wanted a bullet point on their resume for promotion, or they wanted that pay bump.

But those members aren't the ones putting in the time, energy, and effort as they continue through their careers. Unfortunately, they're not supportive of the team, especially during training and even more so during an actual call. You need to find members who are passionate and excited about their craft. They might not have much knowledge initially, but they have that engagement and passion. So flat out, that's the one word: passion. One chapter, one word.

Now, assessing a candidate's ability to perform under extreme stress - that took me a second to think through. I'm just going to quickly read off what I typed up and then I'll spitball on it. An effective way to evaluate this is through previous knowledge and interviews.

Typically, our hazmat team members are more senior; they're two, three, even up to five years on the job, sometimes many more. So, we already have experience and knowledge of how they've performed under stressful conditions. We've seen them on fires, we've seen them on CPR calls, critical trauma events, and we've observed whether they stepped up or shied away during these incidents. So, through an interview process - and there are agencies and entities that do this; FEMA USAR teams are a good example - it's not just about seniority, it's about the interview because that's an elite, national-level team. Knowing their background and having seen them on previous calls is the best way to accurately assess their ability to perform under extreme stress.

One thing that drives me nuts about some fire departments is the idea of "butts in seats". The seat I'm sitting in isn't just literally a seat - yeah, it's physically a seat - but the capabilities of the office and position I'm in, whether it's the right seat of a fire engine as an officer, an engineer in the left seat, or a third or fourth firefighter-paramedic, we don't all have the same skills and attributes. You've gotta have those rock breakers, without a doubt. The rescue tech team needs to have the rope-dope, that guy who just knows how to tie ropes, who knows how to hit concrete. The hazmat team needs that kind of person as well.

We need the hazmat tech who just wants to get in the suits. He's the one saying, "I'm in, boss - I want to get into that hot zone, I want to get wet, I want to get nasty, I want to get dirty." Likewise, you need the nerd - the one who knows and understands everything about chemistry, who knows the reactions, who's been through the NFA classes and all the national-level courses. They can recite the entire periodic table and explain covalent and ionic bonds, whereas the suits-and-boots guy is like, "Um, salts and non-salts, that's it." So, you have to have diversity.

That's what makes a well-rounded team - especially having the tech-savvy member who can handle all the digital computer things. They might not be great in suits, and honestly, you don't even want them in suits. Instead, you're going to want someone who has good command, control, and leadership.

Rob Rezende

In hazmat, there is no box to think outside of - you're always outside of it. We challenge our candidates with problems that don't have a clear-cut solution, asking them to think critically and creatively.

Curiosity is key. I look for people who dive into everything the department does. Whether it's technical rescue, USAR, bomb squads, or arson investigations, I want someone who isn't just checking off boxes but is eager to explore every facet of the job.

In training, I love seeing candidates take on different roles. I'll assign things like Hazmat Group or Tech Ref to those who always want to be the ones suited up. But here's the catch: I pair them with a senior member. They'll struggle a bit, but we won't let them drown. It's about growing through the discomfort.

Every team member has strengths and weaknesses. I focus on leveraging their strengths - whether that's handling projects, conducting research, developing training, or leading during high-risk incidents. But I also push them outside their comfort zone, creating safe spaces for them to tackle areas where they're less confident. Whether it's on the training ground or standing in front of a group to give a lecture, the goal is to fortify those weaknesses

Bob Royall

Hazmat teams are absolutely critical, no doubt about it. My career in this field kicked off with the Houston Fire Department, and I can tell you, that's one of the busiest, most accomplished hazmat teams in the country. Why? Well, it's the sheer risk and responsibility of the Houston and Harris County area. Houston HazMat has been at it since 1979, and back then, we were looking for people with mechanical aptitude - folks who could think on their feet, handle problems in real-time, and who were genuinely passionate about hazmat work, not just seeking a job. We didn't want anyone just showing up for a paycheck; we needed people who wanted to stick around because we invested a lot in them, almost like training fighter pilots.

The focus was clear: we needed highly motivated individuals who might not have been top of their class in high school, but who had the mechanical know-how and the drive to get things done. Those were the qualities we were looking for, and that's how Houston Hazmat built our team.

In the early days, we had the luxury of handpicking the best candidates. But, as you can imagine, that didn't sit well with everyone. As a union guy, I understood the resistance to that approach. Grievances were filed, and that led us to move to a more formal selection process. But even with that, the interview process often allowed us to steer things in the direction we wanted. We would have the team interview candidates to see if they had that "can-do" aptitude. If we collectively felt they'd be a good fit, we'd offer them the job. I still think that approach is crucial today.

The landscape today has changed, though. When I first came on the job, it was a career - something you did for the long haul, planning to retire with a pension and maybe stick around doing something else afterward. But now, there's a more educated labor pool out there, no doubt about it. However, we're seeing less mechanical aptitude in the traditional sense. Many of today's candidates are more familiar with keyboards than with turning wrenches. So, it's tougher to find those "MacGyver" types, the ones who can improvise and adapt quickly.

Building a team today means diversity - people with different skill sets. You don't want a team full of electricians or pipe-fitters, although those folks are valuable. You need a mix of guys who can build on-scene tools, others who might lean toward research or science, and a few who struggle to even find the "on" button on their computer. It's about finding the right balance.

Take, for example, we looked for people who may have a specialty as they joined the team in Houston. We realized we had certain gaps, for instance we needed somebody with knowledge around farm chemicals and pesticides. We had a guy who gravitated toward that, and over time, became a true expert in the field. If he wasn't on duty, we had his number on speed dial. The knowledge he built up over the years - much of it self-taught - was invaluable. He took classes, sure, but the real expertise came from his interest and experience.

Then there's Bill Hand, who specialized in containers. That guy could identify any container you threw at him - he knew what it was made of, what year it was built, everything. That kind of specialized knowledge is gold in our line of work.

When you're building a team, it's like putting together a baseball team. You need strong starting pitchers, reliable relievers, and solid infielders. If you find someone who fits that perfect niche, don't just brush them off - take a second look. You never know when a key player is going to come through the door. And when they do, make sure you recognize their value.

Bobby Salvesen

One of the hardest parts of building a hazmat team - especially from scratch - is picking the right people. It's way easier when you already have a team in place. The reputation of that crew, of the department, helps draw in better candidates. People want to be part of a good team. But when you're just starting out, man, it's tough. You're drafting in the dark a bit.

To build a solid team, you need a good spread. A mix. That means everything from brand new folks - those who are green but eager - to the seasoned vets who've been around the block a few times. You want guys who've been in a firehouse forever, or working in an ER, who carry that institutional knowledge. They're the ones who know how to lead, how to manage the chaos. They've seen enough to offer some perspective when the wheels start to wobble.

At the same time, I *want* those newer members. Because when you've got new people on the team, it forces the experienced ones to step up and teach. Now you've got learning happening. You've got knowledge being passed on, and new folks seeing the expectations modeled right in front of them. It's not just classroom theory - they're witnessing what we *actually* expect of them in the field.

And then there's perspective. I always say, you and I could give the same exact presentation - same slides, same topic, doesn't matter - but the delivery? Totally different. Why? Because we see things through different lenses. And that's *critical*. You need people on your team who see the world differently.

You want the strong guy. The communicator. The chemist. The one who's brilliant at researching obscure stuff. The plumber who just *gets* how things flow. The tech nerd who can make gadgets talk to each other. You're not looking for clones - you're looking for a range. A team with all those skillsets, those viewpoints, those angles.

That's how you build a hazmat team worth having.

Doug Schick and Mark Zilch
Doug:

Recruitment's tough. Especially for hazmat. You know, the guys who are really gung-ho, the ones that want to be out there grinding, they're usually not drawn to hazmat - at least not in CFD. It's not the flashy spot. Most of them want to be on a busy fire company or a rescue squad, someplace where things are always happening. And honestly, I was the same. I was on rescue squads, did a little hazmat stuff here and there, but I didn't want to be on a hazmat company until later in my career. Eventually, I ended up captain of Hazmat, but it took time.

Hazmat's just a different mindset. When I was a squad officer, I could drill all day and guys were into it. And the ones who weren't? I'd just say, "Hey, no problem. I've got twenty guys lined up who'd kill to be here." But with hazmat, it's different. You've gotta be more intentional. I always say: *you've gotta know what you're selling*. As an officer, you've got to recognize what kind of company you've got and lead accordingly.

I've seen it before - really motivated hazmat officers working their teams hard, maybe too hard, and they end up driving off their most experienced people. That's not how you build longevity. My backgrounds in physics, so hazmat was always something I thought about. And I've always appreciated how people bring their different strengths - plumbers, chem majors, tradespeople - they all add something unique.

When it comes to recruitment, I do what I can. For us, hazmat techs - the top tier in our system - get a pay bump, whether they're on the hazmat company or not. So I'll pop into those hazmat tech classes, introduce myself, talk about the team. I'll be honest with them: "I know a lot of you are here for the bump in pay - nothing wrong with that, I'd be doing the same. But if you're genuinely interested, reach out. We can set up a detail, give you a chance to see what it's really like."

That approach has brought in a few folks over the years. Not a flood, but some solid people. Still, it's a challenge. Just yesterday, I was talking to the captain at 512 about this vacancy order we've got. He's worried - and rightly so - that people might apply for the wrong reasons. I get that concern, but here's the thing: if a guy gets through the interview, has the certs, checks the boxes - what do you do? Turn him away?

Sometimes, even if they're here for the wrong reasons, if they stay long enough, they'll pick stuff up. They'll learn the layout, the equipment, the rhythm of things. That's more than you can say for someone who gets detailed in once every few years and barely knows what we do. Knowledge comes with time.

Now, there are two ways into hazmat with us. First is the temporary detail route - basically, you're sitting with us indefinitely, but you don't have a permanent spot, so you can be bumped back. Second is going through the vacancy order. Both require certs, but the permanent slot also comes with an interview. These days, it's way more formal. Used to be, the chief could say, "Nah, I don't like that guy," and that was that. Now, you've got standardized interviews, IG reps sitting in, everyone gets the same questions. If you pass, then it comes down to seniority if there are more candidates than spots.

But again - it comes back to what you're selling as an officer. When I was on a squad, I could push hard because people wanted in. With hazmat, if you push too hard, you might be pushing people right out the door. And then who's coming in to replace them? That's where things get tricky.

Mark:
Yeah, and on top of that, you've got to talk about proficiency standards. When I first got into hazmat, I was detailed in under Captain Scheurich. He was all about proficiency. Didn't matter why you were there - if you weren't willing to drill, teach, or at least contribute every day, he was on you.

You didn't get to just chill because hazmat doesn't get as many runs. If you weren't pulling your weight, he'd run you out. That approach, it worked. The guys who really cared, who felt called to this kind of work, they stuck around. They got good at it. They drilled, they taught, they learned the meters inside and out. And yeah, it took time, but that's how you build real capability.

So to Schick's point - yeah, some people might come because they think it's going to be a slower pace. And maybe it is on calls, but we drill. Three hours a day sometimes. You *better* be proficient. You *will* be held accountable. That's the kind of message we need to send right up front.

That's how I got in, actually. I came in as a temp detail, learned the meters, realized I liked it, and then I went through the interview. But even now, one of the biggest hurdles is just getting guys interested. Hazmat's intimidating. Most of them joined to be firemen or EMTs. They didn't sign up thinking they'd be dealing with chemical threats and meters and technical decon. It's a different world.

But if you can show them the value, show them the challenge and the purpose behind it, you can win some of them over. It's just not going to happen with every guy. And that's okay - because the ones who do stick with it? They're the ones who make this team strong.

Jason Zeller

When standing up the 24th WMD-CST from scratch, I knew this team couldn't be staffed with average performers - we needed professionals with an exceptional mix of discipline, technical skill, and mental toughness. I wasn't just building a team; I was building a specialized capability ready to face the worst-case scenarios.

Drawing from my prior experience as a member of one of the first WMD-CST teams in the country - formerly known as RAID teams - and having responded to real-world WMD incidents, including the terrorist attack on the World Trade Center on 9/11, I knew exactly what kind of Soldier and Airman we needed. We had to create a high-performing, tight-knit environment built on trust, competence, and endurance.

Character came first - integrity, accountability, and a strong sense of duty were non-negotiable. These missions require trust - you must know the person beside you will act decisively and ethically under pressure.

I also prioritized adaptability and intellectual curiosity. Operating in a highly technical and ever-evolving space means you need people who can problem-solve in real time, not just follow procedures.

Mental and physical resilience were critical. In chaotic situations, in harsh environments, dealing with hazardous materials and unknown threats for extended periods - there's no room for hesitation or breakdowns under stress.

Lastly, I looked for a team-first mindset. No matter how talented someone was individually, they had to be able to integrate into a cohesive, mission-focused unit. In CST operations, success depends on communication, mutual support, and total trust.

The assessment phase for selecting team members for the 24th WMD-CST was deliberate, rigorous, and purpose-built to identify individuals who could thrive in the most demanding conditions imaginable. We weren't just looking for qualified personnel - we were identifying those capable of functioning and leading in high-stakes, high-stress environments involving chemical, biological, radiological, nuclear, and explosive threats.

It began with an extensive board interview process, focused on evaluating not only the candidate's experience but also their problem-solving ability, judgment, and emotional intelligence. We asked hard questions and listened closely to how they thought under pressure.

From there, candidates entered a tough indoctrination phase, which included high-intensity physical workouts, often conducted in full PPE. This wasn't just about fitness - it was designed to simulate operational fatigue and evaluate mental resilience, stress response, teamwork, and composure under duress.

Those who advanced were sent through an elaborate array of specialized training, both military and civilian. This included core courses like HAZMAT Technician, Civil Support Skills Course (CSSC), U.S. Army Technical Escort Course (L3 Skill Identifier), and advanced radiological/nuclear operations courses. But we also incorporated training from the Federal Law Enforcement Training Center (FLETC) for maritime operations, as well as using our State Fire Training Academy to certify as rope rescue technicians and Confined Space Rescue, and a variety of medical courses to build well-rounded, cross-functional operators capable of responding to dynamic and multi-domain threats.

The entire pipeline was built to expose a candidate's limits, reinforce excellence, and ensure that by the time someone earned their spot on the team, they had proven their capability across physical, mental, and technical dimensions. You can't teach grit, and you can't simulate courage - but through this process, we found the individuals who brought both to the fight.

Diversity of skills is absolutely critical in building a well-rounded and effective hazmat team. In the context of a WMD-CST, we weren't just looking for individuals who could perform a singular task; we were building a multi-disciplinary unit capable of tackling a range of complex scenarios. Every person on the team needed to bring something unique to the table.

From the very beginning, I knew we needed technical specialists - experts in CBRN - but we also needed problem solvers who could think outside the box and rapidly adapt to unpredictable situations. We had team members with skills in tactical operations, medical expertise, and communication, and we made sure to include those with strong backgrounds in leadership and operations, who could coordinate during high-stress operations.

Incorporating this diversity of backgrounds meant that our team could leverage a wide variety of approaches to address threats. For example, while a hazmat technician might be focused on containment, a tactical medic's expertise could prove crucial in the event of a mass casualty situation, and our engineers would step in for problem-solving and equipment maintenance. On a larger scale, some of our team members had backgrounds in law enforcement, military strategy, maritime operations, Fire/Rescue, and Special Operations, which brought an additional layer of versatility when we were conducting joint operations or responding to complex multi-agency incidents.

A diverse skill set also fosters innovation and cross-training - each individual is capable of stepping into a different role if needed. When every member has a unique, well-developed specialty, but also understands the broader team's mission, the cohesion and adaptability of the group improve exponentially. It's about creating synergy, where the whole is greater than the sum of its parts.

Ultimately, having a team of specialists from varied backgrounds provides the flexibility and depth required to respond to ever-evolving and unpredictable hazmat incidents. That diversity of expertise allows us to adapt quickly, leverage the best skills for any given situation, and ensure that we're prepared for any eventuality.

TRAINING

"Individuals play the game, but teams beat the odds."
-SEAL team saying

Dan Baker

An effective hazmat training program needs to balance two critical standards: OSHA 1910.120 paragraph Q and NFPA 470. But equally important, your training needs to be tailored to your team's actual equipment, specific protocols, and - most importantly - the real incidents you're responding to day in and day out.

This approach must be data-driven. Look at the calls you're handling regularly and let those statistics steer your training priorities. This doesn't mean ignoring JPRs on things you've never encountered - you just shouldn't give them equal emphasis. For example, on our team, the lion's share of our calls involve transportation incidents, specifically LPG and flammable liquids. Knowing this, about half our training hours are dedicated to these types of incidents, with the remainder addressing less frequent scenarios.

Over the years, we've made a significant shift away from heavy classroom-based learning. Sure, textbooks and theory matter, and we expect our students to do their reading and come prepared. But in-person training time is far more effective when devoted primarily to hands-on skill building. Theory can be studied independently and then verified through testing, but skills? They need repetition - and lots of it. Competency must be demonstrated and verified firsthand.

To accomplish this, we rely heavily on props - and whenever possible, they're real-world, not fancy "store-bought" models. Our academy is stocked with every type of specification cargo tank you'd encounter in the field - all authentic, all operational. And whenever we can safely manage the risk, we prefer performing skills under real-world conditions. For example, when we're training on propane transfers, we use actual propane. Realism drives home the lesson and significantly boosts competence.

There are exceptions, of course. We won't mess around with materials like gasoline, where the risks far outweigh any training benefits (seriously, it's sketchy stuff - don't go there). But generally, we've found that training under realistic conditions makes lessons stick and accelerates competency.

Bottom line: your training should be grounded in the standards, but driven by data and reality. Prioritize the incidents your team is most likely to face, emphasize hands-on skill development, and whenever safely possible, train under actual operating conditions.

Mike Callan

Let me put it this way: when I first started training, things were a lot simpler, but definitely more hands-on. My "training" at the beginning involved me holding up construction cards shaped like diamonds - basic, paper cards. I'd hold up a green diamond, and then I'd ask the class, "What's the chemical?" People would try to guess. It was the early '80s, around '81 and '82. Back then, there weren't placards, and we didn't have the kind of training tools we have today. The placards didn't even come around until '75. So, we did the best we could with what we had - just a handful of books, maybe six at most. They focused on recognizing and identifying chemicals: container shapes, sizes, markings, colors, placards, labels, and shipping papers. It was all about getting the name of the chemical. We didn't have what we have now in terms of detailed training, but at least we understood the basics.

I can still remember my first hazmat call. I got sick from nitric acid. Before that, I'd done a little hazmat work, but this was a wake-up call. In fact, before we had placards, the only "hazmat" we'd deal with was something like class B or C ~~buyers~~, fires or class D's - mostly electrical. That was the extent of it. Chemical spills? Those were rare. But once placards came out, we finally had something to study, something to build on. We started learning about hazard classes - what each one meant, what chemicals fell under each class. I remember my first FIC - Fire Instructor Course - was in Memphis. We drove four of us out there, and on the way, we stopped in the middle of Tennessee. A truck driver carrying explosives got turned away from McDonald's just because he had an orange placard. They didn't know what it meant, so they asked him to leave. It made me feel bad for the guy - he just wanted to eat!

Anyway, that awareness training then evolved into recognition training. Once we had the placards, we could start identifying chemicals. But it also became about getting the right equipment. Hazmat teams wanted suits. Everybody wanted to wear suits because that made you look like a real hazmat team. So, suits became part of the identity of what hazmat response was.

I think that's where we started formalizing things, and in Connecticut, when we first began offering hazmat training, it was designed to be around 40 hours. We'd get responders ready for small spills, equip them with level B gear and respiratory protection, and then teach about the high-level stuff - level A, which was reserved for the big incidents. The second week of training was all about chemical-specific knowledge. I'd take groups to places like American Cyanamid Chemical, where we'd learn about monomers and plastics, or go to Ensign Bickford to study explosives. We'd go to Waterbury to learn about acids and bases. The goal was to understand chemical problems and train people to respond appropriately. But it was basic, hands-on learning, just books and manuals, which were cumbersome but essential at the time.

Today, looking back, I think about how far we've come. Now we have videos and online programs, and there's virtual reality. Training is much more advanced, but it still boils down to the same core principle: teaching responders how to assess and respond to hazards. We might have more sophisticated technology today, but the core concepts remain the same. When I'm training, I see the same passion in those first responders today as I did in the '80s. And when I talk to someone programming my training materials for 2025, I realize how much easier it is for them. They've got access to so much more than we ever had.

But here's where I get frustrated: refresher training. It's a joke. You can give someone 24 hours or even 8 hours of refresher training, but if you look at the standards - like 1910.120 - there's no real guidance on how long refresher training should last. It just says "sufficient content and duration to assure competency." Well, what does that mean? If someone gets hurt or blows themselves up, does that mean they weren't competent? I've seen people in old, disposable Level A suits who didn't even know how to wear them properly. There was one guy who wore his suit inside out with "extra large" on the back, and he was a certified tech. I've got pictures of it. Another guy didn't know that a whistle was supposed to go off on a rebreather, and it nearly led to a dangerous situation. These are the kinds of things that make me shake my head when I think about the state of refresher training.

One thing I always say at conferences is that no one knows who Ludwig Benner is, and they should. If you don't know Benner's work - especially his investigation into firefighter fatalities during hazmat incidents - you're already behind. Benner was crucial in understanding what we needed to do in hazmat response. He taught us the importance of analyzing incidents like Kingman, Arizona and Waverly, Tennessee. A guy like Mike Hildebrand, who worked with Benner, helped bring this into focus. Benner's insights are key, and anyone who doesn't recognize that is missing a big piece of the puzzle.

If there's one thing I think everyone should understand, it's flammables. How much do you know about them? It's the one chemical that's been the number one release for the past 19 years. It's the same thing I used to say: find a town that can handle a gasoline tanker and make sure they have enough foam. But even foam has become a problem - nowadays, it's frowned upon to use it because of environmental concerns.

It all boils down to this: training is a continuous ladder. You climb up, but there's always a plateau you can't quite reach because we don't practice enough. In many cities, firefighters start their careers on ambulances, so by the time they get to hazmat training, they've already spent several years doing something else. It's frustrating because it means we lose out on valuable experience. But you can still teach. You can still make a difference. It's just about making sure people get the right tools, the right foundation, and the right understanding to face whatever challenges come their way.

John Cassidy

When we zoom out and look at the broader picture - say, the 550 hazmat techs citywide, whether they're assigned to rescue companies, squad companies, hazmat engines, or Hazmat 1 - it becomes clear that formalized training is absolutely critical. And for Hazmat 1 specifically, every member has to go through that training process *before* they step into the company.

When someone joins us, they're handed the sign-off binder on day one. That binder lays out exactly what they need to do - it's not a mystery. But here's the thing: there are no deadlines. There's no "you must complete X by month three." What we *do* track, though, is initiative. If you've been here a month and haven't signed off on anything yet? That's a red flag. I'm not chasing you down - you should be coming to me, saying, "Hey, can I get signed off on this?" That's how we start to gauge your motivation and work ethic without saying it out loud.

We've got a literal binder in the office - paper and pencil. At any time, I can pull it off the shelf and look at three candidates. One has 20 sign-offs after three months. Another has three. Guess which one's more likely to succeed? It's not rocket science. The sign-off process isn't just training - it's also an evaluation tool.

Now, when it comes to the training itself, the way we design our hazmat technician course reflects how adults actually learn. With the exception of Day One, which is all lecture (because we have to lay down the theoretical foundation), every day from Day Two to Day Fifteen includes hands-on components. The class will be divided into three teams for the hands on lessons. The small group learning model encourages dialog between the students and the instructor.

The teams will train together for three weeks like a fire company. The final certification exam has three Haz Mat scenarios that the team is expected to solve. At the conclusion of the course the team will have utilized all of their individual skills and lessons to completely manage the three incidents modeled after real responses.

We bring that same logic into the company-level training. When a member presents a tool or a meter, it's not enough to just talk about it - they've got to show it. Explain the theory *and* demonstrate the practical. If someone's explaining a catalytic bead flammability sensor, not only doI want to hear the science - but I also want to see you power it on and operate it properly. Around here we call it "buttonology" - the art of knowing which buttons to push and when. If you can tell me how the sensor works but you can't operate and trouble shoot problems then you aren't going to be successful.

Now, you brought up a great question about building a well-rounded team: what role does diversity of skills and experience play?

I think it's huge - and I'd even go beyond just "skills" to talk about *experience*. On our team, we've got folks with the minimum five years on the job required to even apply, and we've got others with 20 years in the department. That's not just a range of time - it's a range of wisdom. Of exposure. Of judgment.

Then there's the skills side - sure, you've got someone who's a plumber, another who was in the military, maybe someone else was an electrician. All of that adds value. But here's the reality: we can't go out and build the "perfect" team. We're working with the candidates who raise their hands and say, "I want to be here." I can't post a job ad that says, "Seeking hazmat technician with journeyman-level electrical experience." We work with what we've got.

So we do ask about your background in the interview - because it matters - but ultimately, it's about how you show up, how you train, and how you contribute once you're here. Skills and experience help, but it's the drive and follow-through that separate the good from the great.

Dave DiGregorio

At the state level, we had a training coordinator and an assistant training coordinator, plus three additional training coordinators in the office who helped assist the teams with their monthly drills and anything else they needed. So, at both the team and state level, there was support for training. But, more than anything, these coordinators had to know their equipment inside and out.

With technology advancing so quickly, especially in Massachusetts, where we had a good budget to work with, when something new came out and it was something we needed, we got it. And that's great - having access to top-tier technology is huge. But here's the kicker: Do the guys actually understand what that technology means?

It's one thing to press a button, but do they know when not to press it? Do they know when a piece of equipment is the wrong choice for a specific scenario? Let me give you an example. This was about four or five years ago, and it wasn't my A team responding. We got a call about Mercury, and when I arrived, the team was wearing P-100s. I called them back and said, "What's wrong with this picture? What's the P stand for?" Blank stares.

It stands for particulate. And what's Mercury throwing off? That's right - it's a vapor, not particulate. So they had done absolutely nothing to protect themselves properly. We quickly realized that this needed to be added to our training curriculum. If that mistake could happen once, it would happen again, and we had to address it.

That's where After Action Reviews (AARs) come in. During each drill, team leaders would conduct AARs from the past months incidents so that we can debrief and learn from what happened. And often, as part of this session, we'd make sure there was a section for "three ups, three downs" - a review of what went well and what didn't. It's vital for continuous improvement.

When I started really pushing the training side of things, I ran into a challenge. Some of the older, more experienced guys - the veterans in the fire and hazmat world - were hesitant to get involved. They didn't want to be embarrassed, and I get that. You have to respect the experience they bring. But how do you get them to engage?

Here's what we did: Every team had in-person drills once a month. And to make it work, we introduced a round-robin style format. With 45 guys per team, we'd set up to nine different stations, with as few as five people rotating through each one. This way, everyone got hands-on time with the equipment and didn't just stand on the sidelines. If you tried to run a class with 45 people watching five guys use a piece of equipment, you wouldn't get the results you wanted.

So, we broke them up into smaller groups - no more than six or seven per group. Then we'd rotate them through different stations: one station for fiber tech, one for ramen, and so on. Even with tanker drills, we'd incorporate grounding and bonding as part of the exercise to make it more comprehensive.

Some people are great at picking things up through online learning or reading, but for most hazmat guys, hands-on training is key. I'd say 75% of the team needed that hands-on experience to really understand and retain what they were learning. The remaining 25%, the science geeks, were more inclined toward the academic side, but that's the minority.

We also tried hybrid training, blending online courses with hands-on sessions. This worked well for a time, though it eventually became difficult to coordinate with everyone's schedules. But the value of hybrid learning is undeniable, especially for the awareness-level courses.

For example, hospitals are required to do eight-hour awareness-level training every year. The emergency manager at the hospital governs that training, ensuring it meets their needs. This type of training needs to be flexible and fit within the scope of what's necessary, and I think moving toward more hybrid or blended learning in hazmat training is the future. It gives you a combination of both the theory and the practical experience to really get the job done.

Dave Donohue

When it comes to training, the first step is making sure that what we're practicing reflects the types of calls and hazards we're actually going to encounter. If you can't handle the routine, everyday incidents smoothly, there's no reason to expect success when things get more complicated. Once you've got the basics down - your bread-and-butter operations - then you can start adding complexity. Start introducing scenarios that throw in the unexpected, like dealing with unexpected twists (think "nuns and orphans").

Once you have a solid grip on the routine operations and can handle the curveballs, it's time to throw in some rare or high-stakes situations - things you might face when responding as mutual aid. But remember, mastering the basics before you scale up is key. You need to ensure the team has a strong foundation before jumping into the more complex incidents.

At some point, it's also essential to build in scenarios that challenge the team in unexpected ways - what I like to call "Disney" training. This is where you run scenarios where key players might make unexpected moves, like taking an unplanned vacation. This forces members to step into roles they don't normally fill, broadening their skill sets and, in the process, preparing future subject matter experts (SMEs) who can add depth to the team.

I'm a huge advocate for hands-on training, but it's got to come with a solid knowledge foundation to make it stick. From a learning theory perspective, skills are learned best when they're paired with the knowledge behind them. I focus on making sure everyone understands why we're training - ultimately, we're training so that the skills and knowledge can be recalled, applied, and adapted to new situations. To be able to improvise and adapt on the fly, there needs to be a solid knowledge base.

So, the training process should involve introducing the knowledge first, then applying it, and reinforcing it with recall. As training progresses, both knowledge and skills should be revisited, applied, and used in increasingly complex and unique scenarios. This ensures the team is ready for anything.

Rick Edinger

At the end of the day, when you're managing any kind of special operations team - hazmat, tech rescue, dive rescue, whatever - it all comes down to three things; people, time, and resources.

How much money do I have to get people to training? And how much time do I have to pull them out of service, backfill positions, and make all that happen? That's the balancing act. Once I know what I've got to work with, then I look at the hours we've got available and start shaping a training plan around that.

You've always got to strike a balance between knowledge and skills. There's the mental side - what they need to know - and then there's the hands-on side - what they've got to be able to *do* in the field. So, for me, it always goes back to: what are our hazards and risks? What do we think we're going to run into? And what do we need to be ready for?

We start with the basics, get that foundation solid, and then we look beyond that. When we get to drill days - remember, we've only got so much time - we're not like some of these national teams where training is the full-time gig. That kind of setup is rare. Most of us are trying to carve out time wherever we can.

Talk to other folks in the business, and you'll hear the same thing: refresh the fundamentals regularly, make sure your baseline is good, then dip into specialized topics when you can. Right now, everybody's chasing the battery and stored energy stuff. That came out of nowhere. Nobody anticipated the scope of that issue or how fast it would grow. So, just like that, your training priorities shift.

Same goes for changes in your response area. A new plant opens up, a rail siding goes in, or you've got new freight coming through on the highway - suddenly, you've got new risks to factor in. So, your training's always going to be a mix of bread-and-butter basics plus whatever emerging hazards and risks are on the horizon.

Now, in terms of *how* we train - what's most effective - I think simulation and virtual reality are the next wave. They're not perfect yet, but they're coming along. Whether it's simulating meter readings or putting on a VR headset and running through a scenario, that tech is evolving fast.

I think about EMS - years back, we started seeing computer-based training where you could sit by yourself and go through almost hands-on skill sessions. You didn't need to round up a whole crew or spend tons of money. Hazmat's heading in the same direction. I see computer-based simulation and VR as tools that are going to enhance what we're already doing with practical training.

The tricky part with hazmat, though, is that it's complex. It's not like a fire scenario where you can tell the computer, "I open the nozzle, fire goes out." Hazmat isn't linear. You've got various layers of decision-making, chemical reactions, environmental factors - all kinds of variables. So building truly realistic simulations is still a challenge. But once we cross that bridge - once the tech catches up - it's going to be a game-changer.

John Esposito

Everybody wants training. Nobody wants crap training. I always say there's pre-9/11 and post-9/11, and training is one of those areas where 9/11 was a major wake-up call. It showed us that you can't simulate your way through real problems. Guys want to train, but they want to train for real. They don't want some watered-down version of the job. They want sweat. They want heat. They want to feel the weight of the gear and the stress of a real scenario. If you're going to call it training, then make it worth something.

You've got to put them in suits. Get them crawling through smoke. Give them real tools and real situations. That's how they learn. But the key is that the department has to care, too. If leadership treats training like a checkbox or gives it the ol' wink and nod, then the members know that - and they'll treat it the same way. But when you make it important, when you put the time and the money behind it, the guys show up, and they get after it.

Look at what we've built. The fire academy has a shipboard firefighting simulator. A subway simulator. We've even got a damn airplane now. A *real* airplane. I love telling that story - JFK calls and says they've got a plane for us. We're thinking it's a section of fuselage or a mock-up we can throw on a flatbed. Nope. Full plane. The real deal.

And we're working on getting a pool. Sounds funny - "a pool for school" - but that's what we need for water rescue and ice rescue training. Our guys are in the water constantly. Not just the Marine units - squads, companies, across the board. And they're not afraid of it because we train them for it.

It's about making the training real, making it consistent, and building buy-in. Because once officers and firefighters start owning it - once they believe in it - they don't need to be told anymore. They start doing it themselves. That's when it spreads. That's when the whole thing takes off.

I'll give you a perfect example. Back when I was a lieutenant in Squad 18, one of those blistering summer days - like 8:30 in the morning and already 90-something degrees. We had a good relationship with the folks over at Carmine Street Pool, so I said, "Let's go." The pool didn't open until noon, so we showed up at ten. Freddy LaFemina calls and asks, "What are you doing?" I said, "We're going to Carmine for water rescue training." And that's exactly what we did. We jumped in, dragged guys around the pool, practiced techniques. Sure, it felt like swimming, and it was - but it was also training. And the lifeguards loved it - they were doing their own training, too. All it took was a couple of t-shirts to get access to the whole setup.

Now, hazmat - hazmat is its own beast. It's tough. I taught hazmat. I was in hazmat training. But I'm not the charismatic one. You guys - you found the Holy Grail. I sat in on one of your classes down in Baltimore, and you had the jacket on like a professor, the whole thing. And it was fun. That's the secret. You made it fun.

I still remember Hazmat Jeopardy with LaRocchia - stuff like that sticks. That's how you sneak it in. You sneak hazmat into their brains when they don't even realize it's happening. And suddenly, they're learning. They're actually learning this stuff and not dreading it.

That's the real challenge: not boring the guys. And hazmat has every chance to be dry and miserable. But if you make it real, make it engaging, if you show them that it matters - because it *does* matter - then they'll get it. Because at the end of the day, if we get it wrong, people get hurt. It's all good and fun until it isn't. And when someone gets seriously hurt, suddenly everyone wishes they'd paid more attention.

So yeah - training has to be effective. And the hardest part isn't delivering the content. It's getting people to want it. But when you do, man... it changes everything.

Brandon Fletcher

Establishing baseline Job Performance Requirements (JPRs) for every member and position within the hazmat team is critical. You need to clearly outline the expectations for each role and how to achieve them. To make this work, you'll need to identify how you will provide the pathways to meet those expectations: Will the department deliver in-house training with its own instructors, or will you rely on outside sources? If you're using external training, which sources are acceptable? (e.g., NDPC, State Academy, Private Industry, etc.) Vet all training, no matter the source. And don't forget to include a plan for ongoing education to ensure skills stay sharp.

Balance is key when it comes to training. Hazmat training has many technical aspects that require classroom learning, and it's essential to explain concepts and theories before diving into hands-on practice. The problem with lecture-heavy formats is often poor delivery. Just because someone has valuable knowledge or certifications doesn't mean they can convey it effectively or in a way that's engaging. You need to be deliberate about who you put in front of the class to teach. A good classroom instructor has to be able to "perform" and "entertain" in order to make sometimes dry content stick with students. HazMat can't be learned just by reading or listening to a lecture - it has to be hands-on.

Here's my approach: I like to explain a concept, either in a classroom or an improvised field setting, and then immediately jump into the hands-on component while the material is still fresh. I believe in a logical flow - Skill A is necessary to perform Skill B, or Skill B builds upon Skill A. Once students understand one, the other makes more sense. This requires the instructor(s) to deeply understand the material and put in significant prep work before class. Without that prep, the training loses its effectiveness.

Once we've covered the concepts and can perform the hands-on skills, we move into scenarios where we put those skills together in a logical sequence. There's no such thing as advanced firefighting, rescue work, or HazMat; everything is built on basic skills and concepts, applied in the right order. Unfortunately, in many "check-box" training programs, particularly certification classes, the focus is on passing written tests and practical evaluations, with little emphasis on applying those skills in real-world incidents.

Technicians become truly good when they understand not just how to do something, but when and why to do it.

Chris Hawley

I've always admired the California hazmat model. They seem to get everything done at once, and they do it right. A California hazmat tech is usually sharp, and those teams are high-speed, well-educated, and on top of things. That's one of the reasons I enjoyed teaching at their Continuing Challenge; they would really challenge me as an instructor. On the East Coast, I could walk in and get by with minimal prep, but in California, you've got to be on your game.

They're not just relying on firefighters - there are actual scientists on their teams. For example, LA has biologists and chemists right there in the firehouses. We had a chemist, but he was an industrial guy we borrowed, so having someone like that in the classroom, constantly asking questions, really keeps you sharp. It's an eye-opener, for sure.

But here's my issue: I'm not a fan of a responder just getting 40-hour training. I don't think it's enough, even if you cover the basics. Forty hours is just not enough to make someone competent or comfortable in the field. You've got to ensure they're proficient and ready to handle situations when they're out on a rig. It's not just about theory - it's about being able to get into a suit, operate the equipment, and handle the basics, like using a 4-gas meter, a PID, and an oxidizer paper. And you have to understand enough chemistry to know what you're dealing with when you're handling hazardous materials - whether it's a leaking 55-gallon drum or a tank truck. In a 40-hour training class how much time do the students spend in protective clothing and get hands on experience with detection devices?

The problem is that there's always this push for more knowledge - too much chemistry, too many high-end detection devices - but what I really want is for my hazmat techs to be able to suit up, operate basic equipment, and do the job. I want them to be able to identify what's going on, whether that's a leak, a chemical spill, or something else, without needing a PhD in chemistry. They don't have to interpret every result in minute detail, but they do need to know how to use their meters, gather the data, and hand it off to someone who can analyze it.

One of my goals with being involved with the NFPA 470 committee is I wanted to simplify the process for technician training. I wanted to simplify the process. You can't expect every tech to be an expert in everything. What we really need are specialists in key areas, but generalists who can hold their own in a variety of scenarios. I'm lucky in that I had some excellent connections - when we did tank truck training, we didn't just look at slides. We went to a chemical plant, climbed on real tank trucks, and handled the equipment firsthand. We had that advantage, and it was invaluable. Not every department has that luxury, but if you can make those connections and get your hands on real-world scenarios, it makes all the difference.

Now, don't get me wrong - technology has its place. Virtual reality (VR) training is incredible, and it's something I've been excited about for years. It's an area I've been waiting to see take off, and I've seen some promising demos, especially from FDNY. With VR, you can create realistic environments where you can use meters, see readings, and engage with the scenario as though it's real. It's not perfect, but it's a step toward replicating the pressure of a real-life hazmat situation without the risk. In theory, VR could simulate the situation well enough to give someone the feel of the scenario. But at the end of the day, it's still not enough on its own - you need that hands-on experience. VR can get you close, but it's no replacement for being on top of a railcar, dealing with a real chemical, or managing a live spill.

In my experience, you can't rely solely on virtual training. You have to go in, physically engage with the equipment, and experience the conditions. For example, during my time in Baltimore, we had a situation where a chemical plant was bringing in 90-ton railcars of oleum (concentrated sulfuric acid). We had to figure out how to deal with it since we hadn't worked with oleum before. The manufacturer told us not to put water on it, and they advised using a special extinguisher to stop the vaporization and form a crust. But when we tried it, we found that the crust wasn't enough - you still had to deal with the oleum underneath. So, we tried different methods, experimenting with neutralizing the spill using soda ash. That experience gave us real-world knowledge on how to deal with an oleum spill, which you can't just read about in a book or simulate in a video. We had to physically handle the material and figure out the best approach.

And this is where I disagree with some approaches to hazmat training. If you only use videos or mock-ups, you're not preparing your team properly. There's no substitute for the real thing. Just like we don't train firefighters without using real fires, hazmat training needs to include real chemicals, real situations, and real consequences. You have to get up close, get your hands dirty, and understand how things react in the real world. That's how you prepare your team - not by relying on the safest, least risky training scenarios. You've got to push the envelope a little and make sure your team is ready for whatever comes their way.

At the end of the day, it's about getting comfortable with the uncomfortable. You need that confidence to handle real-world situations, whether it's a railcar full of chemicals or a hazardous materials leak in a confined space. Virtual reality is a great tool, but there's no replacement for the experience and skills gained from hands-on, in-person training.

Mike Hildebrand

When we first started, we didn't really know what our core competencies were. We thought we did. Some of the stuff we tried worked, some of it didn't. But over time, we learned - core competencies aren't about theory, they're about what you *actually* need to do in the field.

Take chemical protective clothing, for example. Yeah, most people can put it *on*, but that's not enough. You've got to *function* in it. I've run into a lot of folks who couldn't. Claustrophobia, for one. Seen it a lot in breathing apparatus classes. But I've also seen people get over it. Same thing with acrophobia. These are problems you *can* work through. But you've got to be honest about where the baseline is. Core competency means mastery. Period.

I remember doing a team assessment at a oil refinery. Looking at their training records - and right there in the books, they had auto extrication listed as part of their emergency response training. I admit, it was cool. I like busting stuff up as much as the next guy. Using a force multiplier to pick up eggs with the Jaws? Fun stuff.But... the speed limit in a refinery is 10 mph. When exactly are you doing auto extrication in there? Meanwhile, something like putting out a pump seal fire? That's a *core* skill. You should be able to do that in your sleep. That's where the focus has to be.

Thankfully, we've got NFPA standards that define the baseline. Maybe not every competency listed there fits your exact mission - say you don't have intermodal containers in your jurisdiction - but the idea is, start simple and build too complex. Get the bread-and-butter skills down first. And that list of bread-and-butter skills? It's bigger now than it was 30 years ago, and it'll be even bigger in another 40. So, the real mission is to build smarter people who can adapt.

That's where hands-on work comes in. Everything needs a tactile piece to it. Even chemistry. You talk about organic acids, then you peel an orange, squeeze the mist through a lighter, and boom - there's your flash – organic acids are also flammable. You think they'll remember that? Of course they will. They'll go home and try it out. Maybe on the family dog.

The same thing applies to air packs. How long before that skill degrades? It depends on the department. If you're donning gear every day, no big deal. But a volunteer department that rarely trains? That skill's fading fast. So, you've got to integrate these core competencies *into everything*.

It's great to have advanced skills - like drilling tank trucks without hauling in a whole convoy of contractors - but don't skip over the basics. If your bread and butter is handling diesel fuel saddle tank leaks, every team member should be able to do that cold. And then teach someone else how to do it too.

Start with the simple, master it, then build up. That way you can expand endlessly - because there's *always* something new. Once you've nailed the core stuff, that's when you add failure into the training. Pull the "who's-a-whatsit" tool and let it "accidentally" fall into a sewer grate. What now?

Pilots do this constantly. Once you learn to fly, you train for everything that can go wrong. When I used to teach breathing apparatus at the fire academy - we'd bet money on who could suck the last breath of the moldiest air through a filter at the end of a class. That kind of stress inoculation? It works. You don't panic when you've practiced failure. Frank Brannigan used to say that "Panic's okay - as long as you're not the *first* one to panic."

Scenarios are great for this. People remember them. A solid scenario can reverse-engineer a whole lesson. Something goes boom, or doesn't, and then you dig into the chemistry behind it. Someone who's motivated? They're always thinking up scenarios. Driving around, watching for hazards. My wife always knows when my wheels are turning - "You're thinking about hazmat again, aren't you?" Yep.

Chemical plants run scenario talks at the start of shift. Toolbox talks. Everybody gets a turn. You bring in an article, a weird idea, toss it out there. It's expected and part of their culture. "Time to throw the linguine at the wall." You need to create space for offbeat ideas.

And sometimes, the best idea comes from the least likely person. But if the culture doesn't make them feel safe to speak up? You'll never hear it. That's why team culture matters so much in hazmat. Go back to my Colonel Beckwith Delta Forece or S.A.S. examples earlier, they have created a culture that works for their mission. Small specialty teams need to adapt and overcome problems they can't even imagine, but they always do it with a Core Competency Skill Set backing them up.

In the conventional fire department rank and file, a basic firefighter would never walk up to a battalion chief on the fireground and say, "Hey, maybe we shouldn't go interior on this basement fire?" Not unless you want a short career. But in special operations - hazmat, tech rescue - that kind of pushback is essential. Most of the time, we show up and the situation gets *worse* once we start touching things. The spill spreads. Someone walks through it. Something unexpected ignites. So I want people who will say is, "Hey, wait a minute."

You see it all the time after the fact - terrorist attacks, mass casualty events - someone always says, "I noticed something weird but I didn't say anything." That can't happen on a hazmat team. We're asking people from a completely different fireground culture to step into this special ops world. It takes effort to bring them alongside.

When someone comes into a hazmat team, they might be used to hierarchy - do what you're told, no questions. We have to flip that. As a Team Leader, I'll say, "Here's what I think we should do. Now shoot holes in it." And I mean it. I want the pushback. I want the person who says, "Yeah, that made sense an hour ago, but now the conditions have changed."

We've got to make decisions based on *facts*, not assumptions. I'll never forget this: I was part of the investigation team for the 1984 Phoenix Fire Department toluene tank explosion that resulted in the Line of Duty Death of firefighter Ricky Pearce. This was a confined space incident with a worker trapped inside. They were cutting into a tank with a saw creating sparks with a flammable atmosphere inside. When the battalion chief showed up, he asked a firefighter to go check if a vapor test had been done.

But by then, the scene was already rolling. More people kept showing up, assuming the test had happened. It hadn't. No one ever did it. And had that chief gotten there just four minutes earlier, he might have stopped the operation altogether. But he didn't. Because the momentum was already there - and decisions made prior to his arrival were based on assumptions, not facts.

So yeah, facts matter. And team culture matters. Because when someone's gut is screaming "This is wrong," I want them to say it. And I want everyone else to listen.

Bob Ingram

To build a truly effective hazmat team, a comprehensive approach is necessary, starting with a solid understanding of the team's response area. It's essential to assess the risks and hazards present, as well as the scope of potential incidents, to ensure that training and preparation are aligned with real-world needs. A clear, well-structured response plan must be in place, outlining the mission and defining the roles of various entities within the jurisdiction. This ensures a coordinated and efficient approach when responding to emergencies.

Training is key to success, and it should be multi-tiered to cover the full range of necessary skills. At the foundation, recruits should receive operational-level training, followed by basic and advanced technician-level courses for hazmat team technicians and support company personnel. Additionally, Hazmat Officer and Hazmat Safety Officer training should be included to ensure all team members are prepared for leadership and safety responsibilities.

Ongoing training is equally critical. Annual refresher courses should be conducted to keep knowledge and skills up to date, while in-service training ensures continuous development. Standard Operating Procedures (SOPs) should also be developed to guide operations and build a base of successful tactics.

To create effective training programs, balance is important. Introducing topics related to specific missions helps team members understand how different components work together. This can then be followed by skill stations or scenarios designed to practice those missions, with repetition until the entire team has mastered the necessary knowledge and skills. However, it's important not to overwhelm participants with too much information in a single session. Core technician training should be no more than 2-3 weeks in length to allow for enough practice to absorb the content effectively.

Training constraints, particularly in terms of time and funding, are common challenges that can hinder the delivery of core hazmat training. Local teams often face budget limitations, which may force them to make do with fire training facilities that are not ideal for hazmat operations. Ideally, training facilities should be purpose-built for hazmat scenarios, such as the LA County HM training facility, where teams can train in realistic, specialized environments. With limited budgets, however, simulation tools can be a useful alternative, providing controlled environments where students can practice decision-making and interpret data, though hands-on training remains essential to make it truly effective.

Ultimately, developing a successful hazmat team requires a mix of proper assessment, structured response plans, tiered training, and continuous, realistic training opportunities. By balancing foundational knowledge with specialized skills, developing SOPs, and ensuring that resources - whether physical or technological - are used effectively, teams can be well-prepared for the complex challenges of hazmat response.

Documentation of personnel status, equipment maintenance, completed training, and individual and team assessments are critical components to any good HazMat program.

Phil McArdle

Before diving into training questions, it's crucial to recognize that every addition to your Haz-Mat team - whether it's a new policy, procedure, tool, piece of equipment, or protective clothing - requires proper training, with no exceptions.

Start with the basics: understanding the distinctions between Hazardous Materials, Hazardous Substances, and Hazardous Wastes, and why these differences matter. It's all about the product's life cycle and the regulations that apply at each stage. A product is a hazardous substance when it's being made, a hazardous material during transportation (regulated by the DOT under 49 CFR), and once stored, it's again a hazardous substance. When it's no longer usable for its intended purpose or leaks, it becomes hazardous waste (regulated by the EPA under 40 CFR). Knowing these distinctions helps identify the right regulations and ensures you're handling each type of material appropriately.

Understanding the product, container, and environment you're dealing with is crucial to successful hazardous materials response. Your adversary isn't just the product itself, but how it interacts with its surroundings. Mishandling hazardous materials can lead to harm, death, property damage, and environmental destruction, so every situation should be treated with the seriousness of a battlefield.

Training must reflect what individuals will actually encounter. Are you responding to labs, bulk storage facilities, or highway incidents? Knowing the hazards, terminology, and types of hazardous materials specific to these environments is critical. Training should align with your organization's Emergency Response Plan and comply with relevant laws, regulations, and directives.

It's important to understand that knowing a task doesn't automatically make someone competent at it. For instance, simply understanding how a monitoring device works in the classroom doesn't ensure someone will be able to position the probe correctly, maintain it during a live operation, and interpret the data accurately. Competence comes from translating theory into practice under real-world conditions.

Risk assessment is another essential element of training. Can individuals be injured during training or operations? What steps are being taken to mitigate these risks? Supervisors must be trained to at least the same level as those they supervise, if not higher. A demonstration I gave once to a chief involved using a monitoring device in his office, where he thought I was performing the task correctly - only for me to point out everything I had done wrong. Supervisors need to know the procedure inside and out to spot and correct unsafe actions before they occur. This is connected to the concept of "Span of Control," where a good ratio is 5-7 people per supervisor, but in high-risk situations, fewer people should be supervised for closer oversight.

Training isn't just a one-time event; it must include both initial and refresher training, along with ongoing updates to cover new technologies, equipment, policies, and PPE. Evaluating competency through self-assessment, after-action reporting, and performance testing is vital for maintaining high standards.

Competency testing can be challenging to design, but it must be objective, fair, and credible. When creating test questions, be mindful of difficulty levels - questions that are too easy or too hard can signal issues with the material or the test itself. Performance-based testing needs clear criteria so evaluators know exactly what to look for in a candidate's performance.

Laws, regulations, and standards form the foundation of your training framework. Understanding the hierarchy of documents and how they interact - especially when conflicts arise - is essential for compliance. For example, in some cases, standards of care may take precedence over regulations, particularly regarding protective clothing, which can also impact liability in lawsuits.

Balancing classroom training and hands-on experience is essential. Classroom sessions are best suited for understanding laws, regulations, standards, and policies, as well as reviewing case studies and risk assessments. Hands-on training, however, is necessary for mastering tools, equipment, and protective clothing. Scenario-based training combines both, simulating real-world conditions to provide comprehensive preparation.

Finally, as the saying goes: "How do you get to Carnegie Hall? Practice, practice, practice!" Site visits and preplanning are invaluable for identifying potential challenges in real incidents. These visits help you assess conditions like lighting, space, setup time, and communication needs. Familiarizing yourself with the sites and jurisdiction you'll be working in ensures that you're better prepared and can tailor your training effectively to the unique challenges you'll face.

Adam McFadden

A comprehensive hazmat training program isn't just about checking boxes - it has to be immersive, balanced, and rooted in both theory and real-world application. The goal is simple: build firefighters who aren't just familiar with hazmat concepts, but who can confidently apply them when it counts. To do that, training needs to bring together five core components: classroom learning, case studies, department-specific procedures, hands-on practice, and interactive scenarios.

We start with a strong theoretical foundation. Firefighters have to understand how hazardous materials behave, what makes them dangerous, and how to approach them safely. That includes chemical properties, exposure pathways, mitigation tactics, toxicology, and classification systems like NFPA 704 and DOT placards. It's not just memorization - it's about building a working knowledge of how these elements play out on scene.

Next, we bring in real-world case studies. Reviewing past incidents - industrial spills, chemical explosions, transportation accidents - gives context to the theory. It shows what went right, what went wrong, and how decisions made under pressure impacted the outcome. Those lessons stick. They make the training personal and relevant.

We also ground everything in department policies and SOPs. Every agency has its own response playbook, mutual aid agreements, and jurisdictional expectations. It's critical that firefighters are trained within the framework they'll be operating under. A solid understanding of departmental procedures ensures consistency and cohesion when the tones drop.

Then comes the hands-on training, which is non-negotiable. This is where concepts become muscle memory. We run reps on:

- Donning and doffing PPE and SCBA
- Using air monitoring and detection equipment
- Controlling leaks and containing spills
- Performing decon operations, including mass civilian decontamination
- Applying specialized techniques for CBRNE threats

Finally, interactive tabletop exercises are where everything gets tied together. These sessions push teams to think critically, make decisions under pressure, and walk through hypothetical emergencies as a group. It's low-risk but high-impact - giving firefighters a space to test their decision-making and refine their strategies in a controlled environment.

To keep training dynamic and engaging, I use a rotating format: start with a couple hours of classroom instruction to introduce new material, then head straight into the bay for a hands-on scenario. After the drill, we debrief back in the classroom, break down what worked and what didn't, and then gear up again. That back-and-forth keeps the pace up and reinforces learning in real time.

One thing I've found especially effective is beginning each block with a refresher on core strategies, tactics, and team roles. It sets the tone, builds confidence, and ensures everyone knows their lane before the scenario kicks off. Then we'll throw in a curveball - something like a suspicious package, an active threat, or an unexpected shift in the scene. Suddenly, what started as a standard hazmat call becomes a simulated intentional event. That kind of escalation forces the team to adapt fast, which is exactly the kind of critical thinking and situational awareness they'll need when the real call comes in.

At the end of the day, the best hazmat training isn't static - it's layered, evolving, and scenario-driven. When it's done right, it prepares firefighters not just to respond, but to lead, adapt, and succeed under pressure.

Mike Monaco

Hands down, this is the most critical part of any hazmat training program. I get that there are all kinds of regulations - standards, laws, checkboxes you've got to tick. That's fine. But here's the truth: you can be in perfect compliance with every single one of those, and your program can still fall flat.

If your classroom environment isn't engaging - and if your hands-on training doesn't challenge people to the limits of their ability to think critically and problem-solve - then it doesn't matter how many regulations you follow. The program won't stick. It won't be effective. It won't be *good*.

Obviously, you need classroom time. Maybe not in-person, necessarily, but there has to be a structured way for students to learn the theory. Then you need to push that learning into the real world with hands-on application. The balance between those two - classroom and practical - is all about understanding the difference between knowledge, skills, and the bridge between them.

If a topic doesn't lend itself to hands-on work, then sure, it's fine to keep it in the classroom. But wherever we *can* connect the two, we should. Ideally, I'd say the split should be 50/50. Half classroom, half applied.

Now, is there some magical, innovative training method that's better than all the rest? Not really. What I've seen is that *great instructors* - the truly effective ones - all have their own unique way of delivering material. I knew a guy who would sit on the edge of a desk and just talk. No slides, no handouts - just a conversation. And the next thing you know, you're 45 minutes in and fully immersed. He didn't *lecture*, he *engaged*.

Then I've had instructors who were straight lecture-based, but their delivery was so strong, their energy so focused, that you were locked in the whole time. Totally different style - same impact.

So, all the tools, all the tech, all the methods - those are just extensions of the instructor. The key is finding the approach that lets *you* connect with your students. That's the most effective training method there is.

Chris Pfaff

We need more of it. We need more of it in every realm - facts and the technology we're seeing out there is constantly changing. Critical components of a comprehensive training program - that's the foundation. When you talk to the authors of NFPA 470 and 475, or when you're reviewing OSHA and our state regulations, that's the framework. That's the stage, if you will, for how a team becomes efficient. We have to hit those bullet points and those benchmarks to ensure we're efficient and legally protected from litigation or other issues. But remember, that's not all of it, right?

Even the writers of NFPA 470 emphasize that these standards represent the minimum. We use those standards as our starting framework and then expand beyond them. You absolutely have to look at your community and your response area as a whole.

On the national chat boards, the national instructors say it over and over again - it's something we hear repeatedly. You need to buy monitoring equipment and train specifically for the hazards unique to your community. Do we have waterways? Highways? What commodities are flowing through our jurisdiction, and what should we expect? We need to ensure our training isn't just specific, but even more specific - above and beyond those minimum standards.

As for balancing scenario-based and classroom learning, you've got two different sides of the coin there. It's about finding balance. When I think about it, imagine an agency like Harris County, Texas. They're busy -

absolutely, hands-down busy. They're running hazmat calls every single day. They know exactly what they're doing.

But in my world, I don't get to experience that. What's the most common call I run? EMS calls. Most fire departments, that's what we run. I don't necessarily need constant hands-on training for EMS because that's our bread and butter, but I still need regular classroom sessions to keep updated. It's similar for a very busy hazmat team.

If you're balancing training for a busy team, they might need more classroom sessions just to ensure everyone stays aligned and doesn't start flying by the seat of their pants because they're handling dozens of calls the same way each time. "Oh, we're doing a saddle-tank offload - we do this twice a week." Great, but let's also make sure we're staying compliant with all regulations and standards through regular classroom refreshers. They might not need frequent scenario-based training because they're literally doing scenarios in real-time on daily calls.

However, for the majority of hazmat teams nationwide - especially in smaller jurisdictions that might only handle two or three hazmat calls per year - you've got to get it all. I'd lean heavily on scenario-based training and hands-on skills development for these teams. It's not that classroom learning isn't important - it definitely is - but hands-on, scenario-based practice is much more critical for those teams.

And that brings us to innovation, a perfect segue into this next topic: What innovative training methods or technologies have you found effective for preparation?

In the last decade or so, podcasts and chat boards have changed the game - not just in Hazmat or Tech Rescue or firefighting - but in everything. You can listen to podcasts in long-form or short-form formats. Most folks tune into them during their commute, workouts, daily chores, or other routine activities, enhancing productivity throughout their day. Just make sure you're picking podcasts that are relevant and credible.

Another significant innovation is chat boards. Back in the day, our chat board was the dining room or the local diner. Today, social media platforms serve that purpose - and they're great, but you have to use them with caution. Anybody can put their two cents in, and you'll see arguments bubble up constantly. I'm not saying you'll always find the right answer there, but it certainly sparks discussions - especially for those nagging questions you're hesitant to bring up in a classroom session.

Rob Rezende

Frequency is key! We train the entire team, including relief personnel, every month for four hours. This gives us a chance to connect, interact, and boost team morale while keeping skills sharp.

"See one, do one, teach one" is our mantra. It's all about hands-on learning, with plenty of opportunities to both fail and succeed. And when someone struggles? Don't let them drown. We create an environment where they can work through it and come out stronger.

We train not just for success, but for when things go wrong. The unexpected is bound to happen, and we're ready for it.

Classroom learning is most effective when we guide students to find the answers themselves. We don't just hand them the solutions - they need to discover them. That's where the real learning happens.

A key part of our classroom approach is letting the students take the reins. Have them present a tool or topic without any PowerPoint slides, notes, or crutches - just the tool itself. Give them 15 minutes, followed by a Q&A session. It challenges them, builds confidence, and deepens understanding.

Bob Royall

When it comes to basic training, it's a pretty comprehensive process. In our area, we start with an 80-hour technician program, which is the bare minimum. The 80 hours are dictated by a curriculum that is set by the State Fire Commission. But here's the catch: the curriculum doesn't tell you exactly how many hours you must train to. It just says you need to cover a set of specific competencies. As a hazmat chief or training officer, you've got to break it down - figure out how many hours for contact time, suit time, practical exercises, and so on.

This 80-hour program is enough to get someone started and able to respond to a hazmat incident as a technical resource. But that's just the beginning. There's so much more to it: routes of entry, understanding containers, product identification, product control, chemical protective clothing, and the difference between offensive and defensive actions. It's like training a police officer - teach them the basics, send them out with a field training officer, and hope they don't make any major mistakes. That's pretty much the same situation for hazmat techs. They get the basics, then it's up to their FTOs and experience to fill in the gaps.

Mike Callen, a great mentor in this field, has a saying: "We learn by education and experience. One of them leaves scars." I think we all know which one that is.

In Texas, the state minimum for a hazmat technician course is 80 hours, but when you look at Harris County, we push well beyond that. Our basic hazmat tech course is closer to 161 hours, thanks to extra required time, including field trips. Our training is not just classroom lessons; we get out there and do hands-on training. We'll climb rail cars, touch tank trucks, change valves - things that give the trainees real, practical experience. Some folks might call this "advanced hazmat technician" training, but to me, it's still close to the minimum required to be effective on the job.

I've got some concerns about certain certification programs. There's a 40-hour hazmat tech certification that you can take, but I don't think it's enough. It's easy to hang that certification on the wall and head out to apply for a job. But without the required hazmat training or practical experience, you're not prepared to handle real-world situations. That's the issue we face - just like someone with three months of training in some jurisdictions, they might have a piece of paper, but they still lack the hands-on experience.

I believe the current instructional approach must change, especially with today's workforce. Hybrid training is key. You still need some classroom lecture or small group discussions - those work well with today's trainees where online training has its limits. It can't replace hands-on, technical skill-building. No amount of online learning will teach you how to handle a shovel, climb a rail car, or suit up in the right gear. You've got to get your hands dirty. Suit time, meter use, and real-life training are absolutely necessary.

And one thing that really bugs me is the search for that one "magic bullet" tool, that single instrument that's going to tell you what to do in any given hazmat situation. That just doesn't exist. Instruments are useful - they're another tool in the toolbox - but they're not the end-all solution. You need to be able to read and interpret the data, understand the material you're dealing with, and know how to combat the effects of it. It's one of the things we really hammer home with our team: hands-on experience is irreplaceable. You can't just rely on a meter or a piece of equipment to make decisions for you.

Bobby Salvesen

When we set out to rebuild the FDNY's Hazmat Technician course, what we found - once we really started peeling back the layers - was that the course itself had good bones. It *was* a good course... just a little dated. The problem was that over the years, instead of fixing what was broken, people had just slapped Band-Aids on it. And those Band-Aids? They'd been in place so long, they started to look like the actual structure. But underneath? Still broken.

So we made the call: start fresh. Go back to white paper. Strip it down and build it back up.

That gave us the chance to rethink everything - every piece of classroom instruction, every hands-on evolution, every standard we needed to align with. It wasn't just about compliance. It was about designing a *comprehensive* training program that actually produced the kind of hazmat technician we wanted out there in the field.

And if the goal is to build an *elite* hazmat company, then the training has to reflect that. You've got to work within the framework of known standards and best practices - but also aim higher. It's a balancing act. You're setting the table in the beginning, but you're also designing a meal that's going to feed the kind of technician you want leading your entry team one day.

Our three-week structure worked like this:
- Week One was heavy PowerPoint, laying the foundation, setting the table.
- Week Two shifted to a 50/50 mix - small group, hands-on stuff combined with instructor-led discussion.

- Week Three pulled it all together. Now you're integrating all those modules into a big-picture understanding of what hazmat work really looks like.

That kind of training *builds* better technicians. It forces them to think, to adapt, to *own* their role. And if your training program isn't doing that? Don't be surprised when you're not building a great team.

I get it - budgets are tight. I've heard it a hundred times: "We can only afford the 40-hour guys." But let's be honest here - 40 hours? That's just not enough to build a real hazmat team. Sorry. I know there are people reading this thinking, "Well, we checked the box. They got the patch." Cool. But patches don't mean competence.

I'm not obsessed with the number of hours. I care about *competency*. There's a big difference between being certified and being capable. And if we're serious about building hazmat teams that can handle the worst days - we've got to start acting like it in the way we train.

Doug Schick and Mark Zilch
Doug:

Everybody who comes onto the team is already a certified Hazmat Tech, so that's the baseline. But we really try to push for more than that. Like departments across the country, we're always encouraging guys to take advantage of the DHS-sponsored training - places like Socorro, Nevada, wherever they can get it. That extra training is huge.

We keep training going constantly. I'm always trying to line something up. Like this week, we did an ammonia refresher at a cold storage facility. Next week, we've got railroad training on the books. A lot of it happens at the company level, too. It's on the officers to make sure their crews are staying sharp.

Meters, in particular - those are critical. The guys need to be proficient with every piece of equipment: PIDs, pumps, everything. They've gotta know how to don and doff the suits, run through Level A drills, and be familiar with all the gear like the MT94s - which I know your team's probably been using longer than we have, but we love 'em.

And then there's the simple stuff, like flipping through the ERG or the NIOSH guide. That's easy training. You sit at the kitchen table and just start talking - pick a chemical, walk through what it does, what we should be wearing, what our major concerns are. It gets guys thinking. Gets them used to the software, the references, the decision-making process.

Because hazmat's so knowledge-based, the bulk of our training naturally ends up being classroom. And that's not a bad thing. You can do it right at the station - no big setup needed. But that hands-on piece? Still crucial. You've got to get guys suited up, touching equipment, building muscle memory. It's gotta be both.

Mark:
That balance of operational proficiency and certification is critical. Right now, we're in the process of restarting the state task books that maintain our Ops and Tech certs. So beyond just knowing how to use the tools, we've also got to stay compliant with all the state standards. Because let's be real - if something goes wrong, like a release during an ammonia response, one of the first questions is going to be: *Was this guy up to date? Had he been trained?*

And that's where Chief Schick's really done a great job - keeping everyone refreshed, constantly training, staying sharp.

When we run refresher trainings, we always try to integrate some hands-on work, even if it's a quick drill. Say we're reviewing radiation - what's alpha, beta, gamma, neutron? Cool, now here's the meter. Show me how to turn it on. What's it mean when it beeps? What do the numbers tell you?

I've seen it too many times - guys saying, "I don't feel like getting up today," and then I ask, "What does this do?" and they go blank. That's when you know you've got to get the equipment in their hands, not just talk about it.

The chief's also been helping out with the Vista Forge project – A large scale WMD response scenario for the city of Chicago. Part of the prep includes pushing info on NARAC plume modeling. That's been an eye-opener. It's giving hazmat teams a deeper understanding of what national response might look like in a scenario like that, and how we can use federal tools and partnerships to model and manage it. That kind of stuff isn't on your average training calendar, but it's really valuable

Doug:
Yeah, and we've had some really good multi-agency exercises, too. One that sticks out was a simulated chlorine leak from a tanker. We weren't physically doing anything - it was all tabletop - but it forced everyone to walk through the steps: Who are you notifying? What's your plan? What's the result?

And when it didn't work, we'd rework the approach right there. It got people thinking on their feet and opened up discussions we might not have had otherwise - like, "Should we be calling this agency? What about getting intel from that group?" That kind of thinking is critical in a real-world incident.

We're also trying to build up the new training academy with some solid props and interjurisdictional planning. Because when it comes down to it, we're not operating in a vacuum. Whether it's inside our own city or coordinating across county and state lines, training's gotta reflect how these things play out in real life.

Jason Zeller

A comprehensive hazmat training program needs to be multifaceted, covering technical proficiency, tactical execution, and mental resilience. Hazmat teams face an incredibly wide array of potential scenarios, and it's essential that training prepares team members for anything that may come their way - both physically and psychologically.

First and foremost, technical skills are the foundation. This includes mastering CBRN detection and identification, hazmat handling, decontamination procedures, and chemical defense protocols. Members must be well-versed in the latest tools and technologies available for detecting hazardous materials and understanding their properties.

Additionally, knowledge of safety protocols, risk assessments, and environmental controls is critical to ensuring both team safety and mission success.

Another crucial component is tactical training. Hazmat incidents often require collaboration with other first responders, military units, or federal agencies, so building teamwork and leadership skills within these environments is essential. We put a strong emphasis on interagency coordination, command and control, and communication. Practicing real-world scenarios in live, high-pressure settings allows team members to develop the operational awareness and confidence they'll need when the stakes are highest.

Physical fitness and endurance also play a significant role. Training in full PPE and operating in extreme conditions - including high heat, limited visibility, and restricted mobility - mimics the realities of an actual incident. Our program included physical conditioning as part of the daily training regimen, ensuring that team members could function effectively even when fatigued or under physical duress.

Finally, mental resilience is an often overlooked but vital component. Hazmat operations can be overwhelming - whether from the complexity of the situation, the danger involved, or the unpredictability of the environment. Our training involved stress inoculation exercises to simulate the pressures of real-world incidents. This helps team members develop the ability to think clearly, make quick decisions, and remain calm under intense stress.

In sum, a successful hazmat training program must be comprehensive and adaptable, covering all the physical, technical, tactical, and mental aspects that ensure team members are ready for whatever they'll face in the field.

Balancing classroom learning with hands-on, scenario-based training is all about ensuring that the team is not only equipped with the knowledge but also the ability to execute under the toughest conditions.

When we built the training program for the 24th WMD-CST, it was clear that a one-size-fits-all approach wouldn't work. We needed a well-rounded, dynamic program that prepared the team for any scenario.

Classroom instruction was essential for grounding the team in the technical aspects of hazmat operations: understanding chemicals, equipment, protocols, and response plans. But classroom learning alone wouldn't get the job done. We knew that real proficiency comes from being able to apply that knowledge in high-pressure, realistic environments. That's where the hands-on training came in - putting theory into practice through intense, scenario-driven exercises.

We didn't limit ourselves to just basic technical drills. In addition to standard hazmat procedures, we incorporated rescue operations from specialized rescue training, including water survival and working with PPE while submerged or in maritime environments. Given our maritime operations responsibilities, we ensured that the team was also trained in maritime rescue scenarios and operations. These scenarios included everything from handling hazardous materials in confined spaces on boats to performing rescues from water while maintaining hazmat protocols. The physical and technical challenges of operating in a maritime setting added another layer of complexity and realism to our training.

In addition to the regular drills, I implemented weekly unannounced tests for our downrange operators. These weren't just about equipment or technical knowledge; they were about knowing the team, assessing how they reacted under pressure, how they handled unplanned scenarios, and how they executed the basics under stress. Whether it was a knowledge-based quiz, a rescue scenario, or a challenge in how they handled PPE while in extreme conditions, the goal was to keep them sharp and adaptable.

This combination of classroom instruction, hands-on exercises, and unexpected stress tests created a robust training cycle that ensured the team was always prepared - both physically and mentally - for anything that might arise in the field.

The reality is, in hazmat operations, especially when you're dealing with something as unpredictable as WMDs, there's no room for complacency. We made sure the team was prepared for every angle, from basic technical execution to performing complex, multi-faceted operations under extreme stress.

When it comes to preparing a hazmat team for real-world incidents, the most innovative approach isn't about flashy technology or complicated training methods - it's about staying mission-focused and always ready. Hazmat incidents don't come with a warning, and you need to be able to respond immediately, with full capability, regardless of the time or situation.

One of the core elements of our training was ensuring the team was ready for "no-notice recalls." This meant they had to be prepared to respond at any moment without warning. To make this happen, we used high-intensity, unannounced training scenarios to simulate the stress and unpredictability of real-life incidents. These scenarios weren't just about technical skills - they were designed to test how the team performed under pressure, focusing on mental resilience and staying calm under fire. I made it clear: *if you aren't ready when that alarm goes off, you're already behind the curve.*

Training was tough, and mistakes were expected - but only in the training environment. If we were going to screw up, it had to happen in training, where we could learn from it and adjust. Every time we missed the mark, we went back and did it again - no excuses, no shortcuts. This process of *"fail, learn, repeat"* was critical in making sure we were always improving and fine-tuning our skills. The goal was for the team to be so well-prepared that they could handle any situation, no matter how unexpected.

In addition to the everyday drills and exercises, we sent teams to the Army's premier training facilities, including Edgewood Proving Grounds and Dugway Proving Grounds, where they got the real-world experience of handling live biological and chemical agents. These were high-stakes environments where our operators could practice handling actual threats, gaining exposure to scenarios that weren't just theoretical. By training with live agents, our team gained critical hands-on experience that no simulated scenario could replicate.

As for technology, we certainly leveraged tools like virtual simulations for hazardous environments, sensor-based technologies for monitoring, and thermal imaging to enhance PPE drills. However, we always made sure the most critical piece of the puzzle was real-world experience. Live agents, live situations, and no room for complacency - this is what truly prepared the team for the chaos of a real hazmat incident.

At the end of the day, it wasn't about having the best tech or the fanciest gadgets. It was about creating a culture of mission-readiness, where everyone knew that training was the place to make mistakes, and we were committed to learning, adapting, and always being prepared for whatever came next.

Dan Baker

Every hazmat team should keep certain essential items ready to roll. First and foremost, invest in gear that directly enhances responder safety: solid, reliable communication equipment, individually assigned meters that are simple to operate, proper PPE (individually assigned if budget allows), and devices that significantly boost situational awareness - think drones, cameras, and specialized tools like the CBRN Responder.

When it comes to other gadgets, your purchasing decisions should depend heavily on the types of incidents your team regularly faces and the specific risks involved. The one exception might be large, government-based organizations. For instance, as a state-level team, we sometimes buy specialized equipment that local agencies can't afford or would rarely use enough to justify buying themselves. In those cases, it just makes good sense for a government team to step in and provide those resources when needed.

We always prioritize new gear based on actual response data - plain and simple. But we also keep an eye on what matters to elected officials and the public, because their concerns matter, too. A recent example: we've invested significantly in equipment to handle lithium-ion battery incidents. These emergencies caught many agencies off guard as we moved toward an electrified future, and they've rightly become a hot-button issue worth addressing head-on.

Mike Callan

Alright, let me tell you, if someone is serious about becoming a hazmat technician, there are two tools they need to master 100%, and if they can't, they're not really on their way. Those two tools are the DOT Guidebook and the NIOSH Pocket Guide. That's it. If they don't know how to use these effectively, they're missing the foundation of awareness-level knowledge. And awareness, my friend, that's the heart of hazmat response.

Now, I've had chiefs in my career who didn't even know how to use the DOT Guidebook properly, let alone dive into the specific chemical data that's in the NIOSH Pocket Guide. If you can't navigate those two, you're in trouble right out of the gate. It's crucial. As for other tools, well, that depends on the job at hand. Awareness is built on the basics - the books, the guides, the placards. Operations are more about the defensive systems you have in place: evacuation procedures, containment strategies, damming, or whatever you need to prevent the spread of a chemical hazard. But when you're talking about hazmat technicians, you're dealing with a team of people who know their specific roles. They're all soldiers first. They've got their specialized skills, but when it comes down to it, they can also dig the foxhole and fight the fire if that's what's needed.

Now, if you're working with an underfunded or volunteer team, I'll tell you, it's tough. Budget restrictions are everywhere nowadays. But here's how you advocate for the tools you need: first, look at what's in your community. You can't just ask for money from everywhere. I've learned from my experiences, and I'll tell you – Jack McElfish, my chief for about four years, used to say, "I don't want my people doing anything for an industry that the industry shouldn't pay for."

We got our first meters from American Cyanamid- they gave us the meters so we could verify their readings. That was the kind of relationship we built. If you don't have the budget to buy suits, make sure you're training with the people who do have them, so you understand how to use them effectively. And if you need help, you need to make it clear that those companies should be stepping up to help.

Grants are another piece of the puzzle. They can be a double-edged sword. We were able to get top-tier meters with big grant money, but when the grant money dried up, there was no money left for replacements. This is a huge problem. I mean, we saw it firsthand when we met down in Maryland - one of the reasons their equipment was failing was because they were past their grant funding. So, while grants can help you get equipment, they often don't set you up for long-term sustainability.

That's why, when I was in command, I never wanted to go higher than captain. I knew that if I made chief, I'd have to deal with workplace politics and would probably have to apologize to politicians at least five times (like I've done before). It's not a job I wanted, and frankly, I didn't have the patience for it. But I did what I needed to do at my level, and it worked for me.

When we first started getting personal safety devices, we were incredibly creative. For example, when we bought our first pass alerts in Wallingford, they were $99 each. We bought them for every company and every citizen on Main Street, and we didn't just hand them out - we took pictures of people holding them up, like the local clothing store owners proudly displaying their devices. We got 24 of them, and we got the whole community involved. People were happy to participate because they saw the value in it. It was a way to bring the community together and make them part of the solution.

Sometimes, you have to get creative. If you're not networking and making those connections, you'll be at a serious disadvantage. It's about using what you have and being resourceful. If you wait for everything to fall into place, you might be waiting forever. It's all about building relationships, getting the right people on your side, and finding ways to make things work, no matter the budget constraints.

John Cassidy

Look, we could spend hours talking about tools, but if you're building from scratch - or trying to prioritize within a tight budget - you've got to be smart. You've got to ask: what do we actually use? What do we *need* versus what just looks good on a shelf?

First off, you always start with the tools that keep you safe and allow you to assess the hazard. That means detection and monitoring gear - your multi-gas meters, pH papers, thermal imagers, temperature guns. That's your front line. That's the stuff you're reaching for on nearly every call. If you don't have good hazard assessment equipment, you're flying blind.

From there, you prioritize based on what kinds of incidents you actually respond to. If hydrocarbon spills are common in your area, then pumps, absorbents, and overpack drums need to move up the priority list. If corrosives are a regular thing, neutralization kits and the appropriate PPE get bumped up. This isn't just a gear list - it's a reflection of your risk profile.

And here's where people miss the mark: just because you can *buy* something doesn't mean you can *own* it.

Cost of ownership is huge. Let's say I get funding to buy a top-of-the-line gas meter. Great. But do I also have the money for cal gas, for replacement sensors, for maintenance? If not, I've just bought a very expensive doorstop. That meter might technically last ten years, but without a way to maintain it, it's useless six months in.

It's the same story with exotic sensors. Take something like a phosgene sensor. Sounds great - until you realize the calibration gas for it runs $800 and only lasts six months. Meanwhile, I could use a Dräger tube for 15 bucks. And we're not exactly tripping over phosgene calls every week. So unless you're regularly dealing with that specific threat, it's not worth the upkeep.

This is where creativity and strategic thinking come in. Before you buy something, ask yourself:

- Can I maintain this long-term?
- Is it something I can borrow or request through mutual aid instead?
- Is there a lower-cost, lower-maintenance alternative?

You should have a solid understanding of what resources you can call in - whether it's a neighboring agency or a vendor who can roll in a burn-off kit at 2 a.m. If your local propane supplier can deliver what you need in a pinch, why spend thousands on something that'll collect dust?

Bottom line: don't just chase shiny objects when you get a budget infusion. You've got to be disciplined. Think beyond the purchase - think lifecycle. Think sustainability. And always prioritize what keeps your people safe and what aligns with your actual operational needs.

And yes, don't forget the petty cash fund. You'll always need money for those little things - zip ties, Velcro, spare tubing, whatever. That stuff matters just as much when the clock's ticking.

Dave DiGregorio

Over the years, my perspective has shifted a bit. Technology is great, don't get me wrong, but I've come to realize that having the right tools means nothing if you don't understand how to use them properly. Let me give you an example from my background as a PA. As a medical provider, I ordered all kinds of tests - labs, diagnostics, the works. But those tests were just tools. If I didn't know how to interpret the results, then I wouldn't be doing my job properly. I'd be a lousy provider. You can't just rely on the tool; you have to understand what it's for.

Now, that concept works well in hazmat. Some of the countries I've worked with, especially overseas, don't have the budgets we have here, but they can still do a lot with simple tools - things like pH paper or litmus paper. You can diagnose a lot with basic tools, and it's important to start there. Understand what those basic tools are telling you, and then you can decide if you need something more advanced, like a four-gas or five-gas monitor. You need to know why you're using that technology. For example, if I need a specific piece of equipment, I'll weigh the options. Maybe I'll opt for Ramen or FTIR if that's what's needed. But I tend to favor Ramen because it doesn't have the water signature issues, which can be a big factor.

That said, the tools you choose really depend on the mission you're working on as a hazmat team. The mission in New York, for instance, was a bit different from ours in Massachusetts. We saw some battery incidents, but not nearly to the extent that you did. It was still a priority, and we tried to give it the attention it deserved. Now, under John Davine as the fire marshal, it's really become a top priority. I fought that battle with the previous fire marshal for a while because he didn't think battery-related incidents were a significant problem at the time.

And the thing is, providers often over-order, especially in the medical field. If you look at some of the orders they place, it doesn't always make sense. But they just order everything, not really understanding what each test or piece of equipment is supposed to do. It's the same in hazmat: You've got to know why you're using a particular tool and what it's meant for. For example, if I'm dealing with a highly acidic environment, I need to think carefully about whether the equipment I'm using will hold up. Am I going to burn it out, or is it the right choice for the job?

At the end of the day, the most important tool is the user. The person behind the equipment is the one who makes it work - or doesn't. And part of that is making sure you're getting the right resources. If your team doesn't have someone who can write grants, get someone who can. I can't tell you how many millions of dollars in grants I secured for

Massachusetts. It made a huge difference. Another thing we did was partner with other agencies to get the equipment we needed. For example, I didn't buy robots for hazmat, but I did partner with the bomb squad. They had the robots, and we had the hazmat tools, so we helped each other out. We'd partner on grants, and it worked out well for both sides.

I also partnered on grants for other specialized equipment, like the mobile lab we had. It was a partner grant, and the same went for the CAT bags we had. These partnerships helped ensure we got the tools we needed without having to carry the full financial burden ourselves. So, in a way, having the right people to help your secure grants and form partnerships is just as important as the technology itself.

Dave Donohue

Let's start with the basics. Sure, it's great if you have sophisticated equipment like GCMS and FTIR that can identify the exact material you're dealing with, but the reality is, just being able to classify the material and understand its hazards will get you through most incidents. I've seen teams freeze up when high-tech gear can't identify a material in its library or fails to give an answer, while simple wet chemistry could have provided all the necessary information to contain the situation and reopen a facility or roadway. Sometimes, basic tools and knowledge are all you really need to get the job done.

The second key point is ensuring that team members - and especially operational folks - truly understand the capabilities, applications, and limitations of their equipment. It drives me crazy when teams, or even engine/truck crews, have a 4- or 5-gas meter and have no real understanding of what the readings mean, waiting instead for alarms to tell them what's happening. I've encountered more than one team that mistakenly believes that 100% of the Lower Explosive Limit (LEL) on a 4-gas meter is equivalent to the Upper Explosive Limit (UEL) or that the reading represents the flammable range. For instance, if you're dealing with propane with a 2.5% LEL and your meter shows 2.5%, it doesn't mean you're at the LEL - it's just a reading that needs proper interpretation.

As with everything, this starts with a gap analysis that comes from the Threat and Hazard Identification and Risk Assessment (THIRA). If there's a gap in our capabilities, the team needs to evaluate options for addressing it. Then, we weigh those options, factoring in the features of each tool to find the one that best meets our needs. I also want to balance the need with the cost. If I have multiple gaps, I prioritize based on impact and urgency. For example, if I have a low-frequency, low-impact gap and a high-frequency, low-impact gap but a limited budget, I'm going to prioritize filling the latter.

Additionally, I'm going to look at how and when the tool or technology will be used, and whether there are other agencies I can partner with to share the costs. Law enforcement, public works, sanitation, and the health department might all have similar needs, and if I can work out a cost-sharing agreement, it benefits everyone. Not only does it save money, but it helps the community as a whole.

I also consider where the equipment will be used. If the equipment is facility-specific, I'll try to work with the facility to cover as much of the cost as possible - training and maintenance included. Lastly, I'm looking beyond our own jurisdiction. If my neighboring agencies are in need of a piece of equipment that could benefit both of us, I'll explore whether we can share costs. Sometimes they may already have the equipment, and I might be able to help cover maintenance costs in exchange for access to it. It's about working together and making sure we're getting the most out of every resource available.

Rick Edinger

At the most basic level, if I'm running a hazmat team, I've got to have good PPE and solid detection and monitoring equipment. Fancy trucks and bells and whistles are nice, but if I can't suit up for the hazards I'm facing, or I can't detect what's going on and analyze it correctly, then we're dead in the water. That's where it starts - and ends - for me.

Once that's covered, you move on to the rest: decon capability, specialized tools, more advanced meters. When you get into elite-level teams, like CST, you're talking about top-tier gear - high-end PIDs, FTIR, all the latest tools we didn't even have ten years ago. But they've also got the time, money, and structure to *train* on all of that. They know how to use it, and more importantly, they understand what the equipment is telling them. That's a whole different level.

But that's where we are now. The tech is incredible. The computers, the sensors - it's all evolved way beyond what we were working with back in the '90s, flipping through books and using pH paper and hoping for the best.

But here's the catch - and it's a big one: do we actually know how to use this stuff correctly? Can we interpret what the equipment is telling us? That's the real gap. We've talked about it a lot in NFPA circles. There's this danger of over-reliance on the screen. You see a number pop up, and folks just take it at face value. But are they critically thinking through what it means?

It used to be, we had to synthesize information ourselves – minimally pull from three different research sources, compare vapor pressures, look at how things interact. It forced you to think. Now, newer generations - again, not knocking anybody - but they're used to getting information fast and packaged neatly. And that can lead to trouble if you're not thinking beyond what the machine spits out. That's where I think the standards, like NFPA 470, could do a better job - embedding critical thinking into the training and expectations.

Right now, it's all definitions and checklists: "know what vapor pressure is." But nothing says, "understand how it fits into the entire scenario you're walking into." And I get it - standards are hard to write that way. We're handcuffed by formatting and legal language and how much you can put in an standard's annex. We've tried to avoid being too prescriptive, because every situation's different. You crack a dome cover and what happens next? Depends on a hundred things.

So how do we fill that gap? Experienced trainers. People who've done the job, who've seen things go sideways, and who can communicate those lessons to the next crew. That's what bridges the space between what's on paper and what happens in the field.

Now, when it comes to figuring out what equipment we need - how do I build that list? First, what are we running? What incidents are we responding to regularly? Do I have the proper equipment to manage those incidents effectively? Do I have enough suits? Simple questions like, how many entries can my team make before we're out of gear?

For our team, we knew we had the ability to make two solid entries with what we carried. After that, we were calling for help. But we also had the benefit of being in a metro area - help was coming. So that forms the first list: what we have, and whether we have *enough* of it to meet the team's mission.

Then comes the second list: what don't we have that we actually need? And I break that into three tiers:
1. Must-haves – things we absolutely need to operate safely and effectively.
2. Nice-to-haves – gear that would improve performance, but we can function without.
3. Shiny toys – stuff that's cool, but maybe we're only looking at it because everyone else is buying it.

Then we look at the budget. Where's the money coming from? Is it a line-item buy? Do I need to pitch it in the capital budget? Can I chase a grant? Every item falls into one of those funding categories.

It's a multi-layered approach to prioritizing equipment needs.
And training works the same way. How much can I do? How long can I run it? Who can I train, and where's the money coming from? That whole mix - gear, training, budget, people - it all ties together in how you run a hazmat team.

John Esposito

When it comes to tools, I think every special company's got to have a couple of options to do the same job. You can't just rely on a single method. I mean, take a regular company forcing a door - some guys go for the rabbit tool, some stick with the irons. The important thing is they've got both. And if neither works, they've got backup options. That's the mindset.

Now you look at the squads - maybe they've got two or three ways to tackle a problem. Rescues? They've probably got four or five. Just open up the compartments and you'll see. It's all about the mission. The more specialized the unit, the more gear they carry - because if they don't figure it out, no one's coming behind them to do it for them.

Same goes for hazmat. A lot of the tools we've got, we made ourselves - out of necessity. I remember you guys came up with that propane burn-off rig, right? You ran into a unique scenario, and nothing existed for it, so you made the damn thing. That's what we do.

I'll give you one: I was in the rescue battalion, and there was a call to a high school over by the Brooklyn side of the Verrazano. Custodian's refilling the pool - starts the water, then drops dead on the deck of a heart attack. No one finds him for hours. By then, the pool overflows and floods the basement. Naturally, that's where the shutoff valve is. Now it's underwater. Hazmat gets called in, and they end up going to Home Depot to piece together what they need to stop the flow. That's hazmat for you. Make it up as you go. Figure it out.

Now, we're getting more cautious these days with building tools ourselves. Liability's the buzzword now. We try to move toward warrantied, commercially available gear when we can. But the truth is, a lot of the ideas still start with us - because we're the ones who've seen the problem firsthand. We've stood in the mess and said, "You know what we need right now?"

And even when we do build something, it makes sense to us, but someone from outside the job looks at it and says, "Oh, it's a crowbar." No - it's not a crowbar. But that's the fire service. We see what's needed and we make it work. I still carry my little officer's tool. Greatest thing ever. I can do anything with that. That's the core of it - we're problem solvers. Firefighters are built that way, and the more specialized you get, the sharper that skill becomes. You might have an SOP, but if not, you're pulling the team together and building a plan on the spot. That's the job.

Now, none of this is free. We all have budget constraints. So when we want to expand capabilities or bring in something new, we've got to justify it. Show the need. Show the gap. Show the efficiency. Maybe we say, "Let's take this company and give them some added skills, instead of building a whole new team." Some places split their hazmat people up and bring them together for responses. Others operate as a full-time team. It depends.

But whatever the setup, you've got to show that what you're proposing is better than what's already in place. Are the tools already sitting on a county team's shelf, collecting dust? Are they even getting used? Because if you're going to provide a hazmat response, then there's a minimum standard you've got to meet. You can't call yourself a hazmat team if you don't have **SCBA**, **CPC**, the basic plug-and-dike kits. You might be ops-level trained, but that doesn't make you a hazmat team.

Figure out what your most common calls are. That'll guide you. When I was in the squad, we got great at fuel oil leaks. That was the bread and butter. In the early days, we'd wait for the mothership to show up. But eventually, we knew what to do. We wanted to get in, get it done, and go back in service - because let's be honest, we wanted to get back to chasing fires.

So yeah, it's about minimums. Start with the calls you actually get. Build your toolbox around that. And don't just fill compartments - fill them with purpose.

Brandon Fletcher

"It depends" - and that's the reality when it comes to typing, mission, and target hazards. Every team might wish they had the same resources as FDNY HM1, but the truth is, not only is it financially unfeasible, it's also unnecessary for most teams. The key is to clearly define your mission set, understand what classification you're aiming for (if your state requires it), and identify the major target hazards in your response area. From there, you can build out your capabilities.

At a minimum, teams should be able to perform basic air monitoring, have the correct **PPE**, and ensure they have decontamination solutions that are appropriate for their mission or typing. Research capabilities are a must, and access to **ERDSS** (preferably customized to your agency's specific needs) is invaluable. Having tools and kits to stop leaks is another priority - but they don't need to be the fancy, high-end "hazmat" kits you see in the catalogs. Most of my department's plugging and patching kits are home-built, and the supplies can all be found at your local hardware store! Simple tools like spill containment pools or bladders, chocks, drum upright tools, and basic mechanic toolboxes with regular and non-sparking tools work just fine.

I'm also really impressed with the XplorIR. My agency just got one with the quantification module, and it's quickly becoming an essential tool to boost our air monitoring capabilities.

But, of course, funding is always the big challenge. You need to understand the funding mechanisms that are available to you - and keep in mind, not everything has to come from the FireRescueHazmat store. As I mentioned, your leak-stopping supplies don't need to be part of the priciest hazmat kit out there - build your own! I don't need Snap-On mechanics tools for an incident, especially if I may never see them again. For things like booms, pads, and sorbents, shop around. Those are the easy items to source.

When it comes to funding mechanisms, things get more complicated. Do you have a local LEPC (Local Emergency Planning Committee)? Do they offer funding for tools, equipment, or training? Get involved, and learn the ins and outs. Also, consider public/private partnerships - if there's a major industry in your area that might need your hazmat services one day, reach out. They could provide funding or equipment, either directly or indirectly.

And don't forget to write grants! Research available grants, especially those that may not be specifically hazmat-related. For example, an XplorIR or gas meters have a lot of use in fire investigations, and they're eligible for FEMA's Fire Prevention and Safety (FP&S) grant. These tools also happen to be very useful for hazmat, so they can serve a dual purpose. The most important thing with grants is to read and understand the rules thoroughly. That's what makes all the difference.

Chris Hawley

When it comes to tools, I've always believed you need to go beyond the basics. Sure, most people will just head to Home Depot and grab a basic kit, but that's not going to cut it for hazmat work. You need the real deal, the big tools, the ones that actually get the job done. Take, for example, the three-foot pipe wrench we carried on the first rig. It wasn't pretty, but it worked - and we used it a lot. You need that heavy-duty gear that can handle real-world situations.

Then there's the whole non-sparking tools situation. I always thought it'd be fun to test non-sparking tools to see if they actually do the job. I've always been curious about how effective they really are. It'd be interesting to get someone like Andy Byrnes to test them out and see if they live up to the hype.

When it comes to specialized kits like the chlorine A, B, and C kits, the online debates are endless. We used ours a couple of times a year, mainly because we had some "frequent flyer" customers who always seemed to have leaking railcars. But here's the thing with the chlorine kit: it's designed for a specific pressure range. You can't just slap it on any cylinder - if the pressure is too high, it's not going to work. So, you need to be aware of your risks. What are the facilities in your area using, and do you have the equipment to handle it? And if not, does anyone else have it? Knowing who has the tools you might need, like a big pipe wrench, could save your team a lot of trouble.

Another big factor is the relationship with chemical plants. We had an industrial mutual aid group, which was great because we didn't have to stock everything ourselves. For example, we didn't keep a massive stockpile of soda ash - if we needed a ton of it, we'd just call the plant and they'd have it delivered. The same went for foam. We carried a decent amount, but the refineries and chemical plants had far more. So, if we needed thousands of gallons of foam, we just made a call, and it would be on the way.

It all boils down to understanding your jurisdiction and the risks you're likely to encounter. If you have access to a well-equipped maintenance shop, you're golden. If not, there's always someone in your community who can weld or make custom gear for you. I remember when we first started out, we didn't buy fancy stuff. We used old wire frame trash bag holders for decon, and our maintenance shop made the dome clamps. They didn't look pretty, but they worked. I'm sure those dome clamps, which were made by the shop guys, are still on the rigs today, and that three-foot pipe wrench from 1982? I bet it's still there too.
In the end, it's all about making what you have work for you. You don't need the fancy, high-tech gear - just the right tools, a bit of creativity, and

the willingness to adapt. And if you've got a team that knows how to make things work, you can handle just about anything that comes your way.

Mike Hildebrand

I keep coming back to core competencies - because that's where it all starts. But even before that, you've got to define the *mission* of the team. What are we here to do, exactly?

Are we the SWAT team of the fire department? Are we the crew that rolls in when other firefighters are in trouble? Are we going to be specialists - called in for high-risk, low-frequency events or are we going to be technicians expected to deal with the daily routine calls or maybe both?

What's expected of us?

If you already have heavy rescue squads or support companies trained in basic hazmat, then my specialty team shouldn't waste time duplicating those efforts. Instead, we should develop *focused* competencies. Skills that are truly specialized - things others can't or won't do. I don't need my specialty team practicing plugging drums because that'll be taken care of long before we arrive. But a tank truck leaking sulfuric acid? Yeah, I'll be expected to do something about that. Spill and leak control - that's in our lane.

You've got to be realistic about what your higher skill set actually needs to be.

Relationships matter here, too. We always made it a point to know the hazmat team leaders in the surrounding jurisdictions - on a first-name basis. I'm talking about regular cups of coffee with the guys from D.C., Montgomery County, Anne Arundel, Howard County, Baltimore City. We stayed in touch. Always talking. That makes a huge difference when it's time to call for mutual aid. You trust each other. They feel comfortable calling you in - and vice versa.

Once those relationships are solid, you can start having bigger conversations: Do all five teams in the region really need *the same* piece of specialized equipment? How many robots do we actually need in a region? Or is this just another prestige thing - "Bomb Squad's got a robot, so we need one too"? The same concept applies to HazMat trucks. Bigger than the next team is not necessarily productive.

At some point, someone's got to ask: "Do we really need *two* $100,000 robots?"

Early on in our team, hazmat folks weren't even *allowed* to use robots - too fragile, too expensive. The attitude then was you couldn't send one into a contaminated area to take a meter reading because the bomb squad thought the acid might damage it. But it was OK for the bomb squad to blow up the robot? Totally acceptable. That thinking had to change. These expensive tools? They can and *should* be shared.

And that helps when I'm justifying a purchase to my boss. I can say, "Look, I'm getting you this $20,000 specialty RAD meter, and I'm saving $50,000 because I don't need to buy a second robot to move it into the hot zone - Montgomery County's bringing theirs."

And it's true: I usually don't need that fancy meter *right away*. If I know there's radiation, my immediate job is to isolate and figure out how bad it is, where it's coming from. The specialized equipment can roll in from neighboring teams if needed.

We also had to know what *not* to take on. In Maryland, for example, we made a conscious decision: we weren't going to be the oil spill kings. That was the Maryland Department of Environment's game. They were already established, had the right equipment, and were good at it. So, we worked it out - big spill, they'd handle it. But then something interesting happened. They started calling *us* when they needed hazmat support. That's the value of strong partnerships. The same thing happened with the bomb squad. They started calling HazMat in for support outside the hot zone and it produced so many good results and espri de corps.

Once you've moved past coffee and start pouring Jack Daniels with those folks - real friendships form. And when the ego and turf wars fall away, the resource pool opens up. You start teaming up on grants. That's a force multiplier right there.

When you form relationships with industrial teams, you get similar results. You get access to *real world* info. Not just what's in the books -

but what the operators in the plant *really* do to handle chemical emergencies. And when I say operator, I mean the guy turning the wrench, running the unit. That the man or woman we want to train with. Operators know what happens when you screw up. They will tell you, "Yeah, the book says don't add water to titanium hexafluoride... but under *these* conditions, you'll probably be okay."

That kind of info? Invaluable.

It also matters when that operator shows up at your incident. You might get a company specialist who sounds a little off or is suggesting something that doesn't quite make sense to you. But if the chemical plant's fire chief turns to you and says, "Mike, this guy's solid - I trust him," you've got a basis to move forward. But only if you already have that relationship. If you've never met the guy, that's a whole different story.

And let's not forget - those plants have machine shops. They've got tools you've never seen before, and they *invent* solutions. I've had them make things for us right on the spot - tools that don't exist anywhere else. They'll make it for free or show you how to use it. It's all built on trust and attitude.

When you build your team with the right people and the right attitude, they start breaking down barriers. They stop making excuses. They start calling in favors. And before long, they're solving problems that aren't even in the budget.

Hell, sometimes I didn't even *want* to know where they got it. I'd just say, "Don't ask, don't tell." If it works, it works.

Bob Ingram

An elite hazmat team must have a comprehensive suite of equipment tailored to the wide range of hazards and missions it may face. First and foremost, there should be a closet stocked with ensembles designed for various hazards and missions, ensuring that the team can respond to any situation safely and efficiently. Alongside this, a range of respiratory options should be available to address different threats.

A solid basic detection suite is essential, shaped by a thorough area assessment of hazards. As funding allows, more advanced detection and identification capabilities should be incorporated to handle complex and unknown situations. Sampling equipment for gases, vapors, liquids, and solids should be part of the standard toolkit, along with hand tools for a variety of containment tasks, including plugging, patching, confining, and using overpack containers for various sample types. Additionally, pumps (air, electric, etc.) and fans should be on hand to manage ventilation and containment effectively.

Decontamination equipment must be selected based on the types of decontamination the team will perform. It's important that the team has the ability to work in various challenging environments, including at night, near water, or in tight spaces. The team should also have access to various databases, windsocks, and plume modeling tools to support decision-making in the field. Internet capability is a must to access real-time information and provide remote support.

Building a network of local, state, and federal resources is crucial. Having a reliable hazmat network that is just one phone call away from an answer or experience, can make all the difference in a time-sensitive situation. Specialized tools should be added as the area hazard assessment identifies specific needs, and the Response Plan designates them for the team's mission.

The team should have access to a vehicle designed to carry the necessary equipment and personnel safely, with easy access to everything. Too often, teams are assigned a spare apparatus that is not optimized for their needs, which can be a significant limitation.

Keeping an eye on new tools and technologies is essential. The team should regularly assess emerging tools that can fill any gaps in current capabilities or substantially improve existing ones. Identifying and addressing these gaps is critical, as is enhancing current equipment to meet evolving demands. Leveraging information from the hazmat network can provide valuable insights into whether new tools or technologies perform as expected, their durability, and their shelf life.

Additionally, exploring county and state purchase contracts can help with bulk pricing and offer access to competitive deals. It's also important to verify that any new tool or technology meets appropriate standards when available and has test data to support manufacture claims. Equipment technologies listed on the Inter Agency Board's (IAB) Standardized Equipment List (SEL), or FEMA's Authorized Equipment List (AEL), are updated regularly and very helpful guidance to teams staying current. Listing on the AEL makes equipment and technologies eligible for grant funding.

Finally, when developing specifications for a new hazmat apparatus, it's ideal to ensure that the budget covers not just the vehicle itself but also a full complement of HM equipment. New engines often come equipped with a minimum of new hose, ground ladders, hand tools, and nozzles, often required by consensus standards. It makes sense to ensure that the same approach is applied to hazmat apparatus. The current equipment can then be repurposed for training or used in a preventative maintenance program, ensuring that all resources are utilized efficiently and effectively.

Phil McArdle

Every Haz-Mat team is unique, as each jurisdiction inherits different community characteristics - people, businesses, and potential hazardous materials issues. Depending on the area's proximity to such products and their frequency of use, Haz-Mat teams can vary, ranging from in-house teams to local, regional, state, or federal units. Some teams deal with petrochemical industries, while others are involved with major transportation hubs or freight lines running through the community. Every team's needs depend on the specific types of materials they may encounter and the potential for accidental or intentional releases. Regardless of the situation, all teams must be prepared for identification / damage assessment of containers, sampling, spill/leak control, and decontamination. Ultimately, every team must be able to identify, control or contain, and render safe the problem at hand.

A core need for every team is monitoring and detection equipment. These tools help establish safe boundaries and operating zones by identifying hazard areas. Equipment should be reliable, easy to use, cost-effective, and calibrated regularly. When selecting monitoring devices, it's essential to assess their range, capabilities, and limitations. Consider the hazardous materials that may be present in your jurisdiction - whether gases, liquids, solids, poisons, or other regulated materials - and understand the quantities and frequency of their potential releases. Before purchasing monitoring equipment, ensure you have an up-to-date end-user list of these materials to avoid costly mistakes.

Sampling and testing equipment are also vital for collecting products for analysis to determine hazards and concentrations, as well as for evidence collection. This equipment may be reusable, requiring decontamination, or disposable. Ensure you have enough of it if multiple samples are needed.

Leak and spill control tools are also crucial. Leak control involves managing the product and container, while spill control deals with the product and the environment. Many commercially available leak control kits exist, but sometimes it's more effective to create your own based on previous incidents. The US Navy's damage control manuals can be helpful when designing leak control kits. Additionally, building leak simulators can provide valuable hands-on training for team members.

Spill control requires various equipment types, including vacuum pumps, pads, pillows, and rolls of absorbent materials. The key difference between adsorbents and absorbents is that adsorbents allow the product to stick to the material's surface, while absorbents soak up the material entirely. The quality of these materials can vary, so consider cost, absorbent qualities, and retention capabilities when choosing the right tools for spill control.

Containment and labeling are critical for safely transporting, remediating, recycling, or disposing of hazardous materials. Haz-Mat teams are often responsible for preparing materials for transportation, ensuring the proper packaging and labeling are in place. This step is essential before an incident site can be returned to normal.

Another significant challenge for Haz-Mat teams is accessing critical information for decision-making. Teams must be able to quickly retrieve information on products, containers, regulations, decontamination, and medical treatments. Computers and databases are invaluable tools to ensure teams have the information they need in real-time.

Personal Protective Equipment (PPE) is essential for every Haz-Mat team. The basic equipment includes full bunker gear, often with duplicates in case of contamination. Teams also need PPE to protect against cold, heat, chemicals, corrosives, biological hazards, and radioactive materials. Maintaining and cleaning this PPE is vital to ensure it continues to protect team members effectively during operations. The types of incidents your team responds to will dictate the PPE inventory needed.

When prioritizing equipment, life safety should always come first, including extrication gear and PPE. Next, focus on monitoring and detection tools, as these are critical for ensuring safety. It's also important to evaluate the frequency and types of incidents your team regularly responds to. Based on incident categories, identify the most commonly used equipment, which may require upgrading or replacement sooner than less frequently used tools. Remember, the total cost of equipment includes not only the purchase price but also ongoing maintenance and training.

Adam McFadden

An elite hazmat team can't rely solely on detection tools. While air monitoring and chemical identification are vital components of any response, the job goes far beyond that. A well-rounded hazmat unit needs equipment that supports isolation, evacuation, rescue, ventilation, and incident stabilization - especially when operating in complex environments like industrial facilities or fixed sites.

Here's what I consider essential:

- Detection & Monitoring: Multi-gas detectors, photoionization detectors (PIDs), radiation monitors, and field chemical ID kits give teams the ability to quickly assess what they're dealing with and make informed decisions early.
- PPE & Respiratory Protection: Full Level A and B suits, SCBAs, and decon gear are non-negotiable. Without the right protection, nothing else matters.
- Containment & Spill Control: We rely on absorbents, diking and damming tools, overpack drums, and leak control devices to stop the problem from spreading and buy time for mitigation.
- Rescue Equipment: Rapid Intervention Team (RIT) packs, extrication tools, and specially designed stretchers are essential for removing victims safely and efficiently from hazardous zones.

- Ventilation & Suppression: Positive pressure fans help clear contaminated air, while chemical-specific suppression agents give us options when water won't cut it - or might make things worse.
- Communication & Command: Wireless headsets, drones for remote assessment, and digital reference tools help maintain situational awareness and streamline decision-making under pressure.

The bottom line is this: detection gets you started, but it's everything that comes after - the containment, the rescue, the command - that defines your effectiveness.

Now, in a world of tight budgets and rising costs, we have to be smart about how we invest in new tools and technology. Our priority is always on mission-critical gear that directly supports life safety, incident control, and response efficiency.

We start by identifying gaps - what's missing, outdated, or underperforming - and evaluate purchases based on risk profiles, call volume, and the types of incidents we're seeing more frequently. Multi-use, high-impact tools - like upgraded monitors, new PPE, or containment kits - take top priority.

We also get creative. That might mean applying for grants, partnering with neighboring agencies, or using cost-sharing agreements to stretch our budget further. Preparedness doesn't always mean buying everything yourself - it's about building a network of resources that keeps your team ready, regardless of what shows up on the next call.

Mike Monaco

I don't think there are any one set of tools or equipment.

I think you need to be able to look at what your mission is, you need to be able to look at what your threats are, and you need to be able to have the equipment that's going to match both of those.

For example, New York City doesn't run chlorine through rail, so why have a chlorine through rail kit responding on the hazmat truck?

They're never going to see it. It's not something that should be part of their toolbox. Yet, we have to know it, we have to have it, and we have to train on it.

So, I think that balance between what your potentials are versus what you're required to have, that is what needs to be examined.

Obviously, your things that are required by law, your single gas meter, your monitors, all those things are critical. The types, the styles, what they pick up, what they don't pick up, how they work.

Well, you got to figure that out based upon your team.

Grants, politics, you know, sometimes the top people of a fire department or a team, they are going to. They sometimes are forced to play a political game.

They're going to have to cozy up with council members or legislators to be able to have money flow in the direction of the fire department and specifically the hazmat team.

Educating people on the requirements and the need for these technologies is really important. And then ultimately going after grants because the federal government understands how critical a lot of these tools are to maintain safety both in a national security environment and as well as a local, you know, municipality point of view.

So there's tons of resources out there in the grant world.

Chris Pfaff

I put air monitors as a basic - but not just any general air monitor. I guess because, naturally, when most of us think about tools, we immediately think about monitoring meters. But it's really about identification.

We get so caught up analyzing during the APIE-T method, that whenever we hear "tools," our minds go straight to monitoring and meters. Yet there are plenty of teams out there who are way more hands-on, dealing directly with plugging and patching. It's identification that's really evolved. The change we've seen in the past 10, 15, 20 years - even just the last three to five - is incredible, which explains why so many folks are still fixated on monitors and meters.

If we're going to narrow it down, two main tools I think are essential - but newer tools - are decontamination and multi-threat suits.

Decontamination has undergone a massive transformation in the last 30 years, and there's still reluctance among many hazmat teams to embrace new decon technology. And here's the thing: it doesn't always have to be some name-brand product. You can take the basic framework from these brand-name companies, then piece together your own system using readily available items.

Think about it: how did we approach decon before? We'd look at the HAZWOPER appendix, see the big car-wash style setup, then head down to Walmart and buy a couple of kiddie pools. Swing by the garden section, grab some hoses, and suddenly we've procured our own homemade decon system. So why can't we do something similar with other modern techniques or technologies?

A quick example - I won't throw anyone under the bus by naming them because honestly, I don't even remember - but I saw a video from one of those live-fire cop shows, the newer versions like "Live 9-1-1." They responded to an unknown package, called out the bomb squad because of a potential explosive hazard, and were concerned about white powder contamination. After about three minutes, the hazmat and bomb teams determined the package was totally benign and handed it right back to the homeowner, who didn't even know this package was being shipped from New York down South. "Nope, totally safe package," they said. Then, in the last three seconds, they showed firefighters getting completely decontaminated head-to-toe.

What message does that send? We declare the package safe, but then do a full head-to-toe decon anyway - because we're strictly following policy. I'm not knocking policy-driven response, but when it becomes overly prescriptive ("If you do this, you must do that"), it puts us into boxes. Think about it this way: when I finish using the restroom, I don't jump in the shower unless something extreme happened - I wash my hands because that's what's dirty. It's that holistic thinking that matters when we're talking about technology and decon. What exactly do we clean?

101

Then there's multi-threat suits. I think these are game-changers in hazmat response. Sure, they have limits. But often when folks dismiss multi-threat suits by saying they "can't be used for this or that," they're stuck thinking very linearly. Nothing wrong with specialized thinking, but sometimes when a person specializes heavily in one type of PPE, they believe it's the only or best form of protection, without realizing other hazards or scenarios could be addressed differently.

Here's why PPE matters: Here in Washington State, for example, we previously had regulations requiring verification that our SCBA was chemically resistant for any chemical entry scenario. But most firefighting SCBA manufacturers won't certify their equipment for chemical resistance - they're built for firefighting. So by default, we ended up totally encapsulating our SCBA for every chemical entry because it's the safest route. But in chasing ultimate safety, we risk becoming ineffective. Mike Rowe famously says - though I hesitate quoting Mike Rowe here - "Safety Third."

Now, priorities and budgets for new tools and technologies - this is one of the toughest parts. I'll keep it brief: you need to know your community. We've touched on this already, but specifically, this is where knowing your community's hazards becomes critical. A key piece of that is obtaining a commodity flow report.

Sure, you can easily get these reports from your local rail providers or through tier-two reports, but that's only part of the picture. Those methods are easy buttons. What about highway commodity flow? There's no easy button - you'll literally need someone out there watching placards. States can require facilities that submit tier-two reports to disclose where materials come from and where they're headed, giving you a rough idea of routes - but even that's incomplete.

Tier-two reports only cover materials stored onsite longer than a certain duration - usually about two weeks. But think about places like Amazon warehouses, UPS hubs, and big concrete tilt-up buildings: they often hold massive amounts of hazardous materials below reportable quantities. Those are the unknown hazards we'll never fully capture.

So prioritize based on what you do know about your jurisdiction's environment and transportation routes. You don't need the latest, fanciest gadget just because your neighbor has it. You need it because it genuinely addresses a potential hazard you've identified within your own community.

Rob Rezende

Well-trained firefighters are the backbone of any response team, and we make sure our members are equipped with the latest tools and techniques to stay ahead of the curve.

For instance, incorporating advanced technologies like IR (Infrared) and Raman spectroscopy into our training can significantly improve our ability to detect hazardous materials and assess situations quickly and effectively. These tools add an extra layer of precision to our operations, ensuring we're always prepared.

When it comes to securing funding, we focus on writing strong **UASI** grant proposals that highlight the unique needs and priorities of our team. A good proposal doesn't just ask for money - it tells a compelling story about how that funding will directly impact our team's preparedness, training, and ability to handle hazardous materials incidents.

Triage training and equipment are crucial to moving the team forward, but the answer isn't always the same. Every situation is unique, and the tools or training that are needed will vary. It's important to remain flexible, assess the evolving needs of the team, and adapt accordingly. We keep our approach dynamic to ensure that we are always addressing the most pressing challenges and advancing the team's capabilities.

Bob Royall

You bring up a good point, and we actually went down that road when we had only $80,000 budget to spend on our hazmat program for the year. It really forces you to think about how to allocate your resources efficiently.

It starts with the basics - with simple detection tools. I'm talking about things like reagent strips and papers, pH paper, pH strips, a multi-gas detector, and colorimetric tubes. That's your baseline. You've got to start there, because you can't skip over the fundamentals. Sure, you can throw in the fancy high-tech instruments, but without understanding the basics, those tools are just gimmicks. That's exactly what we did - we began with the low-end technologies and built our cache from there. We started with those basic tools, then moved up to a multi-gas detector, and of course, you've got to include radiation detection at that level, too. Once you've got the basics covered, then you start thinking, "Okay, now I've got a little extra budget. What's next?"

Well, that's when you add a PID (photoionization detector), and then you step it up with a parts-per-billion PID. After that, you start branching out even further - things like Raman spectroscopy or FTIR (Fourier-transform infrared spectroscopy). Those are the tools you can use to achieve more detailed analysis. Be mindful - bio-detection technology, for example, is still lagging behind. It's tough to bring something from the lab into the field, but I was there the day they rolled out the travel IR, and let me tell you, it was a game-changer.

You've got to start somewhere, and you have to get a solid foundation with those basic tools - detection papers, colorimetric tubes (which, by the way, are still good, even if the technology's a bit old). The thing with colorimetric tubes is that you have to carry so many of them, and their expiration dates are short, so you're constantly rotating stock. Then you add a four-gas detector with a PID, and you realize, "Great, now I've got a detector with a PID. But if one of these goes down, I've lost two tools at once." That's when you know you need a standalone PID. From there, you start expanding - maybe you get into FTIR or Raman, or some of the other specialized tools.

The thing is, there are so many different technologies out there that you can invest in. If you've got an extra $100,000 to spend, fine, but you'd better have someone who specializes in operating that piece of equipment. Otherwise, it's just another tool sitting in the box. I would require our guys, at a minimum, use three different kinds of technology for detection and identification. Once they get used to that approach, they realize, "Okay, I'm not sure about this. I might have to evacuate a shopping mall. Maybe I need a couple of 'trust but verify' technologies before I make a big decision like that."

It all comes back to starting with the basics. You can't skip that step. You've got to teach the fundamentals in basic training, and once they have mastered those, then you can start adding layers. It's a progression, and every new piece of technology is just one more tool in the toolbox.

Bobby Salvesen

I've always been a tools guy. Give me a tool, and I'll figure it out. Always have. But when it comes to hazmat, it's not just a preference - it's a necessity. A hazmat company without tools isn't a hazmat company. Just like a paramedic without their gear isn't really a paramedic anymore. Tools define the work.

And I'm not just talking about the stuff we buy. I'm talking about the tools we *create*. That's why, when you're building out your team, having someone like a welder onboard is huge. That opens the door to custom solutions - building gear in-house, modifying what you have, or coming up with something completely new to get the job done.

Hazmat attracts a certain kind of person. We're problem solvers. We're the "get it done" types. Having the ability to innovate - especially when budgets are tight - can be the difference between a workaround and a full-blown solution.

Now, let's be real. You *can't* fabricate every tool. But you *can* do more than most people think - if you've got the right minds and hands on the team. That kind of creativity becomes even more valuable when you're working with limited funding.

But tools alone don't make a great team. Training - *thoughtful* training - is just as important.

I used to get into it with one of my lieutenants about how we split our training time. He wanted to dedicate 80% of our training to the stuff we rarely do. I argued we should focus more on what we do frequently - because that repetition builds instinct. Builds muscle memory.

The problem with hazmat is that we're a high-risk, low-frequency operation. That means we don't get the kind of repetition that burns processes into our mental hard drives. Every incident is different. You might've done 30 gasoline tank leaks, but number 31 will throw you something you haven't seen before.

That's where the danger lies - the *illusion* of experience.

It's the gambler's fallacy. If a coin comes up heads 14 times, you think the next one *has* to be tails. But each flip is still 50/50. Just like each hazmat call. Past success doesn't guarantee anything. And thinking otherwise can get you hurt - or worse.

So we have to *rethink* how we train. We need to constantly reprogram our responses, stay ahead of emerging threats, and update our methods with intention. That doesn't happen by accident. That comes from leadership.

From the top.

If you're running a team - if you're the chief or the training officer - you've got to keep that 30,000-foot view. Look at your incident frequency and diversity. Think beyond just the next drill. Build your refresher programs to reflect the real threats your people might face next year, not just the ones they saw last year.

Because in hazmat, every flip of the coin is a new one. And the stakes couldn't be higher.

Doug Schick and Mark Zilch
Doug:

Protective clothing is obviously essential - we can't do the job without it. But SCBA, that's foundational. Any fire company is going to have that. When it comes to detection equipment though, that's where the conversation has been ongoing. I mean, ever since I became a captain, and probably before that, we've been debating certain things - like Draeger tubes. Do we really need them? Does anybody still use them? When was the last time they actually got pulled off the rig?

Sure, you can always imagine a scenario where they'd be helpful, but practically speaking, how often are we seeing that? Especially now, with the amount of new equipment we've been fortunate enough to get - we've got the latest and greatest meters. Now, I wouldn't call those necessities; most departments can't afford them. They're luxuries. But certain tools? Yeah, they're must-haves.

Five-gas meters? Absolutely. PIDs? Without a doubt. Maybe even parts-per-billion PIDs, depending on what you're doing. And then the colorimetric papers - those are cheap, reliable, and any hazmat team should have a good supply. You can do a lot with just that foundation.

Mark:
What you need really depends on your operation. For us, we handle both non-nefarious and nefarious hazmat responses, especially since we work closely with our bomb techs. I know some places split that - like New York has their CBRN assets with the police instead of fire - but we do both.

So one thing I always push is familiarity with the FBI's 12-step hazard threat assessment protocol. If you just walk through that list, it really gives you a blueprint of what you need. Like Chief said, you start broad - gamma radiation, pH, corrosives, nerve/blister, then multi-gas, then to alpha/beta - and you work your way down to the more specialized stuff, like assay kits and FTIR/RAMAN/GCMS.

That step-by-step process helps you at least rule out the dangerous stuff. You may not know what exactly it is, but you can at least say, *it's not hazardous based on what I'm seeing right now.* And if it does go to the next level, all the FBI really wants to know is: *Which lab are we sending this to, and is it safe to handle enroute?*

Doug:
Right - and on the radiation side, rad meters are absolutely part of my essentials list. We've got new ones now - our RadEyes cover both gamma and neutron. Add in something like the Friskers, and now you've got alpha and beta covered, too. That means we can clear a scene for all forms of radiation before even moving on.

Honestly, we've been really fortunate. The DNC helped us out big time. I had a wish list of meters - MX908, the ExplorIR - and I was actually able to get it all. Not just for one company, but for both hazmat teams. It was like a dream.

But before that? No way. One of my training officers would bring me info on new gear, and I'd tell him, "Yeah, I'd love to have that - but that's a third of my budget for one. And I need two." It just wasn't feasible. That high-end stuff is great, no doubt, but it's not realistic for most departments.

So when you go back to the basics - rad meters, five-gas meters, colorimetric papers - you can still get a lot done, for a fraction of the cost. Last year was the exception for us, not the rule. Smaller departments? They're not getting anywhere near that gear. So it's about being strategic with what you *can* afford.

Mark:
Yeah, budgets are always tight. We've burned through most of our STC funding, so now it's like scraping the bottom of the barrel. We're shifting focus to cover the essentials - the most pressing needs.

Like Chief said, the top-tier meters are great, but we're not chasing shiny objects. We're prioritizing what our folks actually need to do the job day-to-day. That means leaning into the more budget-friendly options.

And honestly, those colormetric papers? In some cases, I think they're just as good - or even better - than some of the high-end meters when it comes to categorizing. You don't always need a $30,000 meter to make the right call. Sometimes, simple works just fine.

Jason Zeller

When you're dealing with hazardous materials, the right tools make all the difference. For an elite hazmat team, a combination of specialized gear is essential to stay safe, make accurate assessments, and respond effectively. Here are the top essentials that I consider critical:

Multi-Gas Meters:
One of the most important tools is a multi-gas meter. This piece of equipment can detect a range of gases - Oxygen (O_2), Carbon Monoxide (CO), Volatile Organic Compounds (VOCs), Lower Explosive Limit (LEL), and Hydrogen Sulfide (H_2S). The meters need to be flexible, with interchangeable sensors for detecting specific agents. Being able to measure contaminants at the parts per million (ppm) and parts per billion (ppb) levels is vital for both safety and accuracy. These meters help you monitor the environment continuously, ensuring your team is working in a safe zone.

Remote Detection Capability:
Remote detection systems are also a must-have. These allow the team to assess potential hazards from a safe distance, especially if you're dealing with airborne agents or unknown substances. Early warning systems are crucial for minimizing risk and helping you make a more informed approach. You never know when you're going to be called out for an unexpected event, and this tech gives you that extra layer of safety.

GCMS (Gas Chromatograph-Mass Spectrometer):
For a more in-depth analysis of substances, a GCMS is a game-changer. Whether portable or stationary, it helps you identify the chemical composition of unknown materials accurately. This tool is crucial when you need to pinpoint exactly what you're dealing with on-site. Knowing the specifics allows you to respond more effectively and with confidence.

FTIR (Fourier Transform Infrared) Spectroscopy):
Another critical tool is FTIR spectroscopy, which identifies chemicals based on how they absorb infrared light. This is especially helpful for analyzing a wide range of organic and inorganic compounds. It's a great way to quickly identify chemicals, especially if you're dealing with chemical warfare agents or hazardous materials that are hard to identify with other tools.

Radiological Detection Equipment:
On the radiological side, you'll need radiation identification devices like the IdentiFinder or something similar. These tools help you measure radiation levels and identify the specific types of radioactive material involved. It's also essential to have personal dosimeters to keep track of radiation exposure. Having the right monitoring tools helps ensure that your team stays safe, especially when dealing with alpha, beta, or gamma radiation.

Personal Protective Equipment (PPE):
As far as PPE goes, you need to make sure your team has reliable respirators and self-contained breathing apparatus (SCBA). You don't need to overcomplicate things with different types of suits, but you do need to make sure the team has solid, effective gear for the task at hand. Every team has its preference when it comes to gear, but for us, we kept it simple and dependable.

One thing I'd definitely recommend - if the budget allows - is the rebreather. This equipment extends operational time significantly - from a typical 1-hour bottle to 2-3 hours, depending on the system. This extra time gives your team more breathing room, literally and figuratively, especially during long operations. It's not that you'll be working in Level A or Level B suits for 3 hours, but having that extra time can make all the difference, particularly when you're conducting more detailed tasks like sampling operations. It allows you to stay focused and not rush through critical steps.

This is actually a tough question for me because when I was leading the 24th WMD-CST, we had the advantage of being federally funded through the Department of Defense. That gave us a different kind of budget than, say, your local fire department or a volunteer hazmat team, so we had more flexibility and access to resources that most teams don't. Being federally funded definitely gave us more opportunities to invest in the best tools and technologies available. We were able to work within that structure to ensure we were always mission-ready, without having to sacrifice on quality. We could prioritize acquiring critical gear - like multi-gas meters or rebreathers - by putting together strong cases for the essential nature of these tools and their direct impact on team effectiveness and safety.

However, I know that's not the reality for most teams, especially those in smaller or less-funded departments. For teams in resource-constrained environments, I'd say the key is strategic planning. You have to assess your team's immediate needs and what will give you the biggest return on investment. It's about balancing the essentials - things like detection equipment, PPE, and communication systems - with the long-term benefits of advanced tech. It's not just about keeping up with the latest and greatest gadgets; it's about ensuring that your investments actually make a measurable difference in your team's ability to respond to incidents effectively and safely.

In that type of environment, I'd also recommend leveraging partnerships and grants wherever possible. Working with local, state, or federal agencies and applying for funding can provide some much-needed resources. I also found that a lot of equipment manufacturers are willing to work with teams on discounts or trial programs to help them get the gear they need at a lower cost.

So, while my experience with budgeting and prioritizing for new tools was a bit more fortunate due to federal funding, I think it's still about focusing on the most critical tools that will enhance your team's capabilities and safety while also seeking out every possible opportunity to maximize your budget.

Dan Baker

Fifty calls a year might not sound like a lot, but consider this: we only get called when things have truly gone sideways - incidents that overwhelm local departments, have statewide implications, or extend across multiple operational periods. In most communities, these are the incidents labeled as "the big one." That reality shapes how we approach preparedness in a few major ways.

First off, there's our response time. Our coverage area stretches nearly 55,000 square miles, and we've got around 50 responders scattered all over the map, constantly moving between training assignments. Every call is a bit of a gamble - we cross our fingers hoping that when the pager goes off, we've got people close enough to make a timely difference.

Then there's geography. Our massive territory means we have to keep our main equipment caches strategically placed - right now, we maintain two major caches, one on the east side and one out west. To fill gaps in between, we rely on smaller, squad-level caches spread around the state. The capability is uniform, but availability can fluctuate depending on location and timing.

To keep sharp, we train in-person, as a complete team, at least quarterly. Sure, from an outside perspective, once a quarter might seem infrequent. But consider this: our folks aren't sitting idle between calls - they're actively teaching hazmat courses and demonstrating skills nearly every day. These team sessions build on that constant skill reinforcement, giving us essential opportunities to practice working seamlessly together and using equipment that occasionally differs from our standard training gear.

One significant advantage we have as a state-level agency is that we can devote time specifically to staying ahead of emerging threats. We have dedicated personnel whose full-time job is tracking new technologies and evolving hazards that the fire service might soon face. These staff members pay close attention to developments in alternative energy, renewable technologies, transportation, and other sectors where new risks frequently pop up. Their insights help shape the fire service curriculum across the state and drive our own training and equipment investments, making sure we're ready when new, challenging situations arise.

Adapting proactively to emerging threats isn't just good practice - it's critical. If resources allow, every hazmat team should dedicate effort to this area. It ensures your responders are prepared not just for the incidents they face today, but also for whatever comes tomorrow.

Mike Callan

When we talk about specialization, it's a lot like comparing general practitioners to surgeons. Both have scalpels in their offices. But there are some people who are really good with that scalpel, and then there are others who, when you hand them the scalpel, will say, "Doc, can we put that away? It's just a hangnail." It's the same in hazmat work. You get people with all kinds of equipment, and they want to try it out, even when it's not needed. I laugh sometimes because I'll ask, "How many times do we actually use this tool?" And the usual joke is, "Well, counting today..." as if that somehow makes the number more impressive. But honestly, you probably haven't used it that many times. A hundred times might sound like a lot, but it's really not that much, considering the range of scenarios that can unfold.

A perfect example of this was just before COVID, when we were talking about foam. There was a real lack of understanding on how to calculate how much foam you'd need. Someone might say, "Well, I have two trucks," but that doesn't tell you everything. If you've got a tanker with a quarter-inch depth of fuel, you're going to need a lot more foam than you would for a 60-foot tanker on wheels. It's not as simple as just having the equipment - it's about knowing how to apply it to the specific situation. That's a gap I've seen in training, where people are handed the tools but don't fully understand how to use them.

It's the same with batteries. I'm on the fringes of understanding batteries, but I remember doing a class on them over 20 years ago when I was training on sprint and telephone systems. I held up a AA battery and said, "This is a small battery," and then held up a 1.5V and said, "This is a big one." It sounds simple, but the point was to show how much we need to understand about the various sizes and types. Recently, I asked someone if they knew what an ESS was, and I got the classic "deer in the headlights" look. I told them there was one just five miles away, and one day they'll have to respond to it. It's a massive system, and it's going to look like a huge, unmarked tractor-trailer with a door but no other distinguishing features. People don't realize how much we're surrounded by these potential hazards - just like when they put up chains around substation gates. The fences aren't there to keep the electricity in; they're to keep people out. But we don't think about these things until we're in the field.

I always say, "As bad as things may seem, I can always give you a scenario where it's worse," and most of the time, I'm involved in that worse case. But when I think about how things are changing, I realize we're at a point where the public is getting smarter. They have the internet now, so the level of awareness is shifting. Pretty soon, we'll be in the same boat as police officers, facing increasing scrutiny from the public. You don't even have to believe me - just look at what's going on in California. People aren't just grateful anymore. They've started demanding accountability. And let me tell you, there's always a group that will say, "Someone has to pay for this," and that's when things get tricky.

When something goes wrong on a big scale, there's always going to be a push to find a scapegoat. And while there might be some culpability, it's rarely as simple as assigning blame to one person or group. In fact, when an incident reaches national significance, it's not just about one person - it's about how much of the blame pie each of us gets. Sometimes it's not even about the actual blame; it's about the perception of accountability. Take, for example, a friend of mine who was head of an electric company for only two weeks before a major snowstorm hit, knocking out power for most of the region. He was fired because the company wasn't prepared, even though he had only just taken the job. But in the eyes of the public, they needed someone to be responsible. It was easier to fire him, and it made people feel like something was being done.

I guess that's what I'm getting at. There's always this pressure to fix things, and often, the solution is to assign blame to someone. It's not always fair or accurate, but it's the reality we face in these situations. So, while I'm not sure if this directly answers your question, I think it captures the essence of the changing dynamics we're seeing today.

John Cassidy

If you're building a hazmat team from the ground up, one of the smartest things you can do is start with a reality check: what's actually in your area?

That's going to drive your planning and purchasing more than anything else.

Start with the railroad - does it run through your district? What kind of commodities are moving through? Pull the local Tier II reports. Talk to your fire department's dispatchers and figure out what types of calls you're actually getting. This gives you real data to guide your priorities.

And it's not just about the everyday stuff. Hazmat's full of low-frequency, high-consequence events - the kind that might never happen, but if they do, you better be ready. That's the tough part: balancing preparation for both ends of the spectrum.

For high-frequency calls, the challenge is complacency. You've seen that 20-pound propane cylinder a hundred times. You "know" it's safe. But then one day, you walk up to it and it's got a green valve - something's different. You skipped a proper hazard assessment because it felt routine. That's when things go sideways.

On the flip side, the rare events are where hazmat shines. After 20+ years in the fire service and hazmat, I still come across things I've never seen before. And that's exactly why process matters so much.

It's our anchor. We fall back on the same system every time - hazard assessment, team meeting (our "hazmat bubble huddle," for those of you who listen to the podcast), execution, evaluation, and adjustment. That process carries us through both the common and the unknown.

When COVID hit, or when we were dealing with Ebola, we didn't reinvent the wheel. We followed the same playbook. We did our assessment. We reached out to people who knew more than we did. We gathered intel, built a plan, shared it, and executed. That system is what let us scale up and adapt quickly - and it works whether we're talking about a chlorine leak or a pandemic.

Now, when it comes to keeping the team sharp, especially for those rare high-consequence events, training becomes critical.

Take Level A suit work. If you're doing your hazard assessments right, you probably don't wear one in the field very often - maybe once a year, maybe less. So we train in them regularly. It's part of the annual refresher at the academy, but in the company, we run those drills more frequently - and we make them count.

We don't just suit up and take it off. We give members tasks to accomplish in the suit - fine motor, gross motor, communications, teamwork. The whole deal. We make the training realistic and challenging, because when the real thing hits, we want them ready. And we don't want their first real challenge to be in a hot zone.

That kind of immersive training ties into how we adapt to emerging threats too. For anything big and new, we'll run just-in-time training. When COVID came on the scene and guidance was changing daily, our hazmat training group - Bob and I were heavily involved - put together fast-turnaround training.

For example, when we learned that surface disinfection was important for COVID, we started sending teams to disinfect firehouses where a member had tested positive. We had to build and deploy that capability in real-time. So we created a quick training module based on CDC and federal guidance, and boom - we were out there doing it safely and effectively.

Having a mechanism for this kind of rollout is critical. It might be formal - coming to the academy for a structured class - or something more casual like a Teams meeting or even a group text. In our case, we used a GroupMe thread. A firefighter puts a new tool on the rig? That goes in the chat. Now even if I'm on vacation, I see it and stay up to speed.

That's how you stay ready - not just for the routine, but for the surprises too.

Dave DiGregorio

Over time, my approach has evolved. In the past, we would tailor our training based on the types of calls we were getting. If we had a lot of calls related to fentanyl, meth, and other similar substances, we had to make sure the team knew how to respond to those incidents and use the right instruments for the job. For example, the 908 is a tool that's great for a niche purpose, but we used it frequently for drugs. It's a versatile instrument, but we made sure the guys were proficient in using it, especially when it came to those kinds of incidents.

What we would do is look at the number of calls each year, assess what percentage of those calls fell into different categories - how many tanker rollovers, how many drug-related incidents - and then plan our training accordingly. But we couldn't just focus on the high-frequency calls. We also needed to train for those low-probability, high-risk situations, like nerve agents or organophosphates, which include pesticides. Out in Western Mass, with all the farms, pesticide calls were a real possibility. You've got to account for these things, even if they only come up a few times a year.

Now, trying to fit all that into 12 drills is tough. That's where the round-robin format really helped. It allowed us to get as much training as possible into a single session. Even if the drill was themed around one specific scenario, we'd try to cover multiple areas within that theme. For instance, if we were doing a drill on tanker incidents, we'd incorporate grounding and bonding into it as well. The goal was to maximize the learning, and while it wasn't easy, we made it work.

A big part of my role, especially as the director, was to stay ahead of the curve - anticipating what potential issues we might face in the future. I remember when fentanyl started becoming a serious issue, we knew it was going to affect hazmat teams. The challenge was convincing the higher-ups to take it seriously. My boss thought I was crazy when I started talking about lithium batteries and how they weren't being reported properly. He looked at me like I was out of my mind, but it wasn't in the official reporting system, so of course it wasn't showing up in the data. But we knew it was coming, and we had to prepare for it.

It's the same with things like bird flu. I remember we started looking into that, and before long, we were talking about having hazmat teams decontaminate farm equipment across the state. At one point, they even suggested we be involved in killing the chickens - obviously, I put a stop to that real quick. But we still had to train for bird flu response, come up with policies, and be ready for whatever might come our way.

Since we only had one drill a month, we also offered extra training throughout the year. Depending on the budget, we'd make these additional training days available, and even if we couldn't offer pay upfront, we'd tell the guys, "If we have the budget at the end of the year, you'll get paid." There was never a year I couldn't pay the guys, but I couldn't promise anything until I knew how the budget played out. Even if it meant we'd have to reallocate funds due to unforeseen events, like a large-scale emergency, I made sure they were compensated.

The key was always making sure the guys had the training they needed, even if it meant adjusting on the fly. And those extra training days? They were always full. In fact, I often had to turn people away because they were so popular. Everyone understood that this was a priority, and they made it work, even if it meant a little uncertainty about pay. The commitment to getting the job done right was always there.

Dave Donohue

This is a big issue. I got into hazardous materials back in 1982, and over the years, I've seen the number of incidents we respond to decrease, but at the same time, the need for specialized teams has only grown. We've done a much better job keeping trains upright, adding safety features to facilities and road vehicles, and ensuring better training in the chemical industry. But while we've made these improvements, we've also seen a rise in new kinds of calls - things like powder calls, fire incident support, and dealing with lithium-ion batteries and energy storage systems. From a management perspective, this means we still need to be prepared for the traditional incidents, but we also need to adjust and be ready for new threats as they emerge. And trust me, I've got my eye on hydrogen fuel cells as one of the next big ones.

The team is at the heart of our planning process. They're not just responders; they're actively involved in scanning the landscape and identifying where we need to be focusing our attention. This has a few key benefits. First, it's a form of self-study, where team members are diving into the hazards and impacts they might face, gaining deeper understanding. It also helps foster buy-in for preparation and training. When the team is part of the planning process, they're more invested in the training itself, and that makes it easier to sell the importance of practice, especially when conditions aren't ideal. Plus, it helps build a pool of in-house subject matter experts (SMEs) who can be relied on for their knowledge in specific areas.

Response protocols are continually reviewed. If a protocol hasn't been used in the past year, we pull it out for review and exercise it to make sure it's still relevant. If the protocol has been used, it gets reviewed after every call. This ensures that it stays aligned with reality and, if needed, is adjusted to reflect any new lessons learned or changes in best practices. This ongoing evaluation ensures that our responses are always up to date and that we're constantly refining our approach to meet the needs of the situation.

Rick Edinger

Personally, I think every team should be solid on the bread-and-butter stuff. I mean, if you're regularly running hydrocarbon leaks and spills - like most of us are - you should be good at it. Doesn't matter who's on duty that day, who shows up - you've got the training, you've got the gear, and you've practiced it enough that it's second nature.

But it's the low-frequency, high-impact events that shake people up. That's where the real challenge comes in - because you might see it once in a career, maybe never, and you've got to ask yourself: are we ready for that?

So it becomes this constant balance. How much time and effort do I spend maintaining proficiency in our everyday calls? And how much do I put into preparing for the rare, but potentially catastrophic stuff?

Some of the bread-and-butter stuff works itself out just through repetition. You've got experienced folks running the same type of calls regularly. But bringing new people up to speed, that's a whole different ballgame. And layering in training for those high-consequence, low-occurrence incidents? That takes careful planning - and should always be driven by a hazard and risk assessment.

What's in your community? What's the likelihood of that worst-case scenario? No sense in spending hours training for something that's never going to happen - unless that one incident could absolutely ruin your day.

Like when a local chemical plant starts a new process. If we know a new chemical or hazard is in play, especially something that significantly raises the risk, we've got to spend time on it. Even if it's just making sure our people are aware of it, that they know what they're walking into. In these cases, surprises are not good.

We used to do site visits - walk the plant, talk to the SMEs. That time spent walking the floor, asking "What could go wrong? What might happen? How are you handling this before we arrive?" - that's incredibly valuable. It builds context, familiarity, and real-world understanding.

And for the big stuff? Scenario-based tabletop exercises, multi-agency drills, programs like the ones rail carriers bring in - they're all good. And beyond that, get your people out to conferences, expos, seminars. Let them hear from folks who've been there - stuff you can't just read in a book.

Like we said earlier, you've got to know what's in your first-due area. You've got to stay plugged in. That means engaging with your LEPC, getting your Tier II reports, staying in the loop with local industry. Work with your emergency management agency, monitor what's happening in your community.

Take lithium-ion batteries - New York was the first to really get hit hard, because of the density and volume they deal with. Now it's a national issue, almost a daily incident. And the only reason other departments are ready for it now is because FDNY shared their protocols and best practices. That kind of information-sharing is huge. We were able to take what they did, tweak it to our setting, and train our people so we weren't going into those scenes completely blind.

You've got to monitor the industry. Read the newsletters, follow the podcasts, subscribe to the updates. Stay aware of what's emerging so you can get ahead of it - or at least not fall too far behind. You start hearing about a new threat, you ask: what do we need to manage an incident like that? Do we need to carve out training time? What's it going to take to get up to speed?

Because it's always something. Over the last 30 years of my experiences, it's just been one thing after another. Flammable train cars, new fuels, lithium-ion, hydrogen - and who knows what's next. Battery technology alone is changing by the day. That's the world we live in now.

As someone managing a team, you've got to be ready for the next thing without losing sight of the current reality. We still have to handle gas tankers and fuel spills on the highway. That's not going away. But we also don't want to get caught flat-footed when something brand new drops in our lap.

It's a constant balancing act - time, people, money. Everyone's dealing with the same constraints. But if you focus too much on one thing and ignore the rest of the picture, something's going to fall through the cracks. And usually, something *does*.

That's why I keep coming back to critical thinking. I don't think we emphasize that enough. We try to teach our people to think in terms of product, container, environment, and behavioral prediction. If you understand how those interact, then even if you've never seen the threat before, you can still analyze what's happening. You're in a much better spot to make the right call.

If everything you do runs through a risk-based response lens, the chances of missing something big, drops dramatically. That kind of mindset is what sets apart teams that succeed under pressure from those that get overwhelmed.

John Esposito

Right, so we're still talking about chem-bio, and I go back to '97, '98 - that was a big push. If you were a special unit, you needed to have that capability. It wasn't optional. But the hard part has always been keeping that readiness for the rare stuff while still staying sharp on what we do every day. And that's not easy.

Look at when our guys get hurt or killed - it's fires. Still. Because we're the fire department. So if we spend all our time obsessing over chem-bio or the next big thing, we lose sight of the day-to-day. And right now, it's not even fires as much - it's gravity. It's falls. People have been dying from falls forever, and it's circled back around to us these past few years.

So yeah, you've got to stay aware of the big threats. If chem-bio pops up on the radar again, you have to talk about it. You've got to be ready. But let's be real - once you've got your SCBA on, you're protected from most of it. Whether it's smoke, CO, or something worse, your bunker gear and SCBA do a lot. Then it's about proper decon, understanding contamination - especially now, with all we know about carcinogens and firehouse exposures. It all ties together.

And I'll say this: the average firefighter today is way more educated than they were in 2001 or '98. Information's everywhere now. They're seeing the threats - drones, for example. That stuff's scary. A drone could drop something on you from nowhere, and you don't even know where it came from. So yeah, decon becomes front and center. Doesn't matter if it's fuel oil, asbestos, or some unknown powder - if we know the process, we can deal with it.

After 9/11, we rolled out the SOC Support Trucks. Now, nearly 25 years later, we've scaled back the rescue side of that. But we *kept* the hazmat piece. Why? Because we need their metering, their decon, their ability to act as force multipliers. We've used them at steam leaks, asbestos jobs, all of it. We gave them ropes at one point - but that wasn't necessary. Rescues and squads already had that covered.

So now it's about sustaining that capability. That's why we've got refresher training going for the SOC supports, keeping the ERP current, updating the CPC program. And one big piece of that is ditching the old Level A suits in favor of the Lion suits.

You know Eddie Ryan, right? He said something that really stuck with me. He goes, "It's basically a truck company with better protection." And when you hear it like that - yeah, that's exactly what it is. Not hazmat techs, but firefighters with gear that lets them operate where bunker gear won't cut it. They can do truck work, they can meter, monitor, search, remove victims - and they're safe doing it. Just framing it that way changes how guys see the role.

And the Lion suits - they're familiar. They feel more like a firefighter's turnout. So instead of, "Put on the moon suit and go check it out," now it's "Gear up and get in there." The PPE has come a long way. And we wouldn't have any of this if it weren't for 9/11 and the funding that followed.

I mean, you remember the GX-91s? Garbage. Total garbage. Now we've got real meters. Built for us, not borrowed from industry. And that matters. Because the fire service doesn't baby equipment - we bounce it, drag it, drop it. Same with our guys. If it's going to live on a rig, it's got to take a beating and still work. Just like the firefighter carrying it.

Brandon Fletcher

Incident infrequency and a lack of diversity in the types of hazmat incidents we face is a major challenge in my county. It's led to a generally lazy approach to hazmat, and it's the very reason why my department even gets involved in hazmat beyond the Operations Level. But within our agency, we've built a strong culture of preparedness. We know that in many cases, we may be on our own for a significant amount of time. This reality drives us to be really good at everything we do - we focus on mastering the basics and honing in on the target hazards in our jurisdiction.

A strong, positive culture within the organization goes a long way in shaping the team's mindset. One of the ways we keep everyone mission-focused is by regularly sharing news and After Action Reports (AARs) from incidents that could very well happen here. It's a constant reminder of why we train and how important it is to stay sharp.

Leading by example is crucial as well. When the officers within the organization take the mission seriously, that attitude trickles down to the rest of the team. It's that leadership that sets the tone and drives the culture forward.

Chris Hawley

A lot of teams fall into a trap when it comes to drills and exercises - they focus too much on huge, catastrophic incidents. You know, the ones where the plane crashes, a tank truck collides with a railcar, and then a school bus full of nuns gets involved. Every year, we put on these big shows for the industrial aid group, and they wanted big, dramatic scenarios too. We'd run some wild exercises, but it wasn't always about training - it was more about the spectacle. Sure, there's training involved, but those big shows aren't necessarily what you should focus on when it comes to building competency.

Here's the thing: I always say if you get really good at handling the small incidents, the big ones will fall into place. A small plane crash, for example - get good at handling that, and when the big crash happens, you'll be more prepared than if you just focus on the extremes. You can look at places like the San Francisco airport. They deal with plane crashes regularly. They're good at it, but when it happens, it's still a chaotic, high-stress situation. No matter how well-trained you are, big incidents are going to be overwhelming. But if you focus on mastering the small stuff, you'll be ready when the big stuff happens.

It's like firefighting - if you take an engine company responding to a bedroom fire, you don't need a ton of discussion. The rig pulls up, the officer gets out, the crew grabs their tools, and everyone knows exactly what to do. That's how hazmat teams should operate too.

We need to know our "bread and butter" hazmat situations - like ammonia, chlorine leaks, or saddle tanks. For instance, with ammonia, the biggest question is: is it inside or outside? Inside, it's a lot more complicated. If it's outside, it's a little less tricky. You need to know your tools, your gear, and the procedures. It should be almost automatic. The team should know who's getting in suits, what equipment is needed, and what the next steps are - no big discussions. But too often, you see "paralysis by analysis."

It shouldn't be that way for the basic stuff. When it comes to a 150-pound chlorine cylinder leaking, there should be no hesitation. The team should already know how they're going to handle it, without second-guessing themselves. In rural areas, ammonia nurse tanks are common, and there shouldn't be any confusion about how to deal with them. Know your risks and prepare for the common hazards you'll encounter, because those will be the majority of the time. You don't need to stock every obscure tool, but you do need to understand the risks in your area. If you're in a rural area with lots of ammonia tanks, make sure your team is prepared for that.

One of the key things in hazmat response is knowing what you're most likely to encounter. You don't need to over-prepare for rare scenarios that are unlikely to happen. Look at your local data: if 70-80% of your responses are to flammable incidents, focus your training on those. But at the same time, don't ignore the other hazards like corrosives or radioactive materials - those still need to be in your toolkit. If you spend your time training for the most common situations, when the rare ones come up, you'll be able to handle them much better.

A great example of this is an exercise we ran with a chemical company. They shipped an empty intermodal container full of water down to Norfolk, Virginia. The container was on a ship, and only the captain and the first mate knew it was a training exercise. When it got to the Port of Baltimore, the first mate discovered that the valve was leaking. At that point, the drill kicked into gear. The team had to respond to this leaking container on top of a ship, with no idea that it was a drill. They had to deal with it like it was a real emergency, which was exactly the point. They learned to respond to a real-world, realistic scenario, and that's something you just can't replicate with a PowerPoint.

Now, not every department has a marine terminal, but every team has access to something that they can use to simulate real-world situations. Whether it's a local trucking company, a gas station, or even a chemical plant, you can find ways to create realistic, hands-on training. It takes a little creativity, but that's what makes training truly valuable - being able to practice in a setting that mirrors what you'll face on the job. And that's what's going to prepare your team for the unexpected.

Mike Hildebrand

You've got to understand the difference between high-consequence and low-consequence events. That's the foundation for everything we do. Most of what we handle day-to-day? Low consequence. It's your bread and butter, and that's where core competencies matter. You drill it until it becomes second nature.

But then you've got your Black Swan stuff - low *probability*, high *consequence* incidents. And when that happens? That's where your culture pays off. Your training, your mindset, the thought process you've built from the ground up - that's what carries you through. Because while the event might be new, your approach to problem solving isn't.

The structure you build around core competencies prepares your team to react *well* when the wheels fall off. That's why tabletop exercises matter. That's why scenario-based training matters. Not because we think we're going to be attacked by Godzilla - but because, like Don Abbott showed us with his HO-scale model of Godzilla torching a town - the skills, decisions, and teamwork needed to handle the *absurd* often mirror what you need when something *real* goes sideways.

I watched that Godzilla tabletop exercise and it was brilliant. And you know what? It worked. It wasn't about Godzilla's dangerous atomic breath - it was about how you solve problems under pressure, with chaos in front of you. That mindset scales across everything. It's all about the decision-making process.

Responsibility sharpens people. Nothing hones a team like giving them ownership of a problem. When I put a team member in charge of the week's exercise, I expect them to do more than just run the drill. They should start with intelligence gathering. And I don't mean reading a bunch of chemical MSDS sheets. I'm talking about *strategic intelligence* - looking ahead, spotting patterns, identifying emerging trends and threats, and recognizing what's brewing on the horizon.

There's tactical intelligence - what's happening right next to me - and then there's strategic intelligence: what's coming down the road? Leaders need to do both. I want people on my team who are tracking emerging threats. Maybe it's the tire fires in California or electric battery fires in New York City. Maybe it's a new weird material popping up in rail transport. Doesn't matter. Someone should be watching.

Look at FDNY and their work on lithium battery fires. They didn't wait around. They started gathering facts. They collected data from every incident, identified patterns, and came up with solutions. Then they shared that intelligence through their weekly hazmat intel newsletter. That's 5,000-foot-level situational awareness - and it's gold.

That kind of information? I'd be talking about that at the start of every shift or team meeting. Maybe not every incident is relevant right now, but when you start tracking something like Novichok - the Russian nerve agents - you quickly find connections to other highly toxic materials. You learn what worked, what didn't. And the next time you face something unknown, your mental playbook's already got pages in it.

There's always a new threat on the horizon. That's a constant in this line of work. Some threats fade away. Others become mainstream. Remember when they invented the train? Early railroads faced significant pushback due to safety concerns, environmental impacts, and societal disruption. People thought going that fast on a train would kill you. Before they dropped the first atomic bomb, scientists warned the president it might ignite the atmosphere and destroy the planet. As smart as they were, they simply did not know what might happen to earths atmosphere.

Same pattern over and over: a new thing shows up, and we're not sure what to make of it. Hydrocarbons, LNG and hydrogen fuel cells, lithium-ion batteries, hypersonic weapons - doesn't matter. The cutting edge is always moving, and if you're not keeping up, you're falling behind.

That's why we always made sure we had at least one person on the team who loved strategic intelligence stuff. Not spy-vs-spy, just industrial intelligence. Someone tracking tech, trends, equipment, threats. Because when 50 hazmat teams are all dealing with the same problem, and 49 of them are doing X and you're the one doing Y - well, that becomes a liability real fast. Not just for you - but for your Chief, your agency, your city. The legal and political heat from being the *one team* that wasn't ready? That's not something you want landing on your doorstep.

So yeah - core competencies, culture, intelligence collection and analysis and information sharing. They're all connected. Train for the likely, prepare for the unlikely, and keep your eyes on the horizon. That's how you build a team that lasts.

Bob Ingram

The impact of effective training and preparation for hazmat teams cannot be overstated. If your team operates in an area with significant interstate traffic and frequent incidents, such as saddle tank breaches, your team's expertise in handling these scenarios should be second to none. They should excel at confining spills, patching breaches, offloading hazardous materials, closing dual tank valves, and absorbing ground spills. In this case, the team is well-prepared and highly capable within their mission scope. However, this level of specialization, while impressive, can also limit the team's diversity in handling a broader range of incidents.

This challenge is a constant balancing act. On the one hand, you may have limited time and resources to train for the team's most common missions, especially with the focus being on the frequent, high-priority events. On the other, neglecting low-frequency incidents could leave the team underprepared for those situations when they inevitably arise. The solution lies in having a training plan that ensures overtime, even the less frequent incidents are covered effectively.

It's important to avoid repeating the same low-frequency incidents to the point where they become monotonous and uninteresting. Training must be short, focused, and targeted at the specific points that need attention. If you can make these sessions engaging, they'll retain the team's interest while ensuring that all necessary topics are covered.

To keep things relevant, try incorporating real-world incidents from around the country, or even globally. Hazmat situations often make headlines quickly, and those incidents provide invaluable learning opportunities. Don't be surprised if some of these low-frequency incidents are more common than you might think - look up statistics on incident frequency to get a better sense of how often they occur.

Assigning research on these incidents to team members not only gives them ownership and responsibility but also strengthens their knowledge base. This approach can empower your team to contribute actively to the learning process. Looking to national organizations such as the IAFC, IAFF, FMs, and others for already-developed programs or research can help provide frameworks for training, saving valuable time and effort.

Resources such as the NFPA, UL, and other testing and standards organizations can offer essential information that helps inform your training and preparation. And when new threats or emergencies arise – for example. when Ebola anthrax threatened the U.S. - the hazmat community network proved invaluable. Within a day or two, plans for PPE, containment, decontamination, and more were rapidly developed and shared across the network. We see that happening again with Lithium-ion batteries.

To stay ahead of new SOPs, strategies, and tactics, it's crucial to disseminate updates quickly and efficiently. Bulletins should be sent to all companies, detailing new threats, successful strategies, and SOP updates based on the latest research and experience. These bulletins should be followed by formal training and practice to ensure the team is prepared to implement the changes smoothly and effectively.

This approach creates a dynamic, responsive team that can handle not only the incidents they most frequently encounter but also those that may be less predictable or less common. By balancing frequent and low-frequency scenarios, providing engaging training, and utilizing the resources within the hazmat community, you can build a more well-rounded, prepared team ready for any challenge.

Phil McArdle

Busy Haz-Mat teams often struggle to find time for drills and training due to the demands of operational responses. With only 24 hours in a day, much of that time is spent responding to calls, maintaining tools and equipment, and handling other firehouse duties like meals and activities. Despite these constraints, this should not be seen as a negative. Every response presents a learning opportunity to reinforce knowledge, skills, and good work practices. Critiques and after-action reports are essential in identifying weaknesses or flaws in responses. These evaluations can lead to the development of new policies or procedures, and each operation is a chance to improve.

The diversity of Haz-Mat incidents can be both a blessing and a challenge. A well-rounded team regularly handles a core set of incidents, which constitute the majority of responses. For these types of calls, the team's preparedness and capability are well-established, and response times are efficient. This allows the team to focus more on the less frequent but high-risk incidents. These are events that may be less familiar to the team and therefore have a higher potential for failure due to the limited experience with these specific situations.

To ensure comprehensive preparedness, it's crucial to track and catalog all events the team responds to. Establishing a database is key for this. Past reporting should capture important event components, such as product information, container types, injuries, property damage, environmental impact, and lessons learned. This database will help develop a training and drill schedule that ensures all necessary skills are covered.

Over time, this database allows you to identify trends and shifts in the types of incidents your team is facing. For example, FDNY Haz-Mat 1 saw a shift in their responses from illegal dumping and aBrandoned hazardous waste to more complex situations such as gasoline tanker overturns, anthrax calls, and terrorism-related incidents. Tracking these changes helps the team anticipate future needs and tailor training accordingly.

Adam McFadden

The frequency and variety of hazmat incidents we handle directly shape our team's preparedness and effectiveness. In our jurisdiction, we respond to everything from natural gas leaks and white powder calls to suspicious packages and, on occasion, live bombs. That volume of diverse calls builds experience fast. It sharpens our decision-making, strengthens team coordination, and reinforces risk assessment in real-world conditions. You can't replicate that kind of exposure in a classroom.

Over time, frequent response turns into muscle memory. Our people know how to move, communicate, and make decisions under pressure. When hazmat runs start to rival - or even surpass - standard fire alarms in volume, that's when you see the team develop a level of confidence and adaptability that formal training alone can't provide. Every incident becomes a learning opportunity, revealing patterns, refining tactics, and exposing new threats. That hands-on repetition is what keeps us sharp and prepared for whatever comes next.

That said, we don't let infrequent but high-risk events catch us off guard. For low-frequency, high-consequence scenarios, we build in regular multi-agency training and large-scale drills. Once a year, we run full-scale exercises with fire, law enforcement, EMS, and emergency management partners to test and fine-tune our coordination. These scenarios are critical - they help align response strategies, ensure communication flows smoothly, and build trust across agencies before the big one hits.

We also maintain operational readiness through consistent skill development. Our team rotates through refresher training on CBRNE response, technical decon, and advanced air monitoring techniques. Tabletop exercises and case study reviews offer valuable insight into past incidents, allowing us to dissect decisions, identify areas for improvement, and reinforce best practices. Interagency meetings and pre-incident planning sessions ensure everyone's on the same page when it comes to roles, resources, and response strategies.

Drills aren't just about tactics - they're about gear, too. We regularly test detection equipment, PPE, and all critical tools to ensure our team stays proficient and confident with what's in their hands. Readiness checks aren't a formality - they're how we make sure we can act without hesitation.

When it comes to emerging threats, especially those linked to terrorism or intentional acts, we adapt quickly. Staying informed on evolving chemical agents, dispersal methods, and delivery tactics is a priority. Our training includes specialized scenarios involving **CBRNE** threats, mass decon operations, and threat-based response. We coordinate regularly with law enforcement, bomb squads, and intelligence agencies to ensure we're prepared for coordinated attacks or complex hazmat-terrorism events.

Protocols are constantly refined to improve situational awareness, accelerate hazard recognition, and support fast, effective decision-making under extreme conditions. We don't just train to the threats we've seen - we train for the threats we hope we never do. That proactive mindset, combined with strong interagency collaboration, ensures we're not just ready - we're resilient.

Mike Monaco

This kind of circles back to the question: *what tools should you have on the rig?* And the answer lies in the same mindset we use when we approach a hazmat scene.

We go in with theoretical knowledge - what the chemical *should* do - and then we confirm what's *actually* happening with our meters. That same logic applies to how we prepare our teams. First, we look at the potential: Tier II reporting, commodity flow studies - those tell us what *could* be in our jurisdiction. Then we compare that to what's actually shown up in our past runs. These two - possibility and reality - are complementary. You need both to really understand: *Is my team ready for what's coming next?*

Because even though history doesn't *repeat* itself, it definitely rhymes.

By comparing what's possible with what's probable, and then building training around both, you're giving your team the best shot at being ready. That means not just prepping for what's happened before - but staying sharp for the stuff that *might* happen. I'd say you should revisit those low-frequency, high-risk events at least quarterly - monthly, if you can swing it. Run scenarios, test their knowledge, challenge their assumptions.

Sure, you might train your entire career for an incident that never shows up. But that doesn't mean it *won't* happen. And if it *does* - you have to be at 100%. That mindset - that commitment to staying sharp for something that may never happen - that's what sets apart a truly prepared team.

Otherwise? People start saying, "This is dumb. This is never going to happen. Why are we even doing this?" But they forget: training isn't the same as experience. Just because you've *trained* for something doesn't mean you've *been through* it.

And when things go wrong - and they will - we do what we always do: adapt and overcome. We break it down. We figure out *why* it failed - was it the tool, the training, the situation, the response? Something changed, something didn't work, and now it's our job to fix it.

Over time - years, decades - things shift. Threats evolve. Tools get better. Environments change. So what worked ten years ago might not be the right move today. And what works today won't be the standard tomorrow.

That's the job: keeping an open mind. Staying flexible. Accepting that just because it *used to* be done a certain way doesn't mean it should be done that way anymore. And being okay with that.

Chris Pfaff

You absolutely have to have it - just like when I mentioned those departments down in Texas, who are constantly busy dealing with petrochemical incidents.

The easiest way for me to relate is by thinking about EMS, simply because of the frequency. I don't need continuous hands-on training for the common EMS scenarios that I encounter every day. Classroom refreshers, though? Absolutely. I need those to ensure I'm still following best practices.

But when it comes to hands-on training, the focus really needs to be on those rare incidents - the toxic industrial chemicals, the WMD events, those low-frequency, high-risk situations we seldom encounter. That's where diversity in training matters most. Spending more time on these infrequent events - I completely agree.

A huge factor here is fatigue and apathy. Teams get tired if we keep training the same scenarios every single week, month, or quarter. We need diverse training experiences to keep engagement high, especially when preparing for these uncommon scenarios. At the same time, we still need to sprinkle in refreshers for the common calls occasionally, just to knock the dust off.

Think about East Palestine - the most recent example - but there are countless others where we've ended up unprepared, and these are the events we remember the most. That's exactly why we must remain ready for those extremely rare, high-risk scenarios.

Now, strategies to keep your team sharp and ready for those low-frequency, high-risk engagements: Expand your team's participation into other types of hazmat incidents. This is absolutely essential, especially for many smaller agencies. Natural gas leaks, flammable liquids, combustibles, petrochemicals - those are our bread-and-butter calls.

Many people assume natural gas or petrochemical incidents are just hazmat ops-level calls. And yeah, mostly we're not plugging or patching. Usually, it's just putting absorbents down, isolating, denying entry - but involving a hazmat technician in these smaller, routine incidents, even something as simple as responding to a legitimate carbon monoxide alarm (not just dead batteries), creates engagement. I've witnessed this firsthand with my own team.

My team might only handle two or three full technician-level hazmat calls per year, yet we handle over 500 operations-level calls annually. If we don't regularly bring our hazmat techs into these operations-level incidents, they're going to get bored, disengaged, and eventually leave the team, thinking these incidents don't matter because they're rare. We have to keep exercising that muscle through regular incident responses and constantly updating run cards to keep techs actively involved - or at least make sure we're pushing ourselves into those discussions.

That leads us to the big question: how do you adapt your training and response protocols to emerging threats and evolving incident patterns?

Stay current. Read trade journals. Seriously, check out publications and trade journals consistently. Many of the folks from podcasts and chat boards also write insightful articles. As responders, even glancing at the news or resources like the Hazmat Hotline can keep us informed about new threats or emerging patterns. Keeping tabs on current tech, trade journals, and industry articles helps ensure we're always prepared for what's next.

Rob Rezende

Frequency and diversity are at the heart of our training philosophy. We prioritize training on the topics we don't encounter as often but know could make a big difference in an emergency. Alongside that, we make sure to discuss lessons learned each month from our everyday calls - those "bread-and-butter" situations that form the foundation of our response.

Our training isn't limited to just drills. We focus on frequent training, walk-throughs, and site visits to ensure our team stays sharp and prepared for any situation. We also invite experts from various industries to lecture and provide insights, keeping the knowledge flowing from the people who are doing cutting-edge work.

We stay on top of industry news, technological advancements, and emerging threats, ensuring we are always evolving with the times. To expand on this, we bring in industry leaders to guest lecture at our trainings, providing firsthand insights into the latest developments.

We don't stop there. We also bring in university professors to speak on where the future of the industry is headed, so we can prepare for the next wave of challenges and opportunities. Additionally, we invite military, FBI, and CST (Civil Support Teams) experts to discuss future threats, giving our team a comprehensive understanding of what may be on the horizon and how to stay ahead of it.

This approach ensures we're always learning, always evolving, and always ready for whatever comes next.

Bob Royall

It all boils down to risk. You've got to ask yourself, "Where's the biggest risk we will face? Which incidents are likely to have the greatest impact?" In Harris County, we don't spend a lot of time focusing on rail incidents. Even though we've got a ton of rail here - more than most places - rail incidents account for only about 3% of our responses. The truth is, rail transportation is pretty safe.

We've been tracking incident metrics since the '80s, so we know exactly what kind of calls we're going face each year and what commodities we'll be responding to. About 60% of the incidents in Harris County and Houston involve some kind of flammable material. So, logically, we focus a lot of our training on how to deal with flammability - not necessarily whether the incident happens at a fixed facility or on the highway with a gasoline tank truck. The training focuses on the common denominator, which is flammability.

Beyond that, we also look at occupancy types or transportation emergencies. Tank trucks, for example - those are a major part of what we train for. We've had incidents involving tank trucks that have lasted three or four days. Another thing to consider is the pipelines - we've got 9,000 miles of pipeline running under Harris County. Other areas might only have a few miles, but here, the potential risk is huge, so we prioritize pipeline response training. Even though pipeline incidents don't happen as frequently, the potential impact is enormous.

At the end of the day, the way we train is based on the risk we face and the potential impact of those incidents. If 60% of our calls involve flammable materials, that's where we focus our training. Whether it's flammable, corrosive, or any other hazard, we need to be ready for whatever comes our way. So, we start with the basics - how to deal with flammable spills and releases - and build from there.

In my time with the Harris County team, we also began focusing on hazmat pre-plans. What's a hazmat pre-plan? It's like a pre-fire plan for a high-rise building or a shopping mall, but specifically hazmat pre-plans focus on fixed facilities that contain hazardous materials. It's about being proactive, knowing the facilities in your area, and having a plan in place for when you need to respond.

We are all hazmat technicians, but within the Harris County team, some of us have a little more specialized training and experience. For example, when I was running the Harris County team, I realized I needed someone to manage our meters. We had a third-party service that came in quarterly to maintain our instruments, including our radiation detectors, but I needed someone who would step in and manage our instruments in between those visits. Someone who could deal with things like bad sensors, gas calibration, and maintenance during the shift. So, I went to the crew and said, "I need a meter guy on this shift."

I met with every shift and told them, "I'll send you to training, I'll buy the equipment, and you'll get the knowledge you need. If you want to use it for side jobs, fine - just make sure my instruments stay operational." We started with four people, but two of them didn't really care for the role. Now, we've got two guys who have become so dedicated to it that they don't want anyone else touching the instruments.

Of course, if you're going to take this approach, you need to have backup instruments ready to go. My guys who manage the instruments check every single piece of equipment at the start of each shift to make sure everything is functioning. It's about ownership and accountability.

One of our guys took an interest in air packs, so I sent him to training and got him the equipment he needed. That's the key - you've got to support your people, encourage them, and give them the resources they need to succeed. If someone wants to specialize in a certain area, like air packs or instruments, you've got to make a commitment to them. You've got to be ready to support them, because once they take on that role, they own it.

You'll hear some people refer to themselves as "specialists" - the air pack specialist or the instrument specialist. But that's not how we see them at Harris County. In our eyes, they're all hazmat technicians. That's the job title, and it's the role they own, no matter what their area of specialty is.

Doug Schick and Mark Zilch
Doug:

Most of what we run into day to day is pretty standard - outside gas leaks, a line hit by a construction crew, fuel spills, maybe a high CO level. That's the bread and butter. And because those are the most frequent, that's where people get sharp and comfortable. But that also creates a challenge - keeping folks mentally ready for the once-in-a-decade type of incident.

Things like a major ammonia leak or a true hazmat release - they *do* happen, but not often. And even white powder calls, which used to be a big deal, we've gotten pretty comfortable with. So the real battle becomes: how do you keep people prepared for the stuff they *don't* see every day?

There's always this debate - do we spend more time training on the stuff we rarely do? Or do we double down on mastering what we handle all the time? For me, the answer's both. We try to keep things fresh with creative drills, tabletop discussions, or just sitting down and talking through things that happened - maybe not even here, but across the country.

Take that compressed natural gas vehicle incident out in California a few months back. We pulled together a bunch of info on that, printed it out, and had a sit-down discussion. Talked about pressure relief devices, the decisions that were made, what we'd do differently. I try to keep my ears open - whether it's listening to your podcast, following the news, or just keeping tabs on what's going on - so I can bring that kind of stuff to the team. Even if we don't drill it, we should at least be aware it's out there.

Mark:

One of our past 510s, Glenn Lyman, did a great job with that. He pushed out a memo about mustard agent. It was like, "Hey, remember this exists?" and encouraged everyone to take a second look at our SOPs and SOGs. Sometimes it just takes that nudge to get people thinking again.

I've been talking to our Assistant Commissioner of Homeland Security about doing more of that - more safety bulletins, just quick hits that get people's attention. The last one we pushed out was on IEDs. The next one we're talking about involves chemical dispersal devices - basically hydrogen cyanide bombs. We've been working to figure out how best to get that information to the field.

Problem is, you can't just blast out sensitive material via email. So what we've done is use our Teams page for the hazmat companies. That's where we post the good stuff - the memos, updates, and anything relevant. That way, it's all in one place and accessible for each unit without pushing sensitive info where it doesn't belong.

And like Chief said, these are low-probability, high-consequence scenarios. You don't want to get caught flat-footed just because it's rare.

Doug:
Electric vehicle fires are a great example. We haven't had as many as you guys, but I spent a lot of time digging into how we'd handle one when it does happen. I reached out, did the research, and we came up with kind of a two-pronged approach.

One part is the Turtle Fire Suppression System - I'm sure you've heard of it - and the other is the fire blankets. We worked pretty hard to get those brought into the city. Right now, we're still figuring out distribution, but we've got a stock of both Turtle systems and EV blankets. It gives us a solid plan, at least.

We're also constantly evaluating new tools for handling smaller battery fires - individual cells and modules. Just a few weeks ago, a company came out to demo some of their new stuff. It's all about staying ahead of the curve.

Mark:

And I think that's the key with any of these emerging threats. People see something new - like an EV fire or a nerve agent release - and they think, "This is completely different, we need a whole new way to handle it." But the truth is, we already have a process.

Like Chief always says, we stick to the fundamentals: isolate, identify, notify, mitigate, terminate. Doesn't matter what it is - that process doesn't change.

Sure, more info on the threat helps. If you've got specifics, that's great. But the backbone of the response is the same. That's what gives people confidence to deal with something unfamiliar. Even if they've never seen it before, they've got a framework to fall back on.

Jason Zeller

The frequency and diversity of hazmat incidents in our jurisdiction played a huge role in shaping our team's preparedness and capabilities. Being stationed in Brooklyn, right in the heart of New York City, we were constantly in a high-traffic area, and that kept us on our toes. We were always on standby for various missions, whether it was supporting the NYPD or other federal law enforcement agencies.

Our team was regularly tapped for a wide range of responses - everything from high-profile presidential support with the Secret Service to operations at the United Nations. Then there were large events like the World Series or the U.S. Open, which required us to be prepared for all kinds of potential incidents. The sheer frequency of these high-stakes operations made us very proactive in maintaining mission readiness. We couldn't afford to relax, because the next task could come at any moment.

Having so many different types of events and incidents - whether it was a planned VIP protection mission or an unexpected hazardous material response - meant our team had to stay diverse in terms of skills and readiness. It was about being flexible and anticipating what could happen next, from routine checks to full-scale emergency responses. This constant state of readiness helped us refine our capabilities and think through all possible scenarios, which, in turn, made us more effective in real-world incidents.

The high frequency kept us sharp and always in *"mission mode,"* while the diversity of tasks helped us build a wide-ranging skill set. It was critical for our team's success, as we had to be ready for anything, anytime.

To keep my team sharp for those rare but high-risk events, we relied heavily on scenario-based training. While we maintained readiness through regular exercises, we also set up specialized, unexpected drills that mirrored the type of high-risk incidents we might encounter but rarely saw. This kept the team on edge and forced them to stay engaged with the procedures they might not use every day.

Additionally, we focused on mental conditioning. It wasn't just about knowing the tools and techniques; it was about maintaining a mindset of constant preparedness, knowing that even if we don't face a particular scenario often, we have to be mentally ready to respond without hesitation when it does happen. This combination of unpredictable drills and mental fortitude helped keep our team ready for the worst-case scenarios.

To address emerging threats, we kept a pulse on trends and intelligence coming from various agencies and organizations. We constantly reviewed after-action reports, tracked the latest hazmat incidents worldwide, and integrated those lessons into our training. Whether it was a new chemical agent or an evolving threat like a biological attack, our training would evolve with the times. It wasn't just about reacting to new threats, but *anticipating them.*

We also adjusted our response protocols based on lessons learned in the field. If we saw changes in incident patterns - like an increase in maritime operations or a new type of attack - we'd rework our procedures to address those shifts. We always made sure to adapt our training scenarios and equip the team with the latest tools to handle whatever might come next, ensuring we were never caught off guard.

SPECIALIZATION

"If opportunity doesn't knock, build a door." —Unknown

Dan Baker

A modern, elite hazmat team needs a few highly specialized capabilities to truly be effective. For our team, expertise in highway transportation incidents is absolutely critical - particularly niche skills, like accurately assessing damage to tankers involved in accidents. Equally important is what I call the "nerd factor": having subject matter experts either directly on staff or on-call 24/7/365. Chemists, radiation specialists, industrial hygienists, and even (god help me) lawyers - every one of these specialists can play a crucial role in our success.

Of course, there's always a balancing act between building a team of specialists and maintaining a group of versatile generalists. It's a tricky challenge, and honestly, we haven't fully solved it yet. We manage pretty well, though, because of a core belief on our team: "All of us are smarter than any one of us." In practice, that means we're never hesitant to ask for help, and we keep a well-stocked rolodex full of experts who are always ready and willing to jump in when we need them.

Specialization also greatly enhances what we can do with technology. Let's go back to that damage-assessment scenario. Imagine a situation where only a couple of our team members have the confidence and expertise to quickly evaluate a compromised tanker. By using advanced tools like CBRN Responder software and state-of-the-art communications gear, our specialists can participate actively in the incident, even when they're not physically on site. That means mitigation efforts can begin immediately, without waiting around, which significantly improves safety - both for us and for the public we serve.

Mike Callan

It's funny when we talk about "mission specialists" because that term gets thrown around a lot, but the reality is, you've got to be careful with it. It's kind of like comparing a general practitioner to a surgeon. Both have scalpels in their offices, but some people are great with it, and others, when you hand them the scalpel, will say, "Doc, can we put that away? It's just a hangnail." That's how it is with hazmat work too. You get some guys who are eager to try every tool and gadget, but often, you're only going to need those things once in a blue moon. I laugh when people say, "I've used this a hundred times," because usually, it's not even close to that many. A hundred might sound like a lot, but it's rarely that much, especially if we're talking about specialized tools that don't come into play often.

A good example of this was just before COVID, when foam was a big topic. A lot of people didn't understand how to calculate how much foam they needed. They'd say, "Well, I've got two trucks," but that's not enough information. You could have a quarter-inch deep tanker that's going to need a lot more foam than a 60-foot tanker. It's not as simple as saying, "We've got two trucks, we're good to go." It's about knowing what you're facing and having the right tools and knowledge for the situation.

I've got a similar story related to training. I remember talking about meters. I had a long conversation with Mike Casper (Connecticut OSHA) back in the day about whether firefighters could use meters, because meters were usually reserved for technicians. Mike came back and said, "I don't have a problem with firefighters using them, as long as they're trained to use them." That's the key - training. He emphasized that if you want your whole department to use meters effectively, everyone needs to be trained in how to use them. So, we made sure everyone was comfortable with combustible gas indicators, and eventually, four-gas meters. I still use them in my awareness training. When I talk about the flammable range, I bring up a slide of a four-gas meter beeping. When that happens, it's telling you you're hitting 10% of the LEL. What do you do? You back up. If your CO meter goes off, and you're just doing a trial check, you're supposed to switch to breathing apparatus immediately. The key takeaway is that when those meters beep, it means there's a problem. You don't wait for it to get worse.

But when you start talking about specialization and mission-specific roles, there's a slippery slope. It's easy to get caught up in being too specific without having your foundation in place. That's why it's crucial to stick to a broad curriculum - one that spans from technician basics to the higher levels of operations. You can wear a breathing apparatus and structural firefighter protective clothing and handle a lot more situations than you could in the past, but you need to understand when it's required. For example, in a fire, we used to call ourselves "smoke eaters" when we didn't wear breathing apparatus. But by the time I left the fire department, if you didn't have one on, you were seen as a fool. It's funny how much things change over 30 years.

Another thing I always tell my crew is about the people who wonder, "Why do I always get this job?" The answer from the officer is simple: "Because I need it done, and right now, you're the one who can do it." The officer doesn't have time to train someone else to do the job in the middle of an incident. Often, the same person gets frustrated when they see a newer firefighter stepping in to do their job. They think they're being replaced, but that's not the case. I've always loved my crew, but there are some I like more than others. It's human nature.

When we talk about being a "specialist," it's important to remember that the term often gets misused. I remember how I became a hazmat specialist. My chief, Jack MacElfish, had been on the job for just a few months when we had a derailment. I got a knock on my door from the cop who told me that I was being called in as the hazmat officer. I didn't know why I was picked, but it turned out Macelfish had said, "Give me another alarm and call Callan." When I asked why me, they said, "You can spell hazmat. Half of these guys can't." I got thrown into the deep end, and that's how I started learning on the job. Networking was crucial at that point too. Just months earlier, I had met Greg Noll, who had introduced me to the "eight steps." That's when I started taking charge of the scene. The first thing I did was clear everyone back. We needed to know what was in those tank cars. They came back and said it was liquefied carbon dioxide, and I remember breathing a sigh of relief because it wasn't as bad as it could've been. But I quickly realized it was cold, and then I thought it might be a cryogenic issue. I didn't think it qualified by definition, but it was still a hazard.

It's funny, but most hazmat guys from my time, and probably even up until the early 2000s, were learning on the job. If you didn't get killed doing it, you ended up becoming an expert. It wasn't so much about formal education; it was about hands-on experience and networking with the right people who could guide you through the tough situations.

The bottom line is that while specialization has its place, you can't forget the basics. You've got to be able to handle the situation with a broad range of skills and knowledge. If you only focus on one small aspect of hazmat response, you'll miss the bigger picture when it matters most.

John Cassidy

When you're running a company, one of your responsibilities as an officer or team leader is making sure all the critical roles are filled - and not just on paper. Some of that happens naturally through self-sorting. You've got that one member who's obsessed with the rig - he's cleaning the windshield, checking the compartments, making sure every little thing is squared away. Great. That's his thing. Let him own it.

Then you've got the meter guys. They're deep into the instruments, they know the specs, they keep up with the tech. That kind of passion should absolutely be encouraged. It creates ownership and pride.

But here's where you need to be sharp as a leader: not every role gets filled through self-selection. Some jobs need to be *assigned.* You've got to look around, identify the gaps, and say, "Hey, I need someone to own this." Whether it's maintaining a specific kit, handling calibration, or managing documentation - you fill the blanks.

Now let's talk about specialization - because it cuts both ways.

It's great when someone becomes the go-to expert on a tool or system. Maybe Bob's the GCMS guy. Maybe he's got the propane burn-off kit dialed in so tight he could teach a master class.

Awesome. But the danger is when *only* Bob knows how to use that equipment. If Bob's off that day, the tool might as well not exist.

That's a fail for the team. Everyone needs to have a solid working knowledge of the core tools, even if they're not the subject-matter expert.

So the approach has to be specialized enthusiasm without functional dependency. Let Bob be the guy who lives and breathes that gear - but make sure everyone else can still run a sample, power it up, and troubleshoot it if needed. That's how you build depth and resiliency into your team.

Same goes for drivers. We all know the driver role comes with certain incident responsibilities, and it's easy for someone to get stuck in that identity - "Oh, I'm the driver, so I don't need to worry about entry work anymore." Nope. Not happening. Rotate them.

Today, you're backup. Tomorrow, entry. Keep people fresh across all skills. Nobody should lose proficiency because of routine.

That's how you balance specialization and generalist skills: you encourage people to go deep where they have passion, but you don't let that become an excuse for gaps elsewhere.

And here's where you really get value - you leverage your specialists as teachers.

Let's say I've got a guy who's rock-solid on meters. I'll pull him aside and say, "Hey, I want you to run a drill on this. I want you to take one of the newer guys into the calibration room and walk him through it. Make him your partner on this." Now, I've taken that specialist and turned him into a mentor. And that generalist? He just got a little sharper.

That's how you spread expertise across the team. That's how you build capability at every level - without burning out your high performers or leaving your bench cold.

At the end of the day, your job as a leader is to ensure no role goes unfilled, no tool goes underused, and no team member gets left behind. The best hazmat teams? They're deep, flexible, and always teaching.

Dave DiGregorio

I don't know how many times I've had this conversation, but it's one I used to have constantly with my deputy and the training coordinators. The issue always comes down to this: You want well-rounded team members. You really do. In Massachusetts, you never know who's going to show up to an incident, so it's important that your team can handle a variety of situations. Everyone's going to have their strengths, of course - some guys will be better at certain things than others, and that's just the way it is.

One idea I really liked, though we never got around to it, was implementing a system of patches. When someone joins the hazmat team, they'd complete the basic 160, 280, or 240-hour training, and after that, they'd get a patch for their uniform. Now, this is where it gets interesting: Guys will run through walls for a patch. It's amazing how much motivation something like that can provide.

The idea was, as they progressed, they could earn specialty patches. If they became proficient in a certain area, they could level up. For example, if they're a basic hazmat tech, they start as a Hazmat Tech 1. After reaching a certain proficiency, they'd become a Hazmat Tech 2, and if they were solid, they could earn the Hazmat Tech 3 patch. This would be visible on their uniform and would indicate their expertise and level of skill. I really pushed this concept, but unfortunately, I left before it could be fully implemented.

Some guys loved the idea, but others weren't as enthusiastic. Some didn't want to push themselves and work toward a higher level. That's always the case, though. You've got two kinds of people in a team: those who strive to improve themselves, and those who try to keep everyone at their level. That's never going to change, no matter what team you're on.

In Massachusetts, when you're dealing with a tiered response system- like a Tier 1 response with five people versus a Tier 2 with 15 - it's crucial that everyone knows their stuff. The last thing you want is a situation where you've got five people on a response and none of them are equipped to handle the instruments. Believe me, I've been there. I've looked at the team responding and realized that, despite being trained, not everyone was at the same skill level. That's when I'd call someone like Travis Rebello, Kevin Galligan, or Mike Camora, my training coordinators in the office, and ask them to head over and help out, just to make sure the incident gets handled properly.

It's always a tough decision. Do you focus on making sure everyone is trained across the board, or do you specialize? We had 45-man teams, and we'd go back and forth: Do we train five guys to be the experts on the instruments? Do we train five guys to be decon specialists? Five science specialists? It's a tough call, because if you start breaking the team up, there's no guarantee that the right specialists will be there when an incident happens. What happens if you get to a call and everyone on the team is a decon expert and there's no one who knows how to run the instruments?
There's no perfect answer. It's a balancing act, and it's one we've gone back and forth on countless times.

Dave Donohue

The roles and specialties within a team depend on the specific needs of the community, the threats it faces, and the Threat and Hazard Identification and Risk Assessment (THIRA)/Response matrix. For example, right now I work in a landlocked county with only one interstate river, and the marine traffic is limited to small boats. In this context, there's no need for a marine specialty. However, I've also worked in areas with large commercial port zones, where there was a clear need for marine hazardous materials expertise.

That said, the roles within any team should reflect the specific threats that the community faces, as well as the common hazards that teams typically encounter. Every community has truck traffic transporting hydrocarbons and acids, so it's crucial that the team is familiar with the containers and products involved. All team members need to have a deep understanding of hazardous materials chemistry. This knowledge is essential - not just the theory, but the practical applications as well. They need to fully grasp the capabilities and limitations of the detection, identification, and monitoring devices at their disposal. A thorough understanding of their equipment allows them to perform effectively under pressure.

In addition to that, team members need to be well-versed in the tactics and tasks they'll likely be called upon to perform in an incident. Familiarity with the protocols and procedures is a must, and they need to be able to execute them at the required level, whether it's under controlled conditions or during a high-pressure situation.

Looking forward, there are new specialized roles emerging, and some of these are already starting to take shape. UAV (unmanned aerial vehicle) operations, robotic control, geospatial integration, and research roles leveraging artificial intelligence are all on the horizon. These roles will be critical as the nature of hazardous materials response continues to evolve.

One of my key principles is ensuring that every subject matter expert (SME) has at least one generalist training to be the next SME. When a specialist is identified, it becomes their responsibility to start training their replacement. In fact, several of the teams I've been part of have built this into the evaluation process. SMEs aren't just graded on their expertise; they are also evaluated on how well they develop their peers and future replacements. This helps build a sustainable team where expertise isn't just retained, but also passed down and expanded over time.

Rick Edinger

At the end of the day, I want critical thinkers. People who can take in information, break it down, build a plan, and then execute that plan with confidence. But that's only one side of the coin.

I also want the MacGyver types - the folks who can adapt on the fly, who know their capabilities and equipment inside and out, who can take a rough idea and say, *"Alright, I can make that work."* They're the hands-on problem solvers, the fixers. So really, what I'm looking for is a mix: thinkers who can see the big picture and plan accordingly, and doers who can step in and put hands on the problem and make it go away.

You spend any amount of time around a hazmat team, and you'll start to see the patterns. You can usually tell within an hour who the thinkers are and who the tinkerers are. The real trick is: how do you build a team with the right balance of both? How do you make sure you've got the coverage you need, no matter the call?

That's where development comes in. It's about knowing your team - what their strengths and weaknesses are, what they're interested in, and where your operational gaps are. Once you know that, you can start tailoring your approach.

We used to send people out for specialized training based on needs we saw in the field. If we realized we were light in a particular area - say, radiation - we'd identify someone who was interested and send them to get more training. They might not be on shift all the time, but we could always get in touch if something came up. That was the beauty of the 24/48 shift model - we had flexibility.

Over time, we tried to balance those SMEs across shifts. If we needed a subject matter expert on duty at any given time, we'd work to spread out that capability. That way, we always had someone ready to step in - someone trained, informed, and plugged in.
But that specialized knowledge doesn't exist in a vacuum. You've got to tie it back to your mission profile. What are your risks and hazards?

What's the level of performance expected from your team? Are you the first-in hazmat team, managing the full incident from start to finish? Or are you more of a containment and handoff group, stabilizing the scene until higher-level resources arrive?

If you've got a clear understanding of your team, your tools, and your mission, then figuring out who you need - and how to develop them - becomes a whole lot easier.

John Esposito

So, this week I was talking with a bunch of different chiefs, each running different models, and it really brought something home for me: if we expect a hazmat team to operate as one cohesive unit - especially in high-stakes, rare events - then they *need* to spend time together. Not just train together occasionally. I'm talking about being in the same firehouse, day in and day out.

You can't just say, "Alright, we're playing baseball today," and then grab one guy from this company, one from that one, and throw them on the field together. Sure, they'll play - but are they going to be effective? Efficient? That's a different question.

You and I both spent years in the firehouse. You know what matters. It's not just the runs. It's the time spent cutting vegetables in the kitchen, talking about yesterday's job, swapping stories, asking, "Hey, what would *you* have done there?" That's where the real learning happens. That's where cohesion is built.

And yeah, every department has to work with what they've got. But I believe the *most effective* model is one where the hazmat team works together full-time. That way, they drill together regularly, build chemistry, and become that force multiplier we talk about. It's the difference between remote work and in-person. Sure, Zoom meetings work - but they don't replace those chance hallway conversations that lead to real progress. Same thing here.

If this role is important - and we all agree that it is - then I also think there needs to be some kind of additional compensation. And if there's not enough hazmat volume to keep a team exclusive, then maybe they don't need to be 100% hazmat all the time. But what I *don't* want is for them to be running 6,000 calls a year. I want them ready. I want them sharp.

We already know hazmat runs can be ten hours long. That's the nature of it. So give them the space to be ready. And that brings us full circle - back to training.

People need to remember: just because you're certified doesn't mean you're qualified. A cert just tells me you sat through a class and passed a test. That's a start - but it's not the finish line.

If you have the training but not the experience, how will you perform when the time comes? That's a question worth asking before the time comes.

Same with hazmat. What I love about our approach is that we bring people into the company *first*. We show them the tools, the way *we* do things. We train them hands-on, right there. Then we send them to the formal classes - either just before, during, or right after. That way, the class makes sense. They've already seen it in action.

We do that on the Marine side. On Rescue. On Hazmat. And even when they come back from school, it's not over. That's when the real work starts. Now it's about proving they're competent. Not just certified - *competent*. That's how you put the whole package together.

Brandon Fletcher

In a small team, everyone must be capable of performing every role that could be expected of them. In smaller or volunteer organizations, you never really know who's going to be available on any given day, so versatility is key. Ideally, it's helpful to have a few people you can count on for the roles of HM Officer, HM Safety Officer, and Research, but even in those specialized positions, flexibility is essential.

At the end of the day, everything still hinges on the basics. A technician doesn't get to discard their operations skill set when they step up to technician duties, and the same goes for specialists or other specialized roles within the team. Designated HM Officers or Safety Officers still need to maintain their entry-level skills - not just to be effective in their supervisory roles but to step in when needed for entry, research, decon, or any other task. Circumstances often require it, and you have to be prepared for that. We make it clear upfront that taking on a specialized role means keeping up with the foundational skills. It's all part of maintaining the capability and flexibility of the team.

Chris Hawley

You've got to have your meter guru. You need someone who knows the ins and outs of your meters, someone who understands FTIR, Raman, and all the important detection devices. Sure, everyone should be able to turn them on and get them working, but I don't expect the meter guru to read a full spectrum. What I do expect is for them to glance at the spectrum and say, "I think this is water, or this is something else," and at least have the knowledge to dig a little deeper. They should know how to reach out to the company's support team, be able to send the spectrum off to get a second opinion, and know where to go for that backup.

In addition to that, I've always liked having someone with a mechanical background on the team. Even though we had a bomb squad, I wanted my hazmat folks to know a little something about explosives. It wasn't about going in to do render-safe work, but more about understanding the materials and being aware of what we might encounter. So we'd pair up the hazmat tech with a bomb tech, throw them into a situation together, and let them figure out what was going on. Having that cross-discipline knowledge was invaluable.

And then there's the tank truck specialist. Every team needs a "Bill Hand" - a tank truck guru. Now, I know Bill probably can't be on every shift, but having someone like that in your back pocket is critical. And if you don't have one, you've got to have the ability to reach out to someone who does. I always considered myself a resourceful guy. I may not be the smartest in the room, but I've got a killer phonebook. If I don't know something about, say, the habits of a wombat, I'm just two calls away from someone who does. I'd call Dr. Christine Baxter, and she'd probably say, "I don't know, but I know someone in Australia who does." It's all about knowing who to call when you need help.

You also need someone on the team who really understands protective clothing. It's not that permeation compatibility charts are difficult, but someone needs to know how to avoid issues like the suit inflating because the relief valve is on the wrong side. And if something like that does happen, you need a team member who knows how to deal with it, and how to fix things quickly in the field.

One way to provide incentive and get the best out of your team is to send those key people for specialized training that others don't get.

For example, if someone's your go-to for protective clothing, send them to Kappler University or another reputable training center. Pay for their training, cover their hotel, and let them spend a week diving into the specifics. Even if they don't come back as an expert on the equipment, they'll have a deeper understanding of how everything works. You can do the same for your meter guru - send them to a Honeywell/RAE class or a similar advanced course. Even though they may not be able to do repairs themselves, they'll come back with the knowledge to handle any issues that arise in the field. It's all about providing that extra value and making sure you've got people who can handle the details when things get complicated.

Identifying the right people and sending them for that extra training will not only improve the overall capabilities of your team, but it'll also create a culture of growth and expertise. Everyone benefits from having those specialized skills, and the more you invest in your people, the stronger your team will become.

Mike Hildebrand

There are certain incidents where failure simply isn't an option.

We all know what they are. We all know our soft spots. Like a propane tank truck in the BLEVE mode flipped at Route 50 and Interstate 495 on a lazy summer Friday - the only route to the beach. That's not just a traffic jam - that's political event that creates its own heat. These big traffic clogging incidents cause people to have heart attacks in their cars, babies are being born in backseats, folks are losing their minds because they're stuck in gridlock for hours. If that scene drags out because we didn't know how to core drill the tank or we ran out of foam concentrate? That's not just a tactical failure - that's a public, political, *leadership* failure.

Remember Chief Alan Brunacini's "Be nice to Mrs. Smith" talks? The public doesn't care why the road's closed. They want to know why it's not *fixed*. And if your hazmat team can't fix it - if you're the bottleneck - it's not just your problem anymore. That's a red flag that you need specialized capability. You need that one tool, that one training gap closed, or that one special team standing by.

Elected leadership - they've all have their own thresholds for what will be tolerated. One time there was a suicidal jumper on the bridge that crosses from Maryland into Virginia. The police had a process for getting the jumper safely off the bridge but that process takes time. All of a sudden you've got radio talk show callers asking why we didn't just *shoot the guy on the bridge* – problem resolved. They're not joking. In their world, their kid is crying, their dinner's ruined, they missed a flight - they want someone to pay for it.

And if there's no plan in place to solve that kind of problem fast, your department *will* own it and wear it.

That's where the fly team or special unit has to come in with solutions, not excuses. If your beanbag gun isn't loaded - or you never bought one - that's a planning failure when they guy is on the bridge ready to jump. It's on us to know where the community's hot buttons are, and to make sure we're ready to step in before they're pushed. A good manager knows how to explain that risk to their leadership. Sometimes it takes painting the full picture.

Sometimes it's not about whether *your* department can justify the cost - it's whether another jurisdiction in the region can afford the tools, and *you* can be the recipient of that capability. Anne Arundel County might own the asset, but if you've got that 20-minute response partnership in place, the region wins.

That's why collaboration matters. I've seen ports shut down, airports paralyzed, highways closed for hours. That's not just an ops issue. It's a political and economic one. And it becomes the justification for long-term investments - new gear, additional personnel, regional capabilities. But only if someone on your team knows how to connect the dots between intelligence, capability, and funding.

You've got to have that person - the one who can turn emerging threats into dollars, resources, and influence. Let's go back to the Colonel Beckwith story about Delta Force. Beckwith was a respected soldier with the skill set to recruit, train, and manage people with special skills, however, he was not very good at standup Pentagon briefings, so he recruited another Army officer that excelled at public speaking at high levels of government. Maybe this means forming partnerships. Maybe that means teeing up a grant. Maybe it's just understanding that *how* you pitch the need matters as much as *what* the need is.

Sometimes you have to work it like the movie My Big Fat Greek Wedding. You don't pitch your idea - you make it *their* idea. If it's your boss's idea, it's an *excellent* idea. If it's your idea? It's just a *good* one. I don't care whose name is on it - as long as we get what we need. But you also need to respect bandwidth. There are only so many hours in the day - and only so much mental space your people have. If your team is crushing the basics - handling bread-and-butter work clean, fast, and safely - *then* you've earned the right to dive into more esoteric topics. That's where specialization comes in.

Specialization is what drives innovation. Take Decon, for instance. It used to be too complicated. Too slow. It was a choke point. Everyone was frustrated that it was taking too long - command, politicians, the public. So we picked two guys. "You're our Decon specialists now. Go fix it." They started from scratch. Back to the basics.

It's like changing a diaper. Don't get it on you. Don't spread it around. Get it cleaned up fast. That's it.

We'd spent a lot of money on Decon setups that didn't work like decon tents. Engineers over-engineered it. It took to many people and too long to set up that tent so it never got deployed. These two guys reworked the whole decon approach and made it simple. They invented tools. Found workarounds. Because they had a clear mission and the freedom to *solve* it, not just train it.

My decon problem example goes back to recruitment. You want people who already come in with real-world skill sets. Electricians. Heavy equipment operators. Coders. Guys and Gals who can weld, wire, fabricate. Those cross-trained minds are worth their weight in gold. You want a team like a Green Beret A-Team. Six people, each with their own specialty like languages, medic, engineers or demolition, but every one of them knows how to use a knife. Everyone's got core skills. Everyone brings something extra.

Appoint a specialist. Give them direction. Let them get after it. They don't just train - they *invent*. And then they start sharing what they've built with other teams who have the same problems. I've solved more issues with one phone call to a buddy on another team than I can count.

Sometimes that call isn't just about solving your problem - it's about backing your solution. I've been on scenes where we were ready to go with a plan, but it was politically risky. The chief needed backup. Not just facts and science - he needed *consensus*. So we make the phone calls. You can speak with confidence at the Incident Command Post "I talked to New York City, San Francisco and Baltimore HazMat Teams. We walked them through the problem. They'd do the same thing we're doing." That carries a lot of weight when you are presenting solutions to management.

With that type of team input that same chief can walk into a press briefing and say, "This is a nationally supported approach." Suddenly, I'm brilliant - not because *I* said it, but because three other respected teams said it too.

Greg Noll had a line I love: *"We need as many bloody fingerprints on the knife as possible."* Get buy-in. Build consensus. Share the risk. That's how you lead a high-stakes operation - tactically and politically.

Bob Ingram

The rapid advancement of new technologies, such as battery systems, hydrogen, LNG, and other emerging fuel and power sources, has underscored the need for hazmat teams to strengthen their capabilities across various response missions. In particular, the need for better field capabilities in biohazard detection is crucial. As new hazards continue to emerge and naturally occurring biohazards persist, the threat landscape is evolving. Increased risks from groups and individuals only add to the complexity. Teams must be equipped to rapidly detect, identify, and contain these biohazards to ensure public safety.

An important area for growth is the need for closer collaboration with manufacturers of new technologies. Gaining a better understanding of the hazards associated with these systems - particularly when they malfunction or are not operating as intended - will significantly improve response times and efficacy. This collaboration should also extend to code enforcement agencies, who can play a key role in ensuring that safety measures are built into the design and deployment of these technologies in structures and transportation. By requiring safety defenses for these systems from the outset, we can better protect people in the event of a malfunction.

Looking back to the mid-90s, the FDNY developed a tiered hazmat response system, recognizing the increased resource needs for large-scale incidents, such as releases of weaponized CBRNE materials. At the time, it became clear that training the entire department to the hazmat technician level was not feasible due to funding constraints and practicality. Instead, the department created different mission-specific roles, each with its own associated training and equipment needs. This model played a significant role in the development of the Mission-Specific Chapter in NFPA 472 and the current NFPA 470.

This same concept can be applied to hazmat team structures today. Identifying team members with a particular background or interest in a specialty area - whether it's a new technology or emerging hazard - allows the team to train these individuals and leverage their expertise for broader team benefit. These specialists should be distributed across shifts, ensuring that each shift has one or two trained members available. Over time, as new technologies or specialties emerge, other team members can be trained in these areas, ensuring a constant renewal of expertise. This approach allows team members to maintain their basic or advanced capabilities while developing specialized knowledge, fostering cross-training within the team. As a result, every member learns not only from specialized experts but also instructs others, elevating the overall competence of the entire team.

A prime example of this approach in action dates to 2012 when the FDNY Hazmat Chief assigned two officers to the Fire Prevention Bureau to collaborate with engineers, chemists, and companies like Con Edison and Tesla on emerging battery issues. This initiative led to early progress in safety requirements and code changes for the installation of battery storage systems in commercial and large facilities. However, despite these advancements, we are still seeing incidents involving smaller mobility device batteries in residential structures. There is still significant work to be done in public messaging to raise awareness and educate the public on these risks.

Ultimately, the key takeaway here is that involving personnel early in the research and development stages of new technologies, while they are still in their nascent phases, will give hazmat teams the foresight and knowledge they need to effectively respond when these systems are deployed and inevitably malfunction. By embedding hazmat professionals in the research, standards development, and policy-making process, we can work to stay ahead of emerging threats, ensuring our teams are ready to respond safely and effectively when called upon.

Phil McArdle

The core mission of any Haz-Mat team remains focused on monitoring and detection, especially for specialized units. Once information is gathered through meters and monitoring tools, it's crucial to act on it, ensuring that the team's main mission - identifying and mitigating leaks, spills, or potential releases - is achieved. Rendering safe and returning to pre-incident conditions as quickly as possible lessens the impact of the event is the goal. This process aims to return everything to pre-incident conditions as swiftly as possible. The need for specialized roles within the team is driven by the specific hazards dictated by the jurisdiction's authority.

To effectively tackle any Haz-Mat challenge, the team must first define its mission clearly. Identifying the goals and the strategies needed to meet those goals is paramount. Each goal may have several underlying objectives, so it's important to prioritize them and monitor progress closely. Stay realistic - understand the difference between what you "need to know" and what is simply "nice to know."

Divide and Conquer: Focus on What Matters Without Overextending
When it comes to hazardous materials response, it's essential to recognize that not every member of the department needs to be trained to the highest level of competency or expertise. To illustrate this point, let's examine a real-world scenario - one faced by FDNY during a high-stakes incident involving large-scale planning, logistics, and resources.

Let's take that scenario, adapt it to your department, and substitute relevant details for your own parameters.

Imagine this:

There's an incident at a major transportation hub - Grand Central Terminal, during rush hour, when thousands of commuters pass through. Suddenly, a number of these commuters are incapacitated by an unknown substance. As good Samaritans attempt to help, they, too, fall victim to the same substance. Emergency calls pour in, and Police, Fire, and EMS units are dispatched to the scene. Upon arrival, the first responders, too, find themselves incapacitated by the same substance. Now, let's break down the key challenges of this situation and think about how to tackle them through specialized roles:

1. Large numbers of civilians are incapacitated by an unknown substance and need immediate help.
2. A significant number of first responders have become part of the problem, incapacitated by the same substance as the civilians.
3. A major transportation hub is shut down, leaving thousands of passengers stranded.
4. An unknown chemical substance with both respiratory and skin-absorbing properties is present. We know this because a simple process of elimination tells us it can't be biological or radiological, which have latency periods. The substance's immediate effects on both civilians and firefighters in bunker gear tell us it's likely a respiratory and skin-absorbing hazard.

At this point, we're dealing with numerous people, both ambulatory and non-ambulatory, who need to be moved out of the hazard area, decontaminated, and treated for exposure. Why move them quickly? Because exposure is determined by the equation: Exposure = Dose / (Concentration X Time).

The Big Question: Can a single Haz-Mat team handle this massive task quickly and effectively? We all know the answer to that.

So, let's look at how specialization can solve the problem:

Not every responder needs to be trained to the technician or specialist level. By training personnel to perform mission-specific functions, you

can reduce training time and material costs while still ensuring safety and efficiency. Here's how we can make it work:
1. Provide personnel with the necessary knowledge and skills to carry out specific tasks.
2. Equip them with the right tools and equipment to perform their tasks safely.
3. Ensure they have the proper PPE for the job to protect them from the hazards they face.
4. Weigh the hazards and risks of each task, with knowledgeable supervisors ready to intervene to halt, adjust, or stop unsafe actions.

When these four criteria are met, personnel can work safely and effectively.

While all first responders should be capable of wearing "Level A" chemical protective clothing, there's no need for everyone to be at the same level of expertise.

What needs to happen?
- Victims need to be moved out of the hazard zone to reduce further exposure. This can be done by training and equipping ladder companies with appropriate tools like stretchers and extrication gear (at the FRA 1st responder awareness level).
- Decontamination must occur before treatment. Engine companies can be trained with decontamination equipment (FRO 1st responder operational level), and once decontamination is complete, victims can be handed over to EMS for further treatment.
- Meanwhile, Rescue and Squad companies can search for any hidden victims and identify suspicious containers, using basic monitoring and detection equipment to define the spill or release boundaries (Hazardous Materials Technician Level).

The Haz-Mat Team, on the other hand, should focus on identifying the product, locating its container, and rendering the area safe using advanced detection and monitoring tools. The team's focus is on these specific tasks, leaving the broader issues to other units. This way, Haz-Mat specialists can concentrate on the core problem at hand - identifying and mitigating the hazards without getting sidetracked. This represents the Hazardous Materials Specialist Level.

Adam McFadden

An elite modern hazmat team isn't just a collection of technicians - it's a coordinated unit built around specialized roles that allow us to manage complex and high-risk incidents with precision. Whether we're responding to a large-scale chemical release or a CBRNE event, having the right people in the right roles makes all the difference.

One of the most critical positions on any scene is the Hazmat Safety Officer. This role is responsible for overseeing responder safety, ensuring proper PPE usage, monitoring environmental conditions, and adjusting operational tactics as the situation evolves. They serve as a real-time risk manager, constantly evaluating the scene and making sure safety protocols are followed. Their presence gives us confidence that responders are protected, and that operations don't outpace safety.

Equally essential is the Research Officer - our go-to resource for rapid data analysis and threat identification. This role taps into chemical databases, safety guides, and real-time intelligence to give the team accurate, actionable information. Whether it's identifying chemical properties, predicting reactions, or flagging secondary threats, the Research Officer plays a vital role in shaping how we respond and mitigate the incident.

Beyond those positions, command-level leadership is the linchpin during large-scale operations. These individuals bring strategic oversight, integrating intelligence, coordinating across multiple agencies, and making high-level decisions under pressure. Their ability to manage moving parts - logistics, operations, communications - ensures the entire response effort stays organized and effective.

While we rely on specialization, we don't silo our people. Every hazmat technician is trained as a generalist first. That means everyone on the team is proficient in detection, containment, decontamination, and PPE protocols. From there, we build out specialized skill sets. Some members pursue advanced training in research and analysis, others in CBRNE response, decontamination leadership, or operational safety. This balance gives us the best of both worlds: deep expertise where it counts and team-wide flexibility for any type of call.

We saw this approach come to life during a recent large-scale hazmat incident. Our Hazmat Safety Officer took immediate control of responder safety and PPE compliance. The Research Sector quickly identified chemical hazards and provided key guidance on mitigation steps. Our EMS and triage team staged in a safe zone, ready to assess and treat any exposed individuals. Meanwhile, the Recon and Downrange teams performed initial assessments, identified potential secondary threats, and fed real-time data back to command. Technicians with specialized training in detection and sampling handled on-site chemical analysis, while our Decon Team ensured decontamination procedures were in place and running smoothly for both victims and personnel.

Because each role was clearly defined and backed by specialized training, we were able to operate efficiently, maintain safety, and respond decisively - even in a high-pressure, high-risk environment.

That's what specialization does for a hazmat team. It creates clarity, improves coordination, and enhances our ability to protect lives while managing complex threats. And when it's built on a foundation of broad competency and cross-trained flexibility, it turns a group of responders into a highly effective response unit.

Mike Monaco

I'm not really a believer in assigning strict specialized roles on a hazmat team. I think everyone should be introduced to, and trained up to, the same baseline level. Specialization doesn't need to be formal - it happens naturally.
When you've got a team of five to eight people on scene, everyone's trained in the same core stuff. But based on personal interests - what people are drawn to, what clicks for them - they naturally start leaning into certain areas. That's where the depth comes from. Not because someone was *assigned* to be "the meter guy" or "the chemist," but because that's where their brain tends to go.

Me? I've always been a chemistry guy. So during training, I paid more attention to the chemistry side of things. Other folks might gravitate toward tools and mechanics. So when we're working a scene together, we're all on the same page with the basics - but the guy who's passionate about tools is going to bring something extra there, just like I might when it comes to chemical behavior.

That's how I think teams *should* function. Everyone's a generalist to start. Then individual strengths emerge based on what people are naturally curious about. That curiosity builds expertise, and that's how you get your specialists - organically.

The danger of assigning specialties too early is that it can box people in. You tell someone, "Hey, you're the XYZ expert," and before long, they start tuning out everything else. They stop learning across the board because they think they've found their lane.

So I always look for well-rounded people. Folks who are capable across the board, but have a deeper interest or strength in a particular area. I'd say I'm decent mechanically - I can use tools, fix things, understand systems - but I'm not a welder or a torch guy. That's not where I shine. My strength is more on the chemistry and research side.

The balance, then, is finding people who are solid generalists, but who bring their own depth in different areas. That's how you build a team that's versatile, adaptable, and truly well-rounded.

Chris Pfaff

I mean, a fire department can absolutely run on core operations alone - they don't necessarily need technicians. But there's this weird disconnect where people think, "Well, I'm a technician, so I can automatically do technician-level tasks."
Not true - you also need the tools. If you don't have the tools, you're not a tech. Period. Take paramedics for example. Paramedics have great minds, but without the tools, on a call they're pretty much just EMTs. If they can't start an IV, secure an airway, push medications - if they don't have those drugs handy - they can't do the advanced procedures they're trained for.

There's been ongoing discussion about this, especially on chat boards. Just now, I got an email regarding mission-specific energy specialists.

There's been a push lately to simplify teams into a "Hazmat Ops-plus" status. But honestly, that's just hazmat operations - plain and simple. NFPA writers and compliance officers emphasize this constantly: you're either operations level or technician level. There's no in-between. Operations mission-specific isn't "ops plus"; it's designed for one specific type of incident or mission. Specialization is absolutely critical.

One gap I've observed repeatedly is that the Fire Marshal's office often doesn't communicate much with the fire department's hazmat or rescue technicians - not intentionally, it's just that they think differently. Hazmat techs and fire marshals approach problems differently. But having someone in the Fire Marshal's office with actual hazmat technician training - not just general hazmat knowledge - is incredibly valuable for pre-planning.

For instance, think about those transitory warehouses loaded with hazardous materials below reporting thresholds - those won't appear on tier-two reports. A trained hazmat tech working in the Fire Marshal's office can spot those hazards during inspections, then walk right over to the hazmat team and say, "Hey, you've got this in your jurisdiction." Then when an incident happens, they're already familiar with the building manager or site supervisor. They have direct contact info and established relationships, which is invaluable.

That's precisely the angle I was aiming for with specialization. Back when I was on a rescue tech team, my team leader described us as a "shotgun approach team." We always had two rescue techs on duty, ready to respond to confined space, rope rescue, trench rescue - you name it. The idea was each rescue technician had to be an expert in every single discipline.

Great idea in theory, but it was doomed before I even joined. Personally, I'd say I'm an expert in confined space and trench rescue. But ropes? I barely know knots - I just tie a lot. Building stuff? Forget it - I'm great at breaking things but don't have the muscle the rope guys do to bust concrete in one swing. I'm simply not an expert in every discipline.

Do I know a little bit of everything? Sure. But teams need specialists. In hazmat, you need someone who's the expert in suits and boots, someone specialized in entries. You need the "nerd" who's dedicated to monitors, ensuring they're always operational and calibrated. You need specialists who know plume modeling and those who understand every detail about chemistry.

It's similar to my experience in the Marine Corps: every Marine is first a rifleman - we all knew the basics. But as we progressed, we specialized based on our strengths and attributes. It's the same idea here - specialization balanced with diversity makes us stronger.

Rob Rezende

Response planning and training for lithium-ion battery emergencies and other alternative fuels are critical in today's evolving landscape. As these technologies become more common, the risk of incidents involving them grows. Our training addresses these specific hazards so that our team is prepared to manage these types of emergencies with confidence and precision.

We also emphasize incident command training, ensuring that every member understands how to work within the incident command structure. Leadership takes practice, and by practicing incident command, we make our responses smoother and more coordinated. This builds confidence in our incident commanders, allowing them to make quicker, more effective decisions during high-pressure situations.

We place a strong focus on rewarding specialists with continuous training support, empowering them to become experts in their fields. Their deep expertise doesn't just benefit them - it strengthens the entire team, as their knowledge and skills naturally flow down to the "generalists."

Our specialists don't just accumulate knowledge - they share it. We lean on specialists to lead training sessions for the general team on their preferred topics, helping elevate the entire team's capabilities.

Additionally, specialists are often assigned to maintain, calibrate, troubleshoot, and research tools and technologies related to their specialty. This ensures our team stays up to date, ready to respond, and that our equipment remains in top shape. By putting the specialists in charge of these tasks, we stay on the cutting edge and prepared for whatever we may face.

Bob Royall

At Harris County, we're all hazmat technicians. Some of us just happen to have a little more training or experience in certain areas, that's all.

Take Harris County, for example. I'll just tell you straight - I needed a meter guy. We've got a third-party service that comes in quarterly to check all our instruments, even our radiation meters. But I needed someone for those in-between times. You know, when a sensor fails, or the span gets off, or maybe you need some cal gas and need to reset some stuff - someone who knows how to deal with that stuff when it comes up unexpectedly.

So here's what I did. I went around to every shift - four shifts total - and I said, "I need a meter guy for this shift." I do that kind of check-in pretty regularly with each shift anyways. I laid it out for them: I'll send you out to training. I'll get you trained on a whole range of instruments. And honestly, I don't care if you go use that knowledge for a side gig or not - as long as you keep *my* instruments on the street and working.

We started out with four guys. Now, we are down to two. The other two? Well it just wasn't their thing, and that's fine. But the two that stuck with it, they don't want anyone else touching the instruments now. They'll say, "Don't mess with the span, you'll screw it up. Just leave it on my desk and I will fix it when I get back."

Now, if you're going to let your people take that kind of ownership, you've got to back them up. That means having extra instruments ready to go in case one goes down. And my guys, they put their hands on every single instrument at the start of their shift. I've even got a guy who's all about air packs. He got interested, so I sent him to training. I bought the tools and gear that he needed.

That's the key. You have to *encourage* them and *support* them. You can't just say, "Go do it," and walk away. Do you want a piece of the action? You've got to *commit*. You've got to *have the passion and desire*. And let me tell you, once you bite it off, you better be ready to ride it, because you're gonna *own* it.

Now, internally they might call each other the "air pack guy" or the "instrument guy," kind of as a nickname. But officially, in Harris County, we don't use "specialist." It's not in the job description anywhere. Everyone's a hazmat technician. Period.

Bobby Salvesen

I've always been a little anti-specialization when it comes to *people*, but very pro-specialization when it comes to *tools* and *capabilities*. What I mean by that is, I don't think everyone on a hazmat team needs to be a chemist. In fact, I prefer it that way. I like a mix - a diverse crew with different perspectives. When someone doesn't look at a problem the same way I do, it forces me to see things from an angle I might've missed. That diversity in background and thinking? It's a strength.

But when it comes to tools and response capability? Specialization *matters*. You can't be kind of good at everything and expect to handle complex hazmat calls well. It's just not realistic. You can't master something you only do 10% of the time.

I had the rare privilege of working in a company that *only* did hazmat. No fires. No EMS runs. No building inspections. We didn't even have assigned boxes. We were special-called - brought in only when the regular companies were out of tools or out of options. That meant that every time we went out the door, we were facing something outside the norm. Something that pushed the limits of the typical response.

And that constant exposure to the abnormal? It made us really good, really fast. Because we had no choice. Every run was something new - different chemicals, different environments, different tools. The diversity and frequency of those calls forced us to level up constantly. You either kept up, or you got left behind.

So yeah, I don't need a team full of hazmat PhDs. But I *do* need people who can use specialized tools, master niche techniques, and adapt fast. That's how you build a real hazmat company - by leaning into capability, not just credentials.

Doug Schick and Mark Zilch
Doug:

Ideally, if you could build the perfect team, you'd want a mix of skill sets. One guy who's your chem expert - someone with a chemistry background. Another who knows how to turn a wrench. Someone who's solid on radiation. You're not always going to get that whole lineup working together on every shift, but when you do have people bringing different kinds of knowledge to the table, it makes a huge difference.

We've got a guy like that - he's great with binary chemicals, explosive devices, stuff like that. He's always sending us links, saying, "Hey, check out this YouTube video," and it's something relevant or a new way to look at a hazard. And when we're on a scene or in a training scenario, he'll jump in like, "Yeah, I know how that works," or "I can make one of those." That kind of knowledge - especially when things go bad - can be incredibly useful.

Mark:
It's not just about formal education either. We've got plenty of college-educated folks, but what we could really use more of - especially in hazmat - are people with trade skills.

Think about it: someone who knows plumbing, someone who understands how a semi-truck is laid out, or how to troubleshoot mechanical systems on the fly. That kind of know-how? It's gold. When you're dealing with valves, pressurization, piping systems - having someone who's worked with that stuff firsthand can save a lot of time and guesswork.

Doug:
Exactly. If we had someone on the team who used to be an over-the-road trucker? That'd be amazing. But we don't. And that's a gap. Honestly, one thing I wish we could bring back in the fire service is putting value on trades experience during hiring. If there was a way to give extra points on the entrance exam for having a trade background - plumbing, electrical, trucking, you name it - that'd go a long way. Because those are the people we really need, and we're not seeing as many of them come through the door anymore.

Jason Zeller

For a modern, elite hazmat team, the core is built on expertise in chemical, biological, radiological, nuclear (CBRN) materials - and in our case, high-yield explosives. However, the real differentiator is the ability to integrate seamlessly into a tactical environment, especially when working with law enforcement or military units.

For my team, which was often attached to NYPD Emergency Services Unit, NYPD Counterterrorism, Harbor Patrol, and the United States Coast Guard, we had to be ready for more than just hazardous material containment. We were often tasked with supporting entry teams, clearing atmospheres to ensure it was safe for responders to go in, while also protecting ourselves in high-pressure, potentially hostile environments. This created a unique dynamic where tactical operations and hazmat response had to go hand-in-hand.

A key aspect of our team was the versatility required to handle a variety of situations. We had to be self-sufficient, almost like a *"Jack of all trades."* That included specialized capabilities such as high-angle and low-angle rope rescue, and the ability to operate in challenging environments like industrial sites, underground locations, or urban settings.

Waterborne operations and maritime readiness were also critical. With responsibilities that included responding to maritime incidents, we trained extensively for waterborne hazmat operations - whether it was rescuing personnel from vessels or handling incidents along the waterfront. The ability to perform these operations, combined with the technical expertise needed to address hazardous materials in a maritime setting, added another layer of capability to our team.

Additionally, proficiency with advanced detection technologies like FTIR or GCMS was crucial for us. The ability to operate and troubleshoot this equipment in real time is essential for situational awareness. Specialized medical knowledge for hazmat-related exposures was also key to ensure that we could treat ourselves or others in the field until further medical help arrived.

This combination of CBRN expertise, tactical awareness, maritime operations, and rescue capability made our team well-rounded and prepared for any scenario.

Balancing specialized expertise with maintaining a well-rounded team was essential. With our 22-member team, we were divided into sections to ensure we could cover every aspect of a mission, while also being versatile enough to adapt to whatever came our way.

We had downrange personnel handling the primary operations, but also key sections like medical, communications, and operations. Our medical section was particularly important, with a Medical NCO and a Physician Assistant, but we also had a unique position - a Nuclear Medicine Science Officer who worked inside our mobile analytical lab. This made us more advanced than a typical hazmat response team.

Everyone was trained across multiple specialties, but we leaned on our individual expertise when the situation called for it. This allowed us to be self-sufficient while staying ready to integrate with other agencies when needed - whether it was a hazmat incident, maritime operation, or tactical response.

An example of how specialization within our team enhanced our overall response capabilities can be seen in our unique setup and training pipeline. Unlike civilian hazmat or **WMD** teams, our military unit had very specific requirements that made us better prepared.

One key factor was our requirement for team members to live within 30 minutes of the installation, ensuring that we could mobilize quickly at a moment's notice. This constant availability, combined with our **on-call assets - including waterborne assets - **gave us a unique advantage when responding to incidents.

Another example is our specialized training capabilities. Our unit had the funding and support to consistently send our personnel to high-end specialized training - both within the civilian sector and military. This ensured our readiness was always at the cutting edge.

For instance, we had downrange personnel, communication specialists, and a medical section that included a Nuclear Medicine Science Officer. Our mobile laboratory, equipped with bio-level three capabilities, set us apart from many other teams, providing advanced analytical capabilities in real time during responses. Our robust reach-back capabilities also ensured that we could call upon additional resources and expertise if needed, giving us a comprehensive response structure.

CERTIFICATION

"Genius is one percent inspiration and ninety-nine percent perspiration." –Thomas A. Edison

Dan Baker

Hazmat teams should absolutely require ProBoard National Certification from their members at whatever levels are offered in their jurisdiction. While our team hasn't formally mandated this yet, practically speaking, every member of our team certifies at least at the Hazmat Technician level. In fact, our official job title - Fire Protection Specialist - automatically includes certifications like Officer 1, Instructor 1, Firefighter 1 & 2 at the ProBoard level, along with numerous state-specific certifications required by statute.

Why are certifications so critical? They provide a third-party verification of training against a recognized consensus standard. They also make an individual's credentials portable, so team members can easily transfer their verified training and competencies if they move on. Additionally, certifications offer a layer of protection if training or competence ever comes under scrutiny, especially in the event of accidents or injuries.

As a state agency, our training standards are kept current by default. With NFPA 470 continuously evolving, our members - who also serve as professional instructors - regularly refresh their own training just to stay authorized and prepared to deliver updated courses.

Now, advocating for training beyond the minimum requirements can definitely be a challenge. It often takes multiple attempts to secure approval, particularly when you're looking at out-of-state programs or conferences. This is exactly why it's essential for hazmat team leadership to have - or at least be willing to develop - excellent written and verbal communication skills. We even offer a voluntary writing class specifically for our chiefs, which has been incredibly beneficial for those who've taken it. Clear, persuasive written justifications, followed by straightforward discussions with management, are crucial to securing approvals and ensuring that team members get access to the enhanced education and specialized training they need.

Mike Callan

The first certification I ever got was on October 10th, 1972. The New Haven Fire Department gave me a five-by-seven laminated card that said I was a certified firefighter. That was it. That card got me into the door -

four years later, I could apply to fire departments in places like Houston or a few towns in California when I was looking to move. But, of course, I made a decision that I'd later regret - I didn't want to move, so I ended up joining the Army for three years. Sometimes, I just make bad decisions.

The next certification I went after was in 1980 when I decided to take the Firefighter I test. At the time, some of my colleagues questioned why I would go for that. "You're a lieutenant, why are you taking Firefighter I?" they asked. I said, "Because I want the NFPA certification. I want to know that I can pass it." They didn't understand. They said, "You're already a lieutenant. Why bother?" But for me, it wasn't about the rank or the title; I wanted to be sure that I could pass it, even as a lieutenant. It was just a few months before I started training for the state certification for hazmat, which would be the real focus. I didn't get my firefighter certification until around 1982 or 1983 when I became a chief instructor, but when I did, I had 33 guys in the class, 28 of whom were already captains or higher. Some of them came from cities where they needed Firefighter I certification to take the lieutenant test. It wasn't about competence - it was just a step they needed to take for the promotion.

That's what's wrong with certification today. It's become about the paper, not competency. I see it all the time. Back in the day, when the old house officers would ask, "Do I have to give them a test?" the answer was always yes, but it wasn't about whether they could actually perform; it was just about passing a test. At one point, some parts of the country said, "You can either give a 50-question written test with hands-on, or you can give a 100-question test, but no hands-on," and that was the reality. I've said it before: we have 50 states, and I always tell people, "You want to know how the states do it? Simple. There's 50 ways."

But this whole idea of certification being about paper instead of skill - it drives me crazy. I remember when I passed the test, my older firefighters didn't like it. They didn't like that I went to college. They didn't think that should matter. I kept telling them, "I never graduated, I just went to college." But to them, it didn't matter. What mattered was that I had something they didn't, and they weren't happy about it. But that's the issue with certifications today - it's not about the knowledge, it's just about passing the test and getting that paper.
You can't rely only on book smarts. I had this conversation just this morning. Books are good, but they're not the be-all and end-all. Doctors

don't get to operate just because they graduated medical school. They've still got years of practice before they can actually perform procedures. In the fire service, it used to be all about on-the-job training. But now, people see that term and think it's too basic, too "medial." But if you don't get that hands-on experience, how do you know what you've got? The real problem isn't with the rookie who's learning the ropes; it's with the "old-timers" who've been doing it so long that they start doing everything on autopilot. They think they've seen it all, so they stop thinking. I call them the "super competent unconscious people." They're not thinking critically anymore. It's like driving a car and pulling into your driveway. You get out and wonder, "How the heck did I even get here?" You were on autopilot, not paying attention.

The worst part is that when you're a rookie in a dangerous situation, you have these seasoned guys who aren't really paying attention. And that's a problem. I always said that the guy who does the on-the-job training is not the guy who's too old to care. It's the guy who knows how to do it right. That's why you give it to them. They know what to look out for, they know what to do. But then, those veterans complain, "Why do I always get the new guys?" Well, because you're the one who knows what you're doing. I always used to say, "Let's watch that guy for five minutes." If you're not sure, you'll see why it's better for the rookie to work with someone who's been around.

This all ties back to the question of certification. Too often now, it's just about passing a test on paper, not about knowing how to actually do the job. And that's where the problem lies. If you don't have that on-the-job experience, it doesn't matter how many certifications you collect. You need to practice, think on your feet, and understand that sometimes experience is the only teacher that truly counts.

John Cassidy

When we talk about certifications, it's important to zoom out and look at the bigger picture - especially when you're responsible for a large-scale hazmat training program like ours, with over 550 hazmat techs across the city.

For a while, we operated as a self-certifying agency. You'd complete our internal program and walk away with an FDNY certificate that said you were a hazmat tech. And technically, that's fine - the authority having jurisdiction (AHJ) can certify competence under the standard. But the problem is, that doesn't carry weight outside our bubble. And the real danger? You end up drinking your own Kool-

Aid. You tell yourself, "We're good," but there's no external benchmark to prove it.

One of the proudest moments of my career - and Bob was instrumental in this - was transitioning our program from a self-cert model to a Pro Board-accredited, nationally recognized certification.

That was a heavy lift.

At first, it rattled some cages. "What if people fail?" "What do you mean we're going to be giving written tests?" "Nobody's going to study." There was panic in the ranks. But what happened was the exact opposite: we leveled up. As a department, our training improved, our standards got tighter, and the pride in being a Pro Board-certified hazmat tech became real.

And let's be honest - from a legal and professional standpoint, having that national certification matters. I've been to court on hazmat cases, and when I can stand there and say, "Our program is built on a national standard, evaluated by an independent entity," that ends a lot of arguments before they start.

Now, certification is one thing - but just as important is accurate recordkeeping. You need to be able to pull up a member's file and see what they've done since joining the team. That's how you identify gaps. If Firefighter Smith hasn't been to any specialty schools post-assignment, that's a problem. That's someone we need to coach and push to get more training.

There's only so much we can teach internally at the academy. Our props and equipment fill an important role, but there are limits. For example, when it comes to radiation training, we can use check sources, sure - but we don't have high-energy sources to work with. That's why sending members to external programs like RAD School is critical. The same goes for highway response - our props don't compare to what you'll find at SERTC. Or the NFA Chemistry course, where members are immersed in an environment that's focused, rigorous, and uninterrupted by the daily grind.

So when we talk about continuing education, it's not just about "getting a cert." It's about building capability.

One of the things we're lucky to have is a strong partnership with the New York State Office of Fire Prevention and Control. Before we partnered with them, Pro Board evaluations were kind of like what EMS used to do - individual skill stations where you got signed off for doing one task. Like, "Here's your oxygen tank, give the patient O2." Or, "Put on your Level A suit - good job, pass."

But we took it a step further. We brought our model to the state, and they brought it to Pro Board. Our final scenario is team-based and comprehensive. You don't just do one skill - you do it all:

- Conduct a hazard assessment
- Run a full pre-entry briefing
- Execute mitigation
- Choose and implement decon
- Evaluate and adjust your plan

You don't know which specific skills are being evaluated ahead of time, so you've got to be proficient across the board. That's how you ensure true operational readiness - not just check-the-box proficiency.

And honestly, that outside validation makes a difference. It's nothing new for FDNY members - on the EMS side, the state's been testing us for years. We even joke about it. Behind the scenes, the state is the "bad guy" - they're the evaluators. We're the coaches. Our job is to prepare you, guide you, and help you pass. But the goal is the same: produce competent, confident hazmat techs.

Of course, nothing is ever free. Every training program comes with costs - time, resources, personnel. So how do you sell it to the chiefs?

Get them involved.

If a chief attends the training, they'll see the value firsthand. They'll feel the energy, the passion, the professionalism of the training team. And more importantly, they'll understand the limitations of what we can do in-house. Take RAD training again - if a chief sees that our check source loses effect two inches from the meter, they'll realize why external schools matter. That's how you advocate for time off and support to send people to those "free" schools - they're not just extra. They fill critical capability gaps.

Dave DiGregorio

What I was talking about earlier, about that 40 or 80-hour training, just wasn't enough for us. So, we decided to build our own program. We made it a 240-hour requirement to get onto the team. That way, I knew the guys weren't coming in cold, and they were getting the full picture. The initial 160-hour course was based on the IFSTA curriculum, but we expanded it. The additional 80 hours were focused specifically on Massachusetts policies and tactics. By the time they were on the team, I knew they had the foundational knowledge they needed.

Now, that doesn't mean we didn't recognize other courses. For instance, if someone went to the REACTS RAD course in Tennessee, we'd definitely take that into account - it's an excellent program. Nevada also offers some great classes, and we considered those too. But the main point was that, just like in the military, certifications are great, but they don't tell the whole story. Some people would go through these schools just to get the ribbon or the patch, but they didn't really know anything. We used to call them "PX soldiers," the kind who would go to the PX, buy their ribbons, and wear them proudly, but they hadn't really put in the work.

And it's the same with certification courses - you can sit in the back of a class, learn nothing, party every night, and still walk away with a certificate. So, while certifications definitely played a role, they weren't the be-all and end-all in our hiring process.

Speaking of hiring, the interview process for the JHIRT was insane. It wasn't just a matter of looking at resumes; we went a lot deeper. We'd comb through the resumes first, then choose candidates to interview. The interview itself was intense. We would give each person a stack of index cards, each card listing one of the instruments we used. They had no idea which ones they'd get. We'd tell them to pick eight cards, and then we'd grill them about everything they knew about those instruments. We'd hit them with questions to test their knowledge and understanding. If they made it through that, they'd face the physical test, which, let me tell you, was brutal.

It was set up by the Mass State Police EOD and our hazmat techs, and it was pretty intense. Honestly, I don't think I could do it today, but it was a critical part of the process. It wasn't just about getting through the interview - it was about showing you had the physical and mental toughness to be on the team.

As for team leadership, I didn't pick the leaders directly, but I had significant influence. When teams would decide who they wanted for leadership, I'd be involved in the conversation. We would always ask, "What has this person done to show that they should lead a hazmat team?" It's not just about being a good leader - it's about their willingness to learn and push themselves. If someone was constantly trying to improve, that stood out, and we looked at that favorably.

I also took that mentality into the office. Besides the full-time staff, I had about 25 part-timers who supported the teams, and those were some sought-after positions. We had people, like Al, my logistics specialist, who worked on testing and maintaining the level A suits. He'd go through every suit, check it with meters, make sure it was up to standard. But he couldn't do it all alone, so we trained others to help with that, too.

We also had people dedicated to handling the meters. If a meter needed repair or calibration, someone would be responsible for fixing it. That person would make deliveries to the teams across the state, sometimes coming in once a week, sometimes more often. It was important to have that rotation and training in place, so everything kept running smoothly. We made sure our team members were trained to handle these things, and that was part of the overall process that helped keep everything running efficiently.

Dave Donohue

I'm a big believer in competency over certification. Basic certification should include hazmat technician, EMT or paramedic, and training on highway tank car and rail car handling. Once those foundational certifications are in place, it's the demonstration of competency that really matters. On a national level, there's no universal set of mandatory criteria for certification, so the depth of knowledge and skill among newly trained personnel can vary significantly depending on where they trained and the commitment of their instructor to ensure they understood the job. That's why regularly demonstrating competency is so important. Whether it's through Job Performance Requirements (JPRs), drill days, team rodeos, or recertification programs, it's the ability to show you can perform the necessary competencies, as identified by your community, that should drive certification and assignment decisions.

There also needs to be a constant review of the standards against the needs of the community and the organization to ensure alignment and identify any gaps. This is a dynamic process, as the community's needs can change over time, and the team must stay ahead of those shifts.

Advanced certifications are critical for a few reasons. First, they bring additional depth to skills and knowledge, which is always beneficial. Second, those who achieve advanced training are expected to share that knowledge with their teammates and the organization, helping to spread the learning and raise the overall skill level. Third, the skills and knowledge gained through advanced training might have direct applications for the community, making it more relevant and impactful. Finally, attending advanced training events gives team members the opportunity to connect with others from different organizations, learn about practices from other places, and build a professional network that can be valuable in future operations. This exchange of ideas and experiences is an integral part of professional growth.

Rick Edinger

I'd *like* to think everybody's using NFPA 470 as the foundation for their training programs. That should be the standard. But the reality is, if you're on a local hazmat team – for example in a state like New York - a lot of what you do is dictated by your AHJ. You're probably locked into the state-mandated training framework, whether it's robust or not.

Some states have excellent, well-developed technician programs, and others... not so much. You look at technician-level training and you'll see the hours swing wildly. In places like California, the hour count is high, and rightfully so. But then you see other programs offering a 60-hour tech course and you think - *How is that even possible?* What are you teaching - or more accurately, what are you leaving out?

I get asked that a lot: *Why aren't there minimum hour requirements in NFPA or OSHA?* The truth is, NFPA won't let us dictate hours, and OSHA is pretty ambiguous on training hours. Ultimately, it falls to the AHJ. And the difference comes down to how seriously that agency takes it. Some states are invested and building strong responders. Others seem to be just checking boxes.

Now, at least half the states are Pro Board or IFSAC, so we know they're using certification training material rooted in what used to be NFPA 1072 - now folded into NFPA 470. And if that's the case, I'm confident they're getting some baseline of knowledge and skills, *assuming* the trainers themselves know what they're doing.

Many years ago when I went through tech school in Virginia, it was 120 hours. And now it's more. And frankly, that's what it takes to do it right. You can't shortchange people. If someone completes a 40-hour tech course, I'll just say it: you're either skipping huge pieces of the puzzle, or you're barely skimming the surface. And that's a disservice - because they'll walk into a hot zone thinking they're ready, and they're not. Especially in the complex, one-off scenarios where things go sideways quickly.

I don't ever see NFPA walking that back and saying, "This should be 120 hours." We're just not allowed to write it that way. But everyone in this space knows - you can't build a true hazmat technician in 40 hours. It's just not possible.

So the burden falls on us. Hopefully you've got good training people - folks who are engaged, staying current, going to seminars, building relationships with your certifying body. In our case, we had the capability to run our own tech classes, but we had to prove to the state that we were qualified. Once we got that green light, we still answered to them. If something changed, we adapted.

You can't just run someone through training, hand them a cert, and walk away. "We're good to go, just run the calls now" - that's not how it works.

That'd be like being a paramedic and never doing CE, never learning a new skill. The hazmat industry is changing too fast for that. If you're still doing it the way you did it 10 or 15 years ago, you're already behind.

It's the job of the training cadre to stay in touch with what's happening - and when they do, your team becomes stronger, safer, and more capable. I couldn't always afford to send people out to training on topics that didn't align with our mission. Time and money were too tight. But if it was a real hazard we were likely to face - and I had someone passionate about that topic - I'd send them.

But I don't want to send someone just to check a box. I want them invested, learning, and coming back with something to share. We had a practice: if we sent you to a conference or cert course, you came back and trained the team. You shared what you learned. And that's how we built depth.

I'll say this too - we were lucky. Our chief officers were progressive. Special operations didn't need selling. Our deputy chiefs were the ones who started the hazmat team, and they moved into leadership roles. It was part of the culture.

But I know there are other departments where that's not the case. Where someone's in charge of hazmat just because it was handed down or assigned, and every time they need something, they're begging. In those environments, you've got to make the case. You've got to walk in and say, *"Look, we've got a risk in our community. We're not prepared. Let me send someone to get trained before something happens."*

You can phrase it professionally, but the underlying point is: do you want to be the department that dropped the ball when the critical call came in? Because once it happens, fingers are being pointed, people will want answers, and the budget's going to come up *real* fast.
And look, I get it. It always comes back to backfill and budget. I want to send people, but I've got to fill their spot. For volunteers, it's asking them to give up another weekend, maybe two. Time and money - it's the same constraint everywhere.

But if the only reason you have a hazmat team is because someone before you started it, and you're just checking the box now - don't do it halfway. Either invest in it properly, or stand down and let someone else handle it.

Because this work is too important to do half-assed. It's too important to approach it going through the motions.

John Esposito

For the guys I work with? Yeah, I'll take competence every time. Certification is nice - it shows you studied, passed a test, know the rules. But leadership, real leadership, means applying that knowledge when it counts. Whether it's a leaking saddle tank, which is a pretty standard call, or dealing with a guy who strolls in late, it's not about knowing what *should* happen - it's about doing it.

And real-world execution? That's messy. Sometimes you've got to walk through diesel-soaked mud or climb through garbage to get the job done. That's when we find out what you're made of. You didn't realize you'd be shoulder-deep in sludge? Welcome to hazmat. I'll take a competent firefighter over a certified one if it comes down to that. In a perfect world, you get both. But if I have to choose - competence wins.

Look, there are people out there who are phenomenal on the job who might struggle with reading a test. I don't want to exclude them just because they can't breeze through a written exam. I want them to understand danger. I want them to recognize what *not* to do. But above all, I want them to perform. That's what matters.

I always come back to probie school. Commissioner Nigro said something once that stuck with me, and now I say it to everyone: When you get a new probie assigned to your firehouse, the only thing you know for sure is that they were *minimally competent* enough to graduate. That's it. Even the valedictorian is still just a probie. Your job now is to train them, see where they're strong, where they're weak, and build them up from there. Don't assume anything just because they passed the course.

Passing means one thing: we can't fire you right away. You've got due process now. That's about it. And that applies to all of us - we're all constantly learning. Hell, I'm still learning. I've had plenty of moments where I thought, "Yeah, not gonna do that again."

When I was Chief of SOC, we moved toward Pro Board certifications, and I thought that was a great move. It gave us legitimacy outside the department. It wasn't just, "Yeah, you're good because you've been here a while" or "Bob didn't do great, but he's a good guy, so we'll let it slide." No. Now we had state instructors, outside tests, and real standards. Especially for specialty pay - if you want it, you've got to earn it. You've got to pass the test.

And I always told the guys, "We're going to help you. We're going to give you the resources. We'll give you more than one shot. But if you still can't pass? I don't know what to tell you."

And most of our guys? They rise to the challenge. Every time. You give them a clear expectation, they'll meet it. But you've got to tell them what the rules are. If something's been a sham for years and you suddenly flip the switch, yeah - they're going to push back. But if you're upfront, lay it out from day one, they'll own it.

Those early Pro Board classes, I'd go down there myself. Walk into the room, say, "Look, I'm glad you're here. This is part of your job now. This is the requirement. It's Pro Board certified. State instructors run this. You *have* to read. If you don't read, you won't pass."

And we did it. And I still like the legitimacy of that process. When certification actually reflects competence, that's the sweet spot. But it doesn't always. I mean, look around - how many terrible drivers have valid licenses?

Brandon Fletcher

On the surface, it might seem simple to say that the baseline for hazmat team certification should be technician-level certification. However, what that actually means can vary significantly from state to state and agency to agency. The NFPA JPRs can technically be met in a 40-hour class, but that often comes at the expense of real depth in the material and a nearly complete lack of scenario-based training that teaches the critical *when* and *why* of the skills. Some states and agencies do 80-hour courses, while others may go for 120 hours or more. While the number of hours isn't the sole determining factor, the content and the skills gained from these classes are what really matter and should be thoroughly evaluated.

Agencies must decide what version of technician certification is acceptable to them and what additional in-house training or outside classes will be necessary to cover gaps beyond what's taught in the certification class. Given that nearly every hazmat team will likely deal with highway incidents, the Highway Emergency Response Specialist class from SERTC should be a must-have for team members. Similarly, a Chemistry class from the NFA (or something similar) should be essential. If your team responds to rail incidents, then the Tank Car Specialist class is critical. Rad classes from CTOS should be part of everyone's baseline as well. For teams carrying advanced detection equipment, the Hazardous Materials Technology (HT) class at the CDP is also necessary. Additionally, since hazmat and confined space share many similar elements, cross-training in rope and confined space disciplines would benefit your team.

Remaining current with training is always a challenge, especially in small departments. With fewer people to keep trained, small departments often struggle to stay current in multiple disciplines.

This is where good administration comes in - having a clear training plan for the year, tracking course attendance, and making sure that no one slips through the cracks is essential. When planning for annual refreshers, don't just check the box to say training was done. Ensure that the training is relevant to the team's mission and incorporates updates when standards or industry best practices change. Someone on the team needs to be networking, researching, and keeping a pulse on changes in the industry and ensuring that information is communicated to the decision-makers.

Moving beyond the basics is critical for any team to stay relevant and effective. Selling "extra" training to administration can be tough, especially since nothing is "free." However, as a chief officer who understands the value of training, I know it's not a hard sell. The advice I would give anyone tasked with selling training to their administration is to come prepared with solid facts. What is the training? Why is it necessary? What benefits will it bring to the department or team? What's the cost?

How does it improve safety, effectiveness, and efficiency? And, how does it ultimately benefit the community or customer? Having clear, thoughtful answers to these questions is key. Depending on the size and structure of your organization, you may need to give a brief crash course on what your hazmat team actually does - be sure to do your research and back up your proposal with data and facts wherever possible. Present your proposal with confidence, grace, and professionalism. Be ready to answer questions, and anticipate them ahead of time. After all that preparation, be prepared for a "no" and accept it with dignity - because not every idea or project will be doable at that moment for various reasons. However, handling that response gracefully leaves you in a good position to try again in the future. Don't give up!

Chris Hawley

One of the things that really frustrates me is the number of teams and training programs that aren't following the NFPA standards. When someone tells me they're a hazmat technician, and I ask how many hours of hazmat technician training they've had, and they say "40 hours," I just can't buy it. There's no way you can cover all of NFPA 470 for technician level in just 40 hours. It's not happening. Sure, in theory, you can skim through detection devices in a few seconds, but doing it justice? No way.

I'm not speaking for NFPA here, but the committee's goal isn't to dictate specific hours - it's about competence. But the reality is that very few programs actually meet the full NFPA requirements. You could count on one hand the number of programs that are truly compliant. And even at 80 hours, you're still cutting it close to cover everything. If we were to compare training programs to NFPA 470, it's clear that most don't make the grade.

There's a real gap when it comes to specialized knowledge, like rail training. Take Hawaii, for instance. Hazmat technicians there might not get much rail training because it's just not relevant to the region. But according to NFPA, they're supposed to have some rail knowledge. Now, what happens when that technician moves to LA, where rail is a major part of hazmat response? Suddenly, they're short on rail training. There's got to be a baseline level of training that everyone receives, and then additional training based on what's most relevant to their jurisdiction.

I don't think it's about getting too bogged down with whether you're certified by Pro Board, IFSAC, or whoever. What matters is that the training is realistic and that it prepares people for the situations they'll face. The NFPA is on the right track with their direction, though the jury's still out on whether it's going to be successful. It's written in a way that feels appropriate, but I think we need to be more realistic about what certifying bodies and training academies are doing.

As an example Baltimore County is doing an 80-hour technician class. When I was running the training, we did an 80-hour class, but we added additional days for hands-on work, like tank trucks and railcars. They'd come back for those later, but the initial 80 hours gave them the core knowledge. You can't expect people to become experts in everything in one go, and that's why I like the idea of staged training. Get your initial certification and then add on the specialty training, like how the blue card program works with task books. You do the basics first and then add the more advanced skills as needed.

The point is, every team needs to be realistic about what they can offer, and training needs to be aligned with what the technicians will actually encounter in the field. We can't just rush through training to meet a number - we need to be creating competent, knowledgeable professionals who can respond to real-world hazmat situations.

Mike Hildebrand

Back when we started, there was no national standard, no certification system, no credentials, no official accreditation. You either knew what you were doing, or you didn't - and people figured that out real fast.

Now, the landscape's changed. Certifications, credentials, accreditation processes - they're everywhere. Every state's got their version, and whether you agree with it or not, you're in the system. Legally speaking, once your state adopts NFPA 470, 472, 473, or whatever flavor they pick, you're playing by those rules whether you like them or not.

That doesn't mean I think the standards are perfect - frankly, I think some of them are too complicated - but we're past the point of arguing about it. It's part of the world now.

That said, I don't believe every hazmat team member needs to have Hazmat Tech certification before they join. There are other ways in. I'd rather take a firefighter with a chemistry degree, six years on the job, good performance evals, and the *right attitude* than someone who's already a tech but has no curiosity or drive or willingness to raise the high bar.

You can get a huge multiplier effect by bringing in specialists from outside the usual circles. When we built our team, we *intentionally* recruited bomb squad members. Why? Because when you cross-train the right people, the boundaries start to disappear. Suddenly, the guy who used to say, "We blow things up - you can't use our robot," is now *also* on the hazmat team. Now the barriers start to break down. And if he's in? Maybe the chemist at the community college is next.

You'd be surprised how many highly qualified people would *love* to be part of a hazmat team - PhDs in chemistry, structural engineers, ER doctors. They don't need to know how to pull a hose or make a hydrant connection. They just want to be part of something cool, something meaningful. Let them. Give them an ID, a radio, and a seat at the table. Make them your technical advisor. There's no rule that says everyone on your team has to wear bunker gear.

But to make that work, you've got to have airtight record keeping. Self-motivated people will keep track of their own certs and refreshers, but even then - it's easy for stuff to slip through. You need a system that tracks skills, licenses, special languages spoken, equipment qualifications - all of it. And with today's technology, there's no excuse for not knowing what's in your team's toolbox.

Still, some departments can't tell you who's certified for what because their records are scattered across divisions. The training division tracks one thing, your team keeps another spreadsheet, and nobody's speaking the same language. If training only tracks Hazmat Tech refreshers, but you're the one responsible for keeping your meter specialists up to date, you better have your own system in place.

And here's the thing - those records aren't just useful while you're on the job. They follow you *after* you retire or move on. They can open doors. A clean record shows your commitment. It proves your skillset. Combine that with a mindset of continual self-improvement, and you'll go far.

I've always believed in U.S. Navy Admiral Hyman Rickover's principles – the most important principle is the concept of total responsibility, technical self-sufficiency, and a rising standard of adequacy. That last one is key. It means that "good enough" yesterday isn't good enough tomorrow. You keep climbing.

Certifications help with that climb, especially the higher-level professional ones - Certified Fire Protection Specialist, Certified Safety Professional, Certified Hazardous Materials Manager. These push you past the "this is what the meter does" into "this is *why* the meter behaves this way." That's where you go from technician to professional.

And when you get there, you learn how to speak in *multiple languages*. You can explain the science of a meter to the PhD, and then turn around and break it down for a new recruit. True intelligence is about adaptability. The best people on a team can talk to a medical doctor or a homeless guy and walk away with *useful* information from both.

And you don't need a college degree to get there. There are certification paths laid out step-by-step. You just have to follow them.

But not everyone is driven by the same thing. Some people want to impress their mom. Some want a raise. Some are just naturally curious. Good leadership meets people where they are. You've got to recognize what motivates *each* person and use that to push them forward.

That's tough in a paramilitary structure where time and training budgets are already maxed out. I've had chiefs tell me, "I'm not looking to add more requirements. We can barely meet the ones we have." And I get it. But hazmat gets stuck with everything - from nuclear bombs to rattlesnakes. If no one else wants it, it lands in our lap.

It is important in building a HazMat Team culture to know how to think. I once asked the Godfather of HazMat, Ludwig Benner, who held an engineering degree from Carnegie Mellon, what the most important thing he learned there was. Without hesitation, he said, "They taught me how to think."

That's the goal. Certifications are great, but they're not enough. You need training environments where people learn *how* to think, not just what to do. That's where the magic happens.

And when you do get that knowledge - don't hoard it. Don't be the guy who takes a class, then guards the material to make himself look smart. People see through that. If you're a leader, share it. Offer to teach the class. Bring in a book and say, "I read this, I think it's worth discussing. Let's talk." Leadership isn't one big leap - it's small actions, consistently taken. One conversation at a time. Big victories in life come from small daily victories.

The best team leaders I've seen? They can do everything - from sharpening the knife to building the plan to taking the objective. Sure, someone else might tie knots faster, or run the meters better - but that leader can do it all *well enough*. And more importantly, they *know who's better* and let them lead in that moment.

It all comes back to responsibility. Culture. Curiosity. And building a team that doesn't just do the job - but *thinks* their way through it, together.

Bob Ingram

Certifications in hazmat teams are ultimately determined by the Agency Having Jurisdiction (AHJ), which may vary depending on location and organizational structure. Many large fire departments have developed their own in-house training programs, and while these programs can work well for day-to-day incidents, they may not provide the credibility needed for larger, more serious events. When dealing with incidents involving injuries, fatalities, or incidents requiring mutual aid across jurisdictional, state, or federal lines, it's crucial to have training programs certified by independent organizations.

Certifications such as Ace Accreditation or Pro Board (just two examples I've worked with) not only improve your team's standing in Resource Typing for mutual aid requests, but they also provide stronger legal footing should an incident escalate into a court case. National training facilities' certificates of completion - particularly from **CBRNE** facilities - hold more weight than certifications issued solely by the AHJ. Members certified by manufacturers in the repair and maintenance of critical equipment, such as detection technologies or **PPE** ensembles, adds another layer of legitimacy and ensures that the team can operate complex tools effectively when needed.

But achieving this level of preparedness takes more than just the right certifications - it's about diligence and hard work. Effective tracking systems are essential to maintain an organized approach to training. Training programs should track members' training dates, refresher courses, medical clearances, fit testing, and external training courses attended. These systems should be computerized and include triggers to signal when certifications or testing are due, helping ensure that no critical component falls through the cracks.

Leadership plays a key role in enforcing accountability. Gaps in training, medicals, and fit testing must be addressed promptly to maintain readiness and ensure that the team is always operationally ready.

In terms of policy, teams should follow national standards such as **NFPA 470, 475, ASTM, NIST, FEMA,** and national laws from **OSHA, EPA,** and other agencies. These standards provide a clear, nationally recognized framework for developing and maintaining hazmat training programs. Once you've established those standards, it's important to identify the missions the agency or city expects your team to perform, then assess your current capabilities to meet those expectations.

From there, it's essential to document any gaps that might hinder mission success. Tracking close calls, injuries, or instances where a mission was delayed due to capability gaps can provide valuable data for securing necessary resources or policy and training adjustments. Documenting instances where mutual aid had to be called upon - and the time it took for those resources to arrive - can highlight critical weaknesses in response time, impacting traffic, power, and other vital services.

Finally, performing the legwork to research the required equipment, including initial costs and long-term maintenance, is essential. Never short sell the true cost of equipment, because underestimating these expenses could leave you with a valuable resource sitting unused on a shelf due to a lack of funding to make it operational. Properly budgeting for equipment that can be sustained over the long term ensures the team remains fully functional when called to respond to incidents, avoiding future financial strain or capability gaps.

Phil McArdle

This is a complex question with an equally intricate answer. The final decision usually lies with the authority having jurisdiction, as they determine what their team needs. However, every team, regardless of the situation, must meet certain minimum requirements to operate at the federal, state, and local levels.

Several factors influence this decision, with cost being a significant consideration - who is paying for the training? Is it a one-time expense, or will there be recurring training? Is the training general or highly specific? Are there prerequisites for the training, and are there limitations on course availability? How frequently do these types of incidents occur in the jurisdiction, and does that justify attending the training? How much time should be allocated to training within a year, month, week, or day? How much time away from the team is acceptable? Does every team member need to attend, or can we train the trainer? How does this training benefit the team?

There are many training providers out there - government agencies, public institutions, and private organizations. Ask yourself: *What separates our Haz-Mat team members from every other first responder in our jurisdiction? What unique ability do we have that others don't?* This is the central question: *What ability* are Haz-Mat team members developing that no one else in the jurisdiction possesses? Any well-rounded Haz-Mat team will have attended a combination of schools required by the jurisdiction. It's important to note that training certifications generally don't just cover hazardous materials but also include terrorism components and other emerging threats.

On the federal level, agencies like the National Fire Academy, the EPA, the Department of Justice, Homeland Security, and the DOT offer courses that provide a basic foundation for response, hazard identification, and mitigation. Some of this training is very specific, such as radiation training at the Nevada Test Site, nerve agent training at Army facilities, or railcar training at the transportation test center in Pueblo, Colorado. Other courses, however, are more general in nature.
State courses, often provided by state fire academies, tend to mirror federal training to some extent. These academies offer outreach programs and online training. However, it's critical not to waste valuable training time on redundant courses that duplicate what has already been covered at the federal level.

Local courses or informal familiarization drills are also valuable, as they can address issues unique to the community or jurisdiction. Private training, such as that offered by manufacturers of monitoring devices, PPE, and other equipment, is often highly specific to the tools and technologies the team uses.

This is where a training database becomes indispensable. A dedicated training coordinator can keep an eye on changes to laws, regulations, standards, and emerging threats. They can track curriculum updates and determine whether significant changes warrant re-attending a particular course. Additionally, they can monitor each team member's past, current, and upcoming training to ensure compliance with recertification deadlines and verify that members have the prerequisites needed for upcoming courses.

So, what value is there in pursuing advanced or specialized certifications beyond basic requirements? The answer lies in the very reason Haz-Mat teams exist. They focus on training that goes beyond what other first responders are typically trained for, addressing highly specific hazards and containers. Each community must conduct a thorough hazard and risk assessment to determine which specialties are needed to meet the community's unique needs. This could involve specialized tools, equipment, or knowledge that other first responders don't have, making advanced training essential for team members to perform these specialized tasks.

Adam McFadden

For members of an elite hazmat team, certification isn't just a requirement - it's a foundation. We consider several certifications essential to ensure our personnel are fully prepared to manage the complex and varied threats we face in the field.

At a minimum, every member must hold Hazmat Technician-level certification, but we go well beyond that. Specialized training in Terrorism Response and CBRNE operations is a must, given the evolving nature of chemical, biological, radiological, nuclear, and explosive threats. This ensures our team can respond effectively to both accidental and intentional events with the same level of precision and control.

In addition to these core certifications, our team engages in ongoing training focused on chemical detection, air monitoring, and specialized response tools. These sessions take place daily, monthly, and annually, ensuring our personnel maintain proficiency with cutting-edge detection equipment, sampling techniques, and atmospheric monitoring devices. This regular, hands-on exposure allows us to quickly and accurately identify hazards - and to act fast when seconds matter.

To stay current with evolving standards and certification requirements, we conduct annual refresher training that aligns with NFPA standards and incorporates updates on new equipment, emerging threat profiles, and the latest tactics. This proactive approach means we're not just meeting industry benchmarks - we're staying ahead of them.

We also strongly encourage team members to pursue advanced certifications beyond the basic requirements. These programs deepen our understanding of emerging risks, introduce new technologies and tactics, and ultimately make us more capable responders. The benefit is twofold: our team gains critical knowledge, and our community gains a more prepared and adaptive hazmat unit.

When we present this to fire chiefs and leadership, we focus on the direct impact advanced certifications have on public safety and department readiness. We highlight how they improve operational efficiency, reduce risk on scene, and strengthen interagency coordination. And we make sure to identify cost-effective solutions - grants, regional training programs, and industry partnerships - that allow us to pursue advanced education without straining department budgets.

By investing in continuous training and advanced certification, we ensure our team can meet any challenge - confidently, safely, and effectively.

Mike Monaco

I don't think you need certifications. Honestly, I think certifications are mostly nonsense.

People put so much weight on them - especially things like Pro Board certifications - but when you really look at what they mean, it's just that you passed a test. That's it. It doesn't challenge your critical thinking. It doesn't test your actual ability to perform under pressure or make decisions in the field. It's just a checkbox. And that checkbox can be manipulated.

Now, I *do* believe people need to be trained to certain levels. Absolutely. But I'd take a well-rounded, well-trained, and experienced team over a group of folks stacked with certs any day. I want people who can *do* the job - not just people who've been told they're qualified because they took a test.

There are two sides to this, though. If you bring in people who are self-sufficient and self-motivated, they're going to stay on top of new technologies, new methods. They'll go to conferences, they'll seek out knowledge. But again, that's not certification. That's *initiative*. That's staying sharp because you care about the job, not because someone's handing you a piece of paper.

Now, if you're running a training program, of course you've got to stay current on **NFPA** standards and **OSHA** regulations. That's the baseline. Keep your team compliant - keep them *certified* where it's required. That part's easy. But checking all the boxes doesn't mean you've got a team that can perform when it counts.

I've seen people with 40-hour **OSHA** or Pro Board certifications who couldn't assess a hazmat scene to save their lives. They don't understand the response process. They're not trained in the *why*, just the *what*. And that's not good enough.

So yeah, certifications are fine when required, but they should be taken with a grain of salt. What really matters is *training*. I care about advanced *training*, not advanced *certification*. There's a difference.

When you're evaluating a course, look at what it actually teaches. Then look at your first-due area - your **AHJ** - and ask: "Can we apply this? Does this training make sense for our environment?" And if it does, take it a step further: pull up past runs. Show where that training would've made a difference. That's how you sell it to a chief. You say, "Look, this is the potential for this to happen, and here's where it already has."

Because like I always say - history doesn't repeat, but it sure does rhyme.

Chris Pfaff

I love my "I Love Me" book. It's thick, it's robust, and packed full of certificates. Certification is critical.

And this is coming from a Hazmat technician who's not even IFSAC or ProBoard certified. But still, it's important that our teams get certified - at least to the minimum standards we talked about earlier. Remember, certification sets the baseline. Once we have that paper, we need to recognize there's way more out there - conferences, specialized training, and knowledge coming from around the country.

My agency has hired people whose certificate books were six inches thick, but some of them honestly couldn't do anything practical on a scene. They were qualified on paper, sure, but they weren't competent. There's a big difference between having certifications and having actual competency. NFPA 470 - and pretty much every NFPA training standard - clearly requires competency, not just certification. But competency is harder to measure.

Bottom line, we need both. Certifications prove you've met the minimum requirements, but you have to go far beyond that, adopting a holistic approach to training and continuous learning.

Certifications are crucial at different stages of your hazmat career. As you move forward, pursuing specialized certifications - highway emergency response specialist, tank car specialist, sampling and evidence detection, bomb response - becomes essential. And later in your career, taking Hazmat Safety Officer or Hazmat Officer courses, first to meet the standards, then expanding your skills even further, is critical.

So, how do you ensure your team stays current with evolving certification standards? You keep checking those NFPA standards regularly, alongside your state and local requirements. It's a constant process.

Rob Rezende

As a CSTI Hazmat Specialist, I've had the privilege of experiencing the depth of federal-supported training available across the country. This training is invaluable for staying current with the latest standards and practices.

We train monthly, ensuring our skills are constantly evolving, but we also offer state and federal training opportunities each year to keep our team at the forefront of the industry. These training sessions are crucial for exposing our team to new challenges and techniques, broadening their knowledge base, and maintaining a high level of readiness.

Supporting team members who want to go above and beyond is a powerful way to strengthen both the individual and the group. When we give our motivated members the opportunity to excel, it not only boosts their confidence but also sends a clear message to the rest of the team: the organization values and rewards hard work and dedication. This recognition fosters a positive environment, increases morale, and brings the team closer together. When everyone feels appreciated and supported, the entire organization thrives.

Bob Royall

Let me start by saying that I view entry-level certifications as the lowest common denominator. They are necessary, but they're just the starting point. For example, a basic hazmat technician certification - everyone on my team needs to have that to be part of the crew. It's a minimum requirement, and it's not the end of the road. It's just the start. With that certification, you can actually begin to learn and build on what you know.

Let me give you a few examples. I was a fire officer for 25 years before obtaining the Officer 1 Certification from the Texas Fire Commission because it had not existed previously. But when it was introduced, it became essential for my resume. If I was ever called to testify in court, I needed to be able to prove, "Yes, I'm a fire officer. I've been doing it for 20 years." If you're a chief officer, that certification can be very important. It helps establish your credibility.

But let me be clear - experience counts for a lot. Take the driver operator certification, for instance. It's important. You've got someone running a

$2 million piece of equipment down the road. You want to know that person has experience driving something other than a Prius, right? The certification shows that they've been trained and that they can handle the responsibility.

Another certification that I believe is critical is the Incident Safety Officer. That role is vital because they are always looking at the situation from a different perspective. They are the "eyes in the sky," if you will. The incident commander and even the hazmat officer might be focused on the immediate operations, but the safety officer is monitoring everything from a broader view, making sure safe practices are in place, and ensuring everyone's well-being on the scene.

There are some other certifications I'm less enthusiastic about. For example, the hazmat incident commander certification. To me, if you are the incident commander, then you are the incident commander. You don't have to be a technician to be an incident commander, but it certainly helps. Similarly, the 40-hour hazmat tech certification or the 24-hour hazmat tech certification through OSHA - are pretty much worthless in the grand scheme of things.

The right kind of certifications matter, though. If a certification takes you to the next level, helps you become a better responder, a better fire officer, or a better hazmat officer, then I'm all for it. But if a certification doesn't add any real value or improve your abilities, then it's just a piece of paper.

Bobby Salvesen

One of the most important things we do in this job is *certify* people to perform critical tasks. But let's be clear - certification without *competency* means nothing. I've said it before: I'm not big on the hours game. Hours give you guardrails, sure - but they don't make you qualified. What makes you qualified is your ability to *do the job*.

That's why I care more about competencies than clocked hours. And while people get all wrapped around the axle about Pro Board or IFSAC, let's be honest - those are just testing *methods*. They don't speak to *what* you were taught or *how* well you learned it. Testing is important, but it's only one part of the picture.

That said, keeping up with certifications tied to NFPA and OSHA standards is critical. That's how you keep your team aligned with current expectations and emerging requirements. But the testing itself - whatever system you use - has to be fair, impartial, and consistent. I don't care if you're a rookie hazmat tech or a battalion chief - *everyone* gets in the suit. Everyone checks the same boxes.

Even if the chief is never going downrange, they still need to gear up at least once. Why? Because they need to understand the *reality* of what they're asking us to do. When they see what it's like to move in a Level A, in the heat, under pressure, maybe next to a tanker car or in a basement - they lead differently. They manage differently.

Certifications matter. They're necessary. But I'd go a step further and say this: *atypical* certifications matter too. Things like asbestos abatement, wastewater remediation, industrial hygiene - these aren't emergency-specific, but they broaden the scope of your team's capability. They introduce new tools, new perspectives, and new strategies.

And here's the thing - when you send one person to get a niche certification, they don't come back and stay quiet. They talk. They teach. Around the kitchen table, during truck checks, after a drill - they start injecting that knowledge into the rest of the team.

That's how it spreads. One person learns, five others pick it up.

So yeah - certify your team. But don't stop there. Go beyond the expected. Get them trained in things that might seem left field, because that's where the growth happens. And when you build that kind of culture, competency becomes contagious.

Doug Schick and Mark Zilch
Doug:

So, like I mentioned earlier, the highest state certification we have for hazmat here is Hazmat Tech. That's the big one. We also have an Incident Command hazmat cert. But the Hazmat Tech cert - that's an 80-

hour course, and when you add in the Hazmat Ops prerequisite, you're looking at 120 hours of training just to get started. I know other states go well beyond that for a technician or specialist level, and honestly, I kind of wish we did too. More training wouldn't be a bad thing.

Beyond the tech cert, we really encourage our people to go after additional training - especially the DHS courses. Things like PER-222, the public sampling class - that's a requirement for us. And Mark's been heavily involved with the STC side of things, especially training folks on primary and secondary screening.

All of those are essential in our view. If you want to be on the hazmat team, you've got to be involved in that level of training. And then there's everything the National Fire Academy offers - we're constantly encouraging folks to take advantage of those resources as well.

Mark touched on this earlier, but we've also got new continuing education requirements now - essentially con-ed hours - for a number of our state certifications. This is the first time we've had to do that. It used to be, you got your Hazmat Tech 20 years ago and you were set for life. But now, there's a recertification process, and we've been working on building out a program for that.

Yeah, it's a bit of a hassle, but I think it's a good thing. Even if it's just review, it forces guys - especially the ones who got their tech card and then never touched hazmat again - to go back and refresh their knowledge. You can't put a number on how valuable that is.

That's true across the board in the fire service. Whether you're on an engine company or a hazmat company, you've got to stay sharp. For hazmat, those DHS classes, that extra training - it's what makes you a better technician. It's not just valuable, it's essential.

And I'd say overall, our department's been supportive. We've got an official department memo that lists all the DHS classes we recognize, and they're all covered - no cost to us. I just wish we pushed it a little harder. Some departments might be resistant to the DHS classes, but that's not really the case here. Still, I think we could be doing more to encourage folks to take advantage of them.

Jason Zeller

Certifications weren't just boxes to check - they were operational requirements. Our team wasn't an average civilian hazmat unit. We were a federally funded, military-run, 24/7 on-call, joint-service Army and Air National Guard, active-duty status WMD Emergency Response Team. That meant our bar was higher, and our training pipeline reflected that.

At the core, everyone on the team needed to be certified to the Hazardous Materials Technician level, with a specialty in WMD/Hazmat response.

From there, we built out the expertise based on each operator's section - downrange ops, medical, communications, command, or analytical lab. Critical certifications included:

- Rescue Technician (with high-angle, low-angle rope rescue, and confined space)
- EMT
- Advanced Hazmat Life Support (AHLS)
- New Mexico Tech/DHS Incident Response to Terrorist Bombings (IRTB)
- CIA Small Scale Production Course
- Technical Escort School
- EVOC (Emergency Vehicle Operations Course)
- Commercial Vessel Boarding Ops
- DEA Methamphetamine Clandestine Laboratory Certification

That last one was huge - we had members complete the DEA Meth Lab Course because the threats weren't just international or military-based. The domestic side of WMD is very real. After experience responding to scenes where a clandestine meth lab could look like a bomb-making operation - or a small-scale chemical weapons production process - you'd better know the difference.

That's where street chemistry came in. Our folks were trained to detect small-scale production runs of chemical, biological, energetic materials, and precursors. Pair that with our CIA Small Scale Production cert and the hands-on instruction from places like Dugway Proving Grounds, and we had a level of real-world expertise that separated us from almost every other team out there.

Certifications weren't just about qualifying - they were about surviving, performing, and bringing everyone home.

This wasn't a part-time gig for us - we were full-time, federally funded, and active-duty. That meant there was no excuse not to stay current.

We didn't rely on emails or memos from some outside agency telling us what was changing. We were plugged in - directly tracking evolving standards from DoD, DHS, FEMA, NFPA, and OSHA, especially anything tied to WMD and hazmat response.

We had a dedicated training NCO who maintained a live tracker of every team member's certifications - expiration dates, refreshers, new required modules. If something changed in the industry, it was brought up in the next training meeting. If it was mission-critical, we'd adjust our schedule and get certified immediately.

But honestly, the gold standard wasn't just about checking the box - it was about maintaining operational credibility.

Our medics stayed current on AHLS and EMT recert, our techs on WMD hazmat, Technical Escort, and street chemistry, and everyone knew that if something new came out - whether it was NFPA 472 updates, new CBRN protocols, or emerging threat guidance - we'd be training on it, certifying on it, and validating it with a hands-on evolution.

Complacency kills, and our team never played that game. We didn't just stay current - we stayed ahead.

When we get the call, it's because the situation is beyond what local responders can handle. They're overwhelmed, out of their depth, and facing a problem that's outside their scope of expertise. That's where we come in - armed with advanced technology, specialized knowledge, and capabilities that they simply don't have.

The complexity and danger of the situation require a level of expertise that only a team like ours can provide. It's not just about showing up; it's about having the right tools, the right training, and the right mindset to take control of situations others can't manage.

Our team's ability to respond swiftly and decisively in high-risk environments - whether it's chemical, biological, radiological, or explosive-related threats - is a direct result of our continuous pursuit of advanced certifications and specialized training. We're always pushing the envelope on what we can do, and that means we stay ahead of the curve.

The value in these advanced certifications isn't just in the piece of paper - it's in the capabilities we develop and bring to the table. We don't just meet the bare minimum - we strive for excellence.

The advanced technology and expertise we bring can't be found at the local level. When we deploy, we bring the full weight of our training, knowledge, and specialized skills to tackle the problem at hand.

Convincing the team to pursue these certifications isn't a hard sell. It's about emphasizing the real-world value they bring - not just to the mission, but to their personal growth and ability to rise to challenges.

It's not about getting a certificate for the sake of it - it's about constantly improving ourselves to be the best when it counts.

We do this to ensure that when the stakes are high, we're the ones they can rely on to handle the impossible.

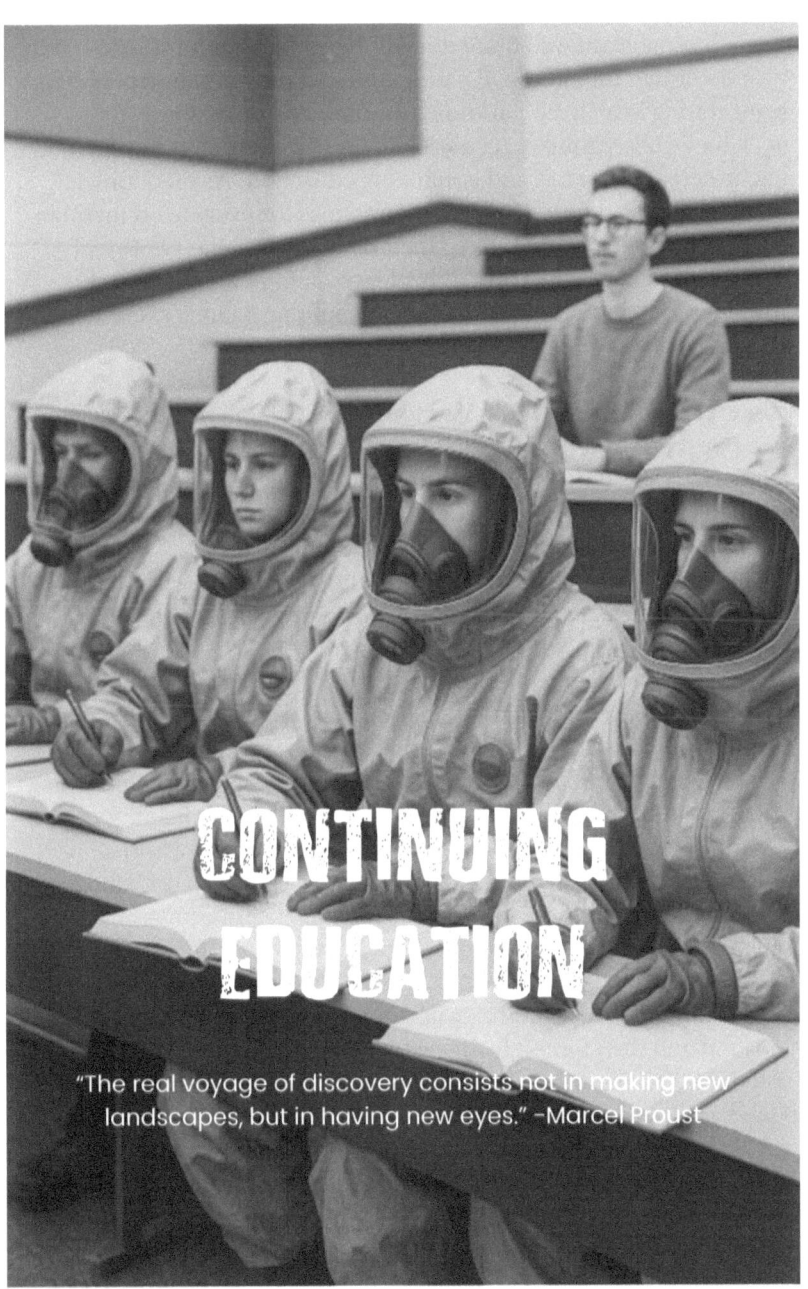

CONTINUING EDUCATION

"The real voyage of discovery consists not in making new landscapes, but in having new eyes." –Marcel Proust

Dan Baker

Keeping a hazmat team well-trained might be a bit easier for a state-level unit with dedicated full-time staff, compared to a busy urban department or a team relying heavily on part-time responders. For us, we've got a Deputy Chief whose primary responsibility is managing all refresher training, in-service sessions, and continuing education. As mentioned before, we schedule quarterly in-person trainings for every team member who actively responds, regardless of their daily assignment. On top of that, our Training DC stays constantly plugged into new educational opportunities, making sure that any valuable info or training events are quickly passed along to the team.

How do we keep the team motivated for training? Honestly, it's a ground ball - we pay them. But beyond financial incentive, most of our folks are naturally driven self-starters, and truthfully, we rarely need to push them towards new or optional training. In fact, usually it's the other way around - they come to us asking about training opportunities, which is always a healthy indicator of strong team culture. If those requests ever start to taper off, that's a clear signal for leadership to start worrying about burnout or low morale.

As an organization heavily focused on training, we create all our own in-service materials in-house. Take this past January, for example - we delivered a team-wide refresher open to the entire organization, including folks not typically assigned to hazmat. While the refresher hit all required OSHA and NFPA points, we built the session around real-world examples pulled directly from the previous year's calls. We drilled deep into staff roles and specific actions taken, making the information meaningful, relevant, and memorable.

Each case study was structured as a tabletop exercise, inviting active participation and direct input from everyone in attendance. The class examined each scenario step-by-step, contrasting what ideally should've happened against what actually did occur. This format achieves multiple objectives: it satisfies regulatory training needs, promotes interactive learning, and keeps folks engaged and alert instead of fighting boredom from a typical classroom setup.

Here's a quick illustration: we'd start by displaying a photograph from a recent incident. Participants would first size up the situation, discussing resources they'd expect to need. Then the instructor guides the group through every phase of the incident, from initial response all the way through demobilization, encouraging everyone to weigh in. This approach not only reinforces critical thinking but ensures that lessons learned genuinely stick.

Mike Callan

You know, it's like doctors - they don't really get grades. They get certificates. And when it comes time to choose one, what's the first thing you ask? You ask around, right? "Who's the best doctor?" You want to know who has the experience, who's trusted. That's the thing. If you're in New York City, and you've got a fire down by the Hudson River, you don't want just any fire department showing up - you want FDNY. You can't just call another town and say, "I don't like my fire department, send me a better one." In most places, you're stuck with your own department. So, you better be good at what you do.

And that's the crux of it, right? Everyone wants to be the best in their field, especially when it comes to a hazmat company. But I'll tell you, even though I've written books on electricity and natural gas, I know that if I stop learning about what's new, I'm going to have problems. Take last year in Massachusetts, for example. I was listening to a guy talk about a new technology, and I was taken by surprise because I didn't have all the details. I wanted to dig into it because my own electric companies were asking, "What do we do with this?" That's why continuous learning is essential.

When I first went to the Fire Academy, nobody wanted to go. But when they found out I was being detailed to the Fire Academy, everyone suddenly wanted to go - of course, they wanted to go on their days on, not their days off. But that's a challenge we face when we don't have flexible training options. The advent of online learning has made a huge difference, especially with the kind of programs you guys are running. Every time I turn around, you're offering something new to keep people engaged.

This year in Baltimore, I wrote a program focusing on a concept I've been wrestling with for years: are we getting better because we're smarter, or are we getting better just because we're luckier? We've seen so much progress in industry safety - things like lockout/tagout systems weren't even around when I started. Back then, we'd take a big bar and shove it into the gears just to stop them from moving.

We didn't have the kind of safeguards that are standard now, and that speaks volumes about how far we've come. But at the same time, industry is always changing, so the question remains: are we really smarter, or just getting more fortunate with the improvements in safety and equipment?

I also think about training, especially refresher training. Can you imagine saying you've been trained to handle a situation, but you haven't had any refresher training in the last 10 years? And then something goes wrong, and you're not prepared. That's a terrifying thought, especially in our field. There are two things that scare me to death today that weren't around when I started: one is third-party diseases. You know, my last call is the only one where I actually worried. I put my hand on a guy's head - just as I was about to head home - and then I thought, "He could have something." That's when I realized how much we didn't know back then. The second thing that worries me today is the tort laws. The way judges handle cases, they only understand what's presented to them. So if you've got all the certificates, you've got your documentation, and you've been practicing, you're covered, right? But the truth is, if you've been doing just one drill a year, you're not really staying sharp.

I always tell industry, don't just do one drill a year - do two. Give me two drills, and I'll put you in the top 10% of cities. Most departments don't even do that - they do the minimum, if that.

Some are doing annual drills, and that's fine, but imagine doing two or three drills a year. You'd get so much better. The key is consistency and practice. And not just practicing the basics - get a third party to come in and challenge your team, test them with their problems. You need to get outside feedback to see how well you can handle real-world situations. I've done that before, bringing in experts to test the team. It's all about measuring how well you can handle problems that you don't already know.

I think the biggest mistake we make sometimes is looking in the mirror and telling ourselves we're doing fine - "Oh, I'm good, I'm on top of it." But when I've done it, I've realized I'm not always winning that argument. There's always more to learn and more ways to improve.

John Cassidy

When we talk about structuring and implementing a robust continuing education program for a hazmat team, it's important to recognize that not all learning needs to come from formal training sessions. In fact, some of the most effective education happens organically, built right into the rhythm of team life.

Let's start with something simple: attrition. Every team, over time, brings in new members. And that's a good thing. Every time a new member joins, the team naturally returns to square one - where things are on the truck, how meters work, how pumps operate. We start from the beginning again. And that creates a powerful feedback loop.

Here's how it works. When a new member prepares a sign-off presentation, they present it to the entire team. On the surface, it looks like an evaluation - the experienced members are there to assess the rookie. But what's actually happening? Everyone's learning. How many times have we sat through a presentation from one of our stronger new guys and walked away saying, "I never knew that"? Maybe it was a technical detail, a historical reference, a procedure tweak - something new. Something valuable.

So even though it looks like we're helping the new guy level up, we're reinforcing the fundamentals across the board. And for your more senior members - the ones who might be drifting or disengaged - it's a subtle but effective way to bring them back in.

You're not saying, "Hey, we're going back to basics." You're just making them part of the process. They get a refresher whether they want one or not.

If I were building a team from scratch, I'd make this part of the culture. Let every new member present to the group. Let them own it. And in doing so, they help elevate the entire company.

Now let's talk about something that's working really well in the FDNY - something that's become a cornerstone of our broader continuing education strategy: "Tips From Training."

FDNY is a massive operation - 300+ companies, five boroughs, multiple shifts. That means a major incident could happen in one part of the city, and the rest of us might never hear about it. There's no water cooler big enough to catch that info. But the Tips From

Training program bridges that gap.

Here's how it works. If there's an unusual call, a close call, a mayday, or just a solid lesson learned from the field, the training division creates a one-page summary. That document explains what happened, what was learned, and what other companies can take away from it. And within 24 hours, it's in the inbox of every single company in the city.

So now, even if I wasn't on duty, or it didn't happen in my borough, I'm still learning from it. I see something like, "Hey, we had a Tesla fire and here's what worked." Or, "We had a ventilation issue in a high-rise and here's how we adapted." That's real-time, relevant, peer-to-peer knowledge sharing - and it's incredibly powerful.

That's what continuing education should look like. Not just scheduled classes and PowerPoint slides, but a living, breathing learning culture. One where we learn from new members, from each other, and from the field.

Dave DiGregorio

Without a doubt, it's absolutely critical. As you mentioned, hazmat doesn't stay the same - there are always emerging threats, new technologies, and shifting priorities that teams need to keep up with. Some people are only going to learn what you give them, and they won't push themselves beyond that. Unfortunately, you can't change someone's attitude if they aren't willing to take the initiative. But then there are others who are eager to learn and constantly seek out new opportunities to expand their knowledge. Those are the people you want to support, so

I always tried to give them opportunities to attend different classes and conferences.

For example, if we had a chance to send a few people to the Baltimore Conference, I wouldn't just send anyone. It was for those who showed they were actively building up their resume, improving their knowledge, and demonstrating their commitment to the team. It was about giving those motivated individuals the chance to grow.

One of the biggest motivators for the team was the JHIRT team. In Massachusetts, it was the elite hazmat team, and guys were eager to join. Getting on that team really helped pad your resume and was a way to demonstrate your skill and ambition. But JHIRT wasn't the only specialty team we had. We also had a maritime team for those interested in maritime operations, and we had a technical specialist team - what we affectionately called the "geek squad." Those guys were all about deepening their knowledge, and they got extra drills - at least four additional drills per year in their specific specialty. It was a huge opportunity for them to learn more, and they knew that. It was a win-win: they got more experience, and we got more skilled, specialized team members.

Creating those "carrots" was key. Giving people something to work toward, whether it was more training, more experience, or a chance to join a specialty team, kept them motivated and engaged. And, as you said, if someone is a natural leader, they can bring others along with them. That's where the real strength of a team lies.

To build the training, we'd start by reviewing the After Action Reports (AARs) from the incidents. Every month, the team leadership would meet to discuss what we had seen across the different districts. We'd share our experiences and ask questions like, "Hey, in District 6, we had issues with Mercury response. Are you guys seeing the same thing?" Some districts would recognize the issue, while others might not have thought about it at all. From there, we'd build training around the issues that were cropping up. It wasn't about throwing anyone under the bus; it was about identifying areas that needed improvement, like how to properly clean a Mercury vacuum, which was often overlooked but caused problems.

Once we identified the issues, we'd make sure the training was system wide. It wasn't just for one district; it was something we'd implement across all teams. Then, we'd schedule the training months in advance - planning it out for April, for example, and making it part of that month's drill.

The real key to it all was finding ways to incorporate these learning opportunities into the budget. Training is critical, but sometimes you need to create those extra incentives for the guys - whether it's the chance to meet others in the hazmat community, gain more experience, or just get away and do something that adds value to their role. Creating those opportunities helped keep the team engaged and constantly pushing for better skills and deeper knowledge.

Dave Donohue

The first step is identifying what's needed in the community and by the organization to meet the mission. Once you have that, you can determine the depth of expertise required across different areas. The areas that require significant depth become mandatory topics for continuing education, while those with less demand are assigned lower priority and integrated as needed.

It all begins with member selection and identifying the qualities we're looking for in a team member. Once that's clear, we work to eliminate organizational hurdles - whether that's issues with funding, staffing, or other constraints - to the greatest extent possible. The next step is offering intrinsic rewards for participation in training opportunities, creating motivation beyond just external incentives.

Every incident gets an After Action Review (AAR) and an Improvement Plan (IP). Each incident is dissected to pull out lessons learned, and these are then incorporated into training scenarios. The goal is to create scenarios that both reflect the original incident and introduce variations to help apply the knowledge in new and unique ways, ensuring the lessons stick. We also compare incidents against Standard Operating Guidelines (SOGs) and protocols to ensure that expectations align with what was actually carried out, helping to identify any gaps or areas for improvement.

Rick Edinger

You've got to run drills - plain and simple. You need to get your people together on a regular basis, make sure they're actually working as a team, not just showing up in the same place at the same time. The key is picking relevant training topics, putting hands on the equipment, and keeping it focused. Don't just go through the motions.

Of course, all that still has to feed into the machine - how much time and money do I have to work with?

When I stepped into the Deputy Chief role in 2015, we used to have this constant battle between our three main special ops teams. We did on-shift training meaning we took companies out of service. The dive team would need a couple of days on the calendar, then tech rescue would come in with a conflict, and hazmat was always trying to squeeze something in between. It was a mess.

So I changed the system. Every September before the new calendar year, I brought reps from all the special ops teams to the table. We mapped out what time was available, let each team identify what they needed, and started putting the puzzle together. We created a system where we weren't bumping heads or scrambling at the last minute. And they're still doing it that way today - it worked.

The other thing: don't just get the team together and say, *"Alright, what do you want to do today?"* You've got to have a plan. Know your subject matter experts. If it's going to be hands-on, make it scenario-based and make it realistic. You've been given the time - use it well. Half-hearted training is a waste of everyone's time and demoralizes your dedicated people.

A big part of all this is passion. I said it earlier - you'll always have a few folks who are in it for the wrong reasons: station assignment, incentive pay, or just convenience. But you'll also see a lot of people who are *truly* into it. You see them at conferences, you see them reading the new material, chasing down expertise, and trying to become subject matter experts. Those are the ones you want to support and grow.

If I can show people that there are opportunities - that we'll support them with time and money, that we're budgeting for new techs to come in, or we're sending folks to training - I think that builds interest and commitment. When the team sees that we're investing in them, they stick around. They stay motivated. They're not just checking boxes.

There are also simple and more structured ways to maintain consistency and continuity within the team. The quick way is through shift change briefings. We had dedicated hazmat stations, so handoff was usually hazmat to hazmat. We made sure we passed along important info - brief, but effective.

The more labor-intensive, but arguably more valuable, method is through after-action reviews. If an incident meets a certain threshold - severity, complexity, however you want to define it - you put together a small group. Some folks who were on the call, maybe a few who weren't, and you build a formal after-action report. You train on it, you disseminate it, and you come back to it.

A month or two later, use it as a drill day. Walk the team through the incident again. Talk about the product or chemical, the decision-making, the response. Let people who were there tell the story, share the lessons learned. That kind of reflection and discussion - that's where the real growth happens. And it's often more meaningful than anything you can pull out of a textbook.

John Esposito

The way I rely on Hazmat One is simple - whatever hazmat situation comes up in New York City, no matter how weird or unique, I expect *them* to handle it. That's the bar. Same goes for Marine - if it's on the water, they own it. And Rescue? That's for the completely fucked-up technical stuff. If it's complicated and no one knows what to do with it, that's theirs.

Now, some people look at Hazmat One and think, "They've got seven guys riding - that's a lot." But out of those seven, even if they're not all specialists, you're going to have four, maybe five, who are. And chances are, at least one or two of them have seen this kind of thing before.

Maybe they've drilled it. Maybe they've just thought it through already. That makes a huge difference.

We've seen that firsthand. Think back to the auto yard - somebody literally pushed a propane tank car off its truck and just left it. Went home. Came back the next morning like nothing happened. That's the kind of stuff we run into.

Now compare that to your average engine or truck company. For them, 98% of what they'll encounter is covered in SOPs. We can train for it. We can script it. But for the special units? That's not how it works. Their world is built around the unknown. Which means it's on *them* to consume everything. They've got to learn everything they can - tools, tactics, meters.

And the meters especially - they need to know those inside and out. What's a real hit? What's a false positive? I used to know all that stuff myself, but now? I've got guys whose *job* it is to know it. Because if I'm still focused on the meter quirks, who's looking at the big picture? That's their lane, and I trust them to stay in it and own it.

And this ties right into education. It's absolutely critical. We've got a lot of great instructors who go out and teach. That's great. That's important. But you've also got to sit down sometimes and be a student. Especially when there's something new. Teaching's great - but learning never stops.

And right on cue - here come the volleys. Wonder what *they're* doing today.

Brandon Fletcher

It's tough to keep everything on track with a volunteer department, and getting everyone in the same place at the same time is definitely a challenge. We train weekly, with a typical month having four training nights: two nights dedicated to firefighting, one to EMS, and one to "special ops." For us, special ops includes hazmat as well as several tech rescue disciplines. That means we've got about 12-13 special ops drills each year, and six of those focus solely on hazmat.

We also run hazmat awareness and operations training for recruits in-house, and a lot of this training takes place outside regular training nights. Members are involved in multiple roles to make sure their skills stay sharp. Whenever we can, we bring in outside training throughout the year. And we actively encourage members to take advantage of training at other agencies or attend NDPC classes whenever their schedules allow.

At the core of our department, training and preparedness are central. Praise and positive attitudes are powerful motivators that drive our members to constantly look for ways to improve themselves and, in turn, strengthen the team.

We also do a "hotwash" after nearly every significant incident we respond to - whether it's a fire, hazmat, or EMS call. We're always looking for areas of improvement, even when the outcome is successful. With hazmat specifically, I keep my ear to the ground and encourage my team to do the same. If there's an incident elsewhere that could easily happen in our area, we jump on it and analyze how we would handle it with our resources. It's a key part of staying sharp and continuously improving our response strategies.

Chris Hawley

This business is evolving so rapidly that it's hard to keep up. I talk to some of the folks who I consider to be the "smart ones" in this field, and honestly, my head starts spinning. These guys are so far ahead of where I was when I first got into this - they're operating meters like it's second nature, hitting buttons and analyzing spectra without even thinking twice about it. For me, it still takes time to go through the process and really think about what I'm seeing. But these guys? They're flying through it. They're comfortable, they've mastered the tools, and they're analyzing data quickly. That's why it's crucial to have those specialists on your team who can handle the technical details.

But it's not just about knowing how to use the technology; it's about continuous education and refresher training. As much as I know how to operate an FTIR and a Raman, I can't be the person to go full throttle with it all the time. These guys who are using the tools regularly? They need to be kept sharp with ongoing training and updated skills. And that's where cooperative training becomes key. I get it - every jurisdiction doesn't have the budget to send everyone to every specialized school, but that's where partnerships and regional cooperation come in.

I've seen it in action. A few years ago, Baltimore City and Baltimore County combined their training programs. All our initial hazmat technician classes were combined. The same went for the refresher courses and even specialized sessions like air monitoring. We would invite other jurisdictions - Anne Arundel County, for example, if they had specialized chemical plants that we didn't have in Baltimore County. If that plant were to have an incident, we could very well be the second due, so it's critical to know the plant and what to expect from it.

Regional cooperation not only saves money, but it also exposes your team to scenarios that other departments might face. Everyone has their own unique set of challenges or facilities - whether it's a specific chemical plant or industrial operation. Being able to train with them means you're better prepared for the unpredictable. And in terms of funding, you can think outside the box. Sure, you can't send everyone to Pueblo or Aniston, but you can work with local industry. Maybe a company like Shell Oil or Baltimore Tank Lines could help cover costs to send a few of your folks to Pueblo. It's about leveraging the resources that are available and making those connections.

The real value of training at places like Pueblo isn't just the course material - it's meeting your peers from other parts of the country. It's the networking. That's where the magic happens. It's the conversations you have in the command post or in the "Ott house" at the National Fire Academy. Those are the moments that shape your understanding of how other teams operate and expose you to best practices. When your folks go out there and come back, they often realize we're not as advanced as we thought we were. That perspective is priceless.

So yeah, sending people to these advanced courses is crucial, but it's the connections they make, the perspectives they bring back, and the collaborative training they engage in that ultimately elevates the entire team. It's not just about checking the box on certifications - it's about continuous improvement and leveraging every opportunity to learn from others.

Mike Hildebrand

Look, shame on you if you can't build training scenarios today.

Seriously. We're in a scenario-rich environment. Just pick up a newspaper, watch the news, scroll through a blog, or read a journal article. The world is *handing you* training material every single day. And with the tech and resources we have now? It's a *double shame* if you're not using it.

When I started, my first fire call was in 1970. You want to know what our training was? *Fire Engineering* and *FDNY* magazine. We would do a weekly hands-on drill, but that was it. In our little small town firehouse in Hagerstown, Maryland, we'd wait for the end of the month to get those well done magazines. By the time that magazine got to the back of the room, pages were falling out of it. If you wanted to be a good firefighter, that magazine was dog-eared. Nobody had to tell you to read it. You just *did*, because you were *motivated*.

Fast forward to today – Mike, guys like you and Bobby – in the instructional world you're the new Greg Noll and Mike Hildebrand. That's a compliment, by the way. What you're doing with podcasts, blogs, video breakdowns – you've reinvented the whole training and intelligence collection model. There are others doing it too – Phil Ambrose from Los Angeles, Bob Coshignano from Orlando – but the truth is, there's no excuse now for not getting training and educated. If you're not using the resources out there to build scenarios and make your team sharper, that's on *you*.

The multiplier effect is real. Guys are taking the content you're creating and bringing it back to their teams. They're training smarter, faster, and more practically than ever before. And scenario-based learning? It's one of the best tools we have.

But it's not just about throwing a situation at people. If you really want scenario-based training to work, you've got to lead it the right way. That means using what I call *learning through inquiry*.

During my 51 year career, I spent close to two decades working with the U.S. intelligence community, I took advantage of every training opportunity even though it was out of my lane. If they would allow me in the class I took it. A lot of our training was scenario-based. One course taught by the CIA that I'll never forget focused on the kidnapping of DEA Agent Enrique "Kiki" Camarena in Mexico - how he was held captive, tortured, and killed. It was a full case study and the class began with students simply reading these case studies that were written by people who went back to the source and interviewed people that were actually there. Every mistake made, every decision that went sideways. You read the case, and the facilitator walks you through it - asking questions, guiding thought, *never* giving answers. It wasn't about whether you were right or wrong. It was about how you *thought* through the problem. That's the Socratic method. That's *learning through inquiry*. And that's what great scenario-based training looks like.

I've been through three-day classes that were nothing *but* scenarios. And the instructor? Never answered a single question. Not one. The instructor knew the answers - but he wasn't looking to lecture. He was looking to see how you approached the problem. Could you articulate a clear, reasonable path forward? Could you make a case, defend a position, think your way through it? Problem solving by *thinking* - What a concept.

Now, in some environments - especially when you're teaching to a standard - you've got time constraints. You're bound by schoolhouse solutions. Confined space rescue is a great example. You've got laws and regulations. If someone's stopped breathing, you've got three minutes before the brain starts to die, maybe five until they're gone. If your average response time is 12 minutes, you're not rescuing anyone. The go/no-go line is clear.

But in real life? People don't always follow that. That's where scenarios matter most - because they let you test decision-making *before* it's real.

So you throw it at your team: what if the guy in the confined space is your good friend Bob? What if it's your brother? Your actual blood brother? In a group of people, you'll feel the shift. Someone in that room will say, "Screw it, I'm going in." And the true leader - the one with the strength to make the hard call - has to be ready to say, "No, you're not. I am. And here's why."

That's what scenario-based training is for. It's not about finding the *right* answer - it's about building the mindset, the culture, and the courage to *ask the right questions.*

Bob Ingram

To keep your team current and ensure that everyone is properly trained, it's important to build a well-structured program that balances both foundational in-house training and external opportunities. Start by focusing on your basic in-house training to ensure all members have the essential skills to handle common incidents. Once that foundation is set, take the next step by sending members to second-level national and private programs to enhance their skills with specialized, broader training experiences.

Identify those team members who are particularly suited for specialized technologies or areas of expertise and follow up with in-house team training to share what they've learned. Encourage participation in hazmat conferences to keep your team current on new response capabilities and insights from teams across the country. These events provide valuable opportunities to network, learn, and bring back fresh ideas for your own team.

Incentives are a great way to motivate team members and encourage growth. Consider creating monetary incentives for various certification levels. This is the approach used in education where teachers earn more for earning higher degrees, such as a master's degree, or doctorate. This keeps team members motivated but can also lead to greater team longevity. It encourages structured career progression and potentially allows new members to enter the team at earlier stages of their career.

Empower your team by giving them a program to manage within the team. People often enjoy standing out in a positive way, so providing them with an opportunity to take ownership of a task or project can increase their engagement. Set a clear end goal, support them through the process, and give them some flexibility to explore how to reach that goal. This approach encourages personal responsibility and growth.

Every new skill, task, or certification must be documented. Documentation not only ensures compliance but also provides a record for future reference. If an SOP (Standard Operating Procedure) doesn't exist for a particular process, use the knowledge of your team to develop one. Similarly, if an existing SOP needs updating due to newly discovered issues or better tactics, engage the team to make those changes, ensuring they are verified repeatedly and approved before being integrated.

Once changes are made, build them into ongoing initial and refresher training so every team member remains informed and aligned. If the changes are urgent and refresher training is still some time off, send out bulletins to keep everyone in the loop. Bulletins should clearly identify what's changed, what works now, and any adjustments to existing SOPs based on updated research or field experience.

Finally, organize a meeting with company officers and team members to discuss these changes in person. This is a great way to address questions, gather feedback, and ensure that everyone understands and is on board with the new procedures. Involving everyone in these discussions helps reinforce the importance of continuous improvement and collective ownership of the team's progress.

Phil McArdle

First and foremost, you must establish the basic minimum requirements that personnel must meet to work in the Haz-Mat unit. At the very least, all personnel need to meet the minimum standards outlined by federal regulations, specifically 29CFR 1910.120 / aka 40 CFR 311. Each potential team member should have training at the Awareness, Operational, and Technician levels, which, according to the most basic minimums, amounts to no less than 48 hours initially. While these minimums are a starting point, any experienced hazardous materials technician or specialist will be quick to tell you that this is far from adequate, but it provides a foundation to build on.

As part of their initial training, personnel should, at the earliest opportunity, apply for and be scheduled to attend schools at the federal, state, and local levels (though these opportunities may be beyond the control of the local jurisdiction and depend on availability from the offering agencies). While waiting for these formal training sessions, an in-house training program should be developed. This program ensures that every tool and piece of equipment carried by the Haz-Mat team is thoroughly familiarized and operable by new members. Personnel should have the necessary knowledge and skills to demonstrate competency in using this equipment effectively. Additionally, any policies, procedures, operating directives, SOPs, or departmental training documents related to the Haz-Mat team should be carefully reviewed by new personnel, who should also demonstrate their understanding of these documents.

Local training within the jurisdiction is essential for familiarizing team members with the unique hazards in the community. For example, what modes of transportation pass through the area, creating a significant hazardous materials presence? Are team members familiar with the different types of motor carriers on the road, their capacities, safety devices, transfer points, and shutoff mechanisms? Do they understand airport operations, the differences between passenger and cargo operations, flightline safety, and special aircraft hazards? What about rail lines, rail yards, railcar types, and industry-specific terminology? Pipelines, shipping ports, and maritime rules and regulations regarding hazardous materials also need to be addressed. Similarly, it's important to assess fixed sites within the community that could present special challenges in the event of a leak or spill. Are you prepared to manage a release at bulk storage facilities, considering factors like the number of tanks, construction types, and fire protection systems? Each facility has unique challenges, and knowing these is key to the team's preparedness. Site visits should be conducted regularly and incorporated into routine training when not responding to active Haz-Mat incidents.

Advanced training goes beyond the basics and covers more specialized topics. This includes training on advanced monitoring equipment, highly technical tools, PPE, and security-sensitive or proprietary information. Some of this material may be restricted to specific team members and compartmentalized for security reasons.

Refresher training and competency evaluation should be continuous and ongoing. It's critical to review every Haz-Mat document, tool, piece of equipment, and piece of PPE in use, ensuring that they are always up to date and that competency levels are maintained.

New technology or policy updates should also be reviewed periodically. It's important to evaluate revised or updated training curricula to understand why changes are being made - whether due to updates in laws, regulations, or standards, or the introduction of new technology that could improve safety and performance.

Adam McFadden

We structure our continuing education program around a deliberate mix of monthly mandatory training and annual multi-agency exercises to ensure our hazmat teams remain sharp, informed, and response-ready.

Each month, we conduct hands-on training sessions focused on maintaining core competencies. Topics include air monitoring, corrosivity detection, radiation refreshers, and new equipment familiarization. These sessions aren't just refresher courses - they're opportunities for real-time skill development that reinforce critical knowledge and keep our responders at peak performance.

Once a year, we bring it all together with large-scale, multi-agency training exercises. These events include fire, EMS, law enforcement, and emergency management partners and are designed to build interoperability and strengthen coordination across agencies. They simulate complex hazmat scenarios, stress-test communication systems, and prepare teams to operate as one cohesive unit during major incidents.

To keep our training relevant, we continuously integrate new technologies, evolving response strategies, and intelligence on emerging threats. This ensures our team remains at the cutting edge of hazmat response and ready for whatever comes next.

We also understand that sustained engagement in training comes from a culture that values professional growth. That's why we motivate team members by offering advanced certification opportunities that not only build skillsets but also boost promotion potential. We support participation through financial assistance, overtime compensation, and incentives for specialized training. This investment sends a clear message: continuous learning is not just encouraged - it's expected and rewarded.

Mentorship, exposure to emerging tools, and access to hands-on learning reinforce that message, keeping our team energized and committed to improving themselves and the mission.

One of the most effective components of our continuing education program is how we incorporate lessons learned from real incidents. We conduct formal post-incident reviews and bring those insights directly into our training sessions. Whether it's a debrief from a recent hazmat response or updates pulled from agency-wide after-action reports, we analyze what went right, where we can improve, and how to apply those lessons moving forward. This process keeps our training grounded in reality - relevant, adaptive, and always evolving with the hazards we face in the field.

In short, continuing education for our hazmat teams isn't just a checkbox - it's a culture of excellence that drives operational readiness, career development, and smarter response in every scenario we face.

Mike Monaco

These days, I'd start by bringing in *The Hazmat Guys* as my training partner. I'd lean on their mix of online and in-person training to keep certifications current and, more importantly, make sure the team's getting solid, real-world education. It's easy, it's accessible, and it works.

When it comes to motivating people - especially in the fire service - there are a few strategies that tend to work, even if they're not exactly pretty. One of the most universally effective? Leading by example.

If I'm the one out there going to conferences, taking advanced classes, asking questions, reading books, staying curious - people notice. That kind of behavior spreads. It gives others permission to do the same. They see it's not only okay, it's expected. That's one way to set the tone.

Then there's the old-school method: ball-breaking. I'll be honest - it took me way longer than it should've to knock out a few of my own certifications. And what finally pushed me? The guys riding me about it. Friendly harassment, constant jabs - "You still haven't done that yet?" Sometimes that's the nudge people need. Not elegant, but effective.

Now, as far as lessons learned? That's all about honesty. You've got to be willing to sit down after a call or an incident, open up, and say, "Here's what I screwed up. Here's what went sideways. And here's what actually went well." That kind of transparency builds trust. It creates a space where others feel comfortable doing the same. And that's how you start embedding lessons - not just from *your* mistakes, but from *everyone's*.

Same goes for when someone comes back from training. Share what you picked up. Say, "Hey, I used to think X, but now I see it differently." That kind of humility and growth mindset sets the tone for the whole team. It tells people: it's okay to evolve. It's okay to learn. In fact, it's expected.

Chris Pfaff

Out here in the West, and really across the whole country, when I look at volunteer hazmat teams, I'm honestly blown away. I'm gobsmacked by the capabilities some of these purely volunteer teams have - their training hours, their knowledge, and their competency often surpass many full-time career teams.

I've seen teams train quarterly, monthly, and weekly. At an absolute bare minimum, you need monthly training. If you're doing training just quarterly, you're basically setting yourself up for failure. You'll see apathy set in, and your team's participation will plummet.

Monthly training is essential because NFPA 470 has so many requirements. Honestly, if we were to cover everything required by NFPA every year, we'd be in class every single day, non-stop.

Think about extreme or uncommon events - going back to EMS examples again since that's the bulk of fire responses nowadays - every three years, I'm required to refresh on OBGYN emergencies. Thank goodness it's not every year, because I don't deal with that often enough. But every year, I absolutely have to refresh CPR, AED, and infectious disease protocols because of their critical importance and inherent risks. Some things you need right at the top of your head; others can be spaced out.

It's the same for hazmat training. Do we really need annual training on using Level-A suits and fully encapsulated entries every single year? For instance, in my area, we'll likely never personally handle certain advanced hazmat kits because there are professional teams nearby, like specialized units from rail companies located in our jurisdiction. Of course, we still need to cover these skills occasionally to meet NFPA 470 check-offs, but yearly? I'd say no. For smaller, less frequent tasks, once every three years could be enough.

Do we need container identification training every year? Probably not. Every few years is fine for these lower-hanging fruits.

But the key is regular engagement and diversity of training topics to maintain readiness. Teams should be deciding what's essential annually versus periodically.

How do we keep our teams sharp and integrate lessons from past incidents? After-action reports - plain and simple. Learning from our mistakes is critical. We need honest, open discussions about how we messed up.

In our alpha-type career field, people don't like admitting mistakes - that's a major obstacle. I usually kick off after-action discussions by sharing my own screw-ups. It's important to acknowledge that we all mess up sometimes. Every member brings their own unique experiences and perspective - we all view incidents through different lenses. Firefighters, law enforcement, hazmat teams - everyone sees the same incident differently.

So we have to listen to each other's perspectives. We learn as much from operations-level responders, law enforcement, and other teams as we do from our own technicians. It's crucial not only to look inward at our team's incidents but also to look outward at trends and incidents nationwide.

We're not blaming other jurisdictions - it's about understanding different approaches, identifying trends, and improving our own response by learning from everyone else's experiences as well as our own.

Rob Rezende

We mandate 24 hours of Continuing Education (CE) annually, with 12 hours required to be completed within the team. This ensures there's plenty of interaction and collaboration, fostering a team-oriented learning environment. It's about more than just ticking boxes; it's about growing together and learning from each other.

Each month, we provide 4 hours of internal training, totaling 48 hours per year. This structured time allows us to build a solid foundation of knowledge, but we also recognize the value of external training. We allow team members to complete up to 12 hours of outside training, giving them the opportunity to bring fresh ideas and insights back to the team. This exchange of knowledge helps prevent "inbreeding" in our training, ensuring we stay connected to the broader industry.

We also bring outside courses to the team to keep things diverse and dynamic. For example, lithium-ion battery training from The Hazmat Guys offers perspectives and expertise from people outside our organization. This kind of training is crucial for keeping us ahead of emerging threats and technologies.

To ensure our personnel can attend training without sacrificing operational needs, we offer funding to cover backfill. This makes sure that attending training doesn't come at the expense of other responsibilities or create gaps in our coverage.

Every month, we dedicate time to reviewing "Case Studies" - incidents from the previous month that provided valuable lessons learned. These reviews involve all shifts, ensuring that everyone has the opportunity to reflect on real-world scenarios and the lessons they offer. This process keeps us sharp, aligned, and constantly improving.

Bob Royall

I guess you could say I'm an anomaly. The Harris County began with just three people. Not three people per shift - three people, period. And that's all we had to work with. So, we had to balance being a technical resource, stepping in to help incident commanders, and actually working the incident with smaller volunteer or paid departments that needed assistance. It was bare-bones from the start, but we also had to build our budget from the ground up, starting with nothing. It helped that I was in control of my own budget - actually, I was the budget control officer for the entire agency.

Now, I'm not saying I took advantage of that situation to make sure I always had enough money, but training and health and safety were always my top priorities. I was programmed that way coming out of Houston. I knew that, as much as we wanted to send everyone to every training course they wanted to go to, that just wasn't feasible. So, I built a multi-year training plan - laying out how many people I could send each year - while taking advantage of every free training opportunity. Just because it's free doesn't always mean it's not high-quality. If there was an opportunity to send someone to a free training session, whether it was in Aniston, Socorro, the Nevada test site, or Pueblo, I was all over that. I had guys waiting for these spots.

And when there was an opportunity to send my guys to industry sponsored advanced hazmat technician school at TEEX or to a transportation emergencies class, I would reach out and ask if I could squeeze a couple of extra spots in from my team. Those kinds of relationships paid double dividends. Not only did it help our training, but it helped us build relationships with others in the field before we ever had to respond together.

You also need to find ways to be creative and stretch your budget dollars. You can't just sit back and wait for someone to knock on your door with a training opportunity. As a hazmat leader, it's up to you to go out and find those opportunities. For example, every year in Beaumont, Lamar University hosts firefighting foam classes. That's another training that I took advantage of to stretch our dollars and get the best training possible.

A big one for me was radiation training. I made sure my team had the chance to train at the Nevada test site. There's nothing like being in a live radiation field, seeing the meter move and knowing you're in a real hazardous environment. You can't replicate that experience at home. That's what I mean by getting out there and finding training opportunities.

But here's another thing - I never took credit for what my guys did. When they accomplished great things, I was the first one to recognize them, put them in for awards, and tell them what a fantastic job they did. A little recognition goes a long way. So, when it was time to send them off to training, they were eager to go. Of course, there were always times when someone would say, "Can I not go this time? Can I go next time instead?" But that's where motivation and support come into play.

You've got to motivate your people and, even more importantly, support them in every way you can. I can't stress that enough - support is the biggest part of being a leader. If you have their back and show them you believe in them their growth and development will come.

Bobby Salvesen

This is something I bring up a lot when I travel and teach around the country. People talk about hazmat certifications like they're the end-all, be-all - but they rarely understand the *difference* between being certified and being truly proficient.

Take the 40-hour hazmat class. Or California's 160-hour technician program. You show up, sit through the hours, do the required checkboxes - and boom, you're a certified tech. Same thing in New York City. You complete our 120-hour course and you're in. You're a Hazmat Tech.

But that's just *technician* level. When someone tells me, "Hey, I'm an FDNY Hazmat Tech," that means you've completed the initial 120 hours, maybe done your annual refreshers - and that's it. And don't get me wrong, that's a solid foundation.

But then I tell them what it takes to become an *FDNY Hazmat Specialist*. That's when jaws start hitting the floor.

It's not a few extra days of class. It's 5,000 hours - on top of the technician certification.

Compare that to California again. Do an extra two weeks - maybe another 80 hours - and you're a "specialist." Meanwhile, FDNY's path to specialist includes:
- Roughly seven additional weeks of school, including:
    - Bomb school
    - Radiological/nuclear school
    - Two weeks of chemistry at the National Fire Academy
    - Live agent training at Anniston, Alabama
- A massive sign-off book filled with detailed competencies

- Live, no-aid oral boards in front of *seven specialists*
    o No PowerPoint. No notes. Everything from memory.
    o They don't just want you to explain a concept - they're going to pepper you with questions to dig into your *depth* of understanding.
    o Most candidates don't pass on their first try. It's not expected. It's part of the process.

All of this adds up to one thing: mastery.

You're not just repeating facts. You're demonstrating deep, conceptual understanding. You've moved beyond "I know what to do" to "I understand why I'm doing it and how to teach it." That's what those 5,000 hours represent.

So, yeah - certification gets you in the door. But mastery? That's earned. It's hard. It's humbling. And it changes how you see the job, how you train, and how you lead.

Doug Schick and Mark Zilch
Doug:

So much of this really comes down to what's happening at the company level. The day-to-day stuff. Are they drilling? Are they training on the basics? Are they checking the meters? Running the equipment they're supposed to be proficient with?

That's where the foundation gets built. And from higher up, there's only so much you can do. Especially when it comes to the DHS classes - we keep circling back to this - you just can't force people to take them. I know your department has the ability to mandate attendance, and that's fantastic. I wish we had that kind of leverage.

On our side, all I can really do is keep encouraging guys to sign up. I'm always nudging them. And with the classes we're trying to set up through the grant funding with you - that'll be huge. If that goes through, it's going to be great for our guys. It'll cover backfill, it'll cover overtime, so there's really no reason *not* to attend. And yet... I know some of them still won't come.

And at that point, what can I do? I can't make them go.

Mark:
Exactly. Like you said, unless it's written into an SOP, it's hard to require that kind of training. And even if it *is* in policy, there's still the issue of logistics. You can put out a requirement, sure, but if you can't staff it, what happens then?

Let's say you mandate training, but you can't afford to pay for overtime or backfill. What do you do when 20 guys don't show up - and that's your whole team? That's the kind of thing we're seeing with the JHAT team right now. We want them to hit a number of trainings a year. But if we can't pay for it, we can't force it. You can't just say, "Okay, you're all off the team now," and be left with two people. Then what? You don't *have* a team.

That's why we try to make the training itself the incentive.

We're nerds - so I try to lean into that. When we go out with the RAP team, I tell them, "Hey, you're going to see stuff nobody else gets to see. Some very exotic material that no one else has - this is next-level." That gets people interested. That makes them show up.

And working with other agencies helps too. Like when the FBI comes in for a joint training - that's a big draw. Guys on the teams eat that stuff up. They ask questions like, "Hey, am I on your FBI watchlist yet?"

Jason Zeller

Continuing education wasn't optional - it was expected. Our training calendar was built to keep every team member sharp in two lanes:
1. Their specialty role within the hazmat/WMD mission
2. Their Professional Military Education (PME) within their respective service branch

That dual responsibility was non-negotiable. You couldn't afford to just be a good hazmat operator - you had to be a well-rounded warfighter too.

Each section - downrange, comms, med, command, lab, logistics, Ops, Admin - had tailored sustainment requirements. Certifications had to be current, hands-on training had to be frequent, and knowledge transfer was a must. If someone attended a high-level course or training event, they were expected to come back and teach the team. That kept institutional knowledge fresh and moving, not stagnant.

We leaned heavily on real-world opportunities - working with places and agencies like Dugway, Edgewood, FLETC, DOE, USCG, FDNY, NYPD, USSS, PAPD - to make sure we weren't just learning from PowerPoints. Our people trained on actual agents, worked with emerging tech, and dealt with real operational scenarios. That matters.

But what really separated us was our culture. We weren't chasing checkboxes - we were chasing excellence. And that meant you stayed a student of the game, always. Didn't matter if you were brand new or a senior NCO - education never stopped.

Motivating people to stay sharp isn't about pep talks or PowerPoints - it's about building a culture where excellence is the minimum standard, not the ceiling.

I never believed in checking boxes just to say we did something. If you wore our uniform, you were expected to invest in yourself, your teammates, and the mission. That's what I mean when I say, *you earn it daily* - that's what I call paying the rent.

We were in the business of saving lives and risking ours. That's not a job you can fake your way through. You had to be mentally, technically, and physically dialed in at all times. If you weren't growing, you were a liability. That's how serious it was. And if that mindset didn't fit, then this wasn't the team for you.

Incorporating lessons learned from real incidents into our continuing education was essential. After every mission or operation, we held detailed debriefs where we looked at the entire response from start to finish. This wasn't just about talking through what happened - it was about digging into the practicalities:

- What tools worked?
- What didn't?

- What did we miss?
- How could we have been more efficient?

Those debriefs became our "live case studies." We didn't just talk theory - we made real-time adjustments to tactics, techniques, and procedures based on what we saw in the field.

Then, we took those lessons and wove them into our training scenarios. For instance, if we encountered a new type of chemical or a situation we hadn't trained for, that real-world experience became a critical learning point for future missions.

Every lesson learned became a building block for making us stronger, better prepared, and more adaptable to whatever challenges would come next.

Dan Baker

Culture is hands-down the most important part of any successful hazmat team - honestly, it's critical for any kind of team. But, man, fostering a great culture can be a constant struggle. For us, the key thing is brotherhood. Our boss always says, "Don't do fake brotherhood." Forget the t-shirts and tattoos if you're not ready to back them up with real actions. True brotherhood means helping your teammates move, checking in on their families when their partners are deployed, or being there when something goes sideways at home. That's how you know you've got it right.

It's easy to see when brotherhood is working. Recently, one of our guys ended up in the ER with appendicitis. By the time I got to the hospital to see how he was doing, another team member was already at his house letting his dogs out. That's brotherhood. Or take the time a tornado ripped through one of our member's homes - by sunrise the next morning, half the team had already arrived with chainsaws, no calls or texts needed. Again, that's brotherhood.

But once you've planted those seeds of brotherhood, leadership has to keep things moving by setting clear expectations of excellence and unwavering commitments to safety. Strong leadership and sensible, enforceable SOGs make that part easier - but remember, culture-building is never "done." It takes continuous effort from every single team member.

Brotherhood and teamwork form one piece of our equation, but equally critical for us is member autonomy. All of our responders also instruct full-time, teaching a packed schedule of classes as their regular day job. Our leadership grants them near-total control over how they manage their weekly responsibilities - where they teach, when they travel, how they organize their classes. This autonomy has been hugely effective for us, not just in empowering individuals but also in building trust and strengthening team cohesion.

We've built our hazmat branch around a clear "three-pillar" strategy rooted in our core mission and our chief's vision. Those pillars are simple and direct:

- Access to Training (for our customers)

- Response Readiness
- Stakeholder Engagement

Underpinning all of that is what we affectionately call our "prime directive": "BE NICE." Be nice to each other, to our customers (whether that's the fire service or the public), and even to management. It's simple, but it genuinely works - as long as everyone actually tries.

And finally - and this might seem minor, but trust me, it's huge - we always break bread together. All of our training trailers and most response units have gas barbecue grills. We don't usually break for lunch to scatter off to restaurants; instead, we cook meals for each other right there, firehouse style. It's surprisingly tough to think someone's an asshole when they just handed you a fresh sandwich or some homemade breakfast (by the way, our breakfast sushi - outstanding, trust me on this).

Culture, trust, brotherhood - it all comes together right there, around that folding table at training or roadside at a response.

Mike Callan

I started thinking about the culture of safety after Wooster, especially in light of the enormous turnout at that funeral - 27,000 firefighters. But when I look back, I wonder how many of them actually knew who the six men were that died. Out of all those people, I'd estimate only about 400 knew who they were. That was the full complement of men in the Worcester Fire Department. Everyone else showed up because the culture told them they had to. But the culture didn't necessarily make them understand who those men were, or why they were important. And that's where we run into a problem - there's a culture of aggressive interior attack in the fire service, but it's hazmat that really gave us the culture of non-intervention.

When I joined the fire department, one of the officers, Clark, wrote a book called *Principles and Practices*. I read it for my test - it was the 1972 first edition - and he only had four classes of firefighting: offensive, offensive defensive, defensive, and offensive defensive. There was no non-intervention, no real thought about pulling back. Defensive firefighting meant just getting as close to the danger as possible and still staying safe. Now, it's all about asking the question, *Is the risk worth the benefit?* And every time I ask that question, I get people in my class who answer with *reward* instead of *risk*. But here's the thing: *reward* is a cookie. Risk is a decision, a serious one, where you're making a choice to do nothing because it's the right thing to do. That takes guts.

I remember one of my first gasoline tank fires. I went to help another city, and the chief asked me, "What do you think?" I said, "Chief, you don't have enough foam. Let it burn. Just surround it. Let it burn." He agreed, but then every so often, someone would get a little too eager and start opening up a nozzle to try to put it out.

And I'd have to yell, "Stop it!" I mean, sometimes you have to let things burn, and you have to make sure everyone understands that. Firefighting has always been about *doing something*, but sometimes doing nothing is the best decision.

Culture is what drives us. It's not about individual attitudes - it's a corporate culture. Take the Marines, for example. They have a culture that's built into them. It's in their DNA. The individual attitude shapes that corporate culture. In our world, as firefighters, we start out with the idea that to be a good firefighter, you need to be aggressive, right? You had to be the guy who could handle the smoke, the guy who could take it all in stride. And then, when you made it to training officer, you earned your stripes because you could eat smoke all week without breaking a sweat. But that kind of aggression is ingrained in us. It's part of the culture, but it's not always the right mindset.

And I always talk about how one person can make a difference. It's not just about what you wear or how you look. Back in the day, there were three guys trying to teach me how to take off my breathing apparatus because I was making them look bad for wearing it. "Take that thing off, you're making us look weak," they'd say. Now, we all know the importance of keeping that gear on. It was stupid not to wear it, but it took a while for that to sink in. And that's the problem with safety culture - it evolves, but it takes time.

It's still evolving, and that's why we have to keep pushing for the right decisions to be made.

I remember a hazmat call where someone had painted the inside of an apartment with all sorts of chemicals. I had my team in there wearing masks, and then an old chief came in and said, "You don't need that." I looked at him and said, "Chief, are you telling me to take it off?" He said, "No, I'm not ordering you to take it off." I said, "Then I'm going to keep wearing it because I don't know what's in there." I told him, "I appreciate that you don't think we need it, but I believe we do." And when the DEP arrived, they all put masks on too. That made me feel a little vindicated, but the bigger picture is that safety culture has come a long way, and we have to keep advocating for it.

Now, I see myself saying things like, "Don't go in there anymore." Back in the day, we didn't have non-intervention. Now, I can actually say, "Get out of the building." And sometimes, I get those radio messages from inside, "Five more minutes, Chief, five more minutes." I would always respond, "You've had it out for 25 minutes and you still haven't put it out, I can't leave you in there anymore."

But that's what we have to remember: crisis management is a second-by-second decision. You can't afford to wait another five minutes when the ice is cracking under your feet. You have to act, or the crisis will take over. That's why we need to back up sometimes, not keep pushing forward.

I know that as I've gotten older, I've become more emotional about firefighter deaths. Bill Hand and I talk about it all the time - it's hard.

Losing someone in the fire service is painful. That's part of the culture, too. It's not just about responding to calls or making sure you have the right tools. It's about the people you lose along the way. The impact of those losses can't be understated. And that's the culture we have now - we care about each other, and we have to keep working to protect each other, not just in terms of safety measures, but also by fostering a culture of accountability and thoughtfulness in every decision we make.

John Cassidy

When we talk about culture - especially a culture of safety, excellence, and continuous improvement - it all starts with the officer. You have to live it. You have to be the example. You can't talk the talk if you're not walking the walk. Around here, we say *complacency kills*, and that's not just a slogan - it's a mindset. You know me, you've worked with me. I don't have a problem being the pain in the ass if that's what it takes. Every run, I'm geared up. Every run, I'm checking the little stuff. Why? Because I'm modeling the behavior I expect from my team.

And in New York, we've got a bit of a unique situation. We've got people who follow us around and film us on runs - literally. I've seen videos posted to YouTube before the company even makes it back to quarters. I subscribe to those channels. We use that footage as training tools. Sometimes those videos catch things we miss in the moment, especially when we're task-focused. Like, maybe the entry team is squared away, full PPE, looking sharp. But just outside the tape line? There's a couple guys leaning in to see what's going on, and they're not wearing proper PPE. That's a reminder that as the officer, I'm not just watching my team - I've got to see the big picture. Sometimes that means stopping and saying, "Hey fellas, back it up." Sometimes, we have to put up our own hot zone tape to protect our own guys from themselves.

It all comes back to being consistent. Model good behavior. Always be watching. Always be coaching.

Now, one of the best parts of our culture is that we expect *everyone* to be a leader. Everyone's an instructor. That expectation alone shifts the mindset. And when you teach, you understand the material at a much deeper level.

Here's the twist - firefighters do one of the most hazardous jobs in the world, right? But public speaking? That's where a lot of people freeze up. They'll avoid it like the plague. But in our company, you can't get assigned until you complete your sign-off book - and that includes probably a hundred presentations. So like it or not, you've been teaching. You just didn't realize you were doing it.

Then we take it a step further. At the school, we've got a mentoring program. We match you with an experienced instructor. Everything's provided. The guys that dive into that? Their performance jumps off the charts. So if you've got high expectations - and a system to help people meet them - you get professional team members. That's the culture we're building.
Now, when it comes to leadership - what really builds cohesion and trust - I think it's simple: do everything you expect your people to do. I was a firefighter in this company before I was an officer. Some of it is

personality, sure, but some of it is just how we operate. Our team positions are entry, backup, decon... plus the officer. And I've heard the guys joke and call me "Entry 3" because, yeah, I'm going downrange in the suit too. I'm not afraid to pick up a tool. I'm in it with them. That matters. That builds trust. They know I'm not just barking orders - I'm right there beside them.

Now look, you asked about dealing with resistance? You've got to be more stubborn than they are. If there's a task nobody wants to do, sometimes the best move as an officer is to say, "Fine, I'll do it." And that shames them into doing it. Suddenly it's, "Wait, the officer's doing *my* job?" Yeah. Works every time.

But beyond that, you've got to be able to explain the *why*. Why are we doing this? Why does it matter? If it sounds like busy work, people resist. If they understand the goal, they buy in. But - every now and then - you've got to put your big boy pants on and say, "Because I said so." Sometimes, you have to *be* the officer. It's a blend. You explain when you can, you lead by example, and when needed, you insist as an officer.

And if you keep all that in balance? That's how you drive the culture forward.

Dave DiGregorio

It's funny, because every one of my six district teams was like a different set of kids - they all had their own personalities, even though they came from the same parent organization. Some of them, I didn't have to worry about. They were solid, always doing their job. Others, well, they were more like the problem children. And, again, because my office didn't choose the leadership, the teams did, sometimes it turned into a popularity contest.

I'd run into this from time to time, where some team leaders would choose people that were just going to make things easier for them. They didn't want to be challenged, so they picked people who wouldn't push them. This created problems in a couple of districts. I remember showing up to a district training once - sometimes I'd announce my visits, and sometimes I wouldn't - and I pull up around 11:30, and they're out for lunch. Fine, I wait. I wait until 1:00, 1:30, and they still hadn't returned.

So, I talked to the team leader and, after a bit of digging, I found out that he let everyone go for the day - no reason, nothing urgent. They were getting paid for a full day, but I was paying them to go home early. That was a huge issue.

So, I had to let the team leader go. Not from the team entirely, but he could no longer hold a leadership role. I couldn't have someone leading a team who wasn't going to hold everyone accountable. In the nine years I was there, I had to make that decision three times, with leaders who just weren't doing their job right. One of those was a training coordinator who put black powder into a Ramen instrument, closed the top, and set it off. There was even a video of the whole thing. Someone warned him about the danger, but he ignored it, and the glass exploded. One guy even got cut in the process. I had no choice but to remove him from the position.

Leadership is key. It sets the tone for the entire team. Take John Davine in District 4 - he and Tim Nelson had a fantastic team. No one questioned them. They did what they were supposed to do, no excuses. But in other districts, where the leader didn't demand as much, the team didn't give as much. If you don't expect much, you can't be surprised when they don't deliver.

Every district had its own personality. Some required a bit more attention, while others were more self-sufficient. District 4 and District 1 were easy; Mike Kelleher, as the team coordinator for District 1, had no issues - everything ran smoothly.

But let me tell you, we had this little mini-revolt when we had to let the team coordinator go. Some people didn't take it well. We had a few others involved who got written reprimands. Here's how it worked: their departments paid them for the drill, and we reimbursed the department. But now I had to go to their department chief and say, "You need to pull four hours off this person's time." You can imagine how that went over. It became a big deal, both for the legal implications and just the overall morale. But ultimately, it set the tone for the future - guys knew I wasn't going to tolerate any nonsense.

Sometimes, when you make a tough move, you have to insert yourself into the team for a while to get things back on track. That's a delicate balance, though, because you don't want to come off as a complete hardass. You don't want to be that person who's constantly cracking down, but when things go south, sometimes you have to step in and make it clear that things are going to change, and they're going to change now.

You're never going to be the most popular person in the room when you're a leader. Some people are going to love you, and others won't. You have to be okay with that and know that leadership involves making decisions that aren't always easy but are necessary.

I had a plaque on my desk that I always referred to when I met new team members: "I promise to treat you fairly, but I don't promise to treat you equally." I would tell them that right from the start. If you're someone who is hungry for knowledge and constantly pushing to improve, I'll give you every opportunity to learn. But if you're someone who just sits back, I'm not going to waste time giving you the same level of attention as the others. That's just how it works. You give me what I need, and I'll give you everything I've got.

Leadership is something that grows over time. I became a sergeant when I was 22, and I had no clue how to lead at that point. Suddenly, I was in charge of guys I used to hang out with. But over time, you learn how to navigate those challenges. The military definitely teaches you how to work through that process and develop those leadership skills, even when you feel like you don't have it all figured out. It's a skill that evolves with experience.

Dave Donohue

It all starts with recruitment, and the recruitment process should align with the culture of the organization. Once the right people are in place, the culture should naturally reflect the team they've built.

I take a page from Lenny Wilkens, the coach of the 1996 U.S. Olympic basketball team. This was the first year NBA stars were allowed to play, and Wilkens was asked how he planned to coach the team, which included legends like Michael Jordan, Magic Johnson, Larry Bird, and Scottie Pippen. His response was simple: "I'm going to give them the ball and let them play basketball." That's how I approach team leadership. I provide the team with the resources - equipment, personnel, training - and set the desired end state, and then I let them do what they do best.

It's important to recognize and embrace that change is constant. We can either fight it, adapt to it, or try to control it, but no matter what, it's going to happen. The key is to stay ahead of it, learn to adjust, and use it to our advantage.

Rick Edinger

The culture of your special operations team - whether it's hazmat, dive, or tech rescue - starts and ends with the culture of your organization. If you've got a crappy overarching organizational culture, it's going to be *really* tough to build something different and successful within your specialty unit.

That said, with strong leadership and some genuine passion, I've seen teams rise above that. When you get the right people together - folks who are committed, who care about the job, who foster a mindset of safety and excellence - you *can* build something great. I've seen special ops teams that lived and breathed their discipline. If they weren't out running EMS or fire calls, they were in the bays working on hazmat. Always learning. Always improving. That kind of culture of engagement and pride - that's what drives a team forward. But it takes the right people, and a ton of buy-in.

Still, your foundation matters. If the organization's core values don't support professionalism, accountability, and teamwork, it's going to bleed into everything - no matter how good your niche team wants to be.

As far as building cohesion and trust, it comes down to the basics:
- Be open and honest.
- Communicate clearly - especially across shifts and divisions.
- Explain the "why" behind decisions.
- Support your people, even when you have to tell them *no*.

That kind of transparency builds trust. And when you have people in leadership positions who've been around, who understand the job, and who've earned that trust - you're already halfway there. People need to know that their leaders will do the right thing, even when it's hard.

Now, how do you handle cultural challenges or resistance to change? That's the $64,000 question, right?

Here's how I've always seen it: if you've built a strong culture, you have to work constantly to maintain it. That means:
- Supporting your people.
- Staying consistent.
- Correcting bad behavior before it spreads.
- Reinforcing standards - even when it's uncomfortable.

I was lucky. I came up in an organization with a very strong, positive culture, built by our founding chief and carried on by the leaders who followed. That gave us a solid foundation. But once that starts to slip, once you start looking the other way, letting things slide - it's hard to claw your way back. It's a slippery slope.

Culture isn't something you set and forget. It's constant maintenance. That means explaining to folks *why* we do things a certain way, or *why* some things aren't allowed. Sometimes that means people leave. And that's okay. We had folks walk because they didn't like our standards. They didn't want to be held accountable to that level. But we weren't going to compromise who we were to keep them.

And the other key to sustaining culture? Consistency. If you've got one group operating under one set of expectations and another getting away with something else - it falls apart. The performance expectations and standards have to apply across the board.

Of course, you also have to adapt. Times change. People change. The folks we're hiring today aren't the same as the ones we hired 10 or 15 years ago. And our organization's evolved, for better or worse, to meet that. I don't agree with *every* change we've made - but I understand why we've had to make them.

Like tattoos. We used to have a strict no-visible-tattoo policy. Now, good luck hiring anyone without ink on their arms. That's just one example of how the world's changed - and how we've had to evolve with it.

John Esposito

Building a culture? It's important - *as long as it's the right culture.* Because, let's be honest, you can build a culture of suckage just as easily as you can build one of excellence. And that's not what we're after.

You could have a hazmat company where the running joke is, "They never call us for anything anyway," so it turns into, "Eh, whatever. Just look sharp when the chief walks by and know how to do this one thing - that's all that matters." Well, guess what? That's a culture too. It's just the *wrong* one.

What we need to be striving for is a culture of competence. Of professionalism. Of *excellence.* And I always say this - especially at promotion ceremonies - every single day, we have thousands of interactions with the public. Now, for us, it's just another call. But for the person on the other end of that interaction, that moment might stay with them for the rest of their life. Even if they don't remember your name or your face, they'll remember how they were treated.

So, what kind of impression do we want to leave behind? For me, it's simple: *Professionalism. Competence. Respect.* That's the culture I want. That's the standard. Know what you're doing, look like you know what you're doing, and treat people with respect while you do it. That's not too much to ask.

Now lately, I've heard people try to twist the words "culture" and "tradition" into something negative, like they're outdated or bad. But I don't buy that. Culture and tradition aren't dirty words - not if you've got the right kind. Different houses have different cultures. That's fine. They've got their own vibe, their own way of doing things. But at the end of the day, there's still accountability. There's still performance. They're still going to put the fire out. They might just do it a little differently.

The goal is to find that balance - preserve the pride, but keep it pointed in the right direction. So yeah, I'm all for building a strong culture. As long as it's built on the *right* things.

Brandon Fletcher

Fostering a culture, whether good or bad, always starts with leadership. And the best way to lead is by example. To foster a culture of safety, excellence, and continuous improvement, you have to walk the talk - there's no other way. I consider myself fortunate in a sense because I work with a small department/team. The culture of our team was shaped from the bottom up several years ago by members who believed that being a volunteer was never an excuse for mediocrity. Luckily, there was a strong buy-in from most of the department at the time, and what started as a movement became the department standard.

A lot of factors drive and affect a team or organization's culture. Sometimes, the right people come together at the right time, and great things happen by chance (luck). Other times, you have to get a little buy-in, get the wheels turning, and then keep pushing forward. We raised our standards and expectations, and along the way, we discovered something powerful: high standards attract high performers and help develop those who are searching for direction.

Letting the team have a voice in where we're headed, while still providing the necessary guidance and course corrections along the way, has been crucial. It's all about creating an environment where people feel invested in the process and know they're part of something bigger.

Chris Hawley

This is a real challenge, and it all goes back to selecting the right individuals. You need to pick people who already have the mindset to be driven, to want to excel, and to improve their craft. And honestly, that comes down to understanding the personality of the person you're bringing on. You've got to be able to recognize who has that intrinsic motivation, that desire to learn and grow.

One of the ways you can attract people and motivate them to be their best is by offering incentives. This was something I used to tell recruit schools - if you want to do the cool stuff, you go to the hazmat team. Sure, if you want to play with rocks, go to the USAR team, but if you want to work with chemicals, blow things up, and use cutting-edge tools, then hazmat is where you want to be. And here's the kicker: we'll send you all over the country to learn your craft, but you've got to prove that you're one of the good ones.

We're not sending just anybody to these advanced training courses. So, it's about building that desire in people to be the best and showing them the rewards that come with it.

This mindset also carries over when you look at hazmat techs transitioning into other roles. I've always believed that hazmat team members and hazmat officers make excellent fireground officers. The skills you learn in hazmat - especially decision-making, risk assessment, and thinking on your feet - translate well to the fireground. Hazmat officers are used to assessing a situation quickly, evaluating the risks, and making decisions fast. That same mindset is exactly what you need when you pull up to a fire scene. It's about risk vs. benefit. Firefighters are typically all about charging in and putting the wet stuff on the red stuff, and they do it without thinking through the risks. But if you take someone who's used to handling hazmat calls, they're going to think about those things right away, assess the situation quickly, and make decisions based on the risks at hand.

I had a conversation with a young lieutenant from a busy engine company once. We were prepping for an oleum training, and he was pushing back a bit, not fully understanding the gravity of the situation. So, I asked him, "Were you the officer on that McDonald's fire last week?" He said yes, and I said, "What did you have when you got there?" He paused, and I pointed out that when they showed up, the fire was through the roof. He didn't need to do much except jump off the rig, grab the line, and go in. But then I asked, "What do we know about McDonald's fires?" He didn't get it, so I said, "Two firefighters just died in a McDonald's fire in Houston because the HVAC system fell on top of them. Same situation - fire through the roof, HVAC loaded on top. You endangered your crew by going in without assessing the risk properly. There was no life hazard, and you risked everyone's life by charging in there."
This is the critical point I was making: just like with hazmat situations, you don't risk everything if there's no life hazard. It's about knowing when to take action and when to step back. And if you're a good hazmat tech, that decision-making ability will carry over to the fireground. Hazmat teaches you to assess the situation and make quick decisions, especially when there's no immediate life risk. Firefighting is no different. Being good at hazmat means being able to make better, faster decisions, and ultimately, that makes you a stronger officer - whether you're dealing with chemicals or a fire.

Ultimately, it's about giving your team the right incentives to improve, providing them with the right training, and making sure they have the skills to transfer across disciplines. If you can cultivate that mentality and mindset in your hazmat team, they'll be excellent in any other role they take on, whether it's as a fireground officer or beyond. It's all about making smarter decisions - faster - and ensuring that those decisions don't put lives at unnecessary risk.

Mike Hildebrand

I don't know everything. I've never pretended to. I'm usually not the smartest guy in the room. But if you've picked the right people and have given them solid training, the solution is already *in the room*. Especially when there's trust. If you've got 20 people on a team - each with a voice, each with respect - you're going to find the answer. And if you compared that to polling 100 people outside the team? I bet the outcome wouldn't be all that different.

Because it's not about the *quantity* of ideas - it's about the *quality* of the environment you create to hear them.

What matters most is *how* you elicit those ideas. If people know they won't be embarrassed or dismissed, they'll speak up. If they know you won't call their suggestion stupid, they'll offer what they're thinking. And that's the environment you need. Everyone contributes. Everyone's respected.

That principle's been at the core of my work for decades - especially through the Yvorra Leadership Development Foundation. We're now in our 37th year. We named the foundation after Jim Yvorra, who was killed in the line of duty in 1988. We traditionally ask each scholarship award recipient to write an essay on leadership. In 2014, I used software to scan nearly 200 What Leadership Means to Me essays for the most common words. And the word that showed up the most, over three decades?

Respect.

If you want to be a leader - if you want people to *follow* you - respect is non-negotiable. You have to earn it one person at a time. People have to respect your fairness. Your consistency. Your skills. Your work ethic. Cultural change is hard. But it starts with principles like that. I've always believed in Admiral Rickover's concept of total responsibility. If something goes wrong and everyone's pointing fingers, then nobody is really accountable.

I learned that lesson early. My dad spent 30 years in the same machine shop. I only saw him truly upset twice - once when his mother died, and once when a co-worker lost a finger in a machine. Even though it was the guy's own mistake, my dad felt *personally* responsible. He carried that weight.

That stuck with me.

In this line of work, responsibility isn't just about your own safety - it's about the safety of the person next to you. That's the beginning of building a real culture. From there, you grow into technical self-sufficiency.

That means if a highway's closed for five hours instead of one, it's probably not because the problem was too big - it's because we didn't have the right tools or people ready. We had to wait for someone from Acme Pump-Off Company to show up.

That becomes a political moment. The chief gets asked, "Why did this take so long?" And now you have a chance to say: "Here's the gap. We didn't have the expertise or capability *in-house.*"

That's when you start pulling bricks out of the wall.

I always go back to a story from a Navy aviator I know named Charlie Plumb. Charlie was shot down in May 1967 over North Vietnam. He spent nearly six years as a POW. He said for the first two years, he built a mental brick wall. Every problem in his life, every frustration, every failure - he turned it into a brick. "My parachute wasn't packed right." *Brick.* "I shouldn't have been on that mission." *Brick Brick.* "My wife left me." *Brick, Brick, Brick.*

But eventually, he realized that wall was keeping him trapped. So he started removing the bricks. One by one. Until he could breathe again. That's what it's like walking into a team with a toxic culture. It's like staring at a massive brick wall. You don't knock it down with a wrecking ball. You take out one brick at a time to rebuild the culture if it even had one to begin with. Sometimes you get lucky - maybe a new chief shows up with a fresh perspective and helps knock out a whole section of the wall. But more often than not, it's slow work taking out one brick at a time.

That's how you shift culture. That's how you build trust. That's how you lead.

Bob Ingram

To effectively lead and build a successful team, it's crucial to set clear standards for what is expected of your team members. These standards should be rooted in experience, AHJ policies, relevant standards, and laws. When establishing these expectations, ensure they are supported by credible sources and can be revised over time through research, diligence, and universal agreement. It's important to adhere to these standards yourself, as leading by example sets the tone for the entire team. Standardized discipline must be in place when these standards are not followed, ensuring consistency and accountability.

One of the keys to success is fostering a team environment that encourages collaboration and learning. Huddling as a team is essential, as no one person, not even the boss, knows everything. Everyone brings something valuable to the table, so it's crucial to assign projects to team members and give them ownership, support, and the resources they need to succeed. Avoid micromanaging - by giving them the space and guidelines, you allow them to develop their own creativity and problem-solving skills. This empowerment will not only boost their confidence but also enhance the team's overall performance.

As a leader, it's essential to keep an open mind. Make it a habit to listen carefully, digest the information, and then either ask more questions or provide a thoughtful response. Refraining from hasty reactions ensures that you understand the full picture before taking action. Listening should be inclusive - hear from everyone, not just a select few favorites. Doing so helps you gain diverse perspectives and ensures all voices are heard, creating a more cohesive and unified team.

When it comes to making informed decisions, doing your homework is non-negotiable. Gather as much information as possible, and ensure your research is comprehensive. Avoid the temptation to only collect positive data that supports your point of view. Balance your research by including data that might challenge your position and actively seek out alternative perspectives or data that refutes the negatives. This well-rounded approach will allow you to make better decisions and mitigate potential risks.

Safety should always be a primary focus, as it's a non-negotiable issue in any team environment. Safety-related data, including lawsuits or liability concerns, must be thoroughly considered as they can pose significant risks to your organization. Understanding the long-term nature of change is also vital - change often takes time, and you need to be prepared for the long haul. Finding funding for any proposed change is another essential step, as financial constraints may be the real reason why a change is not being considered or implemented.

By creating a culture of continuous learning, supporting your team's growth, and staying diligent in your research and decision-making, you lay the groundwork for a resilient, high-performing team. These principles, when followed, not only help you manage effectively but also create an environment where everyone feels valued, motivated, and equipped to contribute meaningfully.

Phil McArdle

As a leader, it's essential to encourage your personnel through personal example. Every team member needs to feel part of the team, and this is achieved through daily participation in tasks like equipment maintenance, in-house training, and recognizing performance excellence. Official recognition, such as unit citations for the entire team or individual acknowledgments, can go a long way. Having a designated area in the firehouse where reminders of team achievements are displayed is another great way to keep morale high. Sometimes, unique opportunities arise, such as special schools or events, where the team needs representation. By sending team members who exemplify the values you want to foster, you not only encourage excellence but also instill a sense of pride and commitment in the team.

Leading by example is one of the best approaches. Take, for instance, the concept of teaching outside the team. When you teach externally, bringing others along encourages their involvement and commitment. Supporting them by encouraging them to apply for teaching positions and introducing them to the people who make hiring decisions shows your support for their efforts. Additionally, offering to cover shifts or exchange tours to support those away teaching demonstrates your commitment to their success. Over time, as more members get involved in teaching, it becomes clear that it benefits everyone. Members gain new knowledge and skills that directly enhance their primary role in the Haz-Mat team. Even those who don't participate in teaching still benefit - filling staffing gaps and gaining shared knowledge, as well as earning overtime compensation.

The beginning stages are always the hardest. Since 1865, the FDNY has been deeply rooted in tradition, with many viewing firefighting as the sole focus, and everything else as secondary. What changes this mindset? Several factors must come together for a new initiative, like Haz-Mat teams, to earn respect.

First, you have to prove yourself every day. As the saying goes, "You're only as good as your last performance." Excellence in operations, where both your superiors and peers recognize your efforts, is vital in gaining admiration and respect. This means demonstrating your value in every operation by making others' jobs easier and showing initiative. Whether it's problem-solving or resolving issues efficiently and safely, your ability to manage the situation shows you're on top of things.

Another important aspect is teaching your peers new tactics and procedures to help make their jobs safer and more efficient. For instance, how do you encourage firefighters to wear Chemical Protective Clothing (CPC) when they're hesitant? By showing them why it matters. For example, if a firefighter becomes incapacitated at a scene while wearing bunker gear, and the Haz-Mat team is unavailable or delayed, the exposed firefighter needs immediate removal and treatment. Time is critical - they can't wait five minutes. The only option is someone who's already there, and that person might be you. No firefighter leaves another behind - it's simply not done. In that situation, the firefighter may not like the idea of wearing the PPE, but they will do it without hesitation to rescue their fellow firefighter.

In these moments, the importance of leading by example shines through. By demonstrating how necessary and effective your tactics are, you can shift the mindset of your team, helping them see the bigger picture and ensuring that safety and teamwork remain top priorities.

Adam McFadden

We foster a culture of safety excellence and continuous improvement by building and maintaining a tight-knit, highly specialized hazmat team within a much larger department. Out of nearly 3,000 members, only 60 to 70 are fully certified hazmat technicians. That exclusivity creates more than just a specialized unit - it cultivates a strong sense of identity, trust, and shared accountability.

Because our team is small, we know each other well. We train together regularly, learn from each other's experiences, and hold one another to the highest standards. That closeness translates into mutual respect, operational discipline, and a shared commitment to doing things right, every single time. Safety isn't just a checklist - it's part of our team's DNA. We pride ourselves on setting the standard for hazmat operations, constantly pushing to improve our skills, adapt to new threats, and support each other in high-risk environments.

Leadership plays a critical role in reinforcing this culture. Our team is guided by a core group of experienced, dynamic hazmat instructors who have been fully invested in the program for years. Their deep operational knowledge and lived experience form the backbone of our mentorship structure. They don't just teach - they lead by example.

This leadership model fosters accountability, respect, and cohesion. Newer members are brought into the fold with a clear understanding of what's expected and what it means to be part of this team. They learn directly from those who've been in the trenches - absorbing not just technical skills, but the mindset and professionalism that define a successful hazmat technician.

Ultimately, what makes our team effective isn't just what we know - it's how we work together. We train like we respond: as one unit, committed to each other's safety and to excellence in every operation. That culture is what allows us to meet the demands of high-stakes environments and come back stronger after every call.

Mike Monaco

I don't know if there's a perfect formula for fostering safety, but I *do* know that excellence and continuous improvement start with being open - open to feedback, and especially open to criticizing yourself.

The second people see that you're okay being wrong, that you don't pretend to be perfect, it shifts the dynamic. You create a space where honesty is safe. That kind of transparency encourages others to open up too - about what they don't know, what went wrong, and where they can get better. And when you've got people sharing that kind of information, everything improves: safety, performance, the whole team culture.

I've always tried to lead with honesty and a sense of approachability. It goes back to leading by example. If *you're* willing to be the first one to admit a mistake, the first one to adjust course, people see that. And eventually, they start doing it too.

Cultural change doesn't happen overnight. It's slow. Sometimes painfully slow. Sometimes it doesn't even happen at all. But if you stay consistent, if you keep modeling the behavior, and people start to see the benefits of that shift, change *can* happen. It just takes time - and someone willing to go first.

Chris Pfaff

We're all used to the traditional classroom method - death by PowerPoint. You know exactly what I'm talking about: a 40 to 48-hour lecture on Hazmat, whether it's operations-level, technician-level, or any variation in between. Someone just flips through slides, throwing in occasional war stories about how they handled a picric acid spill back in 1978. Great. Entertaining, maybe. But it doesn't really engage the learners.

Over my 15 years of instructing, I've definitely seen this shift. My first generation of students didn't just want to hear *what* to do; they needed the *why*. And honestly, that makes sense. When someone understands the "why," it clarifies the "how" so much better.

The new generation of learners - and there's nothing against them - has the attention span of a goldfish. It's just how we're all evolving. Social media and our rapidly changing environment have trained us to avoid boredom like the plague. If someone sits still for 30 seconds, guaranteed they're pulling out their phone. They're not going to sit staring at a blank wall; they're checking social media, news updates, or whatever else is happening in their world.

But there's a positive side to this too. Sure, the short attention span can be a drawback, but the incredible access to information is a huge advantage. Our predecessors back in the '70s and '80s, the ones who laid the groundwork for hazardous materials response - they didn't have this kind of resource. Today, we can literally watch a hazmat incident unfold live from across the country. With news reporters streaming on scene or someone posting videos to TikTok, responders can see calls happening in real-time, all while sitting in a recliner at their station.

A hazmat tech in Washington can watch and learn from an incident unfolding in Philadelphia, Florida, Texas, or Oregon. That is a massive shift in our culture, and honestly, it's an opportunity we've never had before.

Rob Rezende

We prioritize supporting our team in every way possible, whether it's through funding for training, covering backfill when personnel are away, or bringing in external courses that enhance our capabilities. But the heart of this process is requiring members to participate in teaching. Teaching not only boosts their confidence, it also sparks a sense of pride in the team, and that pride is contagious. It strengthens the bond within the team and ensures that the knowledge circulates throughout.

We also make it a point to highlight performers who go above and beyond, issuing citations to recognize their contributions. Recognition fuels motivation and shows that exceptional efforts are appreciated.

Every month, we host a "manager's meeting" with the Captains of the team. This meeting reinforces the idea that they are in charge of the future of the program. It gives them ownership and instills a sense of pride, which naturally trickles down to the crews. When leadership feels empowered, the entire team benefits.

I make it a point to sit down with one crew for lunch each month.

This gives me the opportunity to hear directly from the team - what's working, what's not, and what ideas they have. I make every effort to implement their suggestions when reasonable, so they see that their ideas aren't just heard - they matter. I live by the saying, "I hate ideas with no legs," and I work hard to give those ideas the legs they need, even if that means taking it up the chain.

Inaction is the killer of motivation. Even if the action is simply saying, "Sorry, we can't do that," it's better than radio silence. It shows that you're actively listening and considering every possibility.

Consistency in messaging is key. Change doesn't happen overnight, but if you stay consistent, more people will eventually adopt it. There will be times when you can say, "I told you so," but only if you've been steady and consistent all along. That's how trust and momentum are built within a team.

Bob Royall

What you just described really hits the mark because it all starts as a grassroots effort. It starts with that basic hazmat technician training. And here's where I was blunt with candidates for my team - I tell them straight up, if you don't have a passion for this job, you might as well pack your bags now. This work isn't for everyone. I'm looking for people who are going to commit, and when I say "commit," I mean it's not just about your shift - it's about going the extra mile. It's about outside training, sitting down after tough calls, and discussing how we did.

When you get back from a difficult job, you don't just walk away. You sit down around the coffee table, and that's where it begins. It's not done in a punitive way; it's about building relationships, creating a culture where everyone is aligned and thinking the same way. "What went well?" I ask. It's a simple question. Someone might say, "Well, I think so-and-so did great," but then you get someone who says, "Man, I really screwed up." And I'll ask, "Did anyone know?" "No." "Did anyone get hurt?" "No." "What are you going to do about it?" It's a learning process. You own it, you fix it, and you move on.

That's the way it works. After every incident, the Team will sit down once the rig is restocked and everyone's cleaned up. They discuss what went right, what went wrong, and we throw around ideas for improvement because every person has a voice on the team. It's not just about the boss calling the shots; everyone has a say. And here's the key - I've said this a thousand times, but it holds true: "It's easier to pull a rope than to push one." You get them going, and those values start to stick. It becomes second nature and a part of the Team's culture.

From an early stage, I was trained to ask my guys, "Hey, what did I miss? What's your take?" When you create an environment where everyone feels comfortable speaking up - not just complaining, and offering real input, that's when the magic happens. You might have someone from another shift, maybe even someone from a different background, who pipes up and says, "Hey, has anyone ever done this before?" And the guy who's been around the block, maybe as a side gig, will step in and say, "Hell yeah, I've done that, and we did it like this." Then, they start figuring it out together, "Did it work?" "Kind of, but let's tweak it and give it a shot."

I'll give you an example. One time we had an MC 331 that had a pressure relief device blow out over by the Astrodome, in a populated area. The truck pulled into a Sam's Club parking lot, and we had a vapor cloud coming out of the top. The whole team gathered upwind, and we all kind of looked at each other like, "Uh-oh, what now?" But then, one of our guys - a tank truck guy who had worked a side job out in the industry, steps up and says, "Hey, do we have any of those plumber plugs on the truck? Two-inch diameter?" By now, I'm all ears. He tells us, "We did this at the plant once while waiting to unload the truck." I'm thinking, "Alright, talk to me."

He goes on, "He took one of those plumber plugs, pop the silver disc out of the middle, and then we put an expandable gas plug in it. With a wrench, he can clamp it down and stop the vapor release. But it's going to be tough, and here's what we'll need." So, we had two means of egress from the top of the tank, a standby line to blow the vapor away. He managed to get that plug into the tank. As soon as we cranked it down, the vapor stopped.

Now, the job wasn't done. We still had to move the tank truck to a safer location in a rural area, so we could transload it. That's what I'm talking about - this guy wasn't a techie or a computer guy. He was a tank truck guy. But his hands-on experience, saved the day. That's the kind of problem-solving and innovation we need on a hazmat team. You don't always need high-tech solutions; sometimes, you just need someone who can think on their feet and make it work.

Bobby Salvesen

Back when I talked about personnel selection, this - *this* - is the long game version of that conversation. You can handpick people with great résumés and top-tier certifications, but if you're not building culture, you're not building a team.

And here's the truth any decent manager will tell you:
You can *make* people do things.
But you can't make people *want* to do them.

I've seen it firsthand. There were guys who wore the Hazmat patch, clocked in, did their shift, and went home. As far as I'm concerned, they weren't hazmat techs - they were just *on* the hazmat team. They weren't bad people, but they weren't invested. They were there for the paycheck, for the assignment, for whatever.

Then there were the *other* guys - the ones who left the firehouse and went home to read hazmat books, who talked hazmat on their days off, who *lived* it. Those were the ones who quietly became the North Stars of the company. The ones others looked to, learned from, and tried to emulate.

Because leadership isn't about rank. It's about mindset. It's about consistency. It's about *culture*.

And culture? That starts at the top.

Captains. Lieutenants. Officers. If you're leading a hazmat team, you don't get to pick your days. You *have* to walk the walk - not just most of the time - all the time. When you're in the firehouse, you're in *go* mode. No cruise control. No half-stepping. You set the tone.

And here's the thing: culture is the most *consequential* component of any hazmat company. You can make a few bad calls on personnel. You can recover from that. But if your culture is garbage? So is your team. No skillset in the world can patch over a toxic atmosphere.

So be ruthless about it. If someone is poisoning the culture - cut them loose. Build your team with people who *want* to be there. Who care. Who carry themselves in a way that others want to follow.

Because when you do that?
You get trust.
You get cohesion.
You get flexibility.
And most importantly - you get a team that can overcome things that *shouldn't* be overcome.

If you're building a hazmat team - or stepping in to lead one - culture should be your #1 focus. Without it, everything else crumbles. With it, you can build something exceptional.

Doug Schick and Mark Zilch
Doug:

So much of it comes down to luck - if you're fortunate enough to land a solid core group of people, a lot of this stuff just starts to take care of itself.

When Mark was on the hazmat company, you could feel it. You can hear it even now when he talks - he brought energy, he brought curiosity. He'd come in excited about something new, something going on in the field, and that enthusiasm makes the rest of the team want to know more too. That kind of interest is contagious.

As far as safety goes, a lot of it is just drilling the fundamentals. Constantly reviewing chemical and physical properties, talking about what we need to be worried about, what kind of protection a particular substance requires. Going over things like, "How do we find the IDLH? What does that number mean for us in terms of PPE or operational decisions?" That kind of regular review makes all the difference.

And leadership - real leadership - starts with not asking anyone to do something you wouldn't do yourself. That's something I've always tried to live by.

When I got to hazmat as captain, I wasn't coming in with years of company-level hazmat experience. I'd taught hazmat, I had a physics degree, and I'd always been interested, but I was never a hazmat firefighter. So I had some catching up to do. And I worked hard - reading, listening, going to conferences - and I'm still learning every day.

I think the guys notice that. And I hope it encourages them to do the same. I tell my officers all the time - no joke - "You should be listening to The Hazmat Guys podcast. It's an easy way to pick up a ton of solid info while you're driving." I send out links to good books, videos, anything I think is valuable. Just trying to model the kind of engagement I hope rubs off on them.

Mark:
Yeah, 100%. Chief does a phenomenal job of modeling that commitment and curiosity. Since he's been here, the hazmat teams have never been more cohesive. The interest in training, in going to conferences - it's never been higher. That's leadership, plain and simple.

And like you said, that modeling applies to safety, too. People pick up on that. When the person in charge is clearly invested, it sets the tone for everyone else.

Doug:
And there's something to be said, too, for treating people with respect. Especially in hazmat, where we can't really *make* anyone do anything. If I go out and demand something - "You have to do this" - I guarantee half the guys will go, "Well, I probably *would've* done it, but now that you're telling me I *have* to, forget it."

It's tough sometimes. Sometimes people just don't want to be there. Sometimes you don't win that fight. Usually, you can make some kind of progress with people. But sometimes, no matter what you do, it's just not going to happen. That's why I always tell new officers: don't let the position go to your head.

Just because you've got more time on the job than everyone else doesn't mean you know more than *everyone.* It's possible that you might know more than *any one person,* sure - but you don't know more than the *team.* I try to stay open. If someone sees something, has an idea - speak up.

I loved what you and Bobby used to do with the hazmat huddles. That's exactly what we should be doing. Bring everyone in, talk it out: "Here's what I think we should wear - what do you guys think? Are we all comfortable with that?" Especially for the people who are going in, it's about trust and communication. That's how you build a strong, safe team.

Jason Zeller

To foster a culture of safety, excellence, and continuous improvement within our hazmat team, it was all about setting a standard that was non-negotiable.

Safety was never just a set of rules - it was a mindset. From day one, I made sure every team member knew that their personal safety - and the safety of those around them - was paramount. It wasn't just about wearing the right gear or following protocol - it was about taking responsibility for each other and staying vigilant at all times. Safety was ingrained in everything we did, from training to real-world responses, and that mentality was passed down through every mission we executed.

Excellence was more than just meeting expectations - it was about exceeding them, day in and day out. We built a culture where mediocrity didn't have a place, because when you're dealing with hazmat and WMD threats, there is no room for error. Each individual was challenged to push beyond their comfort zone and constantly evaluate how they could improve.

We held each other to high standards, and we took pride in being the best trained, best prepared, and most adaptable team in the field. Excellence was contagious - it started with leadership, but it spread to every team member who understood that excellence was a team effort, not an individual one.

Continuous improvement was driven by two things:
1. Never accepting that we had "arrived"
2. Recognizing that there was always more to learn

We didn't wait for the next big incident to identify weaknesses - we proactively sought out ways to sharpen our skills. Whether it was through lessons learned after an exercise, debriefing after an operation, or attending advanced training, we were always striving to be better.

That mindset of improvement made us not only reactive to incidents but prepared for any scenario, even those we hadn't encountered yet. It was a constant evolution, and everyone was onboard because we knew it wasn't just about being good at our jobs - it was about being ready to save lives, our own included.

Building trust and cohesion within a team - especially one that operates in high-stress, high-stakes environments - comes down to one thing: being there with your people, not just in command, but in the trenches with them.

In my experience, real leadership isn't about sitting behind a desk or handing down orders from a comfortable office chair. It's about leading from the front, being in the mix, and showing your team that you're willing to get your hands dirty alongside them. Whether it's responding to a hazardous materials threat or handling any other critical mission, you lead by example - period.

Effective leadership is about setting the tone, creating an environment where every person on the team knows they're valued, and no one feels isolated. My team didn't need just commands - they needed to know we were all in it together. I got down and dirty with them, working side-by-side, making decisions on the fly, and being present in every moment, no matter how grueling.

When you put yourself on the line with your team, you show them that you care about them as much as the mission itself.

It's also about transparency and trust. I've always said, *"You're only as strong as the weakest link,"* and when you lead, it's your responsibility to strengthen every link in the chain.

My leadership style was built around:
- Understanding the strengths and weaknesses of my people
- Being their sounding board when needed
- Pushing them to be their best - not because I expected it, but because I believed in their potential

Trust was built through consistent action, not just words. When the situation was chaotic, they knew they could rely on me - and I knew I could rely on them.

Creating that culture of trust and cohesion isn't about making everyone feel comfortable - it's about pushing everyone to be better, together. When we were out there responding to high-risk scenarios, no one was too good to take on any task. We all had each other's backs. And when you show your team that you're willing to stand in the storm with them, they'll follow you into anything.

Overcoming resistance to change is never easy, but it's also one of the most important lessons I've learned as a leader.

When people are comfortable in their ways, they naturally resist the unknown. I get it - change can be intimidating, especially in a high-stakes environment like ours, where the job requires us to perform under extreme pressure.

But here's the truth:

If we're not evolving, we're standing still. And in our line of work, standing still isn't an option.

I've always believed in leading by example. If I wanted my team to embrace a new strategy, technology, or training method, I had to be right there in the trenches with them. I wasn't going to ask them to do something I wouldn't do myself.

That meant taking the same tough training, participating in the same grueling debriefs, and facing the same challenges head-on. If I was going to ask my team to trust me in the chaos of a real-world response, I had to first earn that trust by showing up and putting in the work every single day.

When resistance came up - because it always does - I didn't shy away from it. I made it a point to:
- Sit down with my people
- Listen to their concerns
- Explain the 'why' behind the change

We all knew that the mission was our top priority, but sometimes, that mission required us to change how we operated. If I couldn't clearly articulate why this change mattered and how it would make us better, faster, and safer, then I wasn't doing my job as a leader.

But even more than that, I reminded them of our purpose:

We're in the business of saving lives.

And in order to do that effectively, we had to constantly grow and adapt. Change wasn't about adding complexity - it was about simplifying our response, improving our efficiency, and staying ahead of the curve.

Every time I saw someone hesitate, I knew it was just fear of the unknown, and all it took was showing them that they weren't alone in the process.

At the end of the day, overcoming resistance to change is about trust. It's about showing the team that you're not asking them to do something for your benefit, but for theirs - for the mission - for the people whose lives depend on us. And that's what made it worth it.

The growth, the change - it's all just part of a bigger picture. We don't just adapt for the sake of change; we adapt because lives are on the line, and that's a responsibility we can never take lightly.

When the team saw that I was right there beside them, pushing myself to grow and evolve just like they were, they trusted the process.

We turned resistance into momentum.

And that's the kind of change that moves mountains.

Dan Baker

I realize a lot of what I'm sharing here comes from the unique reality we face as a statewide team, but hopefully many of these insights can translate effectively to other teams. For us, networking is one of the most crucial things we do. Without solid working relationships with the fire departments and local hazmat teams we serve, all our capabilities would essentially be wasted - and here's why.

In a home-rule state, nobody is obligated to use State resources, and we generally have no inherent jurisdiction as an AHJ (there are exceptions, but that's a whole other conversation). If we're called into an incident and local responders either don't know us or don't fully trust us, they can - and sometimes do - send us home, even if the local hazmat team (usually county-based) initially requested us. Building strong, trusting relationships with local fire chiefs beforehand is absolutely critical to our success; if the local chief isn't comfortable, we simply can't operate.

Relationships have to be built long before the tones ever drop, and we're fortunate because our training mission gives us plenty of opportunity to do exactly that. Nothing makes us happier than NOT being called to an incident - because that usually means the local responders are well-trained and prepared (often thanks to us). But when we do get called, arriving in a familiar place, knowing the faces, makes everything easier.

If we show up on scene already knowing the hazmat team leader, the local fire chief, and even the towing company, we can generally predict a successful outcome.

Networking with other agencies isn't just useful - it's mandatory for our team, because we're almost always operating under someone else's authority. Through our training programs, we actively encourage our instructors to facilitate discussion-based learning, creating opportunities where knowledge flows both ways: our customers learn from us, and we absolutely learn from them.

Let me give you a perfect example from February of 2025. We had a propane bobtail rollover incident, and networking was incredibly valuable. The county hazmat team requested us to help out a small local fire department dealing with what was essentially a once-in-a-career event for them - but for us, it was the seventh bobtail rollover that year. I happened to be nearby, so I was the first on scene our team.

Immediately, I recognized the Battalion Chief, and he and I go way back, so the rapport was instant. The rest of the county team members already knew me, and the local fire chief turned out to have attended one of my classes years ago when I was still regularly teaching on the road. So, from the moment we arrived, we were all automatically on the same page - a huge benefit given the complexity and expected duration of the incident.

It also helped immensely that we had a strong relationship with the towing contractor who we've worked alongside multiple times. They're top-notch, equipped with solid gear, and thoroughly understand the nuances of working in a hazmat environment.

Here's how networking genuinely paid off on that job - the incident didn't go smoothly. In fact, pretty much everything we initially tried failed, and the situation dragged on through three full operational periods before we finally got things under control. But here's the key: nobody got frustrated or angry. Because we all trusted each other, the local chief felt confident in our competency, recognizing that the situation itself was incredibly difficult - not that we were messing it up. Despite the prolonged, challenging incident, there wasn't one tense moment due to egos or personalities. And ultimately, that kind of trust and teamwork significantly contributed to a successful outcome - even if it did take a whole day longer than we hoped.

Mike Callan

For me, working in this field has gone through three phases. The first phase was when I didn't know much, and people like Jerry Gray from San Francisco Hazmat were giving me valuable information. Jerry was the first guy who handed me compatibility charts. He had a facepiece crack while he was working on a tank car, and it was a game-changer. The suit worked, but the facepiece didn't. That's how networking saved lives. He told us, "Here's 2,500 feet in all directions," because the first DOT guidebook had a radius of just 750 feet, and the second one increased it to 1,250 feet. Well, I can tell you what happened - the first guide said 750, and something went off at 900 feet. Networking at that level saved us life-saving tips. That was a major turning point.

Then, the third phase came, and I haven't fully lived it yet, but I see it all the time now. It's when you're involved in a major incident, and you're learning from it. I watched the fires in Lahaina, for example, and I knew the area well. It was devastating, and when any firefighter sees a fire coming at them, especially a fire like the one in California where the flames can move horizontally at 80 miles an hour, you know there's nothing you can do to stop it. All you can do is try to save as many lives as possible. We often say it's about being prepared, but really, you're preparing for something that might never happen in your lifetime - a one-in-seven-thousand-five-hundred-million-year event. What are you really prepared for? You can train, but when it comes to such a rare event, it's about saving lives, plain and simple.

I think firefighting and emergency services in general are reactive but also proactive after the fact. We learn from the incident, and we try to be better prepared next time. But the public doesn't always let us be as proactive as we need to be. I had a situation where I was arguing with a staffer from Connecticut, the top guy in the state, about these blue plugs for propane tanks. The idea was to prevent leaks when tanks tipped over. I kept pushing for it, explaining how important it was, and he didn't get it. Then, tragically, two kids died because of a propane tank leak. After that, the guy understood, but it took a tragedy for him to see the value. That's another example of the importance of networking - because when we all know each other, we can get things done quicker. But when we can't agree on something, it can lead to trouble, and sometimes it means apologizing.

It's a good example of how networking helps when you're in a crisis. You can pick up the phone and talk to people you've worked with before. I've spent years doing hazmat classes all over California, meeting people, building connections. Most of the people I worked with during the "heyday" of hazmat training are retired now, but back then, it was a great time to build relationships. When things got tough, I knew I could call someone like Bill Hand. Bill had seen so much as a hazmat specialist, working for Max McCray, who actually helped Houston start their first hazmat team. Bill was one of the go-to people we all trusted. And those are the connections that helped us all get better.

I met people like McGarry, Leahy, Anders, and Dave Anderson - guys who investigated Waverly, Tennessee. I spoke with people who were there during the Kingman, Arizona, incident. These are the people who shaped the future of hazmat response, and when you've worked with them, you understand the depth of their knowledge.

It's through networking that you get to hear the stories that textbooks don't capture. And it's through those conversations that you pick up the real-world lessons that make you better at what you do.

Networking is our language. We don't speak in theoretical terms - we speak from experience. You can read an article about fog and think, "Oh, they used a perfect application of fog," but chances are, they went in with a straight stream first. That's the reality they don't write about in magazines. We don't often share the mistakes we made; instead, we share the lessons learned. That's what networking is all about - it's sharing what worked, what didn't, and making sure that the next person doesn't make the same mistake.

And even when you're in a regional area, networking is critical. You can be dealing with a situation, and it's someone you met at a conference who can help guide you through it. That's the value of these connections - they make you stronger, and they make your response faster and more effective. So, yeah, networking is everything. It's what has allowed us to be where we are today in hazmat response, and it's what will keep pushing us forward as we face new challenges in the future.

John Cassidy

Networking is more than just shaking hands or swapping patches. One of the biggest values of networking is the "phone-a-friend" aspect. And honestly? That can be the difference between success and failure when it really counts.

But here's the catch - it can't just be *my* network. It can't be, "Oh, you have to talk to John, but only I know John," or "You need Bob? You've got to go through me." No. If I know someone who can help, I'm connecting you directly. That's my team. That's our team. And the strength of that team comes from everyone having access to those same resources - not gatekeeping them.

At the school, it's the same idea. Every PowerPoint, every lesson plan, every document - hundreds of hours of content - it's all available. It doesn't belong to *me*. It belongs to the school. It's for *everyone*. That openness is what builds a strong team.

To me, one of the most important marks of leadership is this: make yourself unnecessary. If a hazmat run only goes well because I'm there? I failed as an officer. If a student only gets it because I'm the one teaching it? I failed as an instructor. Same goes for parenting - if your kid can't function without you, then what did you really teach them? Success is making yourself obsolete. That's leadership. That's legacy.

So yeah, networking is critical - but you've got to bring your team into that network with you. You've got to share the connections and the knowledge, not hoard them.

And we back that up with action. One way we do that is through shared resources - like our Google Drive. We've got a whole drive dedicated to lithium-ion response. It's not hidden. It's not locked.

It's open nationally. If someone has the link, they've got access. We learned hard lessons dealing with the rise of mobility device fires, and instead of letting other departments reinvent the wheel, we're handing them the playbook.

People are incredibly grateful. I've had folks reach out and say, "I had no idea this even existed - this just saved us months of headaches." That's the power of sharing what you've got.

Whether it's a cloud drive, a penciled-in note, a group text, or a formal sit-down class - leverage the tech, share the info, get it out there. We even bring that mindset into our trainings. In our hazmat technician school, every class runs a big WMD scenario in the subway. That's built in - it's not a luxury, it's the standard. And because it's part of the program, we can invite outside partners - NYPD, the Medical Examiner's Office, FBI, whoever - to train with us.

That kind of cross-training? That pays off on the street. And it's not just about checking boxes. It's about building real working relationships that matter when the call comes in.

Dave DiGregorio

Networking has always been huge for me, and I've said it a thousand times: I'm not too proud to steal ideas. If someone has a great concept, I'll take it. I'm not the be-all and end-all; I only know what I know. So, if I can learn from someone else, I'm all in. It's that mindset of constantly being open to new ideas and learning from those around you.

One of the best examples of this is when I learned about lithium batteries. I had no idea it was an issue until I talked to you guys. And then it hit me - some of the fires we were dealing with in Massachusetts were related to lithium batteries. That realization was huge. It's like that with so many things - people have different focuses and priorities depending on where they are, and you can learn so much from them. Whether it's someone across the state or across the country, you're always going to pick up something valuable.

When I need help, I don't hesitate to reach out. Whether it's calling you, Christina, or someone else, I'll ask, "Hey, have you seen this before?" It's vital to have that network. And it's not just about having a broad network within the hazmat community - it's about interagency cooperation. I still teach classes on that today. You can't do it alone. Hazmat doesn't operate in isolation. You're dealing with law enforcement, the fire department, public works - so many different agencies. The importance of networking can't be overstated.

You brought up a good point about running a conference. If you're only using internal resources and not bringing in outsiders to teach some of the classes, you're missing out. What are you really learning? You're either repeating what everyone already knows, or if they don't know it, then there's a bigger issue. You need new perspectives, new insights, and you can only get that from bringing in people with different experiences.

Looking back on my time in hazmat, I did a lot of networking, but now, in my new role, I'm realizing just how much more there is out there. For instance, disaster medicine. As a PA, I never got formal disaster medicine training. But now, I'm teaching doctors from places like the UAE, Saudi Arabia, and Indonesia. They never learned about CBRN (chemical, biological, radiological, and nuclear) either, and I'm passing that knowledge on to them. It's wild because even those of us in the military didn't get much exposure to CBRN when we were in.

One thing I emphasize in my hospital assessments is the importance of coordination. How often are hospitals working with the fire department, law enforcement, or even public safety teams? Because when disaster strikes, your small security team won't be enough to manage the chaos. Hospitals need to have those connections established long before the situation arises. Coordination with local agencies like the sheriff's department or police is critical. It's something I always bring up because it's such a vital piece of the puzzle.

Another thing we did, especially when we sent people to conferences like in Baltimore, was require them to teach something they learned when they came back. They weren't just going to go to a conference and come back with nothing. They had to bring something back to the team - whether it was a presentation, a new concept, or a specific skill. And better yet, they had to put together a full training session to pass it on to the rest of the team. That way, everyone benefited, and it kept the learning going even after the conference ended.

Dave Donohue

It's incredibly important. There's an old Amish saying, "The more I learn, the dumber I am," and I think that rings true in hazardous materials just as much as it does anywhere else. The more I learn, the more I realize how much I don't know. Networking both within and outside our discipline helps me identify what I - and the team - are missing and gives us the chance to stay ahead of the Dunning-Kruger curve, where overconfidence can sometimes lead to a lack of awareness.

Locally, this involves things like cross-training, creating opportunities for friendly competition, and offering ride-along experiences. These activities help broaden perspectives and improve the team's skill set. On a broader scale, I try to take advantage of any opportunity to learn from others. When I go on vacation, I often visit different departments to meet with their teams and, when possible, ride out with them. The goal is to learn from their experiences, understand their protocols, and exchange valuable insights. The return on investment for this is twofold: I gain valuable lessons learned, and it opens up more training opportunities for both myself and the team.

I've also reached out on scene to friends in the industry who have faced similar incidents, asking for their advice and perspectives. In return, I've collaborated with several departments to help them develop protocols, make planning recommendations, and serve as a sounding board for their ideas. It's a mutual exchange that benefits everyone involved and helps us all improve our practices and response capabilities.

Rick Edinger

You can't safely or effectively respond to hazmat incidents by just sitting back and waiting for the tones to drop. Eventually, something's going to bite you. You've got to stay plugged in. You've got to know what's out there.

You and I have been around long enough to remember when there were only a handful of hazmat conferences. There were just a few places to go, a couple of big-name events that people would attend every year. I used to manage the Virginia Hazmat Conference, and that was one of them. But now? There's conferences everywhere. There's podcasts, webinars, online trainings, newsletters - you name it. The volume of information out there is massive.

Now, sure - not all of it is good. That's part of the problem. But there is absolutely no excuse anymore for not knowing what's going on in the industry. Whether it's emerging threats, new equipment, PPE changes, or tactics, there are experts out there talking about it. You just need to find the voices you trust and stay engaged.

Back in the day, if you wanted to stay current, someone had to write a check and maybe only two or three people could get sent to a conference. That was your pipeline to new info. But today? There's no barrier to staying informed. You've got a cell phone. Make a call. Network. Share information. Keep those connections alive.

In Virginia, the state hazmat conference is where everybody came together once a year. The seasoned folks came back year after year, and the new people were brought in and shown the ropes. It wasn't just about the sessions - it was about keeping your network up to date, swapping contact info, sharing lessons learned.

At the regional level, we had morning conference calls between the big departments in the Richmond metro area. Right after shift change, the shift commanders and battalion chiefs from each agency would jump on a call. These days it's probably video, but back then it was a phone line. We'd share what happened overnight - fuel spills, significant calls, who's doing drills, who's out of service. It was basically real-time situational awareness across the region, all within a 24-hour window.

And that ties right into what we've been talking about - "phone a friend" isn't just a saying. It's a system. Between conferences, podcasts, morning calls, and good old-fashioned phone trees, there are a thousand different ways to stay connected.

If something big is breaking - say there's a major East Palestine-type incident - you can tune in almost immediately and start gathering the information you need. You don't have to wait until the next conference to find out what happened. You can be proactive.

We also made it a point to maintain strong relationships with subject matter experts, especially at the state level. We'd bring them in periodically for training - maybe on drill days, or for our annual three-day full-scale drill where we'd get the whole team together. We'd invite people in to run stations, deliver targeted training, or work a scenario with us. We'd also tap into our LEPC, or bring in facility reps, depending on the topic.

Because look, it's like the old saying: *Don't meet the critical people you need at 3 a.m. in the pouring rain.* Meet them beforehand. Build those relationships ahead of time. That way, when something goes wrong, you've already got the network in place.

We had a large DuPont plant in our first-due area - one of the major global producers of nylon, Tyvek, Kevlar - you name it. And we worked closely with them. Their safety teams, fire brigade, our department - we were on the same page. If something was happening, we shared info back and forth. That relationship made us better. It was part of the foundation of how we operated.

Bottom line: networking isn't optional. It's a core function of this job. You've got to build those bridges before you need them.

John Esposito

Its importance can't be overstated - relationships are everything.

Several years back, during my foamy class - 2010, maybe 2011 - I was either a battalion chief or a newly promoted deputy, and General Stanley McChrystal came in to speak to the entire fire staff. And I'll never forget what he said. He started off with: *"Relationships aren't everything. They're the only thing."*

And that line stuck with me. Because it's true. When something goes sideways, when you need help fast, it shouldn't be a cold call - it should be a quick, easy phone call to someone you already know. That kind of connection can calm things down, cut through the noise, and solve problems before they escalate.

We saw it play out for years in our relationship with the cops. Minor issues ballooned into major ones - *not* because of the problems themselves, but because the relationships weren't there. If it's "Hey, this is Chief So-and-So from such-and-such," that's one thing. But if it's "Hey Bob, it's John - we've got a thing," it's smoother. That familiarity makes a huge difference. Especially at the scene of an emergency. Everything's easier when you're not starting from scratch.

And I'll admit - it's still something I need to work on. Do I have the Chief of Department from NYPD in my phone? Yeah, we talk. There are other agencies where I've got good contacts, and some where I don't. It's something we should all strive for.

And on that note - not for the book - but I'll just say it: our new commissioner? Fucking fantastic. If he doesn't know someone, he *wants* to. He makes the effort to learn what they need, what he can do for them, what they can do for us. He's always asking, "So what's going on with X?" And next thing you know, he's picking up the phone, making it happen.

He's got this great blend of curiosity and diplomacy. I remember once, I was going into a meeting with a group from City Hall. He says, "I want you to be nice." I told him I'd *try*. And he looks at me and goes, "No - I want you to do more than try." And we're the same age, but in that moment, I felt like my father was giving me a lecture.

But that's him. That's why he's been so successful - not just as a commissioner, but as a businessman too. He's got people skills. He knows how to play the long game. Meanwhile, I've got that fireman in me - I still want to take a shot at someone now and then. But he won't, because he's thinking five moves ahead.

And that's the lesson - build the relationships. Protect them. Because when the time comes, they're not a luxury. They're the whole game.

Brandon Fletcher

I can't overstate how important networking is in every discipline, especially in hazmat! Most hazmat teams don't respond to calls every single day, so having a strong network of people you can communicate with and learn from is absolutely essential to growing your own knowledge base. General James Mattis once said, "If you haven't read hundreds of books, you are functionally illiterate and you will be incompetent, because your personal experiences alone aren't broad enough to sustain you." This same principle applies to networking - your personal experiences just aren't broad enough to sustain you in the long run.

I'm lucky enough to have one of my best friends on Toledo Fire Rescue's HazMat team. We both geek out over hazmat and tech rescue topics, and we're constantly bouncing ideas off each other. We've implemented each other's ideas in our own departments, which has been hugely beneficial. I also work at the CDP in Anniston, which connects me with a wide network of instructors from all over the country with various backgrounds and experiences. This has given me countless opportunities to learn and collaborate, and I always make it a point to seek out networking opportunities when attending classes.
I encourage my students to stay in touch with one another and share their own hazmat experiences. This ongoing exchange of lessons learned is invaluable. Through all of these connections and opportunities, I've gained more tips and knowledge than I can count - and I'm able to pass all of that back to my department to improve our work and responses.

Networking isn't just about who you know - it's about constantly learning, sharing, and growing together.

Chris Hawley

That's an incredible story! It really highlights the value of having the right contacts and the importance of networking in this field. You can know all the theory and the technical details, but having someone to reach out to who's an expert in a specific area is a game changer. I mean, that's how I was able to help someone when they called me asking about mercury. I didn't know a whole lot about it, but I knew exactly who to call - Bob. He's one of the smartest guys out there, and he's got a brain full of knowledge that you just can't find in textbooks.

When I told this person to call Bob, I warned them - clear your calendar, because Bob can talk for hours but it will be valuable. Sure enough, they came back to me a few days later, saying they had spent six hours on the phone with him and now knew everything there was to know about mercury. That's the kind of expertise that's invaluable in this line of work. I can't tell you how many times Bob helped us out through a career of responses. He not only helped us out but he was always willing to help others who needed information.

But that's why it's so important to have those kinds of connections. The ability to refer people to the right experts can make you look like a hero, even if all you did was make a quick phone call. In this case, I looked like the guy who knew how to handle mercury issues because I had Bob's number and knew exactly who to turn to. That's the kind of networking that's invaluable, and it shows just how powerful having the right contacts in your corner can be.

It's the same with conferences. You can get amazing training, but the networking and connections you make are just as important. The National Fire Academy is great for building skills, but conferences give you the chance to meet people from all over, learn from their experiences, and build relationships that can help you out in the future. You never know when you're going to need to reach out to someone for that one piece of expertise that can turn a situation around. And having those connections can make all the difference in the world.

Mike Hildebrand

The best-in-class teams? You know them when you see them. Just like in the business world - there are good companies, and then there are companies everyone admires. Companies people *wish* they worked for. They've got something extra. And a lot of times, we joke about it, but the examples are right there in front of us.

Take McDonald's.

Say what you want about the food, but they're a textbook example of a *system-dependent organization*. They built an empire on consistency. How do you make a cardboard-tasting rubbery hamburger *taste exactly the same* 12 billion times in a row? You build a *system*. They've got Hamburger University. They train their managers with step-by-step precision. Pictures of food on the cash register keyboard so you don't even need to read. Their whole recruitment and training process is designed to create a culture - and it *works*.

You don't have to like the food to admire the model.

And here's the truth - it's a lot easier to *build* a new team from scratch than it is to take over an old one that's in need of a culture reset. Anyone who's ever been promoted into a broken unit knows what I'm talking about.

We've all seen it in the fire service. Some companies become magnets for negativity. The same grumpy, toxic people end up under the same officers, and they sit around, wallowing in their misery. Meanwhile, two shifts over, you've got a crew that's laughing, getting the job done, learning new things and sharing the information, and hanging out after work. They know each other's kids' names. They have *fun*. Same department. Same trucks. Same calls.

What's the difference?

Leadership.

That one officer - that one senior firefighter - set the tone. They built the culture. Every shift is its own universe, no matter how much we try to manufacture consistency at the academy.

And when it's done right? It becomes *elite*.

Look at Rescue Companies in FDNY. You don't just apply. You have to be *invited*. And who decides? The company officer. That officer holds the cards. They know who's coming in and who isn't. And I promise you, they're not picking based on resume padding. They're looking at attitude. Reputation. Grit. They're picking the folks who get *stuff* done.

These are the people who'd succeed no matter where you dropped them. Give them a college to run, they'd make it great. Give them a garbage company, it'd be the best-run operation on the block. It's *who* they are.

Because elite teams - whether it's Rescue 1 in Manhattan or a startup hazmat unit in the suburbs - they all have the same thing at their core: leadership, culture, and people who give a damn.

Bob Ingram

Networking, in my experience, is critical for building the "elite" capability of a hazmat team. No single agency encounters every conceivable type of incident with any regularity. In many cases, other teams have already dealt with similar situations and may have developed different, effective responses.

To build a stronger, more knowledgeable team, it's important to commit to involvement at higher levels, outside of your own jurisdiction. Participating in the IAFC's Hazmat Committee provides valuable opportunities to collaborate and learn from others in the field. Joining NFPA and other standards organizations that develop the guidelines in your mission space also helps keep your team aligned with the latest industry standards.

Additionally, leveraging social media platforms that share hazmat information is an excellent way to stay informed. Podcasts like the HM Guys, or HM community groups on LinkedIn and Facebook, provide real-time insights and facilitate connections with other professionals.

Engaging with and contributing to professional magazines that cover hazmat incidents can further broaden your understanding of emerging trends and best practices. Attending hazmat conferences is another essential way to stay current, allowing you to learn from other teams and experts while expanding your professional network.

Phil McArdle

Haz-Mat teams are a vital but small part of the fire service community, and they don't operate in isolation. They regularly interact with other teams, learning from one another and sharing knowledge. Every time team members attend a school, they have the opportunity not only to learn from the instructors but also from their fellow students. Each team has its own unique characteristics and experiences, offering valuable lessons or different approaches to solving problems and handling situations.

When Haz-Mat members are away teaching, it's essential that they don't just focus on instructing. They should actively be learning from their students as well. Every day, they should bring back new insights, techniques, or strategies to enhance their own team's capabilities. If they're not learning something valuable to pass along, then they're missing an important opportunity.

Let's be honest - industry professionals are often more knowledgeable in their specific areas than we are. This makes it even more critical to seize every opportunity to learn from their expertise and experience.

One of the best ways to build connections and improve knowledge-sharing is by visiting other teams at their base locations, and reciprocating by hosting them at ours. These visits can include show-and-tell sessions where teams examine each other's tools, equipment, and PPE. Ride-alongs, where team members observe actual operations, also provide invaluable learning experiences. Participating in after-action reports and critiques after these operations helps refine tactics and improves safety and effectiveness.
Through teaching and attending schools, our members have developed a broad network across the country. They share contact information, swap stories, and offer advice on mutual challenges. This network of shared

experiences and knowledge benefits everyone, helping teams stay current with trends and best practices in the ever-evolving Haz-Mat field.

Adam McFadden

Networking with other hazmat teams and industry professionals is essential for staying ahead of emerging threats, sharing best practices, and continuously improving response capabilities. Through regular collaboration - whether during training exercises, industry conferences, or interagency partnerships - we're able to exchange real-world lessons, keep pace with evolving tactics, and build a more unified response posture for large-scale events.

Strong relationships with regional hazmat teams and subject matter experts directly enhance our preparedness. They give us access to broader knowledge, additional resources, and the ability to scale up quickly and effectively when incidents demand it. This kind of professional network isn't just a bonus - it's a strategic asset in managing hazardous materials incidents with speed and precision.

To facilitate knowledge-sharing, we regularly collaborate on training exercises, review and exchange agency policies, and participate in joint drills. These multi-agency scenarios help ensure consistency in response tactics, reinforce interoperability, and boost regional readiness. By working side by side with other teams in controlled environments, we reduce friction during real emergencies and increase trust across agency lines.

But some of the most impactful connections happen outside the formal training environment. After the scenarios wrap up, we invest time in relationship-building - through shared meals, social events, and informal meetups. These gatherings give our people a chance to connect on a personal level, forging trust and camaraderie with counterparts in EMS, law enforcement, and emergency management.

When those relationships are strong, communication flows faster, collaboration feels seamless, and teamwork is more intuitive during high-stakes responses. By building those bonds now, we create the kind of trust that pays off in the field - where it matters most.

Mike Monaco

It's absolutely critical. There's no way around it - no single team leader, no one group of people, can know everything that's going on at a hazmat scene. It's just not possible.

There've been plenty of times when we had to "phone a friend," where the only way forward was to lean on someone outside our immediate circle. Whether that's someone in another specialty, someone with a different background, or just someone who sees the problem from a new angle - you *need* those outside perspectives. But that kind of help only comes if you've done the work to build relationships - *inside* your team and *outside* your team, *inside* your department and *outside* your department, *inside* industry and *outside* industry.

And it starts with being just as open and honest with people outside your crew as you are with the people on the inside. You've got to show humility. Let folks know you're more interested in finding the *best* way to do something than in proving *your* way is the right way.

For a long time, my team kept our training internal - we didn't bring in outside voices. We used to call it "drinking our own pond water." But everything changed when we started bringing in instructors and subject matter experts from the outside. Our capability opened up in a big way.

We realized there's more than one way to handle a situation. There's more equipment out there than what's on *our* rig. And maybe most importantly - we realized we don't have all the answers. And that's okay. Because when you build a network, and you're humble enough to tap into it, the team as a whole gets stronger.

Chris Pfaff

We don't live in a vacuum. Think about it - Chevrolet talks to Dodge. Not openly about everything, sure, but you bet the Chevy engineers know the Dodge engineers. They might not share every secret, but they understand exactly what's going on in each other's world, and they follow the same SAE standards.

It's the same for us in the hazmat world. I absolutely need to know how Seattle Fire Department handles certain calls. I need to understand how Tacoma Fire Department does things. We have to recognize each other's strengths, skills, and unique capabilities. And it's not just about our local fire departments - we also need connections with other local entities and agencies.

Hazmat wears a different hat compared to every other emergency response discipline because we constantly interact with multiple players - EPA representatives, spill contractors, public works, and law enforcement. Building personal relationships matters. Knowing that Bill's kid just made the football playoffs genuinely helps when you're standing side by side managing an incident together.

Here's an example of how networking directly benefited our team:

We responded to a hydrogen release event involving a 16-gallon drum filled with aluminum shavings in mineral oil. A small amount of water got into the drum, causing an aluminum oxide reaction. Suddenly, this 16-gallon drum turned into a pressurized hydrogen bomb, actively venting gas out of a partially sealed bung cap. That's what triggered the 911 call.

Some junior team members remembered that a neighboring jurisdiction previously dealt with the exact same scenario at this facility back when it was in their response area. We immediately reached out and asked, "Hey, how'd you handle your incident?"

They told us their drum had been a 55-gallon one, and incredibly, the employees had put it on a hand truck and rolled it into the middle of a parking lot - actively venting hydrogen gas under pressure and elevated temperature. Definitely not firefighters - this was the facility's employees.

Using that shared knowledge, even though that neighboring team wasn't physically there at our scene, we collaborated on possible solutions, which ultimately led us to calling out the bomb squad. They deployed their percussion-activated neutralizer - the fancy term for their water shotgun - to safely manage the situation.
By the way, pro tip: don't ever call it a "water shotgun" in front of the media unless you want to see that phrase plastered all over the evening news. That one falls under hard-earned PIO lessons.

Rob Rezende

Huge! That's how important conferences, lectures, classes, task forces, committees - all of it - are in our industry. It's critical to learn from others, share experiences, and stay connected with the broader community.

We make it a priority to place one of our team members in any committee we can - whether it's state, local, or even industry groups like UL. Being involved in these committees gives our team a voice and access to cutting-edge knowledge. We also make sure to participate in hosting and teaching at conferences, sharing our expertise while learning from others in the field.

Networking is a game-changer. I've had the privilege of networking with my brothers at FDNY, and that connection was absolutely crucial in developing our lithium-ion battery program. Without that relationship, we wouldn't have had the resources, insights, and collaboration that made it possible. Building those connections and being actively involved in the larger industry network is how we stay ahead and continue to grow as a team.

Bob Royall

Over the years, we all start building relationships and friendships that go beyond just work. I consider myself very blessed to have developed strong bonds with a lot of great people. That kind of networking is essential because it builds trust so when we respond to an incident, other responders will know that we are all part of one team. For industry, the gates will open wide letting us just fold right into the response. It's seamless and that's invaluable.

I know some will say that's a bit of an anomaly, but the truth is, you can create those kind of relationships even within smaller jurisdictions. Maybe there's a fertilizer plant in your town, and it's the largest employer. If your fire department or hazmat team takes the initiative to walk up and knock on the door, nine times out of ten, they'll welcome you in with open arms. Why? Because you've shown interest. You want to understand their facility, and you're telling them, "If there's ever have an incident, we want to give you the best service possible." That kind of proactive engagement is key to building relationships.

And it's not just about networking with the local industries. It's also about establishing connections with your professional colleagues, too. I'll give you an example: Tim O'Brien with Union Pacific Railroad. He's a close family friend, and after all those years working together, I can tell you, the guy doesn't like coffee - but he loves diet Cokes. That seems like a simple thing, but it speaks volumes. Over time, you get to know other's likes, their dislikes, their strengths, and their weaknesses. And that kind of knowledge builds a level of trust that can't be replicated.

When you go to a conference, you go for a reason. It's not a paid vacation, and it's certainly not an excuse to hang out in the hospitality suite. Sure, there's plenty of networking that happens there too, but the real connections happen in the hallways, in those informal conversations. That's where you really get to know people outside of the formal settings. That's where the true value of networking happens.

Bobby Salvesen

This is something I think is *really* important.

I didn't truly start growing as a hazmat guy until I got out of my own department - and out of my own head - and started seeing what the rest of the world was doing. Traveling, teaching, working with other agencies... that's what opened my eyes.

I still teach with another company out in California - not just because I enjoy it, but because I *respect* how they operate. And every time I go, I learn something. It's a constant reminder: the sun doesn't rise and set on the FDNY.

I say that as a joke, but I mean it. California does hazmat differently. Arkansas? Different. Michigan? Totally different. Canada? Completely different again.

And if I had never gotten outside my little New York bubble - if I didn't start networking, collaborating, and trading ideas with *really good hazmat people* from all over - I'd still think there was only one way to peel a banana. Or, you know, one correct way to hold pH paper. (Yeah... that one actually blew my mind.)

When you get out there and start engaging with people from different backgrounds - military, police, private industry - you start to see how much there *is* to learn. You share ideas, you get challenged, and you realize that your way isn't the only way - or even the best way.

And then, when you come home, you bring that knowledge back to your team. Maybe you tweak something. Maybe you completely change a process. Maybe you just start a conversation at the kitchen table that leads somewhere unexpected. Crazier things have happened.

If you want to grow, *really* grow, as a hazmat tech - or as a leader - get out there. Talk to people. Learn from them. And share what you've learned. That's how you move the whole field forward.

Doug Schick and Mark Zilch
Doug:

This is bigger than just hazmat - it's a culture shift. When I started in Chicago back in '96, things were really insular. It was like, "This is the Chicago Fire Department. This is the only way to do it. We don't need to learn from anyone else." That was the mentality of a lot of people. I remember when I first started getting *Firehouse* and *Fire Engineering* magazines. The guys at my firehouse were like, "Why are you reading that? You'll learn everything you need to know on the street or at the kitchen table." And after a while, I kind of bought into it. "We're Chicago. We know what we're doing." I bet New York was the same way, maybe even worse.

But then I went down to the Illinois Fire Service Institute - the training hub out of the University of Illinois - and it was like my eyes got opened. There were people from all over the state, bringing different ideas and approaches. That was the first time I realized, *maybe we don't know everything*.

Later on, when I started teaching in the suburbs, I had this perception - like a lot of city guys do - that suburban departments were soft, didn't even go into burning buildings. But once I got out there, I was blown away. Some of the instructors I worked with were absolutely top-tier. Incredible firemen. I learned a ton from them.

It's the same with hazmat. If you only ever listen to your own crew, your own city, you're missing a ton of value. You need to expose yourself to different regions, different specialties, different ways of thinking. That's how you grow.

I try to bring outside training into our department whenever I can. Sure, I sometimes wonder, "Could we do this in-house?" And sometimes we could - but the value is in those outside ideas and connections. We've hosted folks from Hazard3, we've had Dr. Baxter come out, and another chemist from Wisconsin who Mark mentioned earlier. If someone from another hazmat team is in town for any reason, I'll try to get them into the firehouse just to meet the team. Build those connections.

Because networking pays off. We helped another agency with an incident last year - we actually got to use the G-510 for real, not just in training. It wasn't the G-510 that got the hit though - it was the MX908. Came back with a positive reading for nerve agent.

And because of networking, I was able to call Dr. Baxter. I'd met her through earlier trainings. She picked up immediately, just like she said she would, and we had a great conversation. She gave us valuable insight that directly impacted our response. That right there - that's the power of networking.

Mark:
Exactly. And it's not just about local contacts - it's federal, too. We work closely with our FBI WMD coordinator. She's phenomenal. The expertise and resources that she is able to muster at a moment's notice are invaluable. Having access to that kind of expertise? You can't put a price on it.

It's not just one-off incidents, either. They share intel, training insights, technical updates - stuff you'd never hear about if you stayed siloed.

We've also got a strong relationship with Illinois State Police. They handle CBRN response across the state, and we're plugged into their monthly roundtables and discussions. Just sitting in on those, you pick up so much.

Remember that case, Chief, with the "Wasp dope"? It's that synthetic wasp insecticide they smuggle in - it gets smoked and it's highly toxic. That came from one of those intel shares. I'd never even heard of it before that meeting.

Same thing goes for our CST partners, our Region 5 RAP team - those are our go-to folks when it comes to radiation. If I've got a rad question, that's where I'm going.

The bottom line? You can't just rely on what you know inside your bubble. You've got to build those bridges - with the feds, with CST, with your neighbors in the suburbs. That's where the real strength of a hazmat team comes from.

Networking with other hazmat teams and industry professionals is absolutely essential if you want to build and maintain an elite response capability. You can train hard in isolation, but you'll never truly be at your best unless you step outside your own walls and learn from others. No single team, no matter how skilled, has all the answers. When things go south - and in this line of work, they often do - having relationships with others who've faced different challenges and fought different battles becomes invaluable.

For me, networking was never about handing out business cards or shaking hands at conferences. It was about forging trusted relationships with people across fire departments, law enforcement agencies, military units, and industry partners. I sought out connections with those who were at the top of their game - experts in areas outside our core mission. Why? Because when things go sideways, you want to be able to pick up the phone and speak directly with someone who's been through it, rather than wasting precious time figuring things out on your own while the clock ticks.

Networking also opens doors to superior training opportunities, access to emerging technologies, and new perspectives. Every joint exercise I participated in or collaboration with another agency made me sharper. Observing how other teams approached problems, handled gear, or structured their responses made us better and more adaptable.

At the end of the day, this job is about life and death - not ego. Being elite means staying humble enough to understand that there's always something new to learn from others. That's why I made networking part of our culture. We weren't the team that only reached out for help when we were in trouble - we were the team others called because they knew we stayed connected, relevant, and always ready.

For us, networking and collaboration weren't about convenience - they were part of our mission. Our team wasn't designed to operate in isolation or stay confined to our own lane. We existed to be a resource for the broader WMD and HazMat community. Whether it was offering assistance during an incident, providing technical expertise through our reachback capability, or offering specialized training, we were there to be counted on. That's why being accessible was so critical. If no one knows you're out there or how to reach you when the clock's ticking, you're of no use to the community.

That's why I made it a priority to put ourselves out there. We didn't wait for teams to come to us - we built those relationships proactively. We visited other teams, trained alongside them, offered our support, and ensured they knew exactly what we brought to the table. It wasn't about showing off; it was about making it clear that we were capable, available, and ready to step in when needed. Whether it was a late-night phone call or working together during large-scale training events, we kept ourselves visible.

Ultimately, our team's strength wasn't just in our own capabilities - it was in how we connected and supported the entire hazmat response network. Being a trusted resource didn't happen overnight - it came from consistent presence, reliability, and an unwavering commitment to never turn down a call for help. That's the kind of networking that matters. That's what fosters real partnerships.

Networking didn't just benefit our team - it defined our value and opened doors we couldn't have reached otherwise. There are countless examples where those relationships and our reputation paid off, but what really stands out is how networking made us the team that got called when it mattered most.

From the start, we put in the work - attending courses, working side-by-side with other teams, showing up at conferences, and diving into major training exercises. We weren't there to simply check boxes or collect freebies - we were there to prove ourselves. We made sure the entire **WMD** and **HazMat** response community knew we weren't just another team - we were professionals, ready to lead and ready to deliver. When people saw us in action, they recognized us as sharp, capable, and at the top of our game. That reputation spread quickly.

When real-world incidents hit - like the terrorist attacks on 9/11 - that networking paid immediate dividends. As soon as we arrived on the scene, teams like FDNY, NYPD, FBI, and others were asking, "Where have you guys been?" They didn't need to be sold on who we were - they already knew we were the asset they needed in that moment. That trust and familiarity were the direct result of the groundwork we laid by staying involved in the community before the crisis hit.

From that point forward, it never stopped. Because of the relationships we built and nurtured, we were constantly called upon - not just for emergencies, but for major planned events like the World Series, U.S. Open, NASCAR, POTUS missions, the U.N. General Assembly, and countless dignitary protection details. That didn't happen by accident. It happened because networking made us a known, trusted resource - subject matter experts who could perform under pressure.

Bottom line: Networking didn't just benefit us - it made us indispensable.

CONFERENCES

"Know your limits ... but never stop trying to exceed them."
–Unknown

Dan Baker

Conferences benefit our team in two major ways. First, they give our members an opportunity to showcase their talents and introduce innovative programs on a national stage. We frequently receive invitations to present cutting-edge programs developed by our team, and we actively seek to participate in as many conferences as we can. This helps position us as a leader in hazmat response and highlights our instructors as among the very best in the business.

Second, conferences allow our members to engage in additional training, build valuable networks, and explore new ideas, which are always the lifeblood of these events. Attending keeps us from getting stuck in our own bubble - what I jokingly call becoming "Amish" - by providing third-party validation of our programs when they're timely and effective, or gentle reminders when they're not. Additionally, seeing what's happening elsewhere helps us identify gaps in our own programs so we can bring fresh ideas back to the fire service.

We find training-focused conferences particularly beneficial, primarily because it's easier to justify attendance to our leadership. Conferences in general are currently not very popular with our administration, making it necessary for me to put forward extremely robust justifications to gain approvals. Fortunately, training resonates strongly with elected officials, making it a much easier sell - it's practically a ground ball in terms of justification.

Mike Callan

You know, over time, I've seen how conferences and networking have evolved in this field. In the early years, we used to be the ones running things, but eventually, the chiefs in some areas said, "We can't do this anymore," and that's when the IAFC took over the Redmond Conference with the IAFF. That conference became a chance for everyone to get together, exchange ideas, and network.

What happens at these events is that you get an idea, and you take it back to your department or your region and implement it. Back then, we used to ask for a slide from a presentation. Now, you just get a URL and the best resource for solving your specific problem is right at your fingertips.

We're still sharing visuals, anecdotes, and case histories - those are the things that make a difference.

But what really worries me now is how conferences are tightening their budgets. With this pullback, one critical part of networking is getting squeezed. It sounds weird, but I've always looked at myself and people like us as bumblebees. We fly around, land at conferences, pick up all this "pollen," and then take it to other conferences. So, people might not know the answer to a question right away, but they'll say, "I've heard about these hazmat guys, or I know someone who can help with this." The beauty of networking is being able to connect people, even when you don't know the answer yourself. I remember doing this with Toby Frost. I cornered him one day and said, "Toby, what conference do you want to go to?"

He looked at me and said, "What do you mean? Can you really do that?" I told him, "You'll go to a conference you've never been to, and I'll get you in." That's the first step - getting into the conference and getting your questions answered.

Then you get the guys fighting to get to FDIC. But here's where I get frustrated: when I first started attending conferences, everyone was about sharing ideas and learning from one another. It was an unequivocal exchange of information. Now, as I've gotten older, I've noticed almost every conference I go to has business logos on their slides. And while I get it - everyone needs sponsors - it wasn't always like that. In the early days, it was all about sharing valuable knowledge, not selling products. We've learned that if we don't share our information, someone else will. But I think there's got to be a balance. How do you share this information with your team while maintaining the integrity of the message?

We still have great resources out there - articles, magazines, and books. Even today, books aren't entirely gone, though the format has evolved. I remember reading Eugene Myers' *Chemistry of Hazardous Materials*. The book's first edition is falling apart, but it's one of those core texts that taught me lessons I still reference today.
I see my own handwritten notes in the margins, ideas I thought were mine - only to find that Eugene had written them first. It's a humbling experience, but it shows how long this knowledge has been passed down.

One of the best examples of networking for me was a time I met two guys at a conference in Minnesota. We were sitting at the bar, talking, and one of them says, "I've heard about you." I said, "Yeah, I've heard about you too." That was the first time we met in person.

They were going to teach something unsafe the next morning, but I learned so much from them just by talking. I always say that networking isn't just about getting your questions answered - it's about meeting people who challenge you, make you think differently. It's about learning from those moments you wouldn't have gotten otherwise.

It's funny, but sometimes we get so excited when we see someone in a blue shirt at a conference. It's like seeing a brotherhood. You walk up, and when you're close enough to read the shirt, you form an opinion. But when you see them from afar, they're part of your crew. It's that sense of connection, that recognition that we're all in this together. And that's why the word "brotherhood" is so important - it defines how we act when we know we're part of something bigger.

If I hadn't traveled, if I hadn't been part of this culture, I wouldn't have learned anything. My old chief used to say, "If I'd stayed home,

I'd have spent 20 years sitting on my couch, watching Channel 8, maybe gone on to become a chief, but that wouldn't have been the same." Networking is the difference between staying stuck in one place and moving forward in your career.

So, as I look back on my career, I see how conferences, networking, and the sharing of information have shaped where we are now. It's been about building those relationships, constantly learning, and sharing what we know. Without those connections, we wouldn't be able to grow and adapt to the new challenges that come our way.

Whether it's new technology, a new hazard, or a different way of thinking, it's all part of the journey. And for me, that journey started with networking, and it's still going strong today.

John Cassidy

Conferences are incredibly valuable - but they also present a real challenge for us in the New York City Fire Department. And that challenge doesn't come from within the department - it comes from the City itself.

The City of New York has travel restrictions that limit how many personnel we can send to an event. Right now, the cap is four people. That's not a fire department policy - that's a citywide rule. So when you're only allowed to send four, you've got to be very intentional about who goes. It's not just about who *wants* to go - it's about who's going to bring something back.

Let's say I've got a senior guy on the list. Sure, it might be a great opportunity for his personal development. But maybe I also have a less senior member - someone who's actively teaching, helping shape curriculum, and engaged in the school's day-to-day. Now, seniority absolutely holds value and we respect that in the fire service. But from a return-on-investment standpoint? I've only got four seats. I need to send the person who's going to absorb that information and translate it into value for the whole team.

That doesn't mean the senior guy can't go - but if he does, I expect him to come back and present on what he learned. And if he's not interested in doing that - if he's just looking at it like a personal growth trip - then maybe he's not the right pick this time around. And honestly, sometimes people self-select out when they hear that expectation.

But overall, I think conferences are crucial - especially in hazmat. New York City is a unique place. We've got a specific set of regulations, and there are entire industries we don't have here. So when you go to a national or international conference, you're exposed to problems, solutions, and incidents you'd never see in your home district. That kind of exposure is huge.

It broadens your perspective. It builds connections. And if you bring it back and share it with your team? That's when it becomes truly valuable.

Dave DiGregorio

For about six years, I was a capstone advisor at Massachusetts Maritime, teaching at the master's level in emergency management. When the program went virtual, I said, "I'm done." I just didn't want to continue.

They called me back, and I asked if they had returned to in-person classes. When they told me it was still virtual, I had no interest. The thing is, over 50% of the value in those classes came from having students from all different walks of life coming together in a classroom to talk about emergency management. Virtual just wasn't the same.

In terms of my teams, I also always wanted to give them opportunities to grow. When they went to conferences like the one in Baltimore, I gave them credit for two drills. So, if they attended a conference, they'd get credit for two drills that would count toward their required annual drills. If, for whatever reason, they missed a drill with their own team, this would make up for it. But I always stressed that you can only do so many non-team drills. Training with your actual team is so important for cohesion and performance. You need to be able to work together as a unit when it matters most.

Dave Donohue

Conferences and training events serve as crucial networking and growth opportunities. Not only do I attend these events, but I also expect the same commitment from others. I encourage everyone to engage in after-hours activities, ideally with someone or a group they've never met before. This helps expand their network and exposes them to new perspectives that they might not have encountered otherwise.

When selecting sessions, it's important to carefully evaluate the conference topics and look for gaps in our knowledge or skills, rather than simply focusing on what's a strength or what might seem interesting. There's a natural tendency to gravitate toward classes that align with areas we're already strong in, so I make a point of mixing those with sessions that address weaknesses in either our knowledge or skills. This approach ensures that we are growing and improving in areas where we might be lacking.

For those who attend conferences or training sessions, there's an expectation that they bring back what they've learned and share it with the rest of the team. This ensures that the entire group benefits from the experience and knowledge gained.

It's tough to narrow it down because, in the end, all opportunities for growth are beneficial. Each one offers something that can add value, whether it's new techniques, insights, or connections. The key is ensuring that we're constantly pushing ourselves to fill in the gaps and improve as a team.

Rick Edinger

We always invested in conferences. Like I mentioned earlier, I managed our state conference for several years and our folks were plugged into various support roles. But beyond that, we actively encouraged our members - regardless of their specialty - to get involved at the state and national levels. It wasn't necessarily an expectation, but it was something we culturally supported within our organization.

If somebody came to us and said, *"Hey, I want to get involved with the HAZMAT Conference,"* or *"I'd like to help out behind the scenes,"* our answer was, *"Alright - let's make it happen."* Because the return on that investment? It always paid dividends - both in terms of the knowledge people brought back and the networking connections they developed. The benefits far outweighed the resources we put into it.

When you look at conferences, there are obviously a few major national ones that stand out. You're going to see the best of the best there. The Baltimore conference is probably the flagship event in terms of scale and content. You've got this huge mix of people coming in from across the country, a wide range of topics, and instructors you won't find anywhere else. That's the value of the national level - you're exposed to big-picture thinking and people you wouldn't normally cross paths with.

On the flip side, there's a lot of growth happening right now at the state and local levels. Just in the last few years, we've seen several state conferences pop back up - either restarting after being dormant for a while or launching for the first time. These metro and regional events may be smaller, but the networking is often even more relevant. You're talking to people you're likely to actually work with, and that's incredibly valuable when something happens locally.

So for us, it was never just about sending people to sit in chairs and collect CEUs. It was about building relationships, sharing knowledge, and staying engaged with what's happening in the field - locally, regionally, and nationally.

John Esposito

Just like you need to build relationships with the other agencies in your own jurisdiction, you also need to know what other hazmat teams are doing - what other fire departments are doing. Because chances are, someone else has already solved the problem you just discovered you had. There's no need to reinvent the wheel.

And it doesn't matter whether they're a big city or a small rural department. Take New York City, for example. We *have* a lot of hazmat... but in some ways, we also *don't*. A huge amount of hazardous materials shipped by rail never comes through here. Same with road traffic - companies avoid NYC because of the congestion. Even out on Long Island, if a load wasn't made there and isn't staying there, it's probably not going through there. So in a way, we're a little bit spoiled.

We don't have a chemical plant tucked behind a strip mall, protected by a volunteer department, with some of the nastiest stuff in the country sitting in their first-due area. But those departments do. And when something blows up, they're the ones dealing with it. That's why it's not just about the major metros - you've got to talk to the smaller counties too. What keeps *them* up at night? What threats are *they* training for? Because what's uncommon for you might be routine for them.

That's where conferences come in. Staying informed, keeping up with changes in the field, learning what's new in meters, tactics, PPE, training models - it's all important. A lot of states now have their own hazmat conferences, and of course, there are a handful of national ones. And beyond the classroom sessions and keynote speakers, the real magic happens after hours - in the hallway, over lunch, in the bar. That's where the good stuff gets traded. That's where the solutions get shared.

And the value of *in-person* conferences can't be overstated. You don't build real relationships over Zoom. You can't replace that casual five-minute conversation in the lobby or the introductions that happen when someone leans over during a panel and says, "Hey, I've seen that too."

Because when you run into a complex, wicked problem and you need help, you want to be able to pick up the phone and call someone who already knows your name. You don't want to waste 20 minutes explaining who you are just to get routed to the right person. You want it to be, "Hey Mike, it's John. I've got a situation - have you seen this before?" And go from there.

That's why we make the rounds. I was just at the Metro Chiefs Conference, and after the official stuff wrapped up Thursday afternoon, we had a formal dinner that evening - but those hours in between? You're talking with legends of the fire service. Former fire administrators, longtime chiefs, people with real credibility and insight. That's where the most valuable conversations happen.

And when a conference focuses on the right things - emerging trends, hot topics, honest reviews of recent incidents - that's when it's most effective. We had the Chief from D.C. talk us through the response to a plane crash. Not just the facts, but the *chief's perspective* on the decisions that had to be made. And you know somewhere else, a dive team's probably breaking down that same event from *their* angle.

That's how you grow. That's how you build competence across the profession.

Chris Hawley

That's a great perspective on the value of being both a learner and a teacher. I was never really the expert in my own town, but I had the advantage of being able to hire myself out as the expert. What I would do is hire some of my friends, who were experts in specific areas, to come in and teach the same program I would have done. That way, it wasn't just me, but a whole team of experts delivering the same training I would have done on my own. I'd even go to other instructors departments to train their people because they didn't think their guru was an expert, and that's where I could offer value. We'd make it work so everyone was paid, and we'd deliver the same training - just different faces. And it worked, because I was able to bring the right people into the room, and it added credibility to the training.

That's why sending people away to conferences or to other specialized trainings is so valuable. It's not just about learning from new sources, but about opening people's eyes to the wealth of expertise out there. When you get exposed to those folks, it shifts your perspective a little bit. The best way to grow is by meeting other experts and seeing how they approach things. It's frustrating when you can't get some of the best folks, like Kevin Ryan, to teach at the hazmat conference more often because I know how valuable his insight is. He's got a great team, and they see a lot of complex situations. But getting people to make that jump and become part of the teaching community is always a challenge.

One thing that I've always pushed for is navigating the hazmat grant money. Every state has it, but a lot of teams don't know how to access it. It's all about finding the right funding and using it for training. There's often more planning money available than teams realize, and that can be used for training, too. The key is to be proactive and use what's available. There's always money on the table that doesn't get spent, and your team should be tapping into that as much as possible.

As for attending conferences, it's a little funny when people ask why I go to so many. One of my guys once asked me, "How come you get sent to all these conferences?" I told him, "I'm not getting sent - I'm going." The department wasn't paying for it. I was paying for my own travel, meals, and hotel. The only thing the conference covered was the conference registration. But it wasn't just about attending, it was about improving myself and my work. I wanted to be good at my job, so I invested in myself. It was a way for me to stay ahead of the curve and bring back new knowledge to the team.

There's also the element of marketing yourself. Being at those conferences isn't just about learning; it's also about showcasing your expertise. And as long as it doesn't negatively impact the family budget, my wife supports me going. She knows that it's not just for me - it's for the team too. When I get back from one of those events, I'm able to bring in new training or hire specialists to cover areas I might not be an expert in. It's about constantly improving and sharing that knowledge.

You don't need to be stuck in a box. You can always push forward and grow by teaching, learning, and collaborating. There's no reason you can't do the same. Submit proposals to teach, take on case studies, or simply put your name out there. It's a win-win - your team gets better, and you get to grow as a professional. You just have to be proactive about it and take advantage of the resources and opportunities that are out there.

Mike Hildebrand

Conferences. That's learning and relationship building secret weapon. That's where it all started for us - and that's where you meet the people who'll change the trajectory of your team and your career.

Greg Noll, myself, and a handful of other team leaders - back in the early days - were lucky enough to be plank owners at the first-ever national-scale hazmat team conference. It wasn't flashy. It was small. We pulled together folks from Montgomery County, Prince George's County, Anne Arundel County, and the District of Columbia. We'd already been talking and sharing, so we decided: why not make it official?

It was invite-only. About 50 people showed up. Most of them paid their own way. And what did we do? We sat around, drank coffee, drank beer, and talked. About what worked, what didn't, what we were struggling with. At the end of that first one, someone turned to me and said, "Mike, next year I want you to do a talk on Decontamination." And that was it - we were off and running.

Fifty years later, that same conference is still going strong. Now it draws over a thousand people. And it inspired others - the IAFC Hazmat Conference, the Continuing Challenge, the Hot Zone - all of them influenced by that first gathering. From there, the model trickled down to the state level: Florida Haz Symposium, Massachusetts, Wisconsin - all run by state people, for state people. Taught by the very folks doing the work.

That's where you build your *network*. That's where you meet your people.

And if there's one piece of advice I give younger folks - the closest thing I've got to a "Yoda moment" - it's this:

Show up.

That's it. It's not complicated. You want to succeed? You want to grow? *Show up.* Show up to work. Show up to class. Show up to the conference. The amount of free, high-quality training that goes unused simply because guys "decided to go to the beach that day"? It's insane.

Look at the leaders we talked about earlier - the ones who run the elite teams. Rescue companies. Hazmat units. Bomb squads. SWAT. SEAL Team Six. They're not magic. They're not unicorns. They just *show up*, and learn and practice over and over again. That's the pattern.

If you're a young firefighter or a new hazmat tech, here's how it goes:

You go to a conference. You go to the class. You hang back after the Q&A. You ask one more question. You shake their hand. You get their card. You follow up on a phone call. You're at their next class. And the one after that. And after a while, they know your name. You've got a mentor. You've got a phone number to call when everything goes sideways.

That's how it works.

And while you're there, step out of your lane. I once went to a conference session on hurricane *debris removal* - and thought, "How hard could it be to pick up trash after a storm?" Turns out, it's a science. There are laws, protocols, cross-border shipping rules - Mexico will take certain materials, Canada won't. I learned about sorting hazmat containers, handling legacy waste, managing spontaneous dumps. And I met *experts*. I now have a debris removal contact I can call - something I didn't have the day before.

Sometimes, the best way to grow is to get a *cross-certification* in something totally outside your norm.

But the number one thing I've done to get better over the years?

Read.
Not just the training manuals or SOGs. I read biographies. Intelligence books. History. Fiction. Comics. Mission debriefs. You name it. I've pulled more leadership insight and practical lessons from books than almost anywhere else. The story of SAS training. The failure of the Iran hostage rescue mission. The violinist who became the best in the world

through deliberate practice. There's always something in there to chew on, something you can bring back to your team.

And yeah, even those *fictionalized* SEAL Team Six books from Dick Marcinko - sure, they're dressed up, but the bones are real. They're based on experience, on tactics, on failure and grit and adaptation.

If you want to lead, you never stop reading. You never stop showing up. You never stop connecting with people who know more than you. Successful people read or listen to books - lots and lots of books. It's free learning.

Because in the end, that's how the best teams are built - not through luck, not through budget, but through culture, curiosity, and connection.

Bob Ingram

Conferences play a key role in developing a high-performing hazmat team. Networking opportunities at these events are invaluable, as they allow you to connect with not only the instructor cadre and attendees, but also sales teams from equipment manufacturers. These connections can help you stay informed about new technologies and equipment, keeping your team on the cutting edge.

The lectures and presentations at these conferences offer fresh perspectives and new tactics for handling recurring incidents, as well as emerging threats. They often provide insights that can be applied directly to your team's operations. Additionally, attending these events helps identify instructors who can bring specialized training to your AHJ, allowing you to train your entire team without needing to send everyone to the conference itself.
There are several conferences now specifically designed for hazmat teams across the country, offering targeted learning and networking opportunities that can enhance your team's overall effectiveness.

Phil McArdle

Attending conferences and networking events provides valuable opportunities for Haz-Mat teams to expand their knowledge base. We gain new contacts, see the latest tools and equipment, and hear about emerging technologies and protocols that could enhance our operations. These events allow us to collect pamphlets, brochures, and books, which help to increase our inventory of knowledge and keep us informed about the latest trends and advancements in the field.

To ensure that we're maximizing the value of these events, it's essential to set clear expectations for each team member attending a conference. Provide them with a list of what you want them to bring back, not just for their own benefit but for the entire team. For every resource they gather for themselves - whether it's materials or contacts - make sure they also get something for the team's benefit.

Once they return, require each attendee to write a thorough report detailing what they learned, how it benefits the team, and the potential long-term value of attending such conferences. The report should also highlight any new or additional information that could be useful to the team's operations, training, or strategies.

Special attention should be given to conferences where the specific "tools of the trade" are being showcased. These are the events where cutting-edge ideas, techniques, and innovations in hazardous materials response, mitigation, and remediation are presented. By attending these conferences, we stay ahead of the curve and ensure that our team remains at the forefront of safety and effectiveness in the Haz-Mat field.

Adam McFadden

Conferences play a vital role in the ongoing development of our hazmat team, offering direct exposure to emerging threats, cutting-edge technologies, and evolving best practices from across the industry. These events are more than just educational - they're opportunities to gain fresh insights, network with experts, and bring back knowledge that can elevate our entire team's performance.

Unfortunately, not all fire departments formally support or sponsor attendance at these conferences. In many cases, members have to take the initiative themselves - covering the cost, using personal time, and making professional development a personal responsibility. While that's a challenge, those who invest in their own growth often return with a wealth of information, innovative ideas, and connections that benefit everyone on the team. Their commitment strengthens our collective knowledge base and helps push our capabilities forward.

For hazmat professionals, attending conferences and industry events is essential to staying current. Key events include:

- Health and safety conferences with tracks focused on hazardous materials and responder wellness
- Oil and gas industry forums, which provide insight into industrial risk and mitigation strategies
- Chemical manufacturer-sponsored training, offering in-depth information on specific products and safety protocols
- First responder conferences focused on hazmat, CBRNE, and terrorism response

These events feature hands-on demonstrations, expert-led sessions, and critical networking opportunities that help us stay at the forefront of risk mitigation, technical operations, and interagency coordination. More importantly, they foster collaboration and the exchange of real-world lessons between professionals facing the same challenges across different jurisdictions.

Ultimately, conferences are more than just professional gatherings - they're a critical component of how we evolve, adapt, and maintain excellence in hazmat response. Whether sponsored by the department or pursued independently, participation in these events is an investment in both individual growth and team readiness.

Mike Monaco

It's critical. Absolutely critical.
There are so many great instructors out there, so many top-tier training programs, and conferences are where they all come together. For that one weekend, in whatever part of the country you're in, you've got all that knowledge, experience, and innovation concentrated in one place.

It's where you go to pick up new techniques, learn about new technologies, and see the latest tools and gear hitting the field. It's where you hear about incidents you might've never even known happened - just because you haven't had the chance to network beyond your department or your region.

And that's what makes it so powerful. It's not just about sitting through lectures. It's about exposure - to ideas, to equipment, to people you wouldn't normally cross paths with. That kind of broad perspective can shift the way you approach your job.

For us, the podcast has become a way to extend that experience. We put out real stories - things that went right, things that went wrong - and just let people listen, learn, and reflect. We've always seen the podcast as a kind of virtual firehouse kitchen table. A place where people can gather, be honest, swap critiques, and walk away a little smarter.

It's all about creating and contributing to that larger conversation - because that's how the entire field moves forward.

Chris Pfaff

I love - absolutely love - every single conference I attend, whether it's regional or national. Conferences need to play a bigger role in the growth and success of our teams. I've seen teams grow tremendously by sending multiple members to conferences across the country.

We have to recognize the importance of getting outside our own states and regions. We need to see how other teams and agencies handle hazmat response. What are their strengths? Where might they have weaknesses? And, just as important, how do we compare?

It's not about competing or saying we're better or worse. It's about finding ways to improve and building valuable partnerships and relationships.

When attending these conferences, you get so much value from talking to other teams and team members, exploring the vendor areas to see the newest technology available, and - most importantly - the classes. Hearing from national instructors about current trends and what's coming next is incredibly beneficial.

One key point, though: If you're going to send members to a conference, limit the group size to three or four people. If you send five or more, you've got yourself a structure fire. I've seen it happen - when you send five to ten members from the same team, they end up sitting together, at the same table, in the same row, rarely branching out to meet people from other states or regions. Even at after-hours networking events, large groups tend to stick together, talking about local issues like union contracts. And honestly, we don't want to waste national conference time talking about local gossip or internal issues.

If you're having local conversations at a national or regional conference, it should be about comparing how your team operates - good, bad, or otherwise - with other teams, to learn and grow from those exchanges.

And here's how you maximize the benefit: when your agency or jurisdiction sends three or four team members to a conference, make it mandatory for them to present what they learned at your next team training. It doesn't need to be fancy - a simple rundown of key insights and findings will do. This ensures the entire team benefits from that investment.

Rob Rezende

Attending conferences should absolutely be a requirement whenever possible. These events offer so much value, from lessons learned to discovering new ways of doing business. It's not just about networking; it's about growing and evolving with the industry.

One of the most crucial things we focus on at these conferences is learning how to spot snake oil - the fake solutions that seem too good to be true. We need to be able to differentiate between what's legit and what's just hype.
Another huge benefit is learning about new tech. Technology is constantly evolving, and we want to be at the forefront of that, understanding how new innovations can improve our operations and make us more efficient.

We try to send a few team members to a few conferences each year as a reward for hard work and performance. It's a way to recognize their efforts while investing in their continued growth.

At these conferences, we look for demonstrations of new technology and SME (Subject Matter Expert) panels where we can ask questions directly. These sessions offer invaluable insights and help us make more informed decisions about the tools and methods we adopt moving forward.

Bob Royall

Networking is invaluable. I may be a little partial when it comes to Hot Zone and the Baltimore conference, but I can't stress enough how important those are. We always encourage attendees to meet someone new, strike up a conversation, pick the instructor's brain. You never know. They might know more than you or maybe you've got something they can learn from you. Either way, make the effort to connect and build those relationships.

Look at us now. We're running one of the premier conferences in the world, but it all started with networking. It's kind of amazing when you think about it. If you asked me to list all the great people I have ever met - guys from Phoenix, LA, Seattle, New York, Florida, the heartland - I could go on and on, but at the end of the day, it's all about making those connections, building those friendships. a lot of those start at conferences and training events.

It's not just about the sessions you attend; it's about the people you meet along the way. You exchange business cards, grab contact information, and the next thing you know, you're exchanging emails and staying in touch. And when something unusual comes up, you know exactly who you can call. It's the power of that network.

One of my buddies always says, "I got a guy." And it's true. He might not know exactly who to call, but he always has someone in mind. In fact, we joke that we ought to write a book about it. Networking like that is priceless. It pays dividends in ways you can't always predict but you can always count on it when you need it.

Bobby Salvesen

I think of conferences as *mini-networking with a purpose*. They're like commercial-sized bites of a bigger course - small, digestible pieces of knowledge that can plant a seed. A seed that might grow into a new certification program, a better SOP, or just a realization that there's a big training gap back home.

And that's just the *daytime* part.

What people don't always realize is that the *after-hours* side of conferences might be even more important. You know, the conversations at the bar, or wherever people gather once the classes wrap up? That's where the real networking happens. That's where ideas are exchanged and problems get solved.

And no - it's not about the alcohol. You don't need to drink to participate. It's about being in the room with people you wouldn't normally spend time with. You start talking, someone mentions a challenge they're dealing with, and suddenly you're spitballing solutions or sharing war stories. Sometimes, even when you're not looking for advice, you get exactly what you needed - someone walking you through *their* thought process and expanding yours in the process.

From where I sit - both behind a podcast mic and working the booth - I've thought a lot about hosting a virtual conference. And I've pitched the idea, more than once, to people I trust. Every single time, they come back with the same answer: *"It won't work."*

Why?

Because you can't virtualize the bar.

You can't replicate that spontaneous hallway conversation, that unplanned brainstorm over lunch, that connection made in a class that turns into a friendship or a mentorship. That's what makes conferences *essential*.

I've been to 20+ conferences a year for the last decade. And I still look forward to every single one. Not just to see the latest tech or hear the best speakers - but to meet people. From the wide-eyed junior guys to the senior leaders. I *love* that mix.

And let me be clear - conferences shouldn't be officer-only events. If you're trying to build a strong, forward-thinking hazmat team, you've *got* to send your people to conferences. Yeah, I get the budget challenges, backfill issues, union concerns. I've lived all that. But conferences can be a carrot - an earned reward for the guys and gals doing the right things. A chance to expand their minds.

Look, some people still treat conferences like a paid vacation. But I think that's the wrong mindset. Conferences are *work*. Not the boring, soul-sucking kind - but the kind that recharges your brain, gives you perspective, and sends you home better than when you left.

And when your people come back?

Make them *present what they learned*.

Make them share it.

That's how the whole team gets better.

Doug Schick and Mark Zilch
Doug:

I love conferences - always have. They're some of the best learning and networking opportunities we get. I wish I could go to more. Since I took over as captain, one of the things I've really tried to push is getting more of our people to attend, especially starting with the Midwest Hazmat Conference. It's close, it's accessible, and it's a great entry point.

The Chicago Fire Department never had much of a presence there, which always blew my mind. So I made it a priority. For the last two or three years, I've secured funding that covers the ticket cost for anyone from our hazmat teams, JHAT, or even the squads who wants to go. Last year, we had around 20 to 25 people attend.

For a lot of them, it was their first time at a conference, and it really opened their eyes. So many came back saying, "I want to go to more of these." I usually follow up with a few suggestions - send them an email with some upcoming conferences - but most folks don't end up going. Still, the Midwest one sticks because it's local and they see the value in it.

We also got a few of our people to present last year, which I think was a big deal. It's part of my goal to boost our presence - not just as attendees, but as contributors. I want us to be part of the conversation, not just listening to it. And if everything lines up, I'll be speaking at **WAHMR** this year, and Mark - we've talked about maybe getting you involved to present next year too.

For a department our size, we should absolutely have a stronger presence at these national and regional events. Conferences are where the networking happens, where ideas are exchanged, and where relationships are built that you can lean on later.

And with your classes, if we get the grant funding we're working on, I've already told some of the suburban hazmat and **MABAS** teams, "Hey, I'm reserving extra seats for your people too." It benefits everyone. They get top-tier training, and our folks get the chance to connect, learn, and collaborate.

We've done this before - it works. I remember one class, Mark - I forget which one - but we brought in the Civil Support Team. A lot of our hazmat personnel who weren't involved in JHAT got to meet CST folks, and that's huge. That face-to-face time builds trust for future responses.

Mark:
There were a few. We definitely brought them in for PER-222, the white powder sampling class. And especially with **DNC** support and **NSSE** events, it's just like what New York does - tight integration across agencies.

Bringing the CST in and mixing them with our hazmat folks was a win. Anytime you can break down those walls and get different groups in the same room, it's a big step forward.

Jason Zeller

Conferences play a pivotal role in the growth and development of a hazmat team - not because of the slideshows or the name tags, but because of the connections and knowledge sharing that they truly foster at every level. To me, conferences are an extension of networking. They bring together professionals from all corners of the **WMD** and HazMat world, creating an environment where the opportunities to learn and grow are limitless.

At first glance, conferences seem to be about the latest equipment, emerging technologies, new procedures, and best practices that are being rolled out across the community. These things are critical - staying informed ensures we remain relevant and continue operating at the cutting edge. But if I'm being honest, the real value of a conference happens outside the formal agenda. It's in the lunches, the dinners, the hallway chats, and the casual conversations around a table at the end of the day with a cold beverage in hand. I've always believed - and still do - that more progress has been made at a round table with good people and great conversation than in most formal meetings.

Conferences give you the opportunity to sit down in a relaxed, no-pressure environment with others who truly understand the challenges. You swap war stories, share obstacles, discuss things that didn't go as planned, and learn from what others have figured out through trial and error. That's where trust is built. That's where collaboration starts. And those relationships often become your go-to lifelines when a real-world incident strikes.

I never believed in sending people to conferences just to "show the flag." When we attended, it was all about maximizing every minute and extracting every bit of value for the team. Conferences are filled with knowledge, but if you don't have the right people absorbing the right information, it's all just noise. That's why we were strategic in how we approached them.

I always made sure we sent subject matter experts from each section of the team - DECON, Downrange Ops, Recon/Survey, Medical (including our medic and Nuclear Medicine Science Officer), and members from the command team, whether it was myself, the commander, or the deputy. We didn't send a large group to sit through the same sessions. Instead, we spread out to cover every lane. Equipment updates, new technology briefings, DECON symposiums, medical procedure roundtables - if it could make us better, I wanted someone there to soak it in.

But it didn't stop there. Once the conference ended, we came together for a full debrief. We shared everything we learned, and that's where the real magic happened. We collaborated internally, formed small working groups, and dissected the information. We asked tough questions: Can this make us faster, safer, more efficient? Do we need to add this new tool to our kit? Will this DECON process enhance our capabilities? Can this detection tool save us valuable time downrange?

That's how we made conferences work for us. It wasn't about attending - it was about bringing back actionable knowledge to the team and turning it into a force multiplier. That's how you maximize the value of conferences: send the right people, capture everything you can, and immediately turn it into growth and operational improvement.

Not all conferences are created equal. For hazmat professionals, I always sought out the ones that offered real, operational takeaways - the kind that leave you smarter, sharper, and better equipped to solve problems, not just with a bag full of brochures.

Conferences focused on WMD, CBRNE, and HazMat emergency response were always at the top of the list. These environments brought together the best minds and frontline operators from fire service hazmat teams, military units, law enforcement, and federal agencies. You weren't sitting in a room full of guesswork - you were surrounded by people who had been in the trenches, sharing real lessons learned and offering solutions directly from the field. Those were pure gold.

I also valued conferences that showcased emerging technologies and evolving threats. If you're not staying ahead of what's coming, you're falling behind. Seeing new detection equipment, PPE, decontamination systems, and analytical tools being tested and deployed gave us the foresight to plan ahead and make smarter procurement and training decisions.

Dan Baker

We regularly leverage training with other agencies. While our bread-and-butter is providing training directly to the fire service, we've recognized a gap when it comes to interacting closely with other State and federal partners, agencies we don't routinely engage with outside of emergency situations.

To bridge this gap, we've made it a priority to consistently collaborate - at least once a year - with key agencies such as the State Police, the environmental folks, and the Department of Corrections. On the federal level, we regularly train with our local Civil Support Team (CST) and FBI partners.

We also make it a point to actively engage railroad responders operating throughout our response area. Over just the past year, we've trained alongside teams from **CSX, CPKS, Norfolk Southern, and Amtrak**, tapping into their expertise and reinforcing mutual familiarity.

These cross-training sessions and joint exercises align directly with our core missions: training excellence and effective statewide emergency response. But beyond the obvious operational benefits, there's also a subtler strategic advantage - small "p" politics. Whenever we can demonstrate to the executive branch that we're effectively collaborating across local, state, and federal lines, we build valuable political capital. This capital can be critical down the road when advocating for resources, increased staffing, or funding for new equipment. While these political benefits might seem tangential to building team capability, they're nonetheless crucial to our overall success.

Bottom line: Networking matters, not just for day-to-day response capabilities, but for discovering opportunities and building broader support. Staying connected beyond your team's immediate sphere is absolutely essential.

Mike Callan

When I got started, you really had two ways in - either you were "in the house," or you were "in town." And when I say "in town," I mean you were working near chemical companies. That meant you started learning - really learning - a whole bunch of stuff. That's how it went.

For me, the turning point was a derailment back in '81. Actually, before that, it was an exposure to nitric acid. That's what pushed me toward the fire academy. But I didn't go to the academy for the firefighting - I went to learn chemistry. I wanted to understand what I was getting into. That's where I started learning about oxidizers.

I ended up being the oxidizer guy. Not because I picked it, but because of how things worked in town. Greta handled flammables. Bill Hand had his thing. We all carved out our niches. That's just how it went. So, oxidizers, organic peroxides, monomers - that all landed with me. I was dealing with them because American Cyanamid was cranking out monomers constantly. That's just how it worked.

Even today, in Baltimore, it's me, Kate Silverman, and Bill Cullen - we're still the oxidizer crew. We cover all the energy stuff. Still on the monomers.

Honestly, I should've listened to the old man in *The Graduate*. "Plastics," he says in 1968. If I'd taken every dollar I had and put it into plastics back then... man, that was solid advice. But Benjamin was chasing girls, like any college kid. Can't really blame him.

Now, let me read a few things to you - though I can't read half my handwriting anymore.

Here's one for you: back then, there was *no* outside training on safety. None. If you wanted safety, good luck finding it. I was on the committee for the third edition of *Essentials*. That was the first version with a *chapter* on safety. First one! Out of 20-something folks on that committee, maybe three-quarters joined IFSTA just to be part of that work. Before that, safety wasn't even in the books.

Now ironically, the *Fire Chief's Handbook* had been talking about safety since the 1930s. Safety and instructors - those were the two things they really cared about. Somewhere along the line, we lost both. And that's probably part of why the society got so big - it was filling a void.

FDIC? That wasn't a national instructor thing. It was for your department's training officers only. So if your state had 30 towns, that meant you had 30 instructors. Period. I wasn't even eligible to join the Connecticut Fire Department Instructors Association - despite the fact that I was training people all over the country - because I wasn't the official training officer for my department.

Back then, you only trained on what you needed to survive. And the way you learned was through stories. Somebody always had a slide to show. Like Jerry Gray's slide - his facepiece was totally shattered from some chemical off a tank car. That image made the rounds, scared everyone straight.

Or the Milliken Crossing photo. That one's classic. State trooper standing next to a box truck that got nailed by a crane. That slide came out of the National Fire Academy and got used everywhere in the early '80s. The trooper's standing there in nothing but a uniform.

The hazmat guy's suited up in Level B. Guess who got sick? The cop. No hat. Chemical got absorbed through his scalp. Word was it was methyl bromide - a nerve-sensitive agent. Messed up his eyesight. Wore thick glasses after that.

Videos were gold. If a new one came out, you got your hands on it. One of the best was "Closed Container and Fires" out of Ames, Iowa, from IFST. That was outside training at its finest.

Now, how did you get other people into this? Easy. Conferences.

You show up, you meet folks, and someone eventually says, "Hey, can you do this?" After my derailment, that's exactly what happened. A guy called me up and said, "Can you come talk to us about trains?" I said, "Sure - but why me?" He goes, "Well, you were in charge of that big derailment."

Was I? The chief delegated, but the rest of the officers didn't quite see it that way. Still - nobody got hurt, the railroad guys were happy, and that gave me a reputation. Reputation is everything in this business.

I've got a picture of myself at a command post, and I know for a fact I was standing there thinking, *Well, I haven't killed anyone yet - could be worse.* I lived with that fear constantly. Dosimo said it best: your biggest fear is someone dying on your watch.

You asked about outside training? Here's a good one. Lithium-ion batteries. Back then, guys like you - like I was at your age - we were hungry for information. I've got a letter from my chief, dated 1986. Says, "Mike, we're trying to create the Southern New England Hazmat Team." We didn't use the word "county" in Connecticut - we hate that term - but it was basically a county team. New Haven County.

Budget? $5,000 per town, $50,000 total. Lieutenant Callan was going to present it at the library. That was 1986. And nothing ever happened.

Then one day in the mid-'80s, I get a call: "Somebody said you can help us build a hazmat team." I ask, "Who?" They say, "Chief Strobel." He was one of my rookies! So I say, "Did he tell you I was going to yell at you?" Guy says, "No, but if you do, I'm supposed to tell you this - Chief Strobel says we can pay you." I said, "All right, kid. I'll help. But only this once. Don't screw it up."

From 1986 to 2003 - that's how long it took to get traction. All I ever wanted was a truck that could respond to a gasoline tank fire and put it out. That's it. And if I could have all the meters, all the books, and Level Bs? I'd be just fine.

John Cassidy

When you bring your regional partners into your training programs, there's a serious return on that investment. Let's say we're hosting a drill or an in-service training on a new piece of equipment - if the CST has that same piece of gear, then of course we offer them a couple seats. Same goes for the PD, the FBI, whoever makes sense for that particular class.

That kind of inclusion pays dividends. You're networking, yes - but you're also learning from their experience. And it's not just one-way. The next time the CST is doing a training, they remember we looped them in, and they offer *us* a couple seats. It creates this reciprocal relationship that's good for everyone.

We've got a great setup, for example, where a few times a year we bring in higher-activity radiation sources for our classes. And when we do that, we invite others in to get hands-on with them. That's not just generosity - that's strategy. Because next time they have something valuable going on? We're on the invite list.

Now, yeah, sometimes people will say, "Well, you just gave a spot away that could've gone to one of your own members." And that's technically true - but now I've got someone going to *their* training.

That balance is worth it.

This kind of collaboration makes us stronger on the street. Because when the call comes in, it's not "the FBI showed up" or "ESU is here." It's *Frank*. It's *Randy*. It's *Rain*. You know them. You've trained with them. You've seen that they know their stuff - and they know you do too. That trust cuts through all the interagency friction and politics. You skip the posturing and just get to work. That's what joint training builds.

Now, as for how we find those valuable training opportunities? Obviously, if you buy a new meter, you're going to get some kind of training with it. But what if you're not buying anything and you're just trying to find quality instruction?

That's where technology and social media really come into play.

Follow the hazmat groups - Instagram, Facebook, YouTube, whatever. Follow The HazMat Guys, follow Conti, follow these groups that are plugged in. You start seeing trainings, conferences, even major incident breakdowns in your feed. And now you're aware of opportunities you never would've known about otherwise.

You're not even searching - it just shows up. It's referenceable. It's shareable. You see something cool, and now you can send it to your chief, your training officer, or your crew. That alone has changed the game.

And when you see something interesting? Reach out. DM them. Call them. Hazmat folks - by nature - we want to share what we know. I've found that most people are excited to talk shop. They'll send you a lesson plan, a PDF, whatever. People want to lift the community up.

So, whether it's in-person training, virtual sessions, or just trading resources through social media, that active engagement is how we keep evolving - and keep each other sharp.

Dave DiGregorio

It's a huge challenge to find those opportunities, honestly. I used to try and train with the CSTs every so often, just to give the team a chance to see how they did things, get a different perspective. I've held three different positions with CSTs, and I'll be honest, I didn't agree with a lot of what they did. Their approach was very linear - step-by-step, do this, then this, then this. There was no room for horizontal thinking, no room for flexibility or adapting on the fly.

When I came to hazmat, I made sure that wasn't going to be the case with my teams. Hazmat requires thinking on your feet, and that's something I wanted to ensure we fostered. But finding those diverse training opportunities, that's where the challenge lies. One example we used was UMass Lowell, which has a nuclear reactor. We'd go up there periodically to let the teams train on RAD, but also on reactor response. It taught the teams about RAD, sure, but it also gave them a real-world scenario for how to respond if things went sideways with the reactor.

In Massachusetts, we're lucky to have a lot of educational institutions and resources. Same goes for New York - tons of institutions that are open to having teams come in. We'd partner with industrial companies too, going into places that had a higher potential for emergencies. We'd set up drills, and they'd benefit from the training by being able to say they worked with the hazmat team. It wasn't about paying these industries; it was more about building mutually beneficial relationships. We'd get the chance to practice in real-world environments, and they'd get the added security of knowing they had proper training. We did that a lot - going into factories, seeing the layout, and doing drills there.

Now, with the new group I'm working with - the disaster medicine fellowship at Harvard - they recently started a fellowship with a concentration in CBRN, and they've made me the director of that fellowship. It's a different kind of training, but it's all about pushing the boundaries, finding new challenges, and offering those types of opportunities to the team.

Field trips are fantastic for this sort of thing. They get you out of the office and away from the classroom. You can't replace real-world experience by sitting behind a computer or watching a video online. As a leader, part of your job is getting out there, finding those opportunities, and making sure your team is constantly learning, even if it's outside the traditional training room.

Things can get stale fast if you aren't actively seeking new opportunities for growth. It's easy for routines to become monotonous, and that's where the danger lies - when the team stops pushing themselves, the performance can drop. I've had to go to a lot of planning meetings with multiple agencies, and it's not just about talking shop. It's about networking, asking questions, and looking for ways to bring something back to your team. That's how you continue to grow and evolve. It's about always being on the lookout for the next opportunity to enhance your skills and the team's capabilities.

Dave Donohue

The key to selecting a training opportunity is to first identify what it will bring to the team. We need to assess where the gaps are in our current training and ensure that these weaknesses are addressed through the opportunity at hand.

The first major benefit is the chance to create greater cohesion across disciplines and agencies, which will pay off significantly during an actual incident response. Building those relationships beforehand strengthens the overall effectiveness when the time comes to respond together.

Second, cross-training opens the door to integrating new skills and knowledge into our existing tactics and policies. These new insights can improve the way we approach different situations and enhance the overall capability of the team.

Third, there's always an opportunity to identify mutually beneficial activities, such as in areas like purchasing, response, and planning. By working together with other departments or agencies, we can leverage shared resources and ensure that everyone is aligned on objectives.

As for how I find these opportunities, it's all about networking - word of mouth, internet searches, and asking questions of others in the field. Whether through formal or informal channels, staying connected with peers and continually asking about what's working for others helps me stay on top of potential training and growth opportunities for the team.

Rick Edinger

If you can make it happen, I think it's incredibly important to train with your response partners - the people who are going to be there when critical incidents occur.

Back in Virginia, we had a formal hazmat mutual aid system. The state had it structured, similar to what you see in Massachusetts or California - specific teams designated to respond based on region. Our team could handle most of our incidents internally, but if it reached a certain level, we had Henrico County coming in as our backup. They were the state team for the Richmond metro area.

We couldn't train with them as often as we would've liked - time and budget always being what they are - but we made it a point to schedule joint training days when we could. Because here's the deal: you want to meet your partners before the emergency. Know their names, know their faces, understand what equipment is carried and matches up, and what doesn't. Train together now, so you're not trying to solve compatibility issues during an actual incident. That's the whole point - fix it in training, not in real life.

And hazmat's unique in that it often overlaps with other disciplines. Look at the USAR teams - they always roll with a hazmat tech, because sooner or later, they're dealing with chemicals in collapsed structures. In our case, we had hazmat and water/dive rescue working closely together. They'd help us with boom deployment, we'd assist them with decon. So when there was overlap in responsibilities, we did focused cross-training to make sure we could operate smoothly side-by-side. That paid off more than once.

When it comes to finding valuable training opportunities beyond your own department, it's easier than ever. With the internet, there's no excuse. There's information everywhere. I expect my training officers to be out there watching what's going on, staying connected, talking to the right people. But even if they're not, training announcements are everywhere - National Fire Academy, SERTC, Anniston - you name it.

It's just a matter of monitoring the environment. See what's being offered, figure out what fits your needs, and plug into it. You mentioned it earlier - the federal training programs are gold. They don't cost you anything but the backfill time and maybe a meal or two, and they're well-run, high-quality programs. There's a ton of value there, and more departments should be taking advantage of them.

John Esposito

Having an open mind - it's critical. So last weekend, we had the MSOC conference at The Rock. It's not called MSOC anymore - it's got some new acronym - but it's still medical special operations. And when I spoke to that opening group, I told them: *you're here to learn.* That means having an open mind. If you hear something that doesn't match how *you* do it, don't just dismiss it. Think about it. Ask questions. Talk to the presenter. That's how you grow.

You might do it one way. They do it another. But unless you dig into it, challenge it, explore it, you'll never know which is better - or if there's something in between. And that's especially important for us in the FDNY. We've got to realize that just because we didn't come up with something doesn't mean it's not valuable. That kind of thinking? That's pre-9/11 thinking.

There's plenty to learn from a lieutenant in a small fire department in the Midwest. He might've run into a problem you haven't even thought of yet - and he figured out a way to solve it. And that same mindset applies internally. We've got firefighters and junior officers with sharp ideas, and we need to be open to that too.

Truth is, I haven't ridden a fire truck since 2005. That's a full career ago. So when someone brings up a new technique for a standpipe stretch or something that's evolved since I was on the line, I've got to be honest -

I'm not the expert anymore. And that's okay. It's the same with things like chainsaw training. How often does an urban firefighter use a chainsaw? Not much. So we go to the people who *do* - the New York State forestry instructors. We train with them. Because when a hurricane hits and we've got to put together a chainsaw task force, I want guys who know how to stay safe and not cut their legs off.

That takes humility. You have to be able to say, "I don't know." And the further you go in leadership, the easier it should be to say that. It actually becomes kind of freeing. You're not supposed to know everything. I remember John used to joke, "Oh, what do you think - I know *everything*?" And I like to say, "They don't tell me anything anyway." But the point is - we're generalists. We're expected to know a lot, but we're not specialists in everything.

That's especially true for hazmat. When someone new comes to the team, we're going to teach them *a lot*. We don't expect them to walk in with everything figured out. But we *do* expect them to show up with the basics locked in. A solid understanding of PPE. Familiarity with SCBA - how it protects you, what the alarms mean, how to wear it correctly. They need to be more than minimally competent. On the Rescue and Squad side, we say they need to have *superior firefighting ability*. That doesn't mean superhero - it just means a firm grasp on the fundamentals, because we're about to pile even more on top.

If a new hazmat member doesn't understand how PPE works, how are they supposed to grasp the difference between an APR and a PAPR - or what it means to operate in a fully encapsulated suit? We're not bringing people in to teach them the *basics*. We're bringing them in to *build on* the basics.

And that expectation should be clear from the beginning. If someone's struggling with the new stuff? We'll spend time with them. No problem. But if they're struggling with the stuff they should've walked in with? That's not what we're here for. This isn't a remedial program. And they need to understand that.

At the end of the day, hazmat guys are firefighters. That comes first. They should already know their basic tools. They should know how to use the CO meter. The thermal imaging camera. All of it. Because if they don't know *that*, they're not ready for the next level.

Brandon Fletcher

HazMat training with other departments in my area is something I'm always pushing for. However, aside from getting a little participation from multiple departments in continuing education classes, it's tough to get consistent collaboration. It's an ongoing challenge to bring everyone together for this kind of training.

I'm constantly on the lookout for outside training opportunities, and sometimes those opportunities come through word of mouth via my vast network. Other times, I find out about them through social media or email blasts from associations or state agencies. It's about staying connected and being proactive - taking every chance to expand knowledge and encourage collaboration across departments. This kind of cross-departmental training not only improves skills but also strengthens relationships and ensures we're all prepared for the next big incident.

Chris Hawley

I love what you're saying about how valuable it is to bring in outside experts, not just for the knowledge, but for the way they challenge your team. When you bring in someone who isn't part of the internal politics, it gives the team the opportunity to ask questions they might not feel comfortable asking in-house. It's like you said, sometimes team members might be afraid to push back against their own instructors, even when they have doubts. But when the outside instructor asks tough questions, it creates a sense of urgency. Suddenly, they're thinking, "I need to know this." And that push can make them more motivated to learn and improve.

You're spot-on about how sometimes the internal politics get in the way. If you're the coordinator and you ask a hard question, it could be taken as an attack, which isn't the goal. But when you bring in an outsider, they don't know the personalities, so they can ask those tough questions without the same dynamic. And then, the team feels a little embarrassed if they can't answer, and that embarrassment can turn into motivation. They don't want to be caught off guard again, so they'll study harder, pay more attention, and get smarter.

It reminds me of a situation I had with risk assessments. When I first started doing them, I got challenged constantly, not just by my team but by other teams too. Everyone wanted to do a Level A all the time, no matter the situation. But I knew that wasn't always necessary, so I had to use science and chemistry to prove my point and take away the hysteria. I loved that challenge. I didn't mind the pushback at all because I knew that at the end of the day, when the class was over, people were going to walk away thinking, "Crap, he's right." I really enjoy that kind of back-and-forth - it forces everyone to really think about the decisions they're making.

That's why picking the right instructors is so crucial. They not only bring new knowledge but also force your team to question their assumptions and think critically. Like you said, having the right outside person can create that moment where they challenge what they know. And that's when the learning really happens.

The story about the bomb tech is incredible, too. It really highlights the power of bringing in experts with real-world experience. That guy was obviously a walking encyclopedia on explosives, and his experience was invaluable. It's funny how he answered that question about where he got his knowledge - "I've blown a lot of things up." And the fact that they wanted to do this training even though it was late, and despite the overtime worries, really speaks to the impact an instructor like that can have. When people are excited about the training, it's a win, and they're willing to give a little extra time to get it done.

The key takeaway here is that bringing in the right instructors can motivate your team like nothing else. It's not just about the content they're teaching; it's about how they engage the team and create an environment where people want to learn, ask questions, and get better. But, like you said, finding those instructors is the hard part. It takes work, but when you get the right person, the results can be incredible.

Mike Hildebrand

At the end of the day, you've got to give something to get something. That's just how it works.

People want to know: *What's in it for me?* If I let two of your guys into my class, what do I get out of it? Cross-training should be a no-brainer. If I know my sister county is running a training, I should be picking up the phone and calling them: "Hey, I've got a gal coming down. She's solid. Any chance I can send two of my team members to sit in?"

And usually the answer's yes. Because they know, when the tables turn, I'll do the same. Or I'll film the session and share the video. It's not transactional. It's just good faith. It's *professional courtesy*.

Same thing goes for industry partnerships. That's a big opportunity area most folks don't even think about. I've done a ton of operational readiness reviews for regional hazmat teams, and I'm always surprised how often people overlook what's sitting right in their own backyard.

Take this one chemical plant I worked with - they needed a high-angle and confined space rescue capability. It was required by law. But here's the thing: the law *didn't* say it had to be *their* employees doing the rescue. Meanwhile, the local fire department didn't have the budget for the training or the gear. So what happened?

The plant paid for two firefighters to attend high-angle/confined space training at Texas A&M. Then they bought the rope kits and all the gear. They tagged it up, donated it to the department, and now the city has a first-rate technical rescue capability - for free.

That never would've happened if someone hadn't picked up the phone and started the conversation.

So yeah, partnerships matter. A lot. Sometimes they'll pay for your training. Sometimes they'll lend you their people, their tools, their space. But you're never going to know that unless you ask.

It all goes back to one thing: *who you know* - and how willing you are to pick up the phone and build the relationship.

Bob Ingram

In my experience, opportunities for collaboration and cross-training between teams have often been elusive. Many hazmat teams across the country are regional and face the challenge of managing varying schedules, as well as a mix of volunteer and career personnel. This can make it difficult to establish regular, consistent partnerships. However, one approach that might yield better results is developing partnerships with other cities and cross-detailing team members for a week or two. This arrangement would allow personnel from your team to ride with them and vice versa, offering valuable opportunities for observations, sharing SOPs, and experiencing different types of incidents firsthand.

Familiarization drills between neighboring hazmat teams have been a helpful experience in my case. While some sharing of knowledge and practices does take place, it often doesn't go far enough to establish the level of collaboration needed for sustained improvement.

My personal experience also comes from attending programs at the National Fire Academy (NFA) and other federal training sites. These events provide a chance to meet other hazmat team members, discuss team activities, and share insights on training. They create opportunities to build relationships with state and federal resources, which can be invaluable if large-scale responses require external support in your jurisdiction.

Participation in hazmat committees and networking is another critical component of growth. Through these interactions, you can identify new training that would benefit your current mission space or help you prepare for emerging mission spaces. By staying connected with other teams and national resources, you can ensure your team remains adaptable and ready for any challenge that comes its way.

Phil McArdle

One significant limitation for many teams is the cost of training, and for some, this becomes the primary barrier that prevents them from attending more schools. To overcome this challenge, it's crucial to take full advantage of the training opportunities that are available at little to no cost. Look for schools and training programs that minimize travel expenses, utilize ride-sharing options, and take advantage of schools that offer room and board at little to moderate cost. Train-the-trainer programs are an excellent way to keep costs down while ensuring that all team members can benefit from the training materials without the need for each member to attend separately.

When air travel is necessary, it's important to shop around for the best deals on flights and, when needed, work with experienced travel agents to find the best options. By being strategic about travel logistics, teams can reduce costs significantly.

If your team is the lead agency in your jurisdiction, it's essential to keep elected officials informed about your capabilities and training needs. However, this requires a delicate balance. You must be cautious not to overstep your bounds or create controversy that might reflect poorly on management. Working closely with supervisors and managers and encouraging their support for your training requests or initiatives can make your proposals more acceptable and easier to implement.

Training is not only an investment in the team but also an opportunity to learn about the capabilities and limitations of other responding agencies. Attending joint trainings gives you a sense of who you can rely on in the event of an emergency. It also allows you to identify the unique tools and equipment that other agencies bring to the table, which might differ from your own. This helps clarify whether other agencies have complementary roles or competing functions during emergency responses. Identifying these differences ahead of time allows you to work out potential conflicts so that when real operations occur, roles and responsibilities are clearly defined, preventing delays or confusion during high-stress situations.

Today, computers make it easier than ever to identify training opportunities nationwide. Conducting searches for available courses is simply a matter of knowing where to look. Government websites are often the best place to start, as they provide information about available training, eligibility requirements, and any prerequisites that may be needed.

In addition to traditional in-person training, specialized courses can also be found online. These courses can range from highly specific topics and can vary greatly in cost, from no cost to quite expensive. Online training programs are also an excellent option for those seeking low-cost opportunities and can often be completed from the comfort of home, offering flexibility while still providing valuable learning experiences.

Adam McFadden

Attending conferences and industry events is essential for hazmat professionals who want to stay ahead of the curve. These gatherings expose our team to emerging threats, new technologies, and best practices from across the field. Key events include health and safety conferences, oil and gas industry forums, chemical company-sponsored training, and first responder summits focused on hazardous materials and terrorism response.

Beyond the formal sessions, these events provide critical networking opportunities, hands-on demonstrations, and expert-led discussions that help our team stay at the forefront of hazmat response, risk mitigation, and interagency collaboration. The knowledge and connections we gain translate directly into improved capabilities on the ground.

We also place a high value on cross-training with outside organizations. These opportunities offer more than just technical knowledge - they give us insight into how other teams operate under pressure. Observing different approaches, tactics, and leadership styles strengthens our own adaptability, decision-making, and team dynamics. This kind of exposure builds stronger communication, better problem-solving, and improved performance in real-world operations.

To stay plugged in, we actively seek out valuable training opportunities outside our department. We use a mix of industry websites, social media, and in-person networking at major hazmat and emergency response events across North America. This helps us identify specialized courses, equipment demos, and interagency exercises that align with our training goals and operational needs. By staying connected through both technology and professional networks, we ensure our team remains informed, engaged, and ready to lead in an ever-evolving field.

Mike Monaco

I don't really have a perfect answer for that one - but I *can* tell you this: the benefits of cross-training or joint exercises with outside organizations are huge.

It's funny - we spend so much time training with our own. Firefighters train with firefighters. Hazmat trains with hazmat. But you don't get a real sense of the *big picture* until you start training across agencies. That's when things start to click.

For example, the fire department had its hazmat team. So did the police. So did the Port Authority. We were all operating in the same space, with overlapping missions - but for the longest time, we knew next to nothing about each other. It wasn't until we started joint exercises that we realized just how many moving parts there are in a scene - and how essential it is to understand each other's roles.

I remember training with PD - us carrying meters, them carrying weapons - and it became crystal clear: neither one of us could do the job alone. We needed each other. Those kinds of exercises aren't just about practicing tactics. They're about building *awareness* - about understanding the full scope of a response and where you fit into it.

If you're looking for a place to start, sites like HowToCoin.FEMA.gov are goldmines. They're one of the best resources for finding training opportunities. And conferences? Conferences are packed with instructors, most of whom are giving lectures designed to give you just enough information to spark interest - to show you what's possible, what's new, and what's worth bringing back to your department.

Seeing as many different instructors as possible is key. Almost every single one of them can be hired to come out and work directly with your team. So take notes. Get contact info. And think about how their perspective or specialty could fill a gap back home.

Chris Pfaff

Okay, so that shifts this conversation a little bit - I was initially going to talk about regional training, but bringing in those outside influences is huge. It's an old standard, but it's important.

When we talk about outside-department training generally, we start with the lowest hanging fruit - free training. Think the National Fire Academy and the National Consortium. Any elite hazmat team should have members attending these trainings regularly. Sure, some of that content can feel dated, but they're continuously updating their curriculum, which makes them invaluable.

So having national instructors come in - or sending our teams outside of our immediate region or area code - is absolutely critical. This broadens our perspective and ensures we're not stuck in our own bubble, thinking our way is the only way.

Now, bringing it back to regional training - that's another big thing I advocate for strongly. My team up in the Northwest makes it a priority to organize regional exercises at least twice a year, where we collaborate with 10 to 12 hazmat teams. We run roadshows, rodeos, or training capability assessments alongside CST and FBI teams. These large-scale scenarios never go perfectly - there are always frustrations - but they're incredibly beneficial because we get to understand each team's real capabilities and limitations.

One of the biggest advantages of cross-training and joint exercises is gaining firsthand knowledge about other teams. Across the country, we've got many junior teams still building their capabilities and senior teams with tons of equipment. These exercises aren't about judging or pointing out that "those guys don't know what they're doing." Instead, it's about recognizing, "Hey, this is a new team - how can we support or collaborate with them?"

Maybe their strengths lie somewhere we don't expect. They might have an incredible drone program - even if our department won't touch drones to save our lives - but maybe they lack plugging and patching gear. Meanwhile, we might have all the plugging and patching tools but zero drone capability. Through these regional trainings, we build trust, awareness, and partnerships that let us call on each other's expertise during real incidents.

Remember, just because a team operates from a bread truck or a pickup hauling a trailer doesn't mean they can't be elite.

So how do you identify and pursue valuable training opportunities beyond your own department? Conferences - not just chat boards.

Conferences are huge. Sites like hazmatandrescue.com provide a wealth of information about conferences and networking opportunities. Going to these events, visiting vendor booths, and seeing what's available is helpful - but keep a skeptical eye. Vendors pay for those seats, and they'll tell you their product is the best thing ever made.

Lastly, and this is key: be bold enough to be dumb. Seriously, nobody knows everything. Half the stuff those vendors or instructors talk about might be totally new to you - and that's fine. You've got to start somewhere.

Bob Royall

I think it's absolutely crucial to keep an open mind and keep learning. Afterall, if you turn internal, you don't know what you don't know and you are just setting yourself up to be a danger to yourself and to your team. I really believe that.

That's why we bring in so many guest instructors and subject matter experts for our technician training courses. We don't just rely on our own knowledge; we bring in a rail expert to teach railroad 101, product specialists to dive deep into specific products, and detection experts to help with those critical thinking skills. We do have one strict rule though: you are not here to market your product. You're here to teach our folks. The focus is to help student grow and learn from the best.

Throughout the year, we are always meeting new people at conferences. I mean, do I know every single person who comes to Hot Zone? Hell no. A lot of that is based on recommendations. My guys, Houston's guys - they'll come to me and say, "Hey, you need to check this guy out. He's got a great message." And when they say that, I trust them because they can smell a phony from a mile away. We've all been in this long enough to know who's real and who's just talking. It's that authenticity and experience that we value. That's what makes the difference in training and during response situations.

Bobby Salvesen

I remember coming into Special Operations not long after 9/11. At that time, FDNY didn't really bring in outside vendors. We had this mentality that the sun rose and set on FDNY - nobody could teach us anything we didn't already know.

And to be fair, we *are* a damn good department. We get a ton of reps, and we've got some incredibly sharp people in the ranks. But if I'm being honest, there was definitely some hubris baked into that. A little unspoken attitude of, *"We're unteachable."* I say that jokingly - but only *sort of.*

After 9/11, everything changed. The Trade Center brought in an influx of funding, and for the first time in a while, we weren't strapped for cash. So the question became: *What do we do with it?*

The answer was: *Training.*

We started bringing in outside instructors, vendors, specialists from all over. And that was the turning point. Because once those ideas started flowing in, guys began to realize - *"Whoa... that's actually a really smart way of doing things."* And it spread. It caught fire. More training came in. More ideas. More collaboration.

Now? Outside training is a *cornerstone* of what we do.

Yes, FDNY is solid. Yes, we set the standard in a lot of areas. But there are some incredibly talented people out there, doing amazing work in other departments and agencies - and we'd be fools not to learn from them.

So if you're building or leading a hazmat team, let me give you one piece of advice:

Stop drinking your own pond water.

Get Joe's pond water. Get Sal's pond water. Get *anyone else's* pond water. Fresh perspective matters.

You don't grow by staying in your own bubble. You grow by seeing how *other* people solve problems - and adapting that brilliance to your own context.

Enough with the pond water. You get where I'm going.

Doug Schick and Mark Zilch
Doug:

It's all about opening up conversations. That's how the knowledge spreads - people see different ways of doing things and it sparks a discussion. It's like, "Hey, what kind of setup are you using for that?" Or, "How are you guys approaching this?" And suddenly, you've got a room full of people learning from each other.

I've got guys like Mark and Jeff Hennessy around - Jeff's someone you've probably interacted with online. He's the one who actually brought the AFG grant to my attention. And that right there is a perfect example of why these connections matter.

I already knew you guys were offering all this training, and I wanted to bring it in, but it wasn't in the budget. Then Jeff says, "Hey, we could get it funded through AFG." That changed everything. Without that heads-up, it wouldn't have happened. That's the power of staying connected.

Whether it's being online, on email lists, or following groups like Hazard3 - I try to keep tabs on what's out there. A lot of times they'll send out alerts about upcoming training or free webinars. When I see those, I make it a point to pass them along to the team. Even if just one or two people take advantage of it, that's worth it.

Budget-wise, I'm fortunate enough to bring in outside training from time to time. It's not always full-scale, multi-day stuff, but I can usually swing 4-hour blocks for each shift. We run those across the three platoons to make sure everyone gets something without killing overtime.

But if we *can* make a longer training work - like the three-day classes we've been talking about where everyone's there for 24 hours - that's the sweet spot. Those kinds of immersive trainings are just great. They're the ones where things really click, people bond, and the learning sticks.

Jason Zeller

For us, outside department and agency training wasn't just something we did occasionally - it was a cornerstone of how we stayed sharp and grew as a team. No matter how good you think you are, staying stuck in your own bubble is a surefire way to become complacent. I firmly believed in stepping outside our comfort zone and training shoulder to shoulder with other professionals who brought different skill sets, experiences, and perspectives to the table.

I always made sure we actively sought opportunities to train with other agencies - from local fire departments and law enforcement hazmat teams to federal agencies, special response teams, and military units. Whether it was running joint exercises, participating in large-scale incident drills, or engaging in smaller, more specialized training, every single interaction made us better. It gave us fresh ideas, exposed us to new tactics and procedures, and strengthened our ability to integrate seamlessly when real-world events called for multi-agency responses.

Equally important, it kept us honest and humble. Training with others forces you to test your skills against different approaches. You quickly learn where you're well-prepared and where you need improvement. That was always a valuable lesson for me - iron sharpens iron.

Outside training also built relationships that paid dividends down the line. When you've already trained and problem-solved alongside someone, it makes that phone call during a real event much easier. Trust has already been established. You understand how each other works. This familiarity directly translates to faster, more effective real-world operations.

The benefits of cross-training and joint exercises with outside organizations were endless for us. One of the biggest advantages was that it allowed us to start building real-world procedures and TTPs together *before* the emergency ever happened. It's one thing to have your internal SOPs dialed in - and we certainly did - but when you show up to a major incident, you're not operating in isolation. You're integrating with other agencies and teams. Through joint training, we were able to work out those seams ahead of time and develop combined SOPs that worked for everyone. That way, when the Red Star Cluster popped - when the balloon went up - there was no confusion. Everyone knew exactly how we were going to operate side by side.

Another huge benefit was familiarity and trust. Training with the people you'll eventually deploy with makes all the difference. You're not meeting strangers on your worst day - you're working with familiar faces you've already been in the trenches with. You know how they operate. You know their strengths, their quirks, their expectations, and even their pet peeves. That matters when seconds count, and communication needs to be seamless.

Most importantly, those reps together built confidence - in each other and in the process. When you've solved problems together under stress in training, it translates immediately to the real deal. There's no hesitation, no ego - just execution.

Cross-training didn't just make us better individually. It made us better together. It built trust, sharpened our procedures, and ensured that when the call came, we weren't figuring things out - we were already locked in and ready to go.

Identifying and pursuing valuable training opportunities outside our department really came down to staying connected and being an active part of the community. It goes right back to what I've said before - conferences, networking, and building relationships with like-minded professionals formed the foundation. When you invest in those relationships and establish yourself as someone who takes the job seriously, opportunities start coming your way. People share. They want good teams to be involved. You become part of the trusted circle.

For us, it wasn't about sitting back and waiting for an email to cross our desk. It was about being good stewards of our profession and staying engaged. When you train regularly with other agencies, show up at key conferences, and maintain close ties within the emergency response network, you start hearing about the right opportunities - the courses worth attending, the specialized programs that sharpen your edge, and the national-level exercises where you can really test your capabilities.

Fortunately, we were lucky enough to have a solid budget, which gave us the flexibility to pursue both local and national training. But regardless of budget, it all starts with being plugged in and respected in your community. When you're known as a team that brings value and takes training seriously, people want you involved. That's when the doors start opening.

Bottom line: when you're in the mix, constantly improving, and have your finger on the pulse of your profession, opportunities aren't hard to find. They're everywhere. You just have to be ready to say yes and seize them.

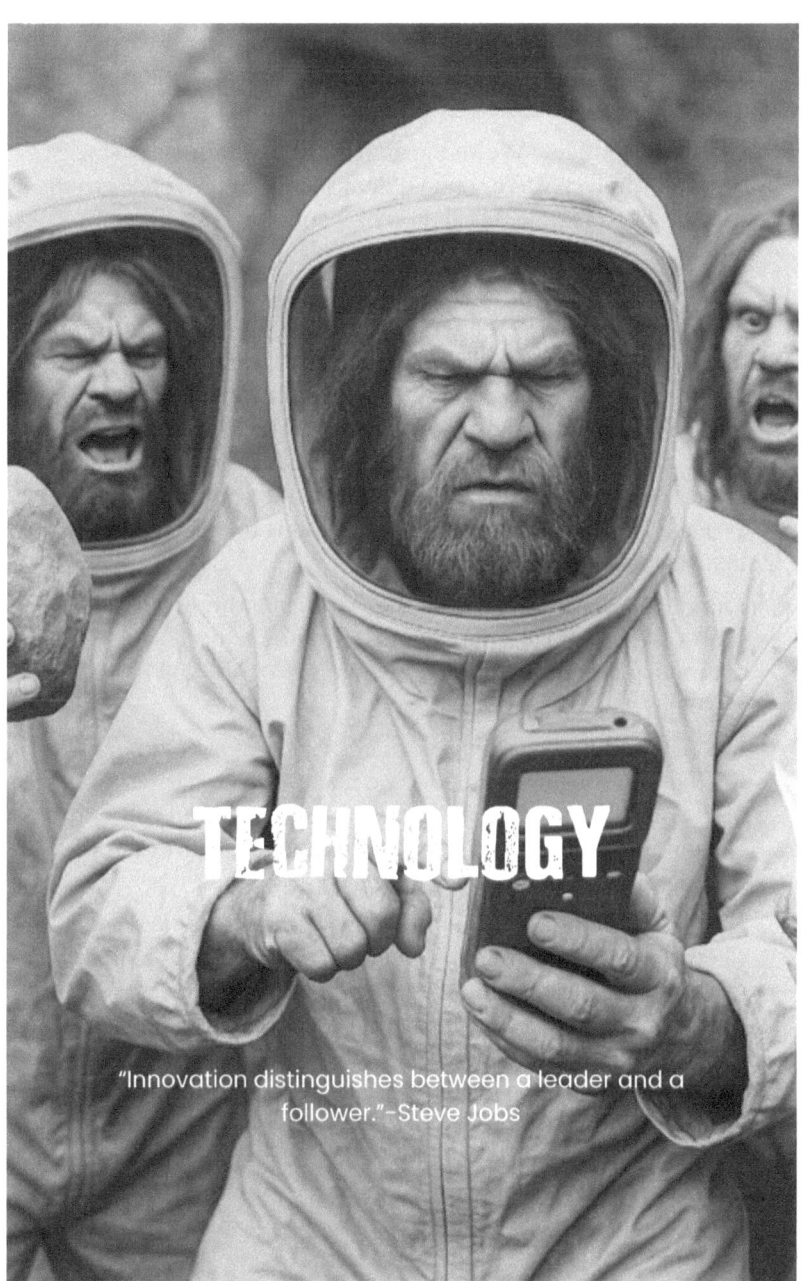

Dan Baker

Technology has transformed our team significantly in recent years - it's really shaping how we approach our mission. Right now, we're especially excited about a few key areas:

- CBRN Responder: We've integrated this tool into every single response. In fact, we've set up a dedicated tech reference group specifically to handle this and other technologies during incidents. We regularly drill with this platform, keeping everyone sharp.
- Starlink: Let's face it, cell service sucks in plenty of spots around the state. Although we often have access to some sophisticated communication systems, Starlink gives us reliable, portable internet pretty much anywhere, anytime. We bring it out on every single run - even when we're not rolling out the full comms truck. (And yes, we typically always have the comm truck available, but sometimes we skip requesting the big interoperable units from our parent agency.)
- Lidar: Anywhere we can get it, we do. Right now, two of our UAVs are fully lidar-equipped, paired with the necessary computing power and trained operators. We absolutely love this capability.
- UAVs and Robotics: At the moment, Special Ops operates 14 UAVs, with roughly half dedicated exclusively to hazmat operations. We're also pushing to add ground-based robots to expand our unmanned capabilities. We're huge advocates of robotics in hazmat.
- Blackline Equipment: This technology offers fantastic responder safety features along with low-maintenance ownership. While we still maintain a significant investment in Honeywell/Rae Systems, we've continued investing heavily in the newer Blackline tech.

Now, the biggest tech-related challenge I'm facing currently involves our robotics proposal. Public perception is tough - especially around the notion of "killer robots" (thanks, NYPD) - and that's made it particularly difficult for us to successfully procure SPOT-style quadruped robots.

Turns out money isn't always the sticking point...

To stay current, we lean heavily on our diverse and tech-savvy staff - our dedicated nerds, basically. Our tech reference folks and their Deputy Chief keep a close eye on emerging technologies, constantly evaluating what's out there. Leadership's job is to sift through the hype and gadgetry, and figure out which new equipment and associated training will genuinely deliver the greatest good for the most people, for the longest amount of time.

Mike Callan

When it comes to technology, I probably wouldn't have even looked up the word if I hadn't thought about what it actually means in the context of my experience. What I've learned over the years in the fire service is that it's not just about having the right tool for the job - it's about having the right tool for the job, with the right person, at the right time. There are certain tools that some people just can't use effectively. For example, I know I'd never send certain people to the roof with a chainsaw. They might come back with one foot! There are good drivers, and then there are those who just want to drive.

And when it comes to technology, the same thing applies. If the information is communicated in a way that benefits education and understanding, it makes all the difference.

Now, I'm not that old, but I see a lot of parallels between today's technology and the past. When Gutenberg invented the printing press, people thought it was revolutionary because it allowed information to be spread quickly. Bibles were printed, but so were "how-to" books - how to plant crops, how to take care of sheep, and all sorts of practical knowledge. People wanted to learn how to improve their lives, and that's exactly what the printing press helped facilitate. This is similar to what we're seeing today with new information systems. When something new comes along, it's powerful because it allows for an exchange of information that can help someone become better than they were before.

People always talk about AI, and a lot of them are nervous about where it could lead. I recently heard someone say that in 30 years, humans might be the second smartest beings on Earth. That's a pretty wild thought. But I've been thinking about AI for a long time, ever since I first saw *2001: A Space Odyssey* back in 1967. In the middle of that movie, there was an

AI named HAL. HAL's whole job was to communicate with the crew, but HAL would say things like, "Dave, I'm upset." HAL had its own mind and made decisions that ultimately led to trouble. I've thought about that a lot, and while AI is powerful, we have to remember to be cautious with it - after all, we're still in control, at least for now.

When I think about education and training, especially in the context of AI, I imagine if I could just plug in a USB port and download everything I've ever seen, done, or learned as a firefighter - every mistake I've made, every positive decision that led to success - I could learn so much faster. That kind of technology, if it existed, would be invaluable in training. But until we get there, the best we can do is focus on sharing knowledge and learning from each other.

Training has always been a part of who I am. I went to school to be a teacher, but after six months, I ended up becoming a fireman. It helped me a lot, though, especially when it came to teaching and training others. My wife, though, didn't want our sons to be firemen. She'd seen me on a roof during a fire, and after she saw me on the roof of a two-alarm fire, she told me she never wanted to go to another call. She didn't want our sons to go into the fire service, either. And I understood that. But the funny thing is, both of my sons became teachers. They never saw me fight fires, but they traveled with me to places like Florida and Sacramento. They'd come along because they were excited to be a part of the experience.

I've been lucky to build a network of good friends over the years, and people like Jan Dumbar, a close friend of mine, have been part of that network. Networking has opened doors and created a family that's not just defined by our work but by the bonds we form with each other. I love the concept of brotherhood and sisterhood. I think the term "brotherhood" works, and I understand the importance of inclusivity, but I haven't quite gotten comfortable with the whole "parentheses, him or her" part. I'll get there, eventually.

So, as I reflect on my journey and the technology we use today, it's all about progress and change. Whether it's new tools or new systems of communication, the goal remains the same: to learn, grow, and share that knowledge to make ourselves and our communities safer. Technology has always been about improving our ability to communicate and make better decisions, and I believe that's what will continue to drive our success in the future.

John Cassidy

After 9/11, there was a huge surge in resources - teams were getting equipped like never before. The ability to acquire, maintain, and upgrade equipment just exploded.

Then with the war on terror, the funding pushed even further. You saw a lot of what used to be lab-based technology transition into portable, handheld, deployable tools that we could actually take downrange. That completely changed the game for hazmat teams.

But all of that comes with its own challenges - especially when it comes to maintaining proficiency. Just because you've got the latest gadget doesn't mean your team knows how to use it. And you can't forget the basics. You can't aBrandon tried-and-true methods like colorimetric tubes or pH paper just because you bought the latest whiz-bang piece of tech. You have to strike a balance.

Procurement is another sticking point. It's a lot like buying a phone - you get the latest model, and a year later it's outdated. But in our world, that "outdated" tool still cost a pile of money. So now what?

You've got to be strategic. You've got to select tech that will hold value over time.

And one thing that absolutely *has* to be built into your procurement plan is training capture. When you buy a new piece of equipment, you usually get some level of factory-supported training. That's great - for the people who are there *that day*. But fast-forward six months or a year, and now you've got new team members. They're not getting that original training unless you plan for it.

So, from the beginning, you've got to secure the rights to keep all training materials. Slides, manuals, whatever. Better yet, record the training. If you're not already doing that, you should be. Set the expectation with the vendor upfront: "I'm going to have my video crew here; I'm going to post this on our internal training portal."

That way, when the next person joins the team, they're not starting from scratch. They're getting the same quality instruction.

And if that costs more? Build it into the price. That's part of making the technology *work* for your team.

I am looking forward to incorporating handheld gas phase FTIR to our hazard assessment tools.

And if you're dealing with natural gas in your area? The laser methane detector is one of the best tools I've seen in a long time.

The price point's high - definitely more than your typical four-gas meter - but the stand-off capability it gives you? That's incredible. One of my favorite tools in the box right now.

But again, this all ties back to those hazmat groups and the broader network. If you're following those communities - on social media, podcasts, forums - you're getting exposure not just to incidents and tactics, but also to *technology*. Some of the best minds in hazmat are active in those spaces. And let's not forget, some of them are sponsors of the Hazmat Guys podcast.

Vendor floors at conferences are another goldmine. You get to see the gear. You get to *touch* it, talk to reps, ask questions without commitment. You're not getting a formal sales pitch in your office - you're one of a hundred people walking by that booth. It's low pressure. You can get a sense of what's out there, what might fit your needs, and if it's something you want to explore further, you follow up later.

That's what I love about conferences. The exposure to new tools, new ideas, and being able to evaluate them without any pressure - that's a win. And the more we stay connected through these channels, the better equipped we are to bring the right technology home and *actually* make it work for the team.

Dave DiGregorio

You're absolutely right about the importance of having backup plans, especially when technology is involved. Technology is a tool, but what happens when it fails? You need to be prepared. If my comms go down, have I trained my guys to communicate using hand signals? If my network crashes, do I have physical books in the vehicles for research? It's all about being ready for Plan B and even Plan C. Sometimes technology doesn't do what it's supposed to, and it happens more often than people realize. We're all so dependent on technology, and when it goes down, people freak out. But my mentality is: figure it out, and adapt. You might have to fall back on something as simple as drawing on the blackboard or improvising in other ways. It's crucial to be flexible when technology fails, and honestly, it's something I've had to do in the past. You can't let it throw off your whole operation.

Now, in terms of technology, I've been diving deep into AI over the last couple of years. Since leaving hazmat, I've learned more about AI than I ever thought I would, and now I use it all the time. Whether it's ChatGPT for creating presentations or using it for logistics, it's here to stay and growing exponentially.

I've even thought about how AI can benefit hazmat teams. A few years ago, I predicted that drones and robots would play a huge role in the future of hazmat response. I knew that using non-human responders equipped with detection and identification technology would minimize risks to personnel while still providing critical information. But now with AI, the possibilities are even greater. We're talking about taking it to the next level. AI can analyze data, predict outcomes, and even help with decision-making on the fly.

I was listening to an audiobook called Scary Smart, and it dives into the future of AI. The first part of the book is pretty alarming, warning about AI learning from negative behaviors, like when people misuse technology. But by the end, it focuses on how AI can be used for good if we teach it right. That really stuck with me. I've even started talking to ChatGPT like it's a person, just to help "teach" it to respond in a more human way. I know it sounds a bit funny, but in a way, I feel like I'm doing my part to make AI a little more empathetic, showing it that people can be decent.

One thing I've learned about AI is that you can give it a specific role. For example, I'll tell ChatGPT, "Assume you are the Hazmat director," and then ask it to help with something specific, like creating a presentation or solving a problem. It really helps refine the output.

A great example of how I've used AI was when I had to conduct assessments for 28 hospitals in Connecticut. Normally, it would take me hours to figure out the most efficient route to get to each hospital, especially with four different people involved. But with ChatGPT, I just gave it the names and locations of the hospitals, and within minutes, it provided a plan with directions, road suggestions, and even hotel recommendations for overnight stays. It saved me hours of work. I use it for things like this all the time, and I feel like a bit of a tech geek, but it's such a time-saver, and the results are amazing.

AI is becoming such a powerful tool in so many aspects of what I do now, and I think it's going to be a game-changer for hazmat teams in the future.

Dave Donohue

New technology has brought both benefits and challenges to our field. Take the introduction of multi-threat garments, for example. They've made wearing PPE much more tolerable - hybrid decon has also helped in this area. But then you look at the high-tech identification equipment. While it has its advantages, it has fostered a dependence on technology that can be detrimental, especially with younger technicians. When the technology fails or doesn't provide an answer, it can throw them into a state of uncertainty, what I like to call "vapor lock." This is something I see a lot of, especially when first-due companies don't fully understand the capabilities of 4/5-gas meters. If you're expected to use a saw on a truck, you damn well better know how to use the meter.

Looking ahead, emerging technologies like unmanned aerial and waterborne devices have the potential to significantly improve our ability to assess, monitor, and enhance safety during incidents. These technologies allow us to place eyes and instruments downrange, providing vital real-time data to support the response. Robotics, too, has the potential to revolutionize downrange operations and reduce the workload for staff. As for artificial intelligence, once it's fully vetted, it has the potential to dramatically improve research capabilities and aid in tactical decision-making. Over the next 5 to 10 years, I expect these technologies to become much more common in our field.

When it comes to incorporating new technologies, the simple reality is that cost, maintenance (both for the equipment and personnel), training, and lifespan are the key factors to consider. The equipment has to be affordable, reliable, and sustainable over time.

But most importantly, it all comes down to training. They have to be skilled in using the technology, not just aware of it. Secondly, we need to create opportunities to use the technology in real-world settings. This means expanding the role of hazardous materials teams. I'm a big advocate for assigning the team to all working fires, where they can take on responsibilities like air monitoring, sample collection, and overseeing decontamination of patients, victims, and responders.

Additionally, the team should support law enforcement by sampling substances to provide presumptive results while waiting for lab confirmation. We can also assist with arson investigations and public health efforts through air sampling and monitoring at various facilities. These roles not only improve the comfort and accuracy of using identification technologies, but they also help support the ongoing purchase, maintenance, and training for such equipment - ensuring that we're all on the same page when it comes to cost-sharing and resource allocation across personnel, training, and equipment upkeep.

Rick Edinger

At a broad level, detection and monitoring is where we've seen the most dramatic evolution in hazmat. You touched on it earlier - FTIR is a great example. Twenty years ago, that kind of tech lived in a lab. Now it's sitting in a box on your hazmat rig. The ability to analyze what you're dealing with - in real time, on scene - and then adapt your incident action plan accordingly? That's a game changer.

I look back at the '90s - we ran so many unknowns. We'd commit two people in a Level A suit into the hot zone, two on backup, maybe 90 degrees out. They'd make entry, come out, and sometimes we'd be only marginally more informed than when we went in. Sure, we'd have a visual, maybe an haze, visible release, or some other clues - but the confidence in our analysis just wasn't there yet.

The technology today has completely shifted that. Yes, PPE has certainly improved, but in terms of game-changing impact, detection and monitoring is at the top. It feels like every few months, there's a new device or an upgrade hitting the market. And the truth is, we're just not walking into as many "unknowns" as we used to. We've significantly reduced that risk - and that's a big deal.

But let's be honest - it's not just about buying the latest equipment. If you need a new piece of equipment or technology, you've got to ask yourself three key questions:
1. Can I afford it?
2. Can I maintain it?
3. Can I train on it and integrate it properly?

Those were lessons I learned early from one of the founding members of our hazmat team - he started as a battalion chief and eventually became my deputy. I remember walking into his office all excited with news of a $10,000 grant. "We're getting this new piece of equipment," I said.

The first thing out of his mouth: "What's it cost to maintain?"

I told him it needed to be sent out once a year, and that was about $1,500.

His next questions:

"How long is it going to be gone?"

"What's the operational impact?"

That conversation stuck with me. Because now, every time we look at new equipment, we're asking:
- Do we need it?
- Can we afford it - not just today, but over time?
- How does it fit into our operations?
- And are we going to train on it enough so our people are confident, not just pointing and clicking?

That's the full picture. Just owning the tool isn't enough.

And then, you've got to think about support. Do you have a reliable vendor or manufacturer rep? Because in this industry, we've all seen companies get bought out or disappear, and suddenly your tech's outdated and unsupported. So you want to build those relationships at the time of purchase. Know who you're dealing with, and make sure there's a support system built into that transaction.

Beyond that, you've got to go to conferences. Talk to other users. Develop some in-house SMEs who understand how the gear actually works. Get them trained up, and let them be the ones who carry the knowledge forward.

**Don't just buy gear - **you need to integrate it into your response model and make sure your people are trained, confident, and ready to deploy it when it counts.

That's it. It's not just about the box. It's about how well that box fits into the bigger picture.

John Esposito

Technology absolutely helps us do our job safer - but let's be honest, I don't even really consider a four-gas meter "technology." That's basic. That's a minimum standard. You can't have a hazmat team without one. And frankly, if you only *have* one, you don't have a hazmat team. Because as we always say: *Two is one, and one is none.* Same logic we use for boats. If we want two, we bring three - because when something goes down, you need redundancy.

Meters are how we stop guessing. If we can't confirm what we're seeing, we're just rolling the dice. And I remember John Cirillo saying this years ago - if this is what it costs to have a fire company, then *that's what it costs*. You can't just throw four guys in a Suburban and say, "Here's your fire company." No. You need the training, you need the equipment, and you need to spend the money.

That said, there's a lot of gear out there right now - some of it solid, some of it smoke and mirrors. I go to conferences, I get the emails, I see the vendors with "the next greatest thing." Some of it works. A lot of it doesn't. So you've got to stay educated, but also skeptical. Know what's out there, but make sure it actually *does* what it says it does. Otherwise, you're spending R&D money without realizing it.

If you're buying a piece of equipment that claims to do A, B, and C - it better do A, B, and C. And not just in theory. You want to hear from real departments who've used it in the field. Is the wireless connectivity reliable? Does it hold up under fire conditions? Does it survive a drop off the rig?

Meters are especially critical - not just to know what's going on, but to protect our people. If we don't know what the meter is saying, or how to interpret it, we're in trouble. In firefighting, the hazards are visible - we see fire, we feel heat, we react. But in hazmat? Most of this stuff is invisible. We don't protect ourselves *until* the meter tells us to.

Which is a little backwards, right? We should be starting with protection. SCBA on, at a minimum. Always. I remember a job right after 9/11 - I was UFO in Squad 18. We got called all the way from Lower Manhattan to Flushing, Queens. Hazmat run. "Chemical odor." Turns out, this guy had been collecting jars of his dog's piss - like, actual mason jars of it. The building reeked, and tenants had finally had enough.

So we get there, meters out, masks on, standard operating procedure. No hits, windows already open. Chief calls up on the radio: "What does it smell like?" I go, "Chief, we're on air. I don't know what it smells like." And I *knew* he wanted me to just take the mask off and sniff it, but I wasn't playing that game. We came all the way out there, we're going to do it *by the book*. Silence on the other end. He didn't know what to say. Eventually we got to the bottom of it. But again - protective equipment, meters, legit process. That's the job.

Technology *can* make us safer and more effective - but you always need a backup. Plan B. Because when the tech fails - and it will - you need something else. Perfect example: thermal imaging cameras. You go too deep into a building, and the TIC craps out? You better have a rope. You better have a plan to get out.

That's the bottom line - trust your tools, but never *rely* on them alone. Know the basics. Know your backups. And make sure your people do too.

Brandon Fletcher

Technology has absolutely transformed hazmat response! We've come a long way from the old 2- and 3-pool shower decon methods to dry and hybrid techniques that are more efficient and safer. PPE has improved dramatically, providing better protection and mobility. Detection, identification, and monitoring have all evolved rapidly for the better, and research has become much more streamlined with the help of new tools. It's an incredibly exciting time to be in hazmat, with so many advancements at our fingertips.

As I mentioned earlier, the XplorIR has me especially excited. The ability to detect, identify, and even quantify products in the gas phase is a game-changer. This opens up a whole range of new possibilities for hazmat teams to respond more effectively and accurately.

That said, funding remains my biggest challenge when it comes to integrating new technologies. It's always tough to secure the necessary resources, but the potential benefits of these tools make it all worth fighting for. Technology is key to keeping up with the evolving demands of hazmat response, and finding ways to fund these innovations is critical to staying ahead of the curve.

Chris Hawley

I love how you bring everything back to the basics and the importance of understanding the fundamentals. It's honestly eye-opening to see how many teams are still struggling with the basics of detection devices, and when you introduce newer, more advanced technology, the gap in understanding can be even more pronounced.

Like you said, those basic devices - like the LEL sensors - should be the first things you grab when you go through a hazmat door. But if people don't understand how they work, there's a real danger, like with MPS LEL sensors. They're great sensors, but they can miss certain things. If they're not detecting the target gas, the sensor will show zeroes, and that's where you end up in a bad situation, not realizing the environment is actually dangerous. Understanding how these and other sensors work is critical, and if people don't get that, it's a recipe for disaster. There are a variety of LEL sensors being sold and you have to understand their individual capabilities and deficiencies.

And you're right - there's a huge gap when it comes to some of the more advanced tech. I mean, I love the new technology, especially the advancements with the RedWave and other vapor detection devices. We're getting closer to being able to detect things at lower concentrations, like down to one part per million. That's huge for situations where you don't know exactly what you're dealing with. But, even with that technology, we still need those basic, reliable tools to guide our first steps.

When you talk about things like radiation, it's another example of how fundamental understanding is often overlooked. Like you said, even something as simple as bananas can set off a Geiger counter. People panic, not understanding that a little spike above background radiation doesn't necessarily mean a danger. I've had similar situations where people call in a radiation concern over something totally benign. That's where a solid foundation in the basics, along with the ability to assess the situation calmly and critically, is so crucial.

The story you told about your HazMat Officer calling you in for the radiation incident is a great example. It's funny how sometimes the simplest solutions go unnoticed - he was walking around the truck with a radiation meter, and the spikes were coming from his own radio! That kind of miscommunication and misunderstanding could have been avoided with a better understanding of how the tools work and how to use them properly. It's about not jumping to conclusions and thinking critically.

And, to your point about incentivizing people to get better and improve their skills, I think you hit the nail on the head. Whether it's sending people to conferences, providing opportunities for specialized training, or just getting them out of their comfort zone to learn from others, those outside experiences can really open people's eyes. You said it best - you might not be the expert in your own town, but bringing in someone from the outside can shake things up, give your team a new perspective, and ultimately improve everyone's knowledge and confidence. That external perspective can push them to ask questions they might never ask their own instructors.

At the end of the day, it's about equipping your team with the right knowledge and tools, whether it's basic sensors, advanced technology, or just having the confidence to ask the right questions. That's how you build a strong, capable team that can handle anything that comes their way.

Mike Hildebrand

I'll be honest - I'm excited about artificial intelligence.
We're right at the beginning of something big. Same way we were with lithium batteries not that long ago. But like anything new, people have strong opinions - especially older folks. And I say that as a member of the Old Guy community.

Change is hard. People don't like it. Especially in the fire service. I once listened to an economist give a lecture on change in the fire department - he had no fire background, just pure data as an ecomomist academic. He'd written a thesis on cultural resistance in organizations and was *shocked* when he learned how long it took fire departments to switch from hard suction to soft suction hoses – it was a 30 year transition.

Thirty years.

Three decades of "I'm not giving up my hard suction." It worked for me. It worked for my dad. It worked for my *granddad.* This new stuff? I don't trust it.

That's where we are with AI right now.

But the reality is, artificial intelligence is going to start guiding decision-making - especially in those low-probability, high-consequence events where time is tight and the margin for error is razor thin. That's where it's going to shine.

Greg Noll and I used to see this in refineries all the time. We'd try to get plant management to change their culture, but they'd always default to their *normal* decision-making model. That process requires studies, meetings, policy development, ordering stuff, and a budget. Problem is, that model was built for daily operations - not for a high-stakes, fast-moving emergency. In a refinery, when things go wrong, you're losing pressure vessels and instrumentation in ten to fifteen minutes. If your response plan is built around a 20-minute timeline? Your whole strategy is an *illusion*.

So we had to get people to see things differently. Sometimes that meant changing the way we explained the problem.

And with AI - or any new tech - the same rule applies: you will never get user buy-in unless the people using it believe in it. They have to think it's going to make them *safer*. Or faster. Or more efficient. Or lower maintenance. Something. There has to be a *payoff* - a reason to suffer through the learning curve.

That's where your early adopters come in. You always have that one guy on the team who reads *Popular Mechanics* on the toilet. That's your test pilot. You send them out. You let them train on it, test it, kick the tires. Then they come back and say, "You know what? I was skeptical - but this thing *works*. And here's how."

Now suddenly, the skeptics start to lean in.

I've been that skeptic. I'll admit it. I was late to the iPhone party. Still had my old flip phone. Walked into the store and the kid behind the counter looked at me like I was holding Eisenhower's battlefield radio.

He didn't hesitate. "*Dude,* you need to upgrade."

Took me a while to cross the threshold, but once I did? You couldn't pay me to go back. That's how it goes with most new tools. You need someone to *translate* it to the team - someone they trust. Someone who can show why this is good for *us*, not just good on paper.

Because not every technology *does* work. Sometimes the shiny new thing is a dud. Like our first Decon setup. Sounded great in theory. Didn't work in the field.

But that's why you test. You evaluate. You adapt. And you learn from others.

The best innovation doesn't happen in a vacuum - it happens in *partnership*. I was at the FBI not long ago, looking at what their technical

Evidence Response Unit was doing. They showed me a piece of kit I'd never seen before. I asked, "Where'd you get this?"

Turns out it wasn't some million-dollar off-the-shelf federal government solution. It was born out of necessity. They had a problem. They called a Tier 1 military team - they had the same problem. No solution existed, so they teamed up. Their engineers collaborated, built something new, tweaked it until it worked. Someday, it'll be for sale. But for now, it's only in that spooky world.

That kind of innovation? It happens when people drop their egos and work together. Military, law enforcement, hazmat - we're all solving the same kinds of problems. Just with different motivations.

In the end, new tools and tech - whether it's AI, robotics, or smart meters - are only as good as the *culture* they land in. You've got to have the right people. The curious ones. The skeptical-but-open ones. The ones who show up, test things, and tell the truth about what works.

That's how change actually sticks.

Bob Ingram

Technology is constantly changing, and it is very difficult to stay current on all relevant components of your team's inventory. New technology usually comes with a high price tag and bugs that must be worked out, as well as additional training requirements.

I mentioned earlier the IAB SEL and FEMA's AEL. These two lists provide a good overview of emerging technologies, their capabilities and limitations, standards they may be tested against, test results, and manufactures working with the technology.

The NFPA and their Fire Research Division are a great source of information on new equipment and technologies as they develop standards for them operationally.

The Department of Homeland Security's (DHS) Standards and Technology office and their Performance testing group have been beneficial to the responder community for the last twenty years since their inception.

Conferences with vendor displays provide a good introduction to new technologies, equipment, and services as well. It is helpful if you are interested, don't just pick up the brochure and free trinkets. Ask questions, get answers, and contact numbers to follow up with. Ask what standards they were tested to, what test results do they have, what limitations are known, etc. Always remember, not everyone at a booth is a scientist. Many are salespeople who want to make a sale.

Finally, you do not need every new technology that comes out. What does your team's response capability gain from it? What gap do you currently have in your mission space, and does this technology fill the gap? Does the added response capability justify the cost? What are the maintenance costs and life expectancy of the new technology? What initial and refresher training requirements and costs come with the technology?

Phil McArdle

New technology is advancing at an incredibly fast pace, and it's something Haz-Mat teams will continuously have to adapt to throughout their careers. Just when you get comfortable with a monitoring device in your inventory, a new device is released that completely outperforms your current equipment with its capabilities. This cycle is something that will keep happening, so it's important to get used to it and adjust accordingly.

Both communications and computers are rapidly improving as well. Most experts in the field of computers will tell you that the lifespan of any computer you purchase today is typically only 3-5 years. This raises the question: how quickly is technology advancing in specific areas, such as monitoring devices, tools, and other equipment? Are we prepared to budget not only for the purchase of new technology but also for the training necessary to effectively use it?

The challenge, however, is whether we are replacing old equipment or adding new items to the inventory. Replacing equipment usually means that a piece of technology or gear is being taken out of service, along with its maintenance and training components. On the other hand, adding to the inventory increases the team's responsibilities for both maintenance and training. Are we ready to incorporate this new technology into our operations? How long will it take to train personnel? And, of course, what's the cost involved?

If we're adding equipment, another factor to consider is whether there is enough space on the current response vehicle for the new items. For instance, a few years ago, a Haz-Mat team was in the position of acquiring containment vessels for compressed gas cylinders. These vessels were relatively large and couldn't be carried on their existing response vehicles. As a result, the team had to bring this essential but infrequently used equipment to the scene in a separate vehicle and trailer.

As part of the ongoing training process, when members attend schools, conferences, or seminars, they should bring back valuable information for the rest of the team to review. No team member should return from training - whether it's education, a conference, or seminar - empty-handed. The team should always benefit from the knowledge and insights gained through these experiences, ensuring that the team stays up-to-date on the latest advancements in technology and best practices.

Adam McFadden

Technology has fundamentally transformed the way we approach hazmat response, dramatically increasing our ability to assess, identify, and mitigate hazardous incidents with greater speed and safety. Today's handheld chemical identification devices, advanced air monitoring systems, and drone platforms provide real-time situational awareness that would have been unimaginable just a decade ago.

One of the most exciting advancements is the integration of AI-driven hazard prediction tools and real-time data sharing platforms. These innovations allow teams to analyze multiple variables on the fly - substance identification, environmental conditions, potential reaction risks - and make more informed decisions faster. Add to that enhanced PPE materials, robotics for high-risk environments, and remote sensing capabilities, and we're operating in an era where safety and effectiveness continue to reach new heights.

However, adopting this wave of new technology isn't without its challenges. Budget limitations are a consistent hurdle, but another often-overlooked issue is the availability of qualified personnel to train our teams on these advanced tools. Manufacturer-provided training is useful, but it rarely goes deep enough. We need instructors who understand both the gear and the operational realities of the field.

To stay ahead, we've built a system of consistent internal updates and targeted training, guided by leadership and input from our hazmat committees. These committees stay closely tied to industry developments and help us assess new equipment, vet updated tactics, and monitor emerging threats. Their insight allows us to focus our time and resources where they'll have the greatest operational impact.

By continuously integrating cutting-edge tools, updated protocols, and hands-on training, we keep our hazmat operations running at the highest level of safety and efficiency. Technology alone isn't the solution - it's how we train with it, implement it, and adapt to it that truly transforms our capabilities.

Mike Monaco

Technology has changed *a lot* over the past 20, 25 years. Honestly, probably a hundredfold in the last four decades. What's wild is how it just keeps getting smaller, more portable, and more powerful. You're able to do more, carry less, and multitask in ways that would've been unthinkable not that long ago. That's pretty damn cool.

One of the technologies I'm most excited about right now is FTIR making its way into the gas phase. That could be a total game changer for a lot of departments and hazmat teams. The ability to identify gases in real time with that level of precision? That's next level.

But, I'll be honest - it comes with a little trepidation too.

Because with technology often comes a certain kind of laziness. Not physical laziness, but mental. The more we rely on tech to make decisions *for* us, the more we risk losing the ability to think critically in the moment. And in our world, that's dangerous.

We don't trust easily in this field. We trust what we've seen work, what we've done with our own hands. So when a new piece of equipment comes along - especially one you're supposed to stake your life on - that trust doesn't happen overnight.

That's why time and training are everything. Introduce the tech, use it in drills, slowly integrate it into real runs. Let people *see* that it works. Let it earn their trust. That's the only way forward.

And if there's one place where you're going to find those kinds of advancements - whether it's new equipment from a vendor or a cutting-edge lecture from an instructor - it's at conferences. Hands down. If you want to stay ahead of the curve, that's where you've got to be.

Chris Pfaff

I still remember when I first joined, talking about infrared spectroscopy - back then, just 20 years prior, it was strictly a lab-based technology. And then you mentioned GCMS - holy crap, GCMS devices are tiny now! There are multiple companies making portable GCMS specifically for responders. Or PCR technology - instead of basic bioassays, now we've got rapid PCR kits in the field. NDIR technology for air monitoring is huge. Additionally, the creation of Laser Spectroscopy Technology to remotely detect gases are total game changers.

There's tons of new tech I'm excited about - I even wrote a list down - but before diving into that, a quick caution: don't buy the newest, shiniest gadget every single time. If you do, you will absolutely blow up your department's budget.

One critical area that's completely evolved is communication. Think about it - I literally have 96% of human knowledge at my fingertips. If I'm en route to a hazmat call, I can jump onto a chat board (not spilling all the details, of course), and say, "Hey, I've got this issue - any thoughts?" Before I even arrive, I've got 15 comments and a dozen discussions. I don't have to read all of them right away, but it's a valuable resource for navigating tough calls. It completely changes the game at a national, even international, level.

Also, GPS and telemetry - huge advancements. Air monitors are now mandatory on every response apparatus. Hazmat teams should absolutely have multiple air monitoring devices. The sensors themselves - NDIR, NPS technology - have improved dramatically. But beyond that, the real innovation is telemetry. Right now, from my cell phone, I can log in and see real-time readings from every single air monitor deployed in my jurisdiction, complete with GPS locations. Sure, there's about a 30-second delay, but that's nothing short of incredible.

Another huge one, recently discussed during a hazmat curriculum validation session, is drones. Drones have so much potential - not just in hazmat, but across all disciplines. Think active-shooter events; law enforcement already uses drones extensively for infrared scanning. Technical rescue teams deploy drones for rapid 360 assessments or even to drop ropes across hazardous areas. Urban search and rescue? Fly a drone over rubble and combine it with remote air monitoring - massive capabilities there.

But bringing drones specifically back to hazmat, even just having visual and thermal imaging cameras is revolutionary. Now add an air monitor. Six years ago, I was in a drone class where we literally taped a standard air monitor to the drone. But how did we read the results? We mounted a second camera pointing directly at the air monitor's screen. Today's air monitors have SIM cards; I can read real-time data directly on my phone without even watching the drone itself. That's mind-blowing tech.

But, a word of warning: new equipment must come with adequate, ongoing training. I've seen plenty of cases where a $50,000 piece of gear ends up gathering dust two offices away because it's too technically complicated. These technologies require continuous training - not just a quick 8-hour intro session. Make sure team members understand what every dot or reading means on their screen. Three dots versus five, two dots versus one - you must integrate sustained training so your crew is confident using it.

Administrative challenges come into play, too, especially with drones. A big roadblock for many departments is deciding who operates the drone. They might say, "Let's have the incident safety officer do it," or "Assign it to research." But safety officers and research personnel are already slammed. Recognize that the drone operator role must be dedicated - someone will always get pulled away to handle that specifically.

On the flip side, though, technology can multiply our force. We can remotely call experts through Zoom, Teams, or controlled chat groups. You don't always need every team member physically at the scene - you can outsource some tasks. This ability to reach out to external expertise in real-time is transforming hazmat response in ways we've never imagined.

Bob Royall

I think the greatest technological advancement in my career is SCBA - Self-Contained Breathing Apparatus. And you might laugh, but it really was a game changer. Up until 1986, there wasn't even a mandatory air pack rule in the Houston Fire Department. That's hard to believe today, but it was true. SCBAs made a massive difference in our ability to protect ourselves in hazardous environments.

Later on, when infrared spectroscopy and Raman spectroscopy came into play, we all thought, "This is it. This is going to change the game. It's going to tell us everything we need to know." But even with those advancements, every technology has limitations. We have stopped short of fully harnessing the power of AI, but I think that's where the next big breakthrough is coming from. Think about it: how valuable would it be if we could feed information from a four-gas meter into AI, have it interpret that data and process it, and then provide us with a list of potential actions, options, or solutions. I believe AI has the potential to take us into a new dimension, but we are just not there yet.

As for robotics, in my opinion, they have been sort of a non-starter. When robots first came out, their capabilities were limited - limited in range, functionality, and battery life. Today we have different types of robotics, but their original focus was DOD and EOD. They were adapted for hazmat operations after Desert Storm. Yes, they have a place in hazmat, but they come with their own set of challenges and limitations.

Biological detection is another area that have never fully developed. We haven't figured out how to take legitimate PCR (polymerase chain reaction) from the lab out into the field. If we could do that, it could be a game changer, especially in a world dealing with viruses like COVID-19, but we are not there yet. We just can't just depend on what's out there and available right now.

Drones are another technology that's starting to be used in ways I never imagined. But they're still limited, especially when it comes to payload. The more sensors you add to a drone, the more the weight. The heavier the unit the less battery life it has. Tethered drones have their own limitations, especially when it comes to distance from the "mothership." And then there are these new robotic dogs, or simulated animals, which are kind of unsettling.

If you add AI to those, though, it could very well be the next game changer.

Technology is evolving so rapidly that your average hazmat guy just can't keep up. Now, it's almost essential to have someone on your team who's a techie - a person who's tracking all the emerging technologies. They need the depth and breadth of knowledge to determine whether a new piece of technology will be useful for your operation or if it's just another gimmick.

Believe me, we have all seen our fair share of "snake oil salesmen" - you know, those folks who show up every time a new gadget hits the market, ready to sell it to us. We've seen them all, but it is critical to be discerning. Not every new tool is going to be the solution we're looking for.

Bobby Salvesen

Technology in hazmat is important - but only *to a point.*

Let me be clear: I'm not anti-tech. I've seen what great technology can do. But I also believe that the *basics* are absolutely critical, and sometimes we lean too hard on the gadgets and start losing our edge.

Take thermal imaging cameras. They've been around for, what - 20 years now? As soon as they came out, everyone started depending on them. And over time, that started to erode some of the core skills. Guys forgot how to search without one. Forgot what to do when the battery dies. That's what I mean when I say we're getting a little *too* tech-dependent. And hazmat's not immune. We've got a mix of low-tech tools - colorimetric tubes, pH and pH paper, hazcat kits - and I'm a big fan of those. Even though the hazcat's a little dated and is being edged out by newer stuff like RAMAN and FTIR, I still think it *has* a place. That kind of basic, hands-on tech is valuable.

Since about 2000, we've seen an explosion of new technology. And here we are in 2025, on the cusp of something big. I think we're about to shift - *really shift* - away from the old school "categorize and generalize" hazmat approach, and toward real-time *identification and mitigation*. Handle exactly what's in front of you. That's exciting.

But... it also costs money.

And budgets are always tight. That's why I don't think you need a million bucks to run a solid hazmat team. You need a solid core kit:

- A 4-gas meter
- A PID
- Some papers
- A decent set of tubes
- Maybe a hazcat kit

If you've got that - and people who know how to *use* it - you're in business.

And here's where networking comes in. Don't have a fancy piece of tech? No problem. If your neighboring department does, then *you* do too. That's how it works.

It's like the old saying:
What's better than owning a boat?
Having a *friend* with a boat.

They deal with the cost, the maintenance, the headaches. You just bring a six-pack and enjoy the ride.

Same with hazmat tech. Build relationships. Share resources. Stay grounded in the basics - and be smart with the toys.

Doug Schick and Mark Zilch
Doug:

I've already talked somewhat about keeping up with the latest technology when we were discussing other topics. By going to conferences, following podcasts, webinars, FaceBook groups, etc. I receive a lot of information about the latest technological advances. Technology is great and it has taken us to levels in hazmat response that we never imagined in the past. For instance, our front line radiation detectors now detect both gamma and neutron. A few years ago who would have thought that every engine in the department would be able to detect neutron radiation?

The one drawback to technology, which is both good and bad, is that it advances so rapidly. It is impossible to keep up with it budgetarily. Last year we purchased a series of new meters and a couple of months later an updated version was announced. Now, I love the advancement of technology and the meters we bought still work great but it's just tough to keep up with it all.

Jason Zeller

Today's technology gives us speed, accuracy, and reach that we've never had before. Multi-gas meters, FTIR, Raman spectroscopy, portable GC/MS, and advanced radiological identifiers provide real-time answers right downrange. You're no longer standing there guessing or waiting for samples to be sent off you're making decisions right there on the X. This not only saves lives but reduces the risk to operators and the public.

Add to that remote monitoring and robotics, which have truly been game changers. Now, instead of putting people in harm's way from the start, we can deploy drones or robots to conduct initial surveys and atmospheric monitoring. This technology buys us time, keeps personnel safer, and allows commands to make smarter decisions without rushing personnel into hot zones unnecessarily.

Looking forward, two big areas excite me: AI-enhanced detection and analysis, and interoperability and data sharing. Imagine integrated systems that not only detect but also interpret, prioritize, and communicate hazards across all responding agencies in real time. This is coming, and it will elevate situational awareness to a whole new level. No more stovepiped data - everyone will have the same picture at the same time, which will save lives and accelerate response efforts.

Another exciting development is wearable tech for downrange personnel - biometric monitoring tied directly to command. It tracks vitals, stress levels, and air usage live. That level of accountability and safety wasn't even imaginable years ago, but it's becoming a reality.

Bottom line: technology has made us faster, smarter, safer, and more connected. It has shifted us from reactive to proactive. And as the threats continue to evolve, so too will the tech - and that's exactly what we need to stay ahead.

Integrating new technology into a hazmat team isn't necessarily difficult - but it does require time, discipline, and smart decision-making. You don't just grab the latest shiny tool and toss it into the mix because it looks cool or promises to do everything. That's not how you build a reliable team.

Every new piece of gear has to earn its place.

The first challenge is time. We don't train to time - we train to standard. This means if we're going to integrate new technology, we need bandwidth to do it right. You can't just hand operators a new piece of equipment and expect them to figure it out on the fly during a real-world response. You have to allocate the time to train on it properly, get hands-on experience, stress test it in scenarios, and ensure it performs as expected under pressure.

Second, you have to be cautious not to overcomplicate your kit or processes. It's easy to fall into the trap of wanting every new tool available - but more isn't always better. If a piece of technology doesn't bring valuable utility, speed, reliability, or enhance your downrange capability, then it doesn't belong. Too many tools slow you down. They create confusion, eat up valuable space, and distract from what matters. Every new tool you integrate must earn its place and make your team better, not burden them.

Finally, once you decide a piece of technology is worth adding, the biggest challenge is integrating it into your SOPs and operations. It's not enough to just know how to use it - you need to know where it fits tactically. Does it improve detection, speed up decision-making, or enhance medical response? Everyone on the team must understand where it fits into the mission, so it becomes second nature, not something you have to stop and think about when the pressure is on.

Keeping my team current with technology was never a challenge - and that's because of who they were and the culture we built. I had hungry, motivated operators who didn't just want to keep up - they wanted to lead. They wanted to be the tip of the spear. Staying cutting-edge wasn't something I had to force on them - they were already leaning forward, always asking, "What's next? What's out there? How can we get better?"

That kind of mindset made all the difference. They understood that having the latest technology wasn't about bragging rights - it was about being the best prepared and most capable team on the ground. They wanted to be subject matter experts, not just for our team, but so they could share that knowledge with other responders in the community. That's what drove them - not ego, but pride in being the team everyone could rely on when the stakes were highest.

I stayed on top of advancements myself, constantly tracking what was emerging across the industry, but truthfully, my team drove a lot of it. They were invested. They brought new ideas to the table, kept their eyes open during conferences, training, and joint operations, and stayed plugged into the professional network.

At the end of the day, staying current wasn't about chasing technology - it was about staying lethal and effective in a world where threats evolve quickly. My team embraced that, and it became part of who we were.

That's how you stay ahead of the curve - you build a team that refuses to fall behind.

Extra Phil Stuff

Force Protection & Multi-jurisdictional Deployments

A key mission objective at every hazardous materials incident, though not always explicitly mentioned, is force protection. One of the most critical aspects of our job is to ensure that areas are safe for other emergency responders to operate in. This responsibility spans not only local operations but also state and federal levels. At times, team members may be asked to operate in other jurisdictions or even become part of federal task forces, such as FEMA's Urban Search & Rescue Task Forces.

State-Level: In 1987, the FDNY Haz-Mat team was deployed to the Bridgeport, Connecticut building collapse, where workers were buried under rubble from the collapse of a building under construction. Haz-Mat's expertise in using thermal imaging equipment, which was exclusive to Haz-Mat 1 at the time, was crucial. The team was deployed for several days to assist in the recovery of bodies, identify potential heat signatures from victims, and provide air monitoring to ensure it was safe for other rescuers to operate in the area.

Federal-Level: During the 1995 Oklahoma bombing, FDNY Haz-Mat Specialists were deployed with New York's Task Force 1. These specialists performed air monitoring and supervised decontamination operations to ensure that the operating forces were not affected by contaminants present at the site. When new hazards were identified, rescuers were temporarily moved away until Haz-Mat specialists could render the area safe and allow others to operate.

One of the most successful initiatives for a Haz-Mat team is having team members pursue second careers as hazardous materials trainers and instructors. This offers multiple benefits. First, teaching external classes requires team members to deepen their knowledge of the subject matter, enhancing both their instructional and technical skills. This, in turn, sharpens their expertise for their primary Haz-Mat responsibilities. Second, teaching provides an opportunity to learn something new each time a class is led, bringing fresh insights back to the team. Third, as more team members become involved in teaching, it creates a ripple effect - leading to better training for everyone, safer operations, and improved morale, bolstered by the additional income generated from teaching roles.

No successful team operates without critique. After-action reports and post-incident reviews are essential for identifying and addressing deficiencies and safety concerns. No operation is ever perfect, and there is always room for improvement. Every incident should be thoroughly examined, and in some cases, adjustments to policies, procedures, strategies, or tactics may be necessary to enhance safety and performance. Recurring mistakes should be treated seriously, as they indicate that lessons are not being learned or that a deeper issue needs to be addressed and resolved.

www.ingramcontent.com/pod-product-compliance
Lightning Source LLC
Chambersburg PA
CBHW021351290426
44108CB00010B/199